Willem de Kooning

The Breakthrough Years, 1945–50

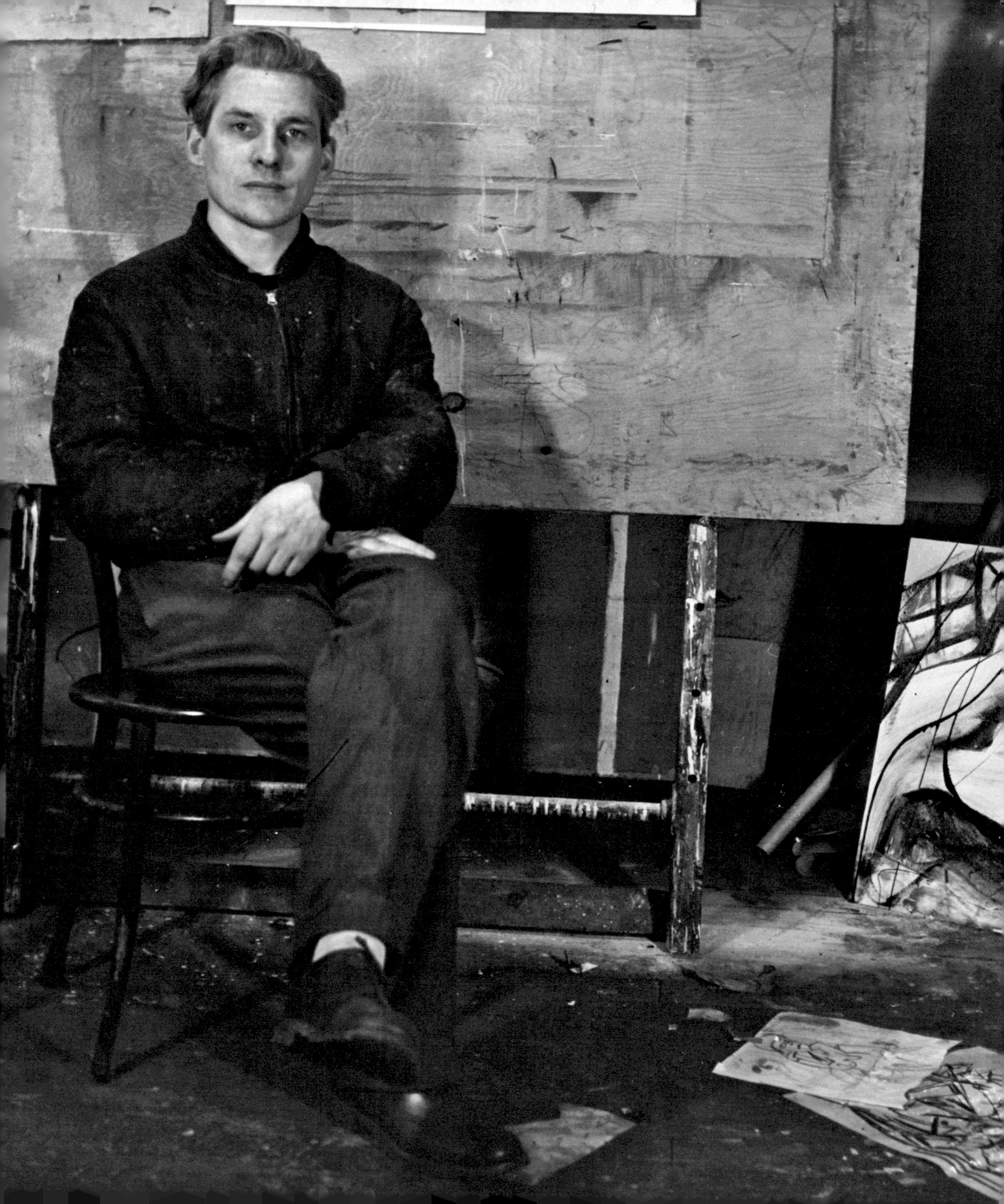

Willem de Kooning
The Breakthrough Years, 1945–50

John Elderfield
Mitra Abbaspour

with Lee Colón

and a contribution by Jim Coddington and Bart J. C. Devolder

Princeton University Art Museum

Distributed by Princeton University Press, Princeton and Oxford

Willem de Kooning

The Breakthrough Years, 1945–50

Princeton University Art Museum

Princeton, New Jersey

March 15–July 26, 2026

The exhibition is organized by the Princeton University Art Museum.

The publication **Willem de Kooning: The Breakthrough Years, 1945–50** is generously supported by The Willem de Kooning Foundation.

The exhibition **Willem de Kooning: The Breakthrough Years, 1945–50** is made possible by leadership support from the Allen R. Adler, Class of 1967, Curatorial Leadership Fund; the Fanzhi Foundation for Art and Education; the Frances E. and Elias Wolf, Class of 1920, Fund; Gagosian; Shelly and Tony Malkin; the Robert Lehman Foundation; and Tom and Mila Tuttle. Additional support is provided by Christie's, Preston H. Haskell III, the Joseph L. Shulman Foundation Fund for Art Museum Publications, the Melanie and John Clarke Exhibition Fund, Mark W. Stevens and Annalyn Martha Swan, and contributors to the Director's Exhibition Fund.

This exhibition is supported by an indemnity from the Federal Council on the Arts and the Humanities.

Published by the Princeton University Art Museum
Princeton, New Jersey 08544-1018
artmuseum.princeton.edu

Project editor: Janet S. Rauscher
Designed and typeset by Katy Homans
Copyedited, proofread, and indexed by Jane Friedman
Prepress and printing by Puritan Press
Printed on Gardapat Kiara
Typeset in Akzinenz-Grotesk

Distributed by
Princeton University Press
41 William Street, Princeton NJ 08540-5237
99 Banbury Road, Oxford OX2 6JX
press.princeton.edu

GPSR Authorized Representative: Easy Access System Europe, Mustam.e tee 50, 10621 Tallinn, Estonia, gpsr.requests@easproject.com

ISBN: 978-0-691-97396-8

Ebook ISBN: 978-0-691-97397-5

Library of Congress Control Number: 2025948273

British Library Cataloging-in-Publication Data is available.

Printed and bound in the United States

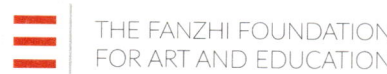

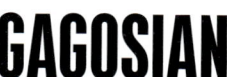

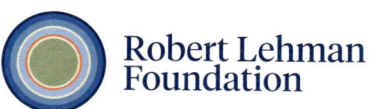

Dedicated to the memory of John L. Eastman

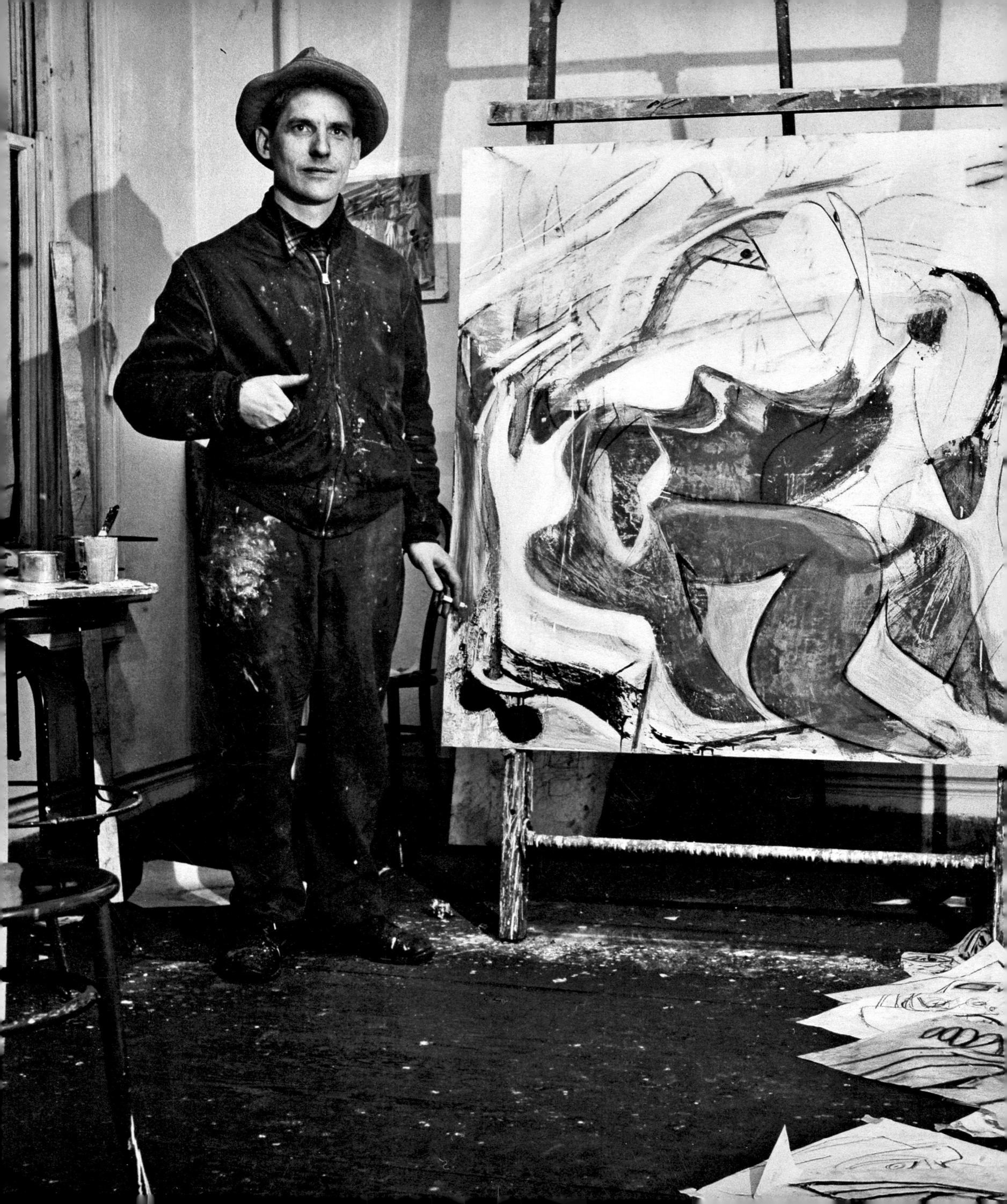

Contents

Foreword

At critical moments over his roughly sixty-year career, the revolutionary American artist Willem de Kooning (1904–1997) made truly transformative paintings that altered the direction of his own practice and deeply influenced the art made by his contemporaries and thus the path of modern art. No works were more impactful than the pictures the artist showed at his first solo exhibition, at the Charles Egan Gallery, New York, in 1948. Among these extraordinary works was the painting *Black Friday,* which entered the collections of the Princeton University Art Museum fifty years ago, in 1976. Like so many of the objects in the Museum's holdings, this spectacular work was donated by a generous alumnus, H. Gates Lloyd, Class of 1923, and Mrs. Lloyd, in honor of the great Class of 1923. I have personally felt a deep connection with the painting for many years, not least as a good friend of the Lloyds' daughter, Prue Rosenthal, but particularly for the impact that the work had on me when it shone in the context of the landmark de Kooning retrospective curated by John Elderfield for the Museum of Modern Art in New York in 2011. Seeing it there was a revelation, and I have since wanted to understand it better.

For nearly fifteen years, then, I have yearned for an exhibition that would center on *Black Friday* and would create an appropriately rich context for it. It seemed only fitting that *Willem de Kooning: The Breakthrough Years, 1945–50* should be the first major temporary exhibition to take place in the purpose-built galleries of the Museum's dramatic new building, which opened to the public in October 2025. *The Breakthrough Years* comprises works by de Kooning that were shown with *Black Friday* in 1948, along with others made both just before or just after the Egan Gallery exhibition. This publication serves as a record of the art that was shown in 1948, and also includes works de Kooning made from 1945 to 1950—a watershed period for both the artist and for American art generally. Shown together, the selected works illustrate the rapidity of de Kooning's development over the span of five years, arguably one of the greatest brief periods of radical change in modern art. Together, the exhibition and this volume address the complexity of de Kooning's growth as he continuously revised his paintings; moved between abstraction and representation; combined the two modes; and was forever inventive in his painterly means.

The exhibition and this publication are to my mind remarkable, and we at the Princeton University Art Museum are honored to have been the catalyst for them. The works brought together for this project will only be shown in our galleries, so those with an appetite for discovering this remarkably rich period in the career of one of the greatest artists of the twentieth century shall have to journey to our new galleries to see them. It is only thanks to the exceptional generosity of the custodians of the major works in the museum and private collections that agreed to part with them for a time that the exhibition has proven possible: Christophe Cherix, David Rockefeller Director, the Museum of Modern Art, New York; Melissa Chiu, Director, the Hirshhorn Museum and Sculpture Garden, Smithsonian Institution, Washington, DC; Max Hollein, Marina Kellen French Director and Chief Executive Officer, the Metropolitan Museum of Art, New York; Jason Linetzky, Director, the Anderson Collection at Stanford University; Katherine Crawford Luber, Nivin and Duncan MacMillan Director & President, the Minneapolis Institute of Art; Daniel H. Weiss, the George D. Widener Director and CEO, the Philadelphia Museum of Art; Rebecca Rabinow, Director, the Menil Collection, Houston; Scott Rothkopf, Alice Pratt Brown Director, the Whitney Museum of American Art, New York; Scott Stulen, Illsley Ball Nordstrom Director and CEO, the Seattle Art Museum; and Billie Milam Weisman, Director, the Frederick R. Weisman Art Foundation, Los Angeles. Particular thanks go to those who agreed to lend works with which they live in profound intimacy—Bettina Bryant; Sueyun and Gene Locks; Linnea and George Roberts; and the Eastman Collection.

We at the Princeton University Art Museum are also indebted to The Willem de Kooning Foundation for their generous support of this publication, without which it might never have come to fruition. The exhibition was made possible by leadership support from the Allen R.

Adler, Class of 1967, Curatorial Leadership Fund; the Fanzhi Foundation for Art and Education; the Frances E. and Elias Wolf, Class of 1920, Fund; Gagosian; Shelly and Tony Malkin; the Robert Lehman Foundation; and Tom and Mila Tuttle. Additional support is provided by Christie's, Preston H. Haskell III, the Joseph L. Shulman Foundation Fund for Art Museum Publications, the Melanie and John Clarke Exhibition Fund, Mark W. Stevens and Annalyn Martha Swan, and the many generous contributors to the Director's Exhibition Fund.

Finally, although it may have been I who long hoped for such a project, the conception of the exhibition and the publication, and the determination to realize them, belong to John Elderfield, an independent scholar who is Chief Curator Emeritus of Painting and Sculpture at the Museum of Modern Art, and was the inaugural Allen R. Adler, Class of 1967, Distinguished Curator and Lecturer at the Princeton University Art Museum, and Mitra Abbaspour, who was Haskell Curator of Modern and Contemporary Art here at Princeton when she began work on this project, and is now Houghton Curator of Modern and Contemporary Art and Head, Division of Modern and Contemporary Art, at the Harvard Art Museums. They have been aided by Lee Colón, research associate at the Princeton University Art Museum, and many colleagues at Princeton and beyond who contributed their expertise and assistance in the development of the exhibition and the publication, and who are thanked in the preface, to which I add my sincere gratitude.

James Christen Steward

Nancy A. Nasher–David J. Haemisegger,
Class of 1976, Director
Princeton University Art Museum

Preface and Acknowledgments

The exhibition that this publication accompanies focuses upon a group of paintings by Willem de Kooning—small in number, large in importance—that are among those he made prior to and after his first solo exhibition opened at the Charles Egan Gallery, New York, on April 12, 1948. The publication is not a catalogue of the Princeton University Art Museum exhibition but discusses many more works that de Kooning made in the years 1945–50 than is possible to include in a focused museum presentation.

The essay by John Elderfield proceeds from a critic's response to the Egan show—that the artist's "subject seems to be the crucial intensity of the creative process itself, which de Kooning has translated into a new and purely pictorial idiom." As such, it follows the development of his creative process over the second half of the 1940s. The essay by Mitra Abbaspour examines the context against which this development occurred—notably, the debates on abstraction versus figuration and on what comprises a specifically American art. These texts are accompanied by a new, detailed chronology of this period by Lee Colón, and a contribution by conservators James Coddington and Bart J. C. Devolder on their study of Princeton's *Black Friday*, which was in the Egan exhibition.

Our work was aided by members of The Willem de Kooning Foundation, especially Executive Director Amy Schichtel, Senior Researcher David Roger Anthony, and Archivist Richard Goldstein; and of the Willem de Kooning Catalogue Raisonné, LLC Project Manager Stephen Mack. John Elderfield's research for his essay was aided by that of Lauren Mahony, Delphine Huisinga, and Jennifer Field, his collaborators on the catalogue of the Museum of Modern Art's 2011 *De Kooning: A Retrospective*; and its composition by his customary first reader, Jeanne Collins. In addition to the team at The Willem de Kooning Foundation, Mitra Abbaspour benefitted greatly from viewing many of the paintings that are the subject of this book with John Elderfield, and from subsequent conversations with him on process and the influences of the era as well as his close reading of her text. Many of the curators and conservators at museums that hold works of this period made their collections and object files accessible and joined in the conversation; Mitra is grateful for this generosity. Regular conversations with Lee Colón regarding archival documents that were the focus of her research were essential to the formation of her essay.

Lee's extensive research for her chronology drew on many contacts: Marisa Bourgoin, head of reference services, Archives of American Art; Jacob Burckhardt and Tom Burckhardt, Estate of Rudy Burckhardt; Shelly Buring, special collections, Research Center, Gelman Library, the George Washington University; Michela Campagnolo, Archivio Storico della Biennale di Venezia, Fondazione La Biennale di Venezia; Alex Paul Chapin, program director, Milton Resnick and Pat Passlof Foundation; Mark Coltrain, oral historian, Belk Library and Information Commons, Appalachian State University; Sarah Downing, retired archivist, Western Regional Archives; Mary Emma Harris; Mahsa Hatam, reference librarian, Getty Library, Getty Research Institute; Michelle Harvey, the Rona Roob Head of Archives Services, the Museum of Modern Art; Grace Hopkins, director, Berta Walker Gallery; Alexandra Katich, photography archivist, the Art Institute of Chicago; Denise Lassaw, Ibram Lassaw Estate and Studio; Jim Levis, Levis Fine Art; Lawrence Lewitin, Estate of Landès Lewitin; Rossy Mendez, reference archivist, New York City Municipal Archives; Cherie Miller, archivist, Western Regional Archives; Lena Newman, Rare Books, Avery Architectural and Fine Arts Library, Columbia University; Rachael Nutt, library collections specialist, Marquand Library of Art and Archaeology, Princeton University; Katy Rogers, programs director and director, Robert Motherwell Catalogue Raisonné, Dedalus Foundation; Jessica Salinas, librarian, The Henry W. and Albert A. Berg Collection of English and American Literature, the New York Public Library; Alice Sebrell, director of preservation, Black Mountain College Museum and Arts Center; Deborah Shapiro, archivist (reference), Smithsonian Institution Archives, Smithsonian Libraries and Archives; Isabella Strazzabosco, library assistant, Newberry Library;

Jillian Suarez, former head of library services, Archives Library, and Research Collections, the Museum of Modern Art, New York; Ashley Swinford, public services assistant, Center for Creative Photography; Kyle R. Triplett, rare book librarian, The Brooke Russell Astor Reading Room for Rare Books and Manuscripts, the New York Public Library; and Jim Zimmerman, photographer/archivist, Provincetown Art Association and Museum.

At the Princeton University Art Museum, our first thanks go to James Steward, Nancy A. Nasher–David J. Haemisegger, Class of 1976, Director, an enthusiastic advocate of the project from its beginning. The exhibition was made possible by the generosity of those who loaned works to it; both the individual lenders and those who facilitated the loan of works from their institutions are thanked in James's foreword to this publication. In Princeton, our work on the exhibition was aided by Cassie DiCarlo, exhibitions project manager; Juliana Ochs Dweck, chief curator; Michael Jacobs, senior gallery designer and manager of exhibitions services; Courtney Lacy, manager of foundation and government relations; Carol Rossi, registrar; and Irma Ramirez, head of graphic design. In the creation of this accompanying publication, we thank Calvin Brown and Matt Ward for their scholarly review of our texts, making important suggestions. And it is with great pleasure that we acknowledge the role of Janet Rauscher, editor, in managing and editing so sympathetically our texts, aided by Jane Friedman, copy editor. And we thank Katy Homans for having produced a beautiful book, the printing of which was overseen with such care by Jay Stewart and his team at Puritan Press.

John Elderfield, Mitra Abbaspour, and Lee Colón

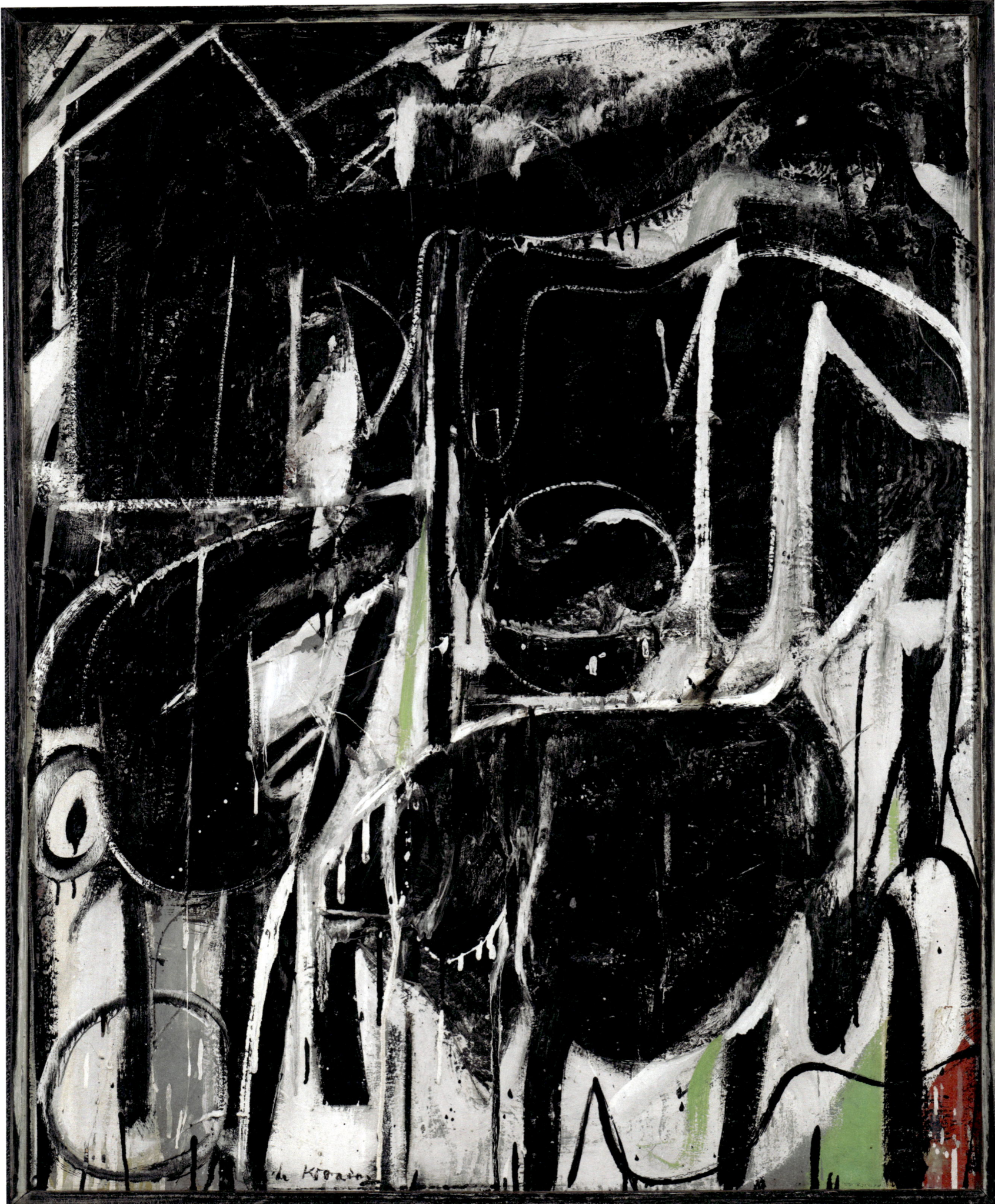

The Creative Process Itself

JOHN ELDERFIELD

Willem de Kooning's first solo exhibition opened at the Charles Egan Gallery in New York on April 12, 1948, twelve days before the artist's forty-fourth birthday. By this point, he already had an underground reputation among the city's artists for single paintings in group exhibitions and from visitors to his studio. "Having chosen at last, in his early forties, to show his work," wrote critic Clement Greenberg, "he comes before us in his maturity, in possession of himself, with his means under his control, and with enough knowledge of himself and of painting in general to exclude all irrelevancies."[1] Featuring paintings that are now among the artist's most celebrated, the Egan show quickly cemented de Kooning's status as a leader among American avant-garde artists. The present publication, and the exhibition it accompanies, is focused around a selection of these works, while also addressing examples of those from 1945 to 1950 that led to and succeeded them.

De Kooning's development over these years belongs among the greatest short periods of radical change in modern art. Moreover, his invention throughout these years was not only *continual*—always underway as, for example, Henri Matisse's transformation of his art step-by-step from 1905 Fauvism to 1910 high decoration. De Kooning's work was one of the few that was also *continuous*—uninterrupted in time and sequence, comprising not the replacement of one style by another but an unbroken process of revising a personal vocabulary with ever-more ambitious results.[2]

In this respect, de Kooning's richly productive period corresponds to that of his peer Jackson Pollock over roughly the same time frame. They differ, though, in one basic way. Pollock's continuous development through the first half of the 1940s was substantially unidirectional, taking him to an increasingly more radical form of abstract painting. In contrast, de Kooning's development was at once continuous and dialectic, moving back and forth between abstract and representational painting.

But that is to simplify a more complex process. Technical examination shows that some of de Kooning's works started out as abstractions but ended up as figurative, and vice versa.[3] Moreover, body parts in some figurative works differ little from difficult-to-describe passages in abstract works. In his review of the Egan exhibition, Greenberg dubbed de Kooning "an outright 'abstract' painter." By surrounding "abstract" with scare quotes, the critic conceded that paintings in the show could be called abstract only because they could not be said to be representational.[4] Neither one nor the other, but both.

Or both separately, at the same time. Indeed, that is how de Kooning proceeded in the years prior to, and during, the years under examination here, begging the question, How best to begin? Before doing so, however, we should bear in mind a far less noticed response to the Egan exhibition, by *Art News* critic Renée Arb, who observed: "His subject seems to be the crucial intensity of the creative process itself, which de Kooning has translated into a new and purely pictorial idiom."[5] According to Elaine de Kooning (neé Fried), his wife since 1943, the artist would come to regard Arb's review as "a prophetic statement about his work."[6] What follows here, as well as throughout the publication as a whole and the exhibition it accompanies, is based on the assumption that it is precisely from concentrated attention on a set of related objects made in a relatively short period that we come closest to understanding how crucial was the intensity of de Kooning's creative process itself.

FIRST PRINCIPLES
A Whole Series of Operations

Before proceeding further, we need to realize that we cannot be sure about the specific dates when de Kooning made his paintings, especially those from this period, including when he completed them. Describing the working method of his friend Edgar Degas, the great critic Paul Valéry characterized "a painting . . . [as] the result of a limitless number of sketches—and of a whole *series of operations.*"[7] Even though, to my knowledge, de Kooning was not aware of this quote, it aptly characterizes his approach. So, too, how Valéry further described Degas: "I am convinced that he felt a work could never be

called *finished*, and that he could not conceive how an artist could look at one of his pictures after a time and not feel the need to retouch it."[8] As far as I am aware, de Kooning's collectors never got to the point of Degas's in hiding his works to prevent the artist's reworking of them; nonetheless, anything in these years that de Kooning himself possessed was never safe from revision.

According to the dealer Allan Stone, who knew the artist well from the 1960s onward, "De Kooning in his prime never felt a painting was finished. He worked and reworked, often painting over a painting many times. It was Elaine [de Kooning] who would often pull him from a painting, declaring it to be 'done,' and it was Elaine who named many of his works."[9] This tendency was true of de Kooning's earlier works as well, as confirmed by his friend Thomas B. Hess, who wrote the first monograph on the artist, published in 1959. As Hess explains, de Kooning's habit of continually revising made it difficult to identify the sequence in which he made his paintings:

> **De Kooning's pictures are worked on over and over again during long periods of time. He did not sell paintings with any regularity until 1954. Old pictures in the studio often were painted out or drastically changed. He does not sign pictures until they leave the studio. He almost never dates them, and in the case of the few dated paintings and drawings, the dates usually refer to when the picture was sold or given away to a friend—which might have been several years after conclusion.[10]**

Hess confessed that, "aside from a handful of works, most [in his book] can be dated only within 18 to 24 months. And a few may be off by 36." His conclusion, which likewise applies to the present publication, was: "This has made the chronology of de Kooning's work a problem of interior stylistic development."[11] In the present case, my account of his work through the second half of the 1940s is, therefore, a historical one, in the sense that James Boswell defined such an approach in his *Life of Samuel Johnson* (1791). Boswell distinguished between

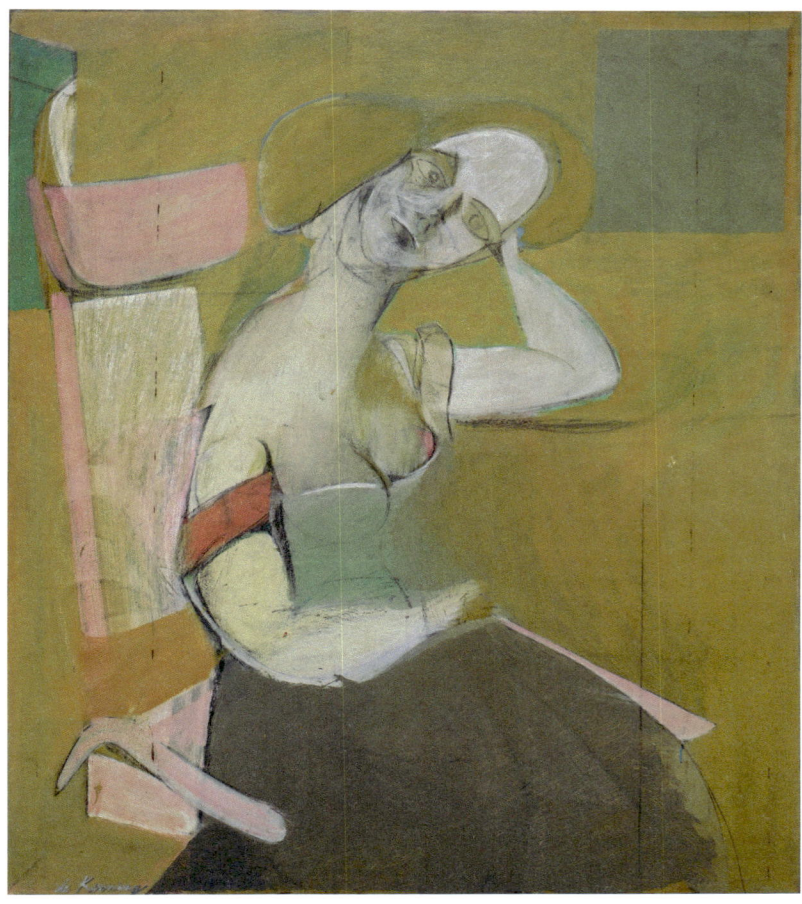

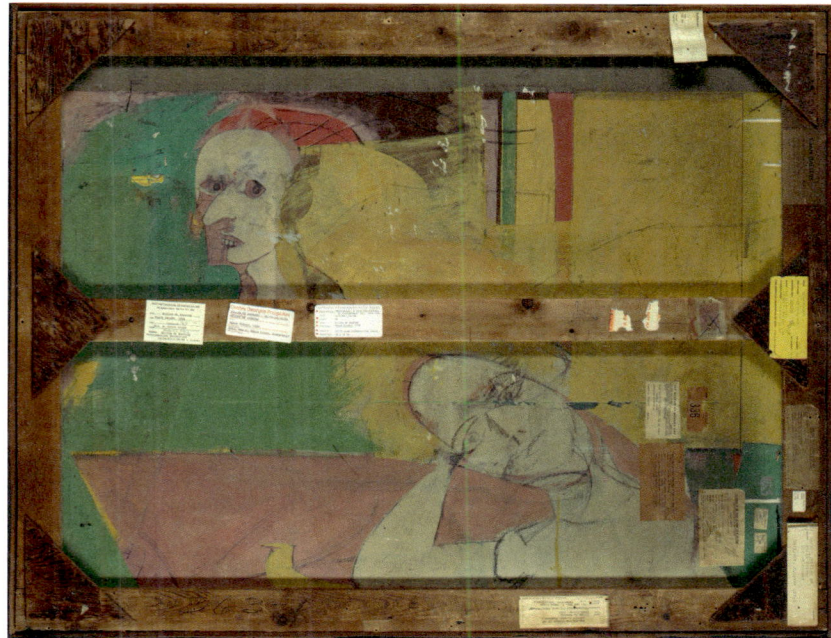

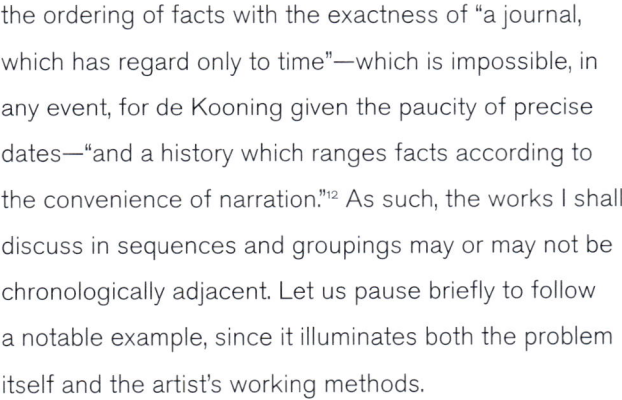

the ordering of facts with the exactness of "a journal, which has regard only to time"—which is impossible, in any event, for de Kooning given the paucity of precise dates—"and a history which ranges facts according to the convenience of narration."[12] As such, the works I shall discuss in sequences and groupings may or may not be chronologically adjacent. Let us pause briefly to follow a notable example, since it illuminates both the problem itself and the artist's working methods.

In his 1959 book, Hess dates the painting *Woman Sitting* (fig. 1) to circa 1939, making it the first of de Kooning's series of Woman paintings. By 1968, however, he had modified its date to 1943–44.[13] To complicate matters, an inverted oil sketch of the woman's head and supporting arm appears on the back of the canvas *Black Friday* (see figs. 2, 28), which was probably painted in 1948. Since it is highly unlikely that the sketch dates to 1948, the canvas must be one of the "old pictures in the studio" to which Hess referred, which "often were painted out, or drastically changed"—prompting us to wonder what may lie beneath the front surface of *Black Friday*.

Figure 1
Willem de Kooning, *Woman Sitting,* 1943–44
Oil and charcoal on composition board, 122.6 × 106.7 cm.
Private collection

Figure 2
Willem de Kooning, Verso of ***Black Friday,* 1948** (see fig. 28), rotated 90 degrees counter-clockwise

Figure 3
Willem de Kooning, *The Wave,* ca. 1942–44
Oil on fiberboard, 121.9 × 121.9 cm. Smithsonian American Art Museum, Washington, DC. Gift from the Vincent Melzac Collection (1980.6.1)

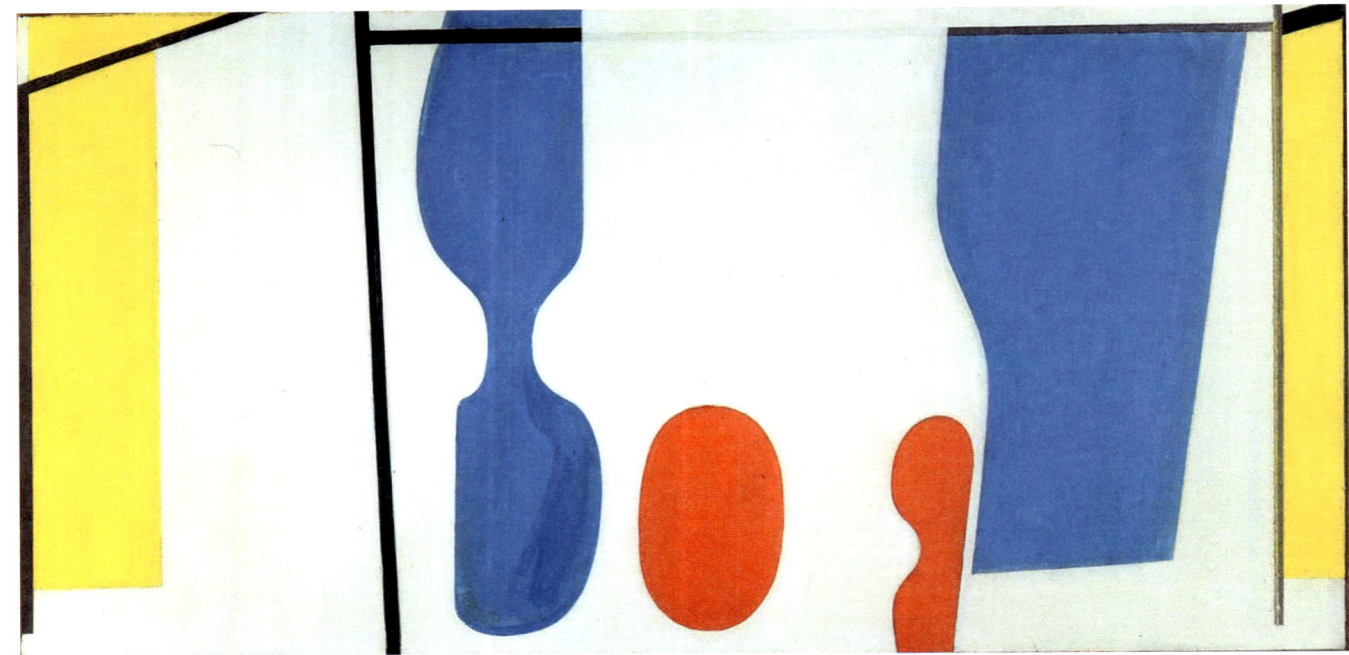

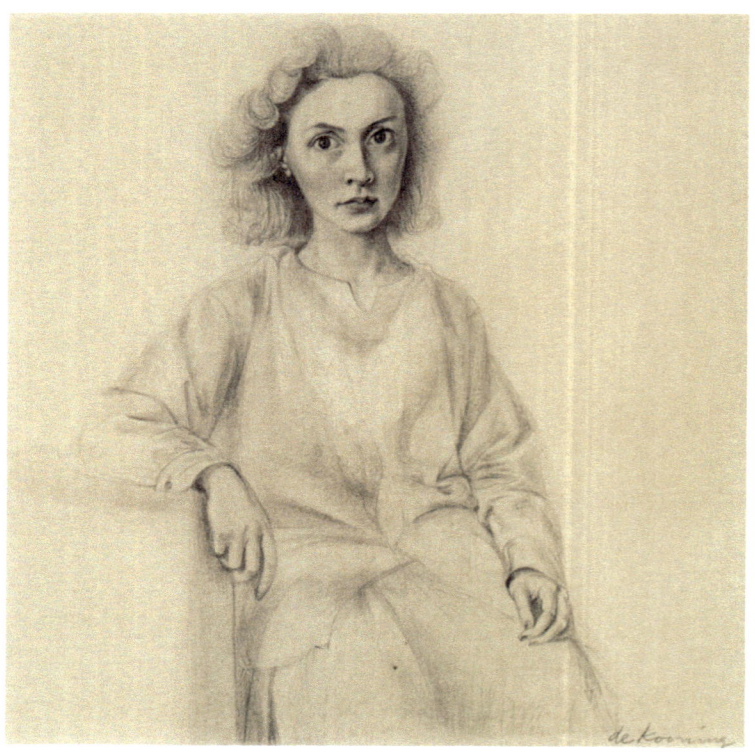

Figure 4
Willem de Kooning, *Father, Mother, Sister, Brother,* ca. 1937
Oil on board, 30.5 × 55.9 cm. Private collection

Figure 5
Willem de Kooning, *Portrait of Elaine,* ca. 1940–41
Pencil on paper, 31.1 × 30.2 cm. Private collection

There is more: *Woman Sitting* is compositionally akin to the abstract painting *The Wave* (fig. 3), which Hess dates to around 1942. The predominantly black curved elements of the abstraction echo the forms of the seated woman; the black teardrop shapes her tilted head. And both canvases have a prominent large rectangle in the top-right corner. Hess tells us that the drawings de Kooning used to make his paintings accumulated on his studio floor to such a degree that he neatly arranged them in portfolios for future reference.[14] So, did he pull out a tracing that he had used to compose *The Wave* to make *Woman Sitting*, or vice versa—either one after the other, or one well after the other had been completed? We will never know.[15]

Woman Sitting and *The Wave* seem, to varying extents, unfinished. In the former, this is revealed by the visible signs of underdrawing not precisely followed as well as passages obviously changed; in the latter, by areas of incompletion. In contrast, the abstractions the artist had made in the 1930s (fig. 4), inspired by recent works by Pablo Picasso, were so carefully composed and rendered that he later conceded they were "timid."[16] Their timidity, it seems fair to say, lies in their being so perfected—because of, not despite, the considerable, extended pictorial invention that gave rise to works of this kind. The same was true of de Kooning's meticulous early-1940s portrait drawings of his wife, Elaine, inspired by the French Neoclassical artist Jean Auguste Dominique Ingres, that attest to his extraordinary facility as a draftsman (fig. 5). De Kooning had studied academic drawing at the Académie van Beeldende Kunsten en Technische Wetenschappen (Academy of Fine Arts and Applied Sciences) in Rotterdam from 1917 to about 1921. There, it seems, a single drawing routinely took three to six months to complete.[17] De Kooning's Ingresque academic drawings, which are widely admired, did not take that long to make, but even so apparently long enough to feel torturous. He said that if he kept this up, he would go crazy, remembered his friend Rudy Burckhardt.[18] It may well have been de Kooning's experience of Surrealism that freed him from his timidity and saved him from that fate.

Surrealism had become a major presence in the New York art world by 1942–44, facilitated in part by Peggy Guggenheim's Art of This Century gallery and the movement's self-appointed leader, André Breton's, activities in the city in these years. De Kooning's *The Wave* was included in Sidney Janis's important publication *Abstract and Surrealist Art in America* (1944) and displayed at Art of This Century's *Autumn Salon* in 1945. Nonetheless, he was uneasy about the expanding, increasingly dogmatic Surrealist circle there, and his friend Arshile Gorky's embrace of it would be a reason for their later estrangement. The one artist affiliated with Surrealism who de Kooning clearly admired was Joan Miró, of whom the astute Greenberg wrote in 1944: "Miró belongs among the living masters. He is the one new figure since the last war to have contributed importantly to the great painting tradition of our day—that which runs from Cézanne through fauvism and cubism."[19] *The Wave* does reveal the influence of some of Miró's works, but a less obvious indebtedness to him characterizes what happened thereafter and led into the principal direction of de Kooning's art in the second half of the decade. It had two prominent features, both of which promoted the realization of previously untapped aspects of his artistic personality.

Automatism and the Grotesque

In 1924, Breton famously defined Surrealism as "pure psychic automatism by means of which one intends to express, either verbally, or in writing, or in any other manner, the actual functioning of thought. Dictated by thought, in the absence of any control exercised by reason, free of any aesthetic or moral concern."[20] Miró's version of automatism found inspiration in the embrace of chance, letting his brush wander over the canvas and playing with his materials, including pasting bits of paper randomly on his canvases or tacking the canvases to the wall to paint from: in either case, freeing himself from conscious control before consciously applying himself to their organization.

Elaine de Kooning recalled that her husband "would begin a picture by writing words across the surface of the canvas. These were very large—one or two to a canvas—hastily scrawled with charcoal or brush using the greatest possible muscular freedom of shoulder or arm. . . . I can almost remember the exact words—one like *hope* clear across the top, and one like *man* across the bottom."[21] He may well have begun *The Wave* in such a way, then filled in the cavities formed by the letters, turning them into shapes that resembled a figure seated in a chair.

De Kooning's early training from 1916 to 1920 at the decorating firm Gidding & Zonen in Rotterdam, where he worked prior to and while at the Academy, provided him with skills in marbling, graining, and composing decorative designs. This experience lay behind his continued interest in lettering, which is evident in his work from the later 1940s as well. His background in commercial art also prepared him for playing with his materials. According to a Dutch friend, artist Joop Sanders, de Kooning "used to do these things that they do in commercial art layouts—they cut out and do a sort of collage, a final paste out. I remember him . . . drawing lipsticks . . . He would make an arrangement by cutting them out and moving them around."[22] Hess elaborated on this point, saying that de Kooning "will do drawings on transparent tracing paper, scatter them one on top of the other, study the composite drawing that appears on top,

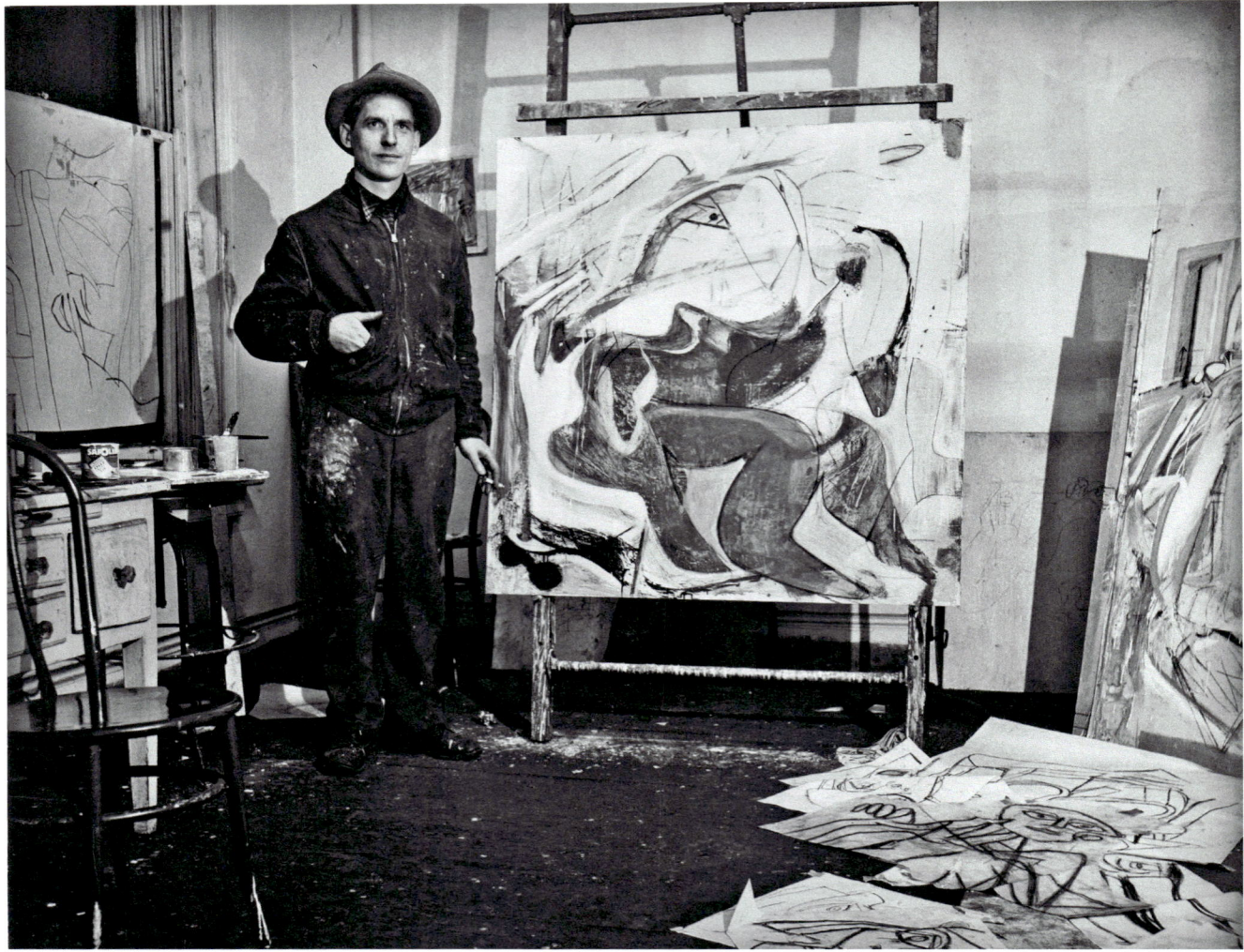

Figure 6
Harry Bowden (1907–1965; born Los Angeles, CA; died Sausalito, CA), **Willem de Kooning's studio, 1946**
Photographic print. Harry Bowden Papers, Archives of American Art, Smithsonian Institution, Washington, DC

Figure 7
Joan Miró (1893–1983; born Barcelona, Spain; died Palma de Mallorca, Spain), ***Dutch Interior (I)*, 1928**
Oil on canvas, 91.8 × 73 cm. The Museum of Modern Art, New York. Mrs. Simon Guggenheim Fund (163.1945)

Figure 8
Willem de Kooning, *Pink Angels*, ca. 1945
Oil and charcoal on canvas, 132.1 × 101.6 cm. Frederick R. Weisman Art Foundation, Los Angeles

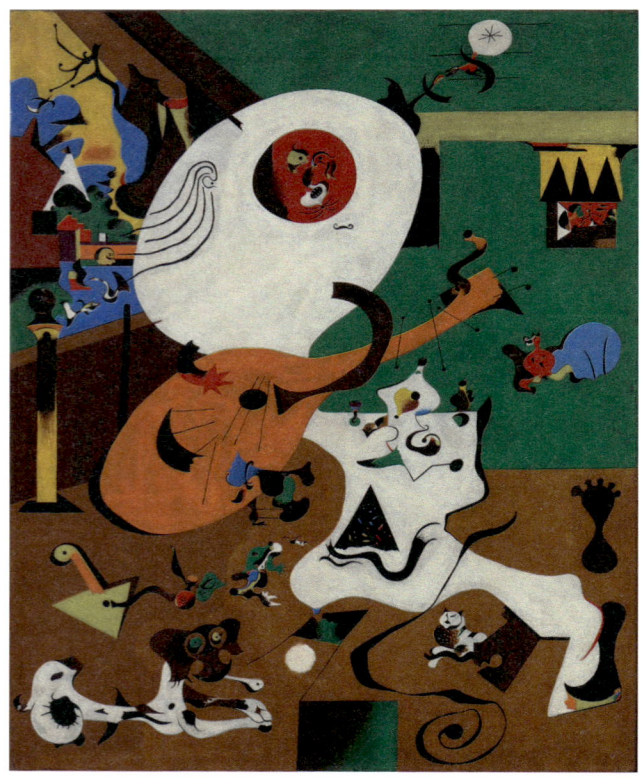

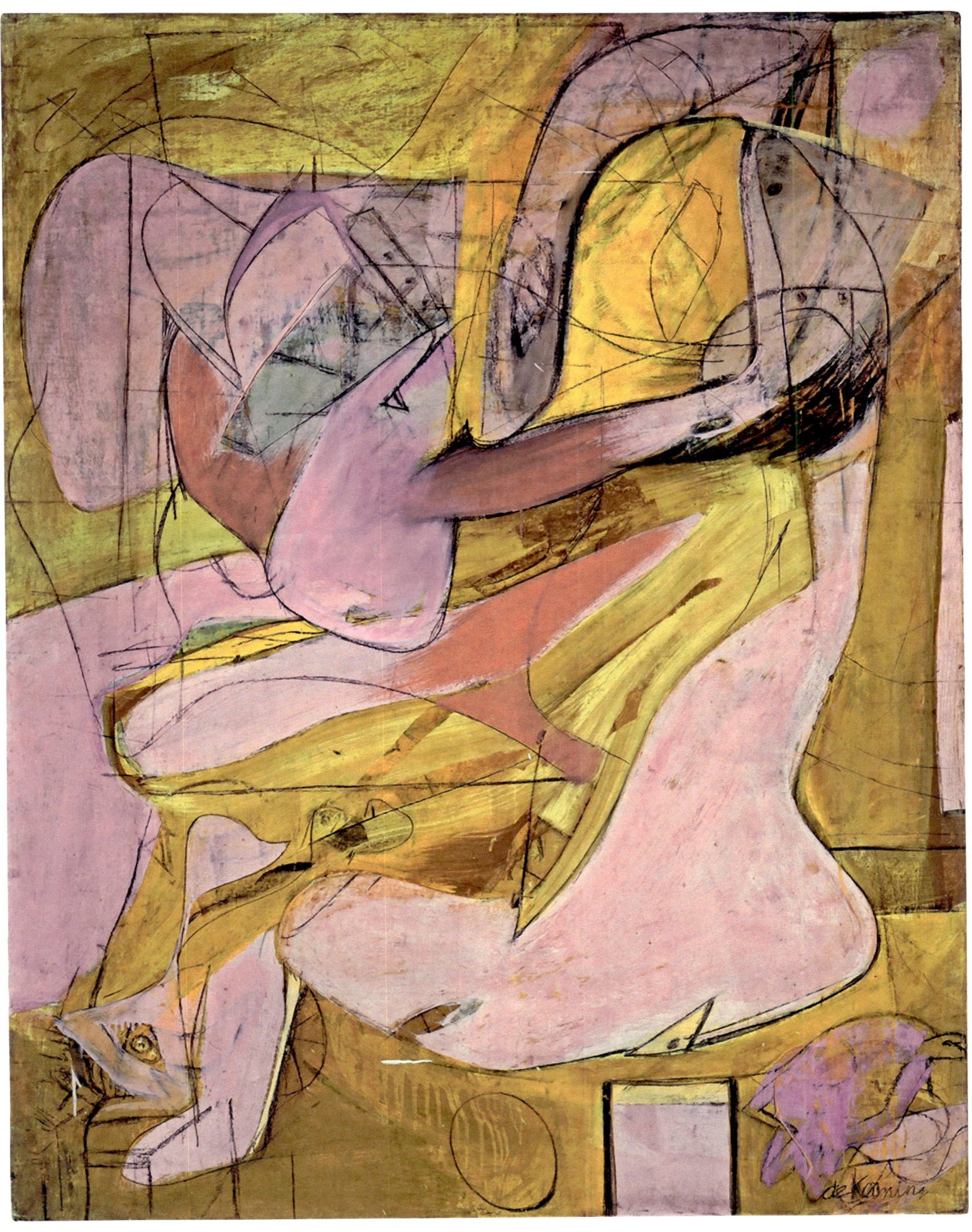

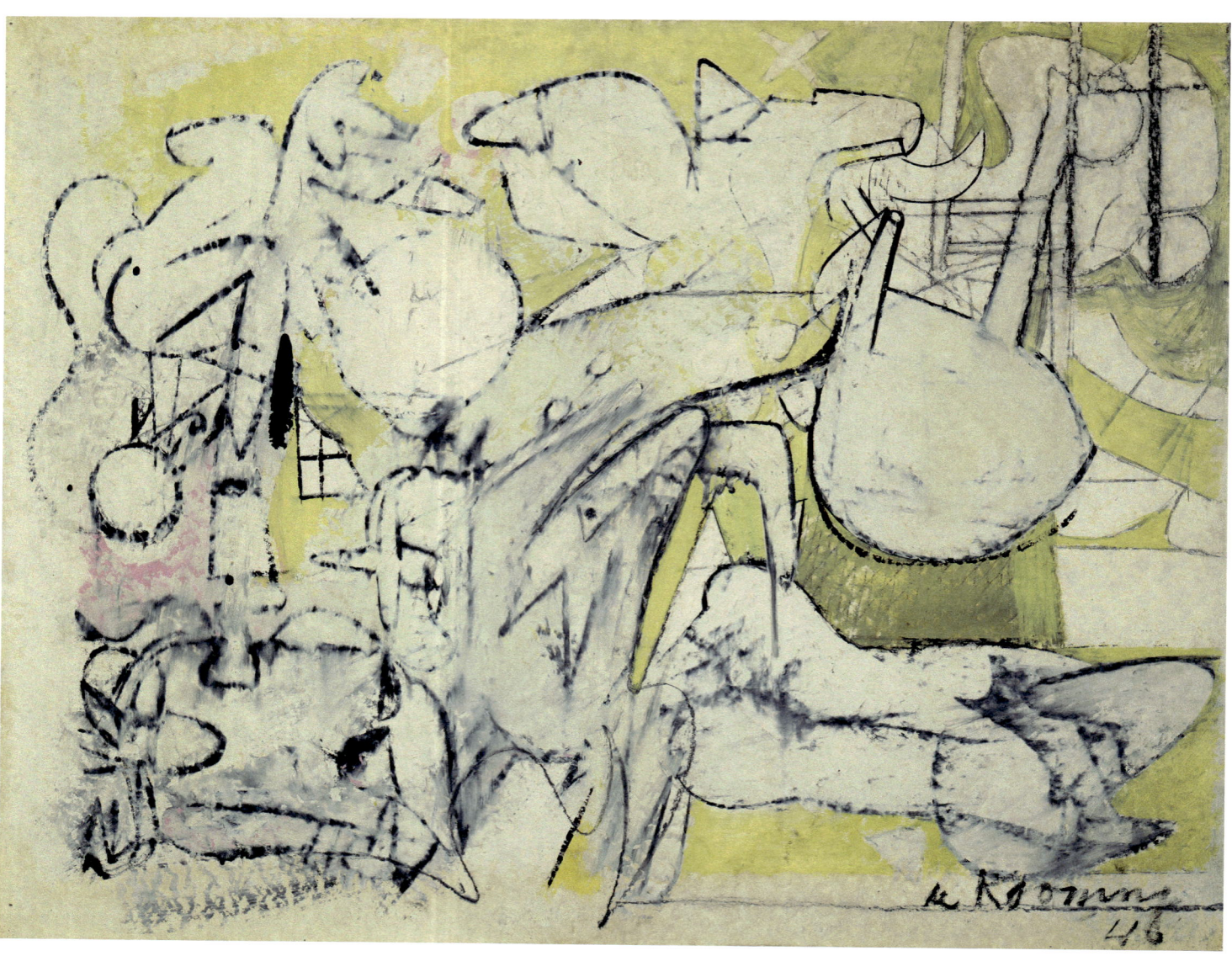

Figure 9
Willem de Kooning, *Special Delivery*, 1946
Oil, enamel, and charcoal on paper mounted on paperboard,
59.4 × 76.2 cm. Hirshhorn Museum and Sculpture Garden,
Smithsonian Institution, Washington, DC. Gift of the Joseph H.
Hirshhorn Foundation, 1966

make a drawing from this, reverse it, tear it in half, and put it on top of still another drawing."[23]

A photograph of de Kooning in his Fourth Avenue studio in November 1946 (fig. 6) shows this kind of composition in process, producing—at least at this stage—an image that deserves to be called "grotesque." The great nineteenth-century critic John Ruskin defined the Grotesque as "composed of two elements, one ludicrous, the other fearful." Wanting it both ways, de Kooning once said, "I like the grotesque. It's more joyous."[24]

Commenting on Ruskin's words in his 1948 book on Miró, Greenberg proposed that the "cheerful flamboyance" of his work was underpinned by hints of the monstrous and the macabre.[25] Miró's *Dutch Interior (I)* of 1928 (fig. 7) was acquired by the Museum of Modern Art (MoMA) in 1945, probably the same year in which de Kooning painted the macabre *Pink Angels* (fig. 8). He appears to have paid attention not only to the overall metamorphic figuration of *Dutch Interior (I)* but also to specific motifs, including the abstracted animals that surround a rectangle on the bottom edge. De Kooning added the features of grotesque animals in the same location in his own cheerfully flamboyant composition. The fish head at lower left and the scurrying, crablike creature at lower right are images derived from Pieter Bruegel the Elder's prints of *The Last Judgment* and *The Seven Deadly Sins* (both 1558),

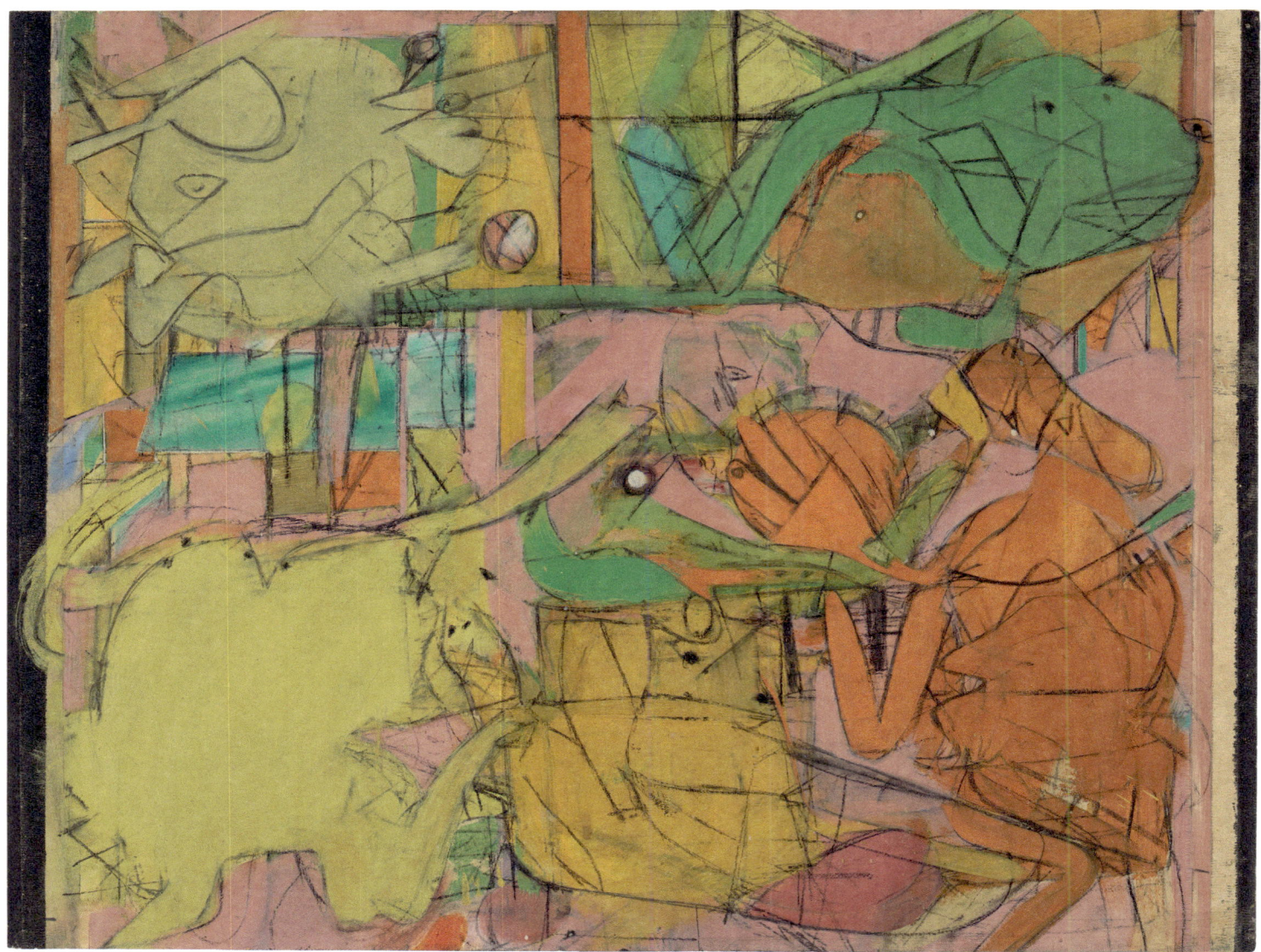

which de Kooning could have seen at the Metropolitan Museum of Art. He positioned these motifs below a drawing of an upturned head that lies just above the knee of the big, seated angel, the latter of which comes from a very different source—Picasso's *Guernica* (1937), which went on long-term view at the Museum of Modern Art on July 26, 1943.[26]

Special Delivery (fig. 9), dated to 1946, transforms such grotesque figural motifs into more ambiguous biomorphic forms, rendered in white on a yellow ground, set in an interior. The composition's lower-left quadrant appears to have been traced from a small painting titled *D* (see fig. 46), which allows us to see how that section depicts an abstracted reclining female figure beneath a lamp and a window. Also that year, such motifs completely filled a composition titled *Judgment Day* (fig. 10),

which de Kooning copied at a greatly enlarged scale in about three days with the aid of fellow artist Milton Resnick, to create a seventeen- foot-square backdrop for a dance called *Labyrinth*, performed on April 5, 1946.[27] Much later, in 1977, he told Hess that the backdrop portrayed the four angels at the Gates of Paradise.[28]

The performance of *Labyrinth* occurred eight months after the United States dropped atomic bombs on Hiroshima and Nagasaki on August 6 and 9, 1945, respectively, and de Kooning was not alone among artists in alluding to these events in their writings or statements. Not unexpectedly, as the Second World War came to a close, news of its carnage, of genocide, and of nuclear destruction gave rise to what W. H. Auden, the British poet domiciled in the United States, called "The Age of Anxiety"—the title of his long narrative poem published in 1947. Set in a bar in New York, Auden's poem—which describes the loneliness and anxiety-ridden purposelessness of its characters' lives and ends with their being drunk on the city's streets—is a dystopic rendering of what the lives of many impoverished artists at the time may have been like. Yet the convenient coincidence that it won the Pulitzer Prize for Poetry in 1948, the year of de Kooning's first solo exhibition, only goes to show that it was not, in fact, solely an age of anxious-seeming art.

De Kooning did refer to Hiroshima, albeit not directly, in a short lecture of 1951 at MoMA, featuring an extremely odd reference to angels: "Eyes that actually saw the light melted out of sheer ecstasy. For one instance, everybody was the same color. It made angels out of everybody. A truly Christian light, painful but forgiving."[29] Unsurprisingly, *Judgment Day* has been associated with that passage, and raises the question, which will continue to require attention, as to the extent to which a work by de Kooning may be judged to be an illustration of the title that he—or Elaine, or someone else—gave it.

I shall return to this topic presently. For the moment, though, I think we must agree with Greenberg's statement in his essay "Abstract, Representational and So Forth" that the value of illustration per se was indisputable, even in abstract art, but "not a value that is realized by, or as, *accretion*"[30]—a nicely put warning against reading too much into imaginative titles. In making this point, the critic observed that a work that "has an allegorical or anagogic meaning does not make it a more effective work than one that has solely a literal one."[31] It seems fair to say that the title of *Pink Angels* is not especially inviting of more than a nominal literal association, given the massively revised surface and complex relationship of figure and ground. In contrast, the tightly,

carefully composed *Judgment Day* seems to encourage an allegorical reading—while the interiors with grotesque inhabitants invite interpretation but refuse to provide it.

Never Empty Perfection

Writing in his journal in 1824, the great French painter Eugène Delacroix warned: "Never seek after an empty perfection. Some faults, some things which the vulgar call faults, often give vitality to a work."[32] Several decades later, he added, more impatiently, "The so-called conscientiousness of the great majority of painters is nothing but perfection laboriously applied to the art of being boring."[33] With rare exceptions, this was de Kooning's creed. He would say:

> For many years I was not interested in making a good painting . . . I didn't want to pin it down at all. I was interested in that before [presumably, meaning his work through the 1930s], but I found it was not my nature. . . . [I worked] [n]ot with the idea of perfection but to see how far one could go, you know—but not with the idea of really doing it. . . . [With] [a]nxiousness and dedication to fright maybe, or ecstasy, you know, like *The Divine Comedy*, to be like a performer; to see how long you can stay on the stage, with that imaginary audience.[34]

Given statements like this, and the fact that so much attention has been paid to de Kooning's willingness to let the process of painting show, we need to be clear that his obvious aim was to produce a work on which he had gone as far as he could go, at which point it was finally done—even if it took someone else to persuade him that it was. To look broadly at the interior stylistic development of de Kooning's work through the second half of the 1940s is to see two basic types of hybrid paintings—neither abstract nor representational, but both—and two kinds of figure compositions, which I will be mentioning a little later. There are very few hybrid canvases in which de Kooning appears to have deliberately set out to make a summative, hopefully not boring,

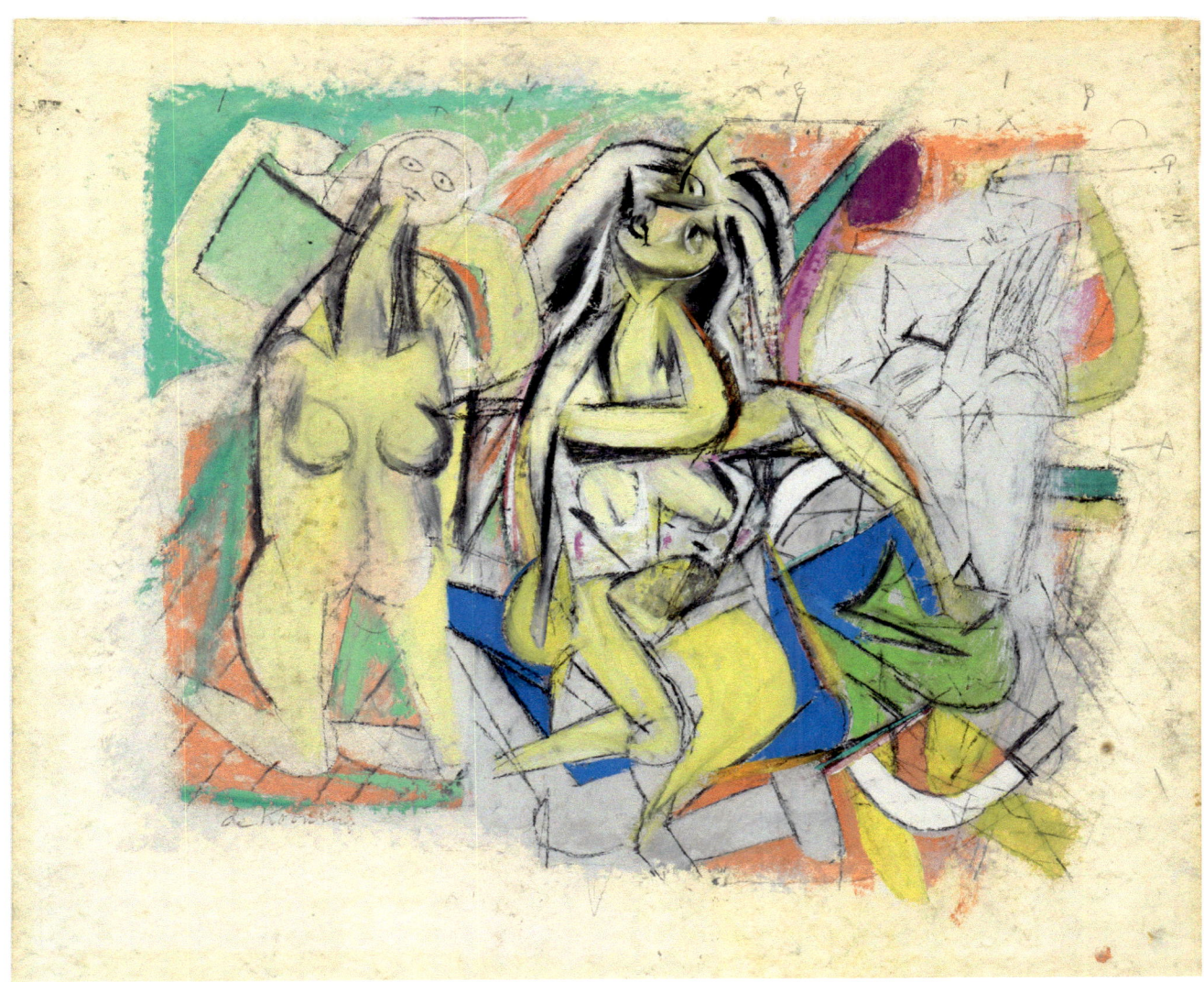

Figure 11
Willem de Kooning, *Untitled (Three Figures)*, 1947–48
Oil, enamel paints, graphite, and charcoal on paper, 52.7 ×
61 cm. Glenstone Museum, Potomac, MD

perfected composition. *Judgment Day* and its enlarge-ment, *Backdrop for "Labyrinth,"* both from 1946, were the least successful and the first of this kind. *Attic* and *Excavation* (see figs. 50, 51), from 1949–50, were the final, widely acclaimed pair. In contrast, most of these works followed the lead of *Pink Angels* in clearly having been declared "to be 'done,'" even though parts of some com-positions may be deemed provisional, while other works managed to appear stopped at the perfect moment with-out looking laboriously perfected at all.

We should remember that *Pink Angels* was likely painted only five years after de Kooning had been mak-ing his "timid" abstractions of the late 1930s and, more recently, the meticulous, Ingres-inspired portrait drawings of his wife, Elaine, from the early 1940s. The radical shift was noted in Greenberg's review of the Egan exhibition: "Emotion that demands singular, original expression tends

to be censored out by a really great facility, for facility has a stubbornness of its own and is loath to abandon easy satisfactions. The indeterminacies or ambiguity that characterizes some of de Kooning's pictures is caused, I believe, by his effort to suppress his facility."[35]

This recalls what T. S. Eliot famously said of poets: that "only those who have personality and emotions know what it means to want to escape from these things."[36] It may be said that only an artist with such a plenitude of draftsmanship skills as de Kooning knows what it means to want to escape from dependence upon them. There is, however, another side to the story, told by Gus Falk, one of de Kooning's students at Black Mountain College

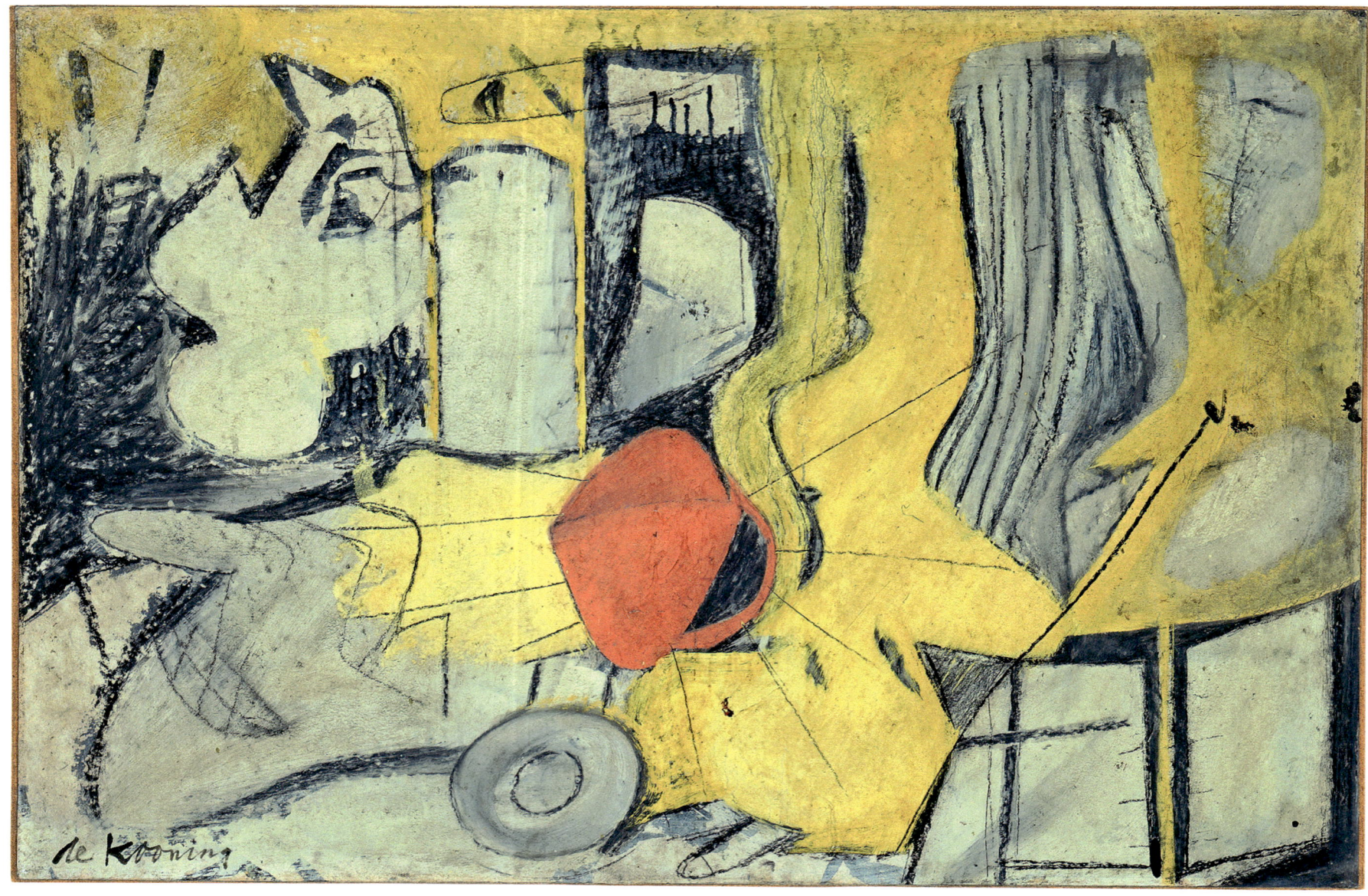

Figure 12
Willem de Kooning, *Secretary*, 1947–48
Oil and charcoal on paper mounted on fiberboard, 61.9 × 91.9 cm.
Hirshhorn Museum and Sculpture Garden, Smithsonian Institution,
Washington, DC. Gift of Joseph H. Hirshhorn, 1966 (66.1193)

in 1948. Falk recounted the artist revising *Attic*, then in
progress when he visited him a decade or so later:
"He made a drawing of it, to work on the parts where he
felt there was a problem. He worked on that picture carefully. 'Maybe I could throw a line here,' he would say. He
would erase parts, redraw it. In other words, he *did* it like
Ingres. It was not throwing his guts on the wall."[37]

What did Falk mean by saying "he did it like
Ingres"? Certainly not like the Ingres of the meticulous pencil drawings. Perhaps, Falk knew that Barnett

Newman had credited Ingres with being a progenitor
of Abstract Expressionism, saying, "That guy was an
abstract painter. . . . He looked at the canvas more often
than at the model. Kline, de Kooning, none of us would
have existed without him."[38] But what Falk describes
could not be further from what the critic Harold
Rosenberg called "action painting."[39] It would be Hess
who more specifically compared de Kooning's methods
to those of Ingres, "like de Kooning an encyclopedic
draftsman, who, once he had established the turn of a
bather's neck or the set of her spine, would rephrase
the shape with constantly re-inspired variation for the
rest of his life."[40] Of course, the result was very far from
Ingres's ever-more polished Neoclassicism. Allan Stone
got it right when he wrote: "De Kooning valued the

24

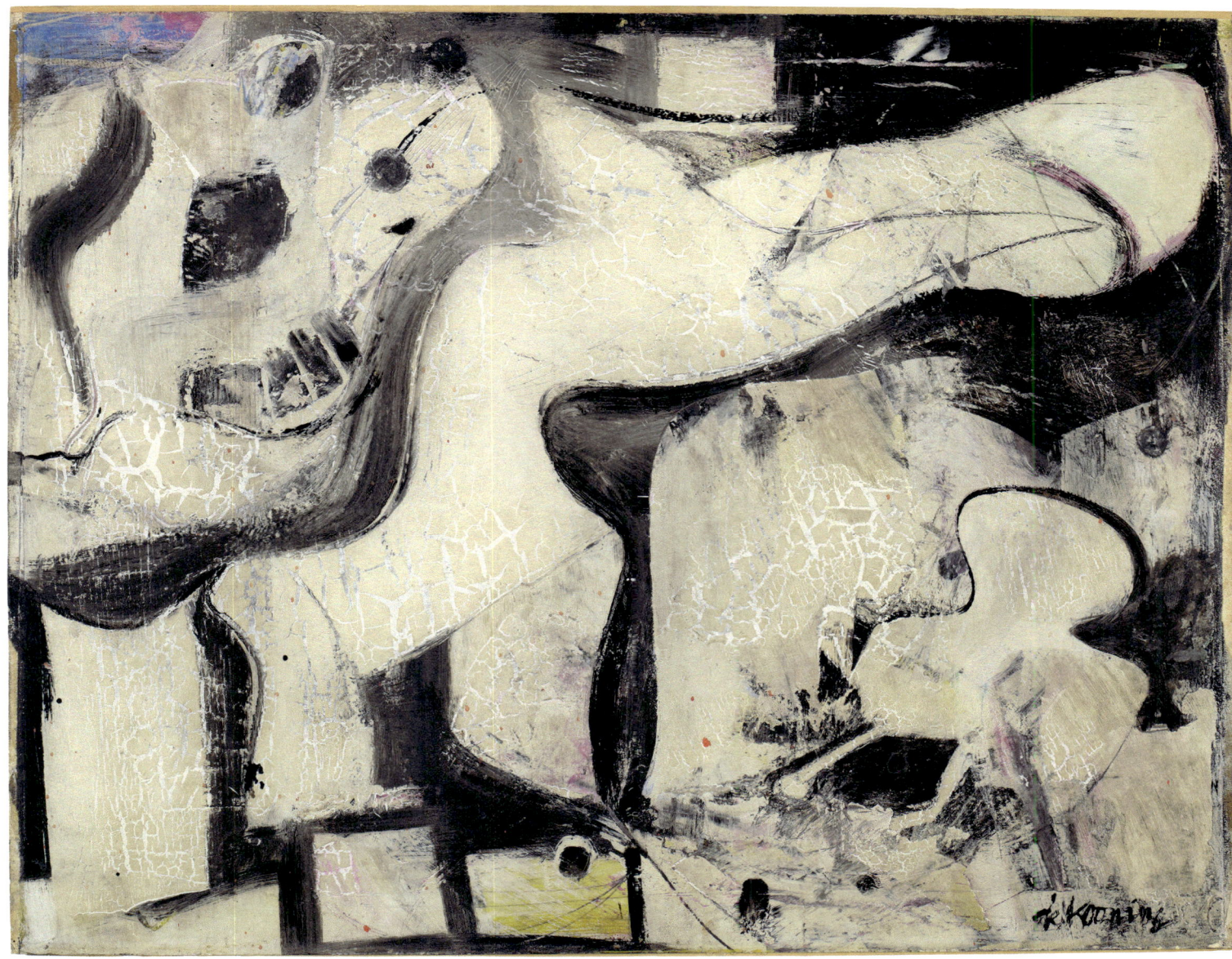

Figure 13
Willem de Kooning, *Night*, 1947–48
Oil on board, 55.9 × 73 cm. Minneapolis Institute of Art.
The John R. Van Derlip Fund and The Ethel Morrison Van Derlip
Fund (63.36)

appearance of spontaneity and pursued the accidental rigorously. He would try out a 'spontaneous' passage on vellum many times before he achieved the desired effect, and then he would meticulously reproduce the passage on canvas."[41]

Stone's assessment seems to reflect what Falk characterized: that it was "the *appearance* of spontaneity" that mattered to de Kooning, however meticulously it was realized. Although Falk was describing the artist at work on the densely composed *Attic* (see fig. 50), this careful additive and revisionary process may be seen in some of de Kooning's figure compositions, most notably, his small works on paper, reportedly from 1947–48, depicting men and women, and women without men (fig. 11). Some of these show de Kooning having dissected figures into

jigsaw-like parts; used tracing to repeat the same leg and arm fragments within an individual work (as he did from one such composition to another); and employed what he would later term "fitting-in" to weave together the body parts.[42] The settings of other works bear an affinity to presumably earlier grotesque interiors including *Special Delivery* (see fig. 9), but they are as splintery geometric as that had been biomorphic.

And such was de Kooning's range in this 1947–48 period that at this time he also made the most grotesque

25

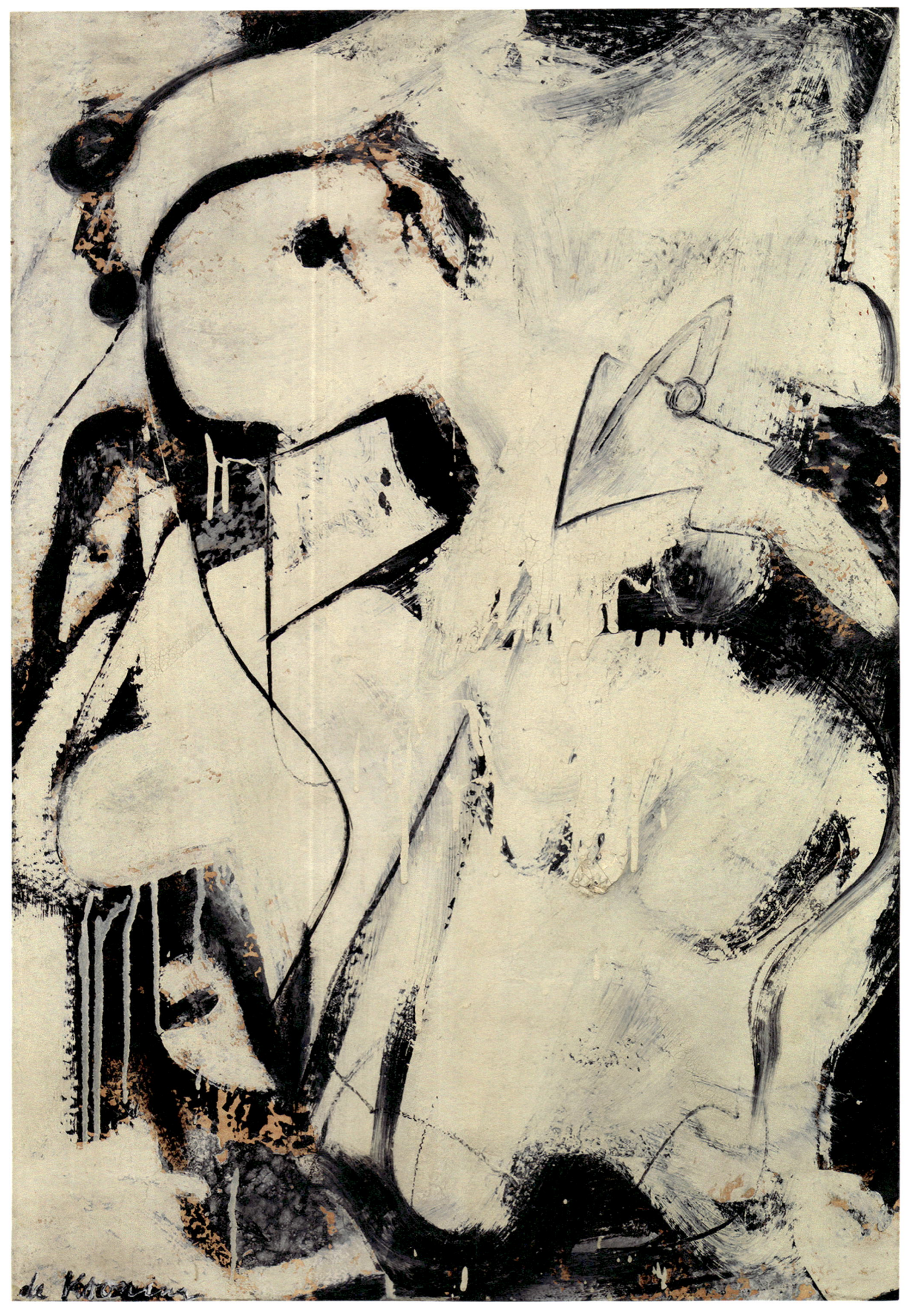

of these interiors: *Secretary* (fig. 12) and *Night* (fig. 13). The former belongs to a small group of paintings on the theme of the young American women who, after the war, entered the labor market to do office work, a theme popularized by *The Secretary's Day* (1947), an instructional film featuring glamorous actresses.[43] De Kooning's office scene is not easily deciphered but seems to picture a falling figure above a smiling face with a large nose; a red, Miró-like sexual symbol above a penis peeping out from below a yellow garment; a door at the top and an open window, or perhaps a notebook, below a falling, pleated gray cloth. Drips going toward the top edge show that *Secretary* was partly painted in an upturned position. If we look at it upside down, we see that de Kooning had traced this composition onto *Night*, or vice versa. *Night* is even more grotesque, with its grinning, ghoulish face set above a two-legged, amorphous creature that leans across the surface. Below it is the falling man of *Secretary* leaning rightward up in the corner. Flashes of blue, pink, and red, especially in the upper-left corner, suggest that *Night* had been a brightly colored composition like *Secretary* before being transformed into a nocturnal scene. De Kooning's Egan exhibition was most frequently discussed as a show dominated by black paintings. However, it seems fair to assume that he left *Night* out of the show because he did not want to include examples of his more macabre compositions.

The same would seem to hold for his omission of the contemporaneous black painting *The Moraine* (fig. 14). It may have been an extremely tactile response to Gorky's smoky-dark *Charred Beloved* paintings (fig. 15), shown at the Julien Levy Gallery in April–May 1946. The painting's title—referring to a flow of debris, specifically rock debris transported by glaciers—aptly describes the composition in its movement of areas of dense, resistant white and black paint across the paper. Close observation reveals that *The Moraine* depicts two figures—a standing, headless man overwhelmed by another with a raised arm. Paint both clotted and freely streaming down within and around the figures makes this the most nomi-

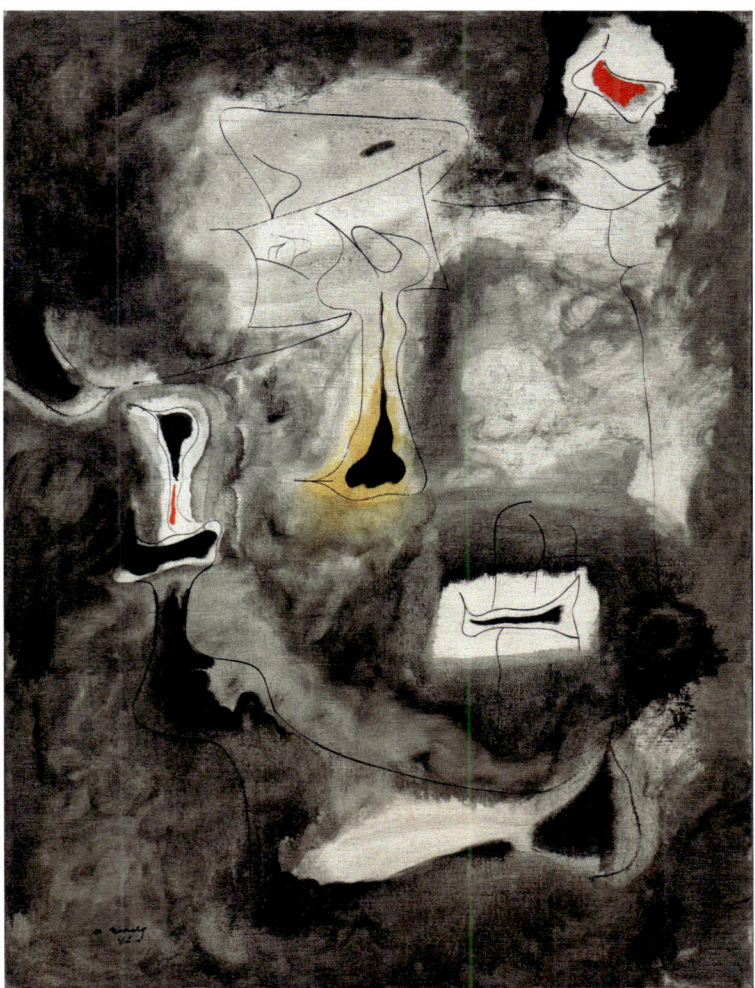

Figure 14
Willem de Kooning, *The Moraine*, 1947
Oil on paper mounted on Masonite, 93.7 × 65.1 cm. Eastman Collection

Figure 15
Arshile Gorky (1904–1948; born Dilkaya, Turkey; died Sherman, CT; active New York, NY, and Boston, MA), ***Charred Beloved No. 2, 1946***
Oil on canvas, 137.3 × 101.6 cm. National Gallery of Canada, Ottawa. Purchased 1971 (16690)

nally unfinished of the series of de Kooning's paintings of grotesque subjects. Evidently, it was initially painted in layers of black, with white over them. These are set on a substrate of perhaps brown (or later discolored) paper, regions of which appear within the visible black paint around the perimeter, while thin black lines describe undecipherable motifs on each side of the composition

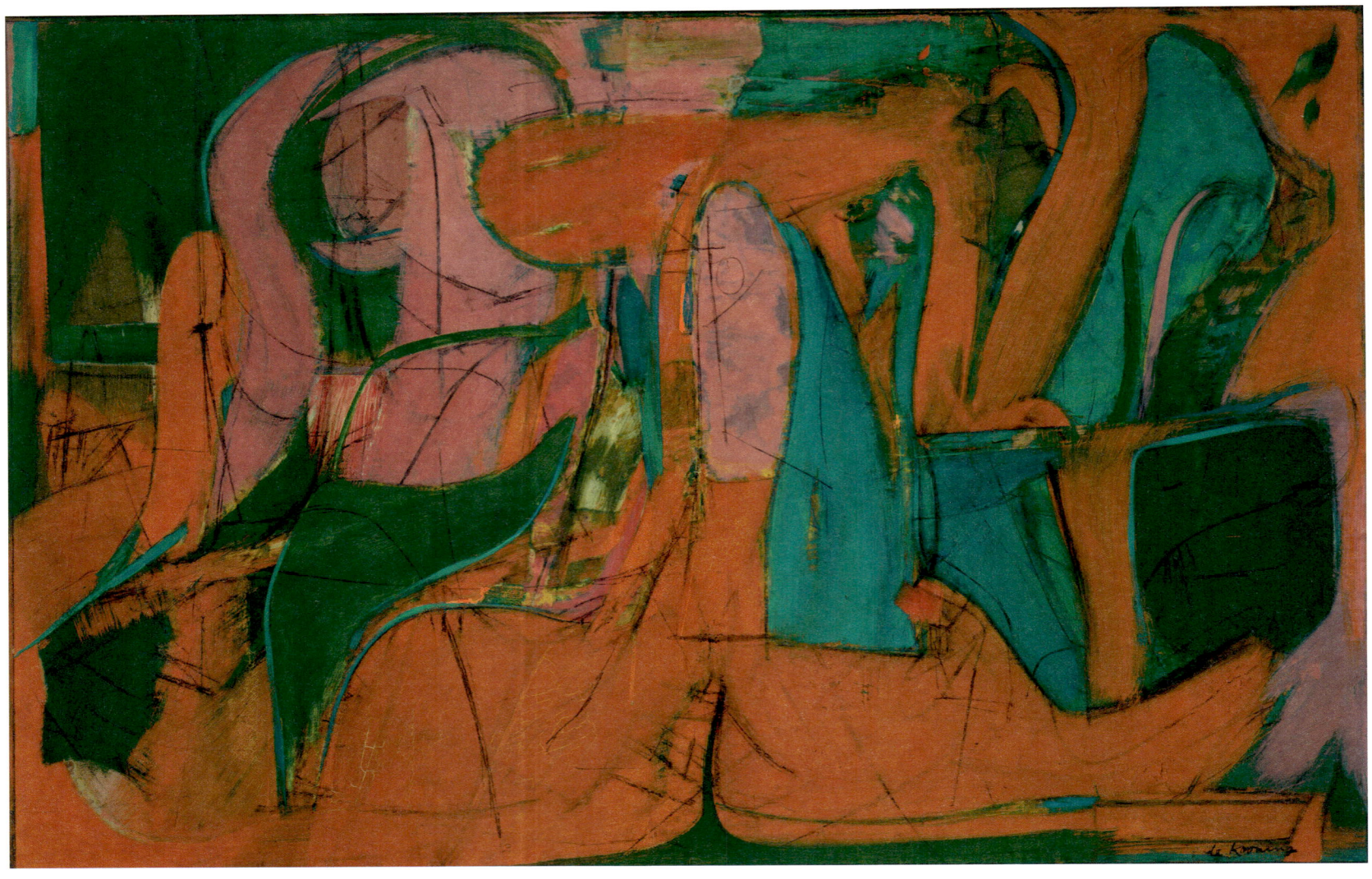

THE FIRST SOLO EXHIBITION
Selection and Allusion

De Kooning's first solo exhibition opened at New York's Charles Egan Gallery on April 12, 1948, and was scheduled to close on May 12. (Monthlong exhibitions were common then.) However, according to Elaine de Kooning, Egan extended the exhibition in the hope of selling more work "until it became an embarrassment to Bill."[44] (It probably closed on June 25.[45]) In fact, the exhibition did receive a reasonable amount of attention, most of it positive, as the documentation in the Chronology (pp. 85–88) here shows; and three of the ten, or possibly more, paintings shown were sold during or shortly after the exhibition, one of them, *Painting* (see fig. 27), to the Museum of Modern Art.[46]

There appears to have been no checklist of the exhibition. Clement Greenberg's review in *The Nation* says that it comprised "ten pictures . . . done within the last year"; that there did "not seem to be an identifiable image in any"; and leaves the impression that most of them were dominated by black and white.[47] Since the review was not illustrated, and other contemporaneous reviews were illustrated only in black and white—critical journals at that time rarely having color reproductions—readers were not able to judge the veracity of Greenberg's two descriptions. As we shall see later, neither was strictly accurate; it is therefore possible that the critic was also mistaken about the number of works shown. Renée Arb's short review in *Art News* was illustrated by *Painting* but speaks of "brilliant hues" as well as black and white; and there do appear to have been some, if not many, bright colors in the exhibition, judging by what the gallerist Charles Egan remembered.[48] As for the

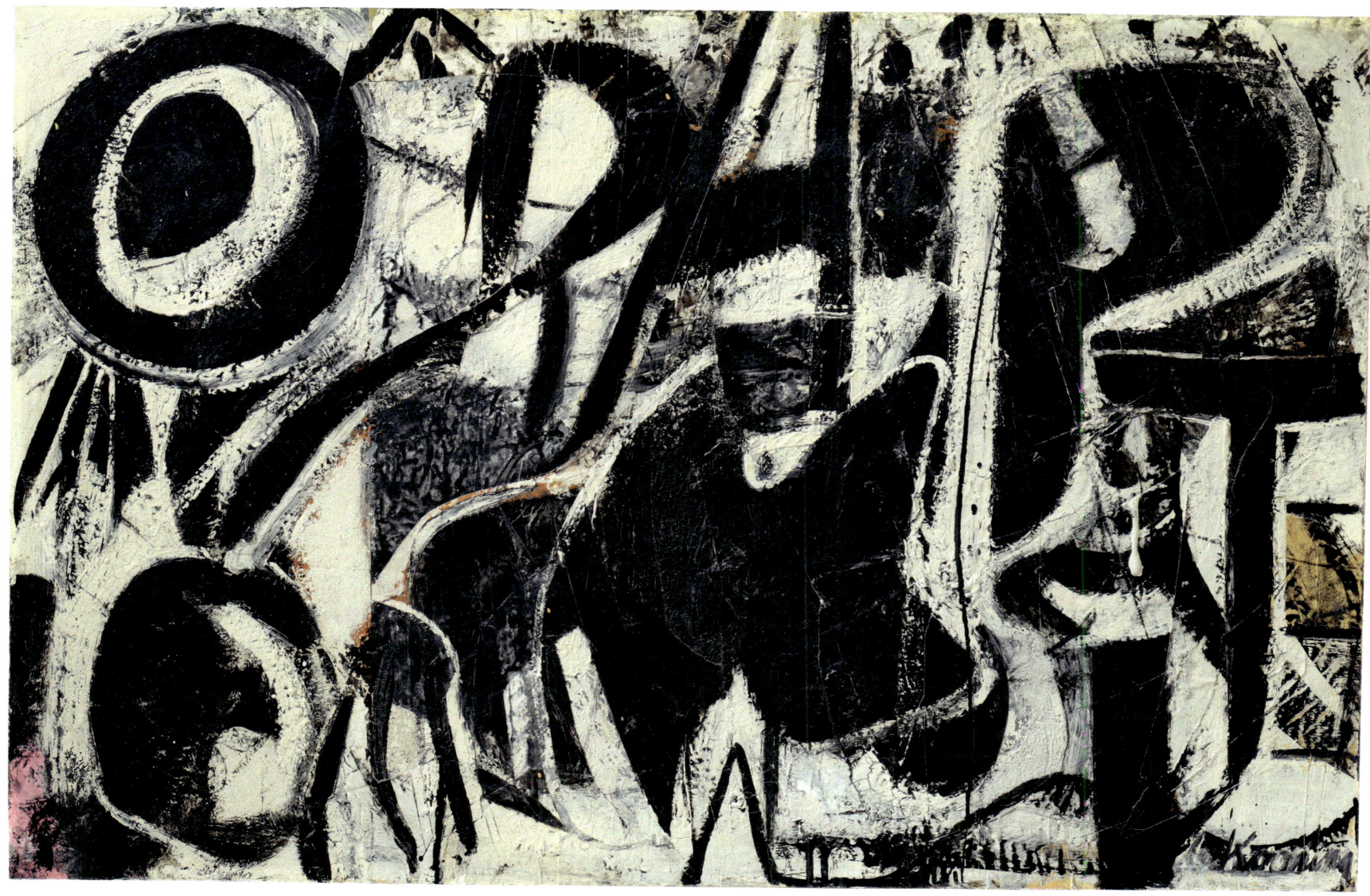

number and the identity of the works shown, we cannot be entirely sure. Nonetheless, we can be reasonably certain of a good number of them.

A brightly colored, untitled painting, now known as *Bill-Lee's Delight* (fig. 16) was illustrated in a black-and-white cartoon by Ad Reinhardt (see fig. 62) published in December 1946 and again, with the untitled work soon to be titled *Orestes* (fig. 17) in *Magazine of Art* on February 2, 1948, two months before the show would actually open.[49] They accompanied a "Biographical Sketch" (see fig. 66) of de Kooning, which announced: "His work is in a number of private collections; he will have his first one-man show this year at the Egan Gallery."[50]

Among the works mentioned after these two was a painting called *Brown and White* (see fig. 29) in one review of the Egan show.[51] *Brown and White* was also

Figure 16
Willem de Kooning, *Bill-Lee's Delight*, 1946
Oil on paper mounted on composition board, 80.3 × 122.9 cm.
Eastman Collection

Figure 17
Willem de Kooning, *Orestes*, 1947
Oil, enamel, and paper collage on paper mounted on board, 61.3 × 91.8 cm. Private collection

one of four reproduced in the newly established *Partisan Review* in August, the others being *Valentine* (see fig. 20), *Zurich* (see fig. 23), and *Painting*, the MoMA picture. It would therefore seem that contemporaneous documentation tells us what were likely six of the works in the exhibition: these four, plus *Orestes* and the work that later became known as *Bill-Lee's Delight*. We are therefore indebted to art historian Charles Stuckey for

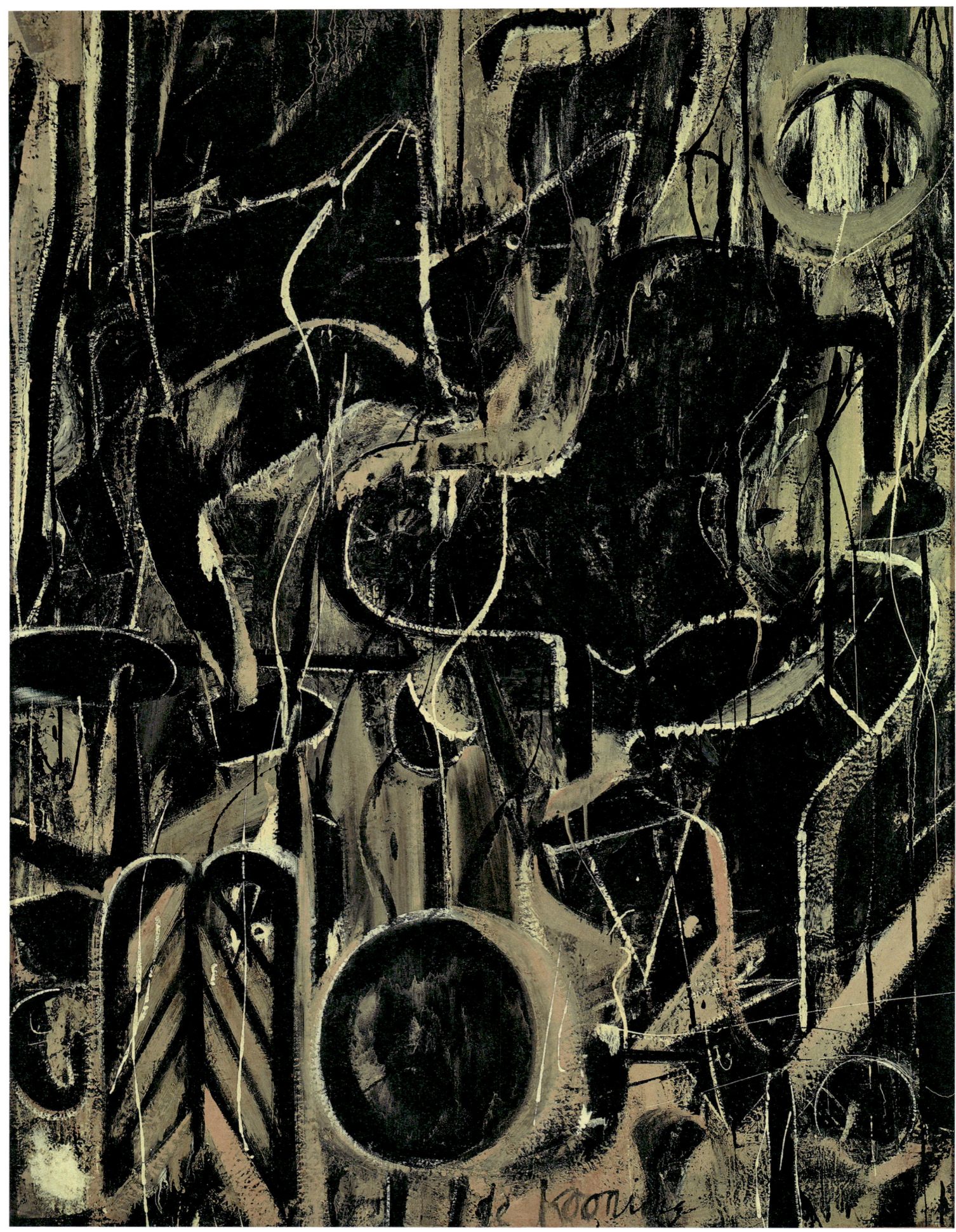

asking Egan if he remembered what was shown, and reporting in 1980 that the gallerist remembered eight: not *Brown and White,* but the other six that were documented early, along with *Light in August* (see fig. 18), *Mailbox* (see fig. 21), and *Black Friday* (see fig. 28).[52] This totals nine works, one short of Greenberg's tally. When working with my colleagues on MoMA's 2011 de Kooning retrospective, we determined that, not only had Egan been forgetful but also that Greenberg may have undercounted and proposed that one or two other works, *Abstraction* (see fig. 31) and *Noon* (see fig. 22), were as likely to have been de Kooning's choices for the show as those that Egan remembered. They have been retained here for the same reason and will be discussed in the pages that follow; recent research does reveal that *Abstraction* could well have been in the exhibition.[53]

We might wonder whether de Kooning's decision to finally have a solo exhibition, at age forty-four, had anything to do with Jackson Pollock's first exhibition of his allover drip paintings at the Betty Parsons Gallery in January 1948. Or whether Elaine de Kooning having that month begun to write reviews for *Art News* caused her to speak to her husband about his needing to get more attention for his work. And whether one or both of these events led de Kooning not to include any recent figurative works in his exhibition, only those in which he showed a more radical face.

Be that as it may, de Kooning's work did begin to attract new attention. In March, just prior to the opening of the Egan exhibition, the recently founded journal *The Tiger's Eye* illustrated the de Kooning painting now titled *Orestes* by the journal's publishers, Ruth and John Stephan.[54] The other work illustrated in the *Magazine of Art* did not receive its title, *Bill-Lee's Delight*, until many years later, after Lee Eastman had become Willem (Bill) de Kooning's lawyer. The remaining works in the Egan show received their titles at a meeting in de Kooning's studio at which Elaine de Kooning, she later recounted, suggested titles to her husband and Charles Egan, and three affirmative responses were needed to determine each title.[55]

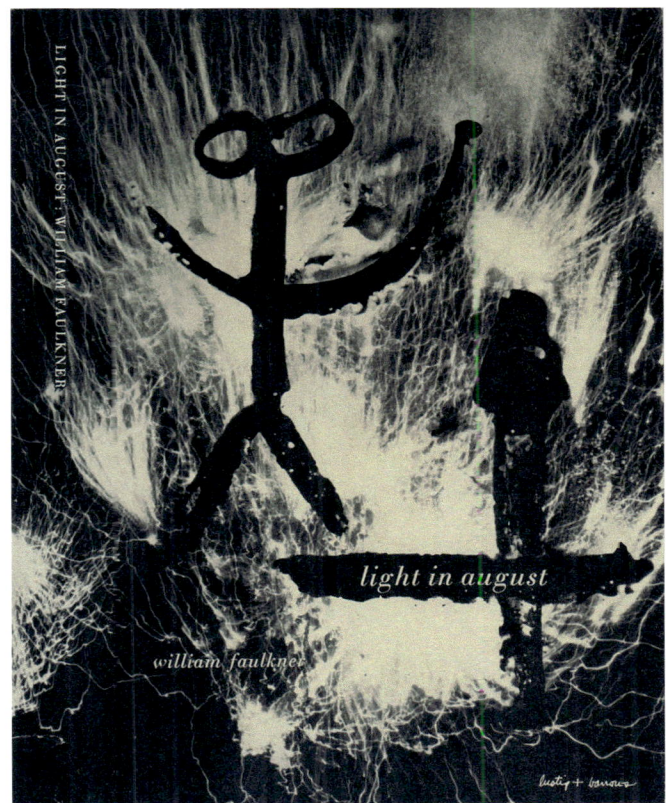

Figure 18
Willem de Kooning, *Light in August*, 1946
Oil on canvas, 140 × 105 cm. Tehran Museum of Contemporary Art, Iran

Figure 19
William Faulkner, *Light in August* (1932; Norfolk, CT: New Directions, 1947)

Abstraction, *Painting*, *Brown and White*, and *Untitled* (the later-titled *Bill-Lee's Delight*) escaped more imaginative titles; *Noon* and *Zurich* received inscrutable ones, unless the "Z" of "Zot," slang for "nothing," and in Dutch, "crazy" or "foolish," at the bottom-right corner of *Zurich* (see fig. 23) was meant to allude to the Swiss city. *Valentine* (see fig. 20), with the pink heart, and *Mailbox* (see fig. 21), humorously titled for the grinning mouths, were fairly obvious choices. This leaves *Orestes,* already titled as such in *The Tiger's Eye*, plus *Black Friday* and *Light in August*, three unexpected titles that, it is reasonable to conclude, did have thematic resonances for de Kooning—although there is no circumstantial evidence to tell us what they were.[56]

In the case of *Orestes*, Elaine de Kooning recalled that because *The Tiger's Eye* was focused on Greek

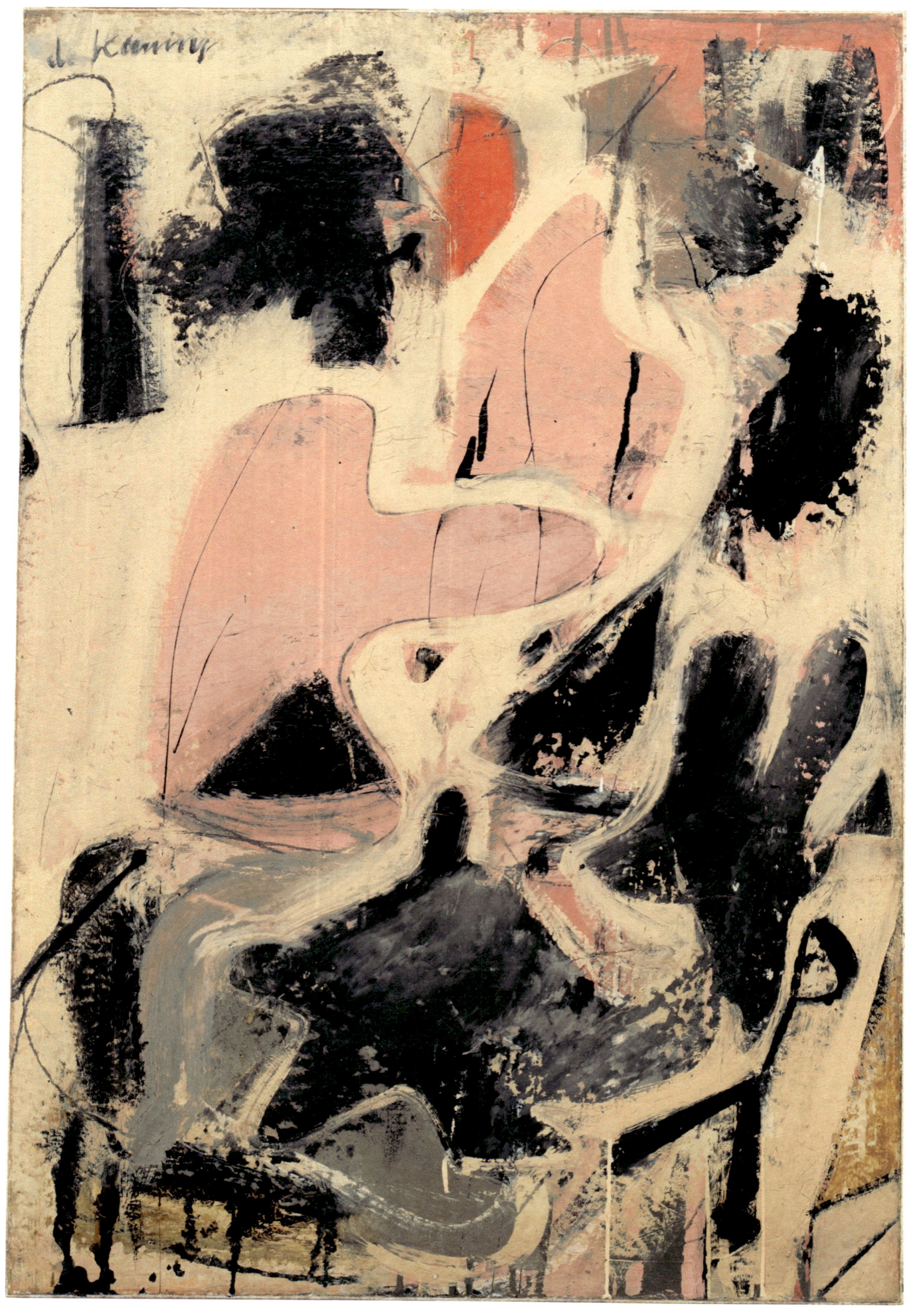

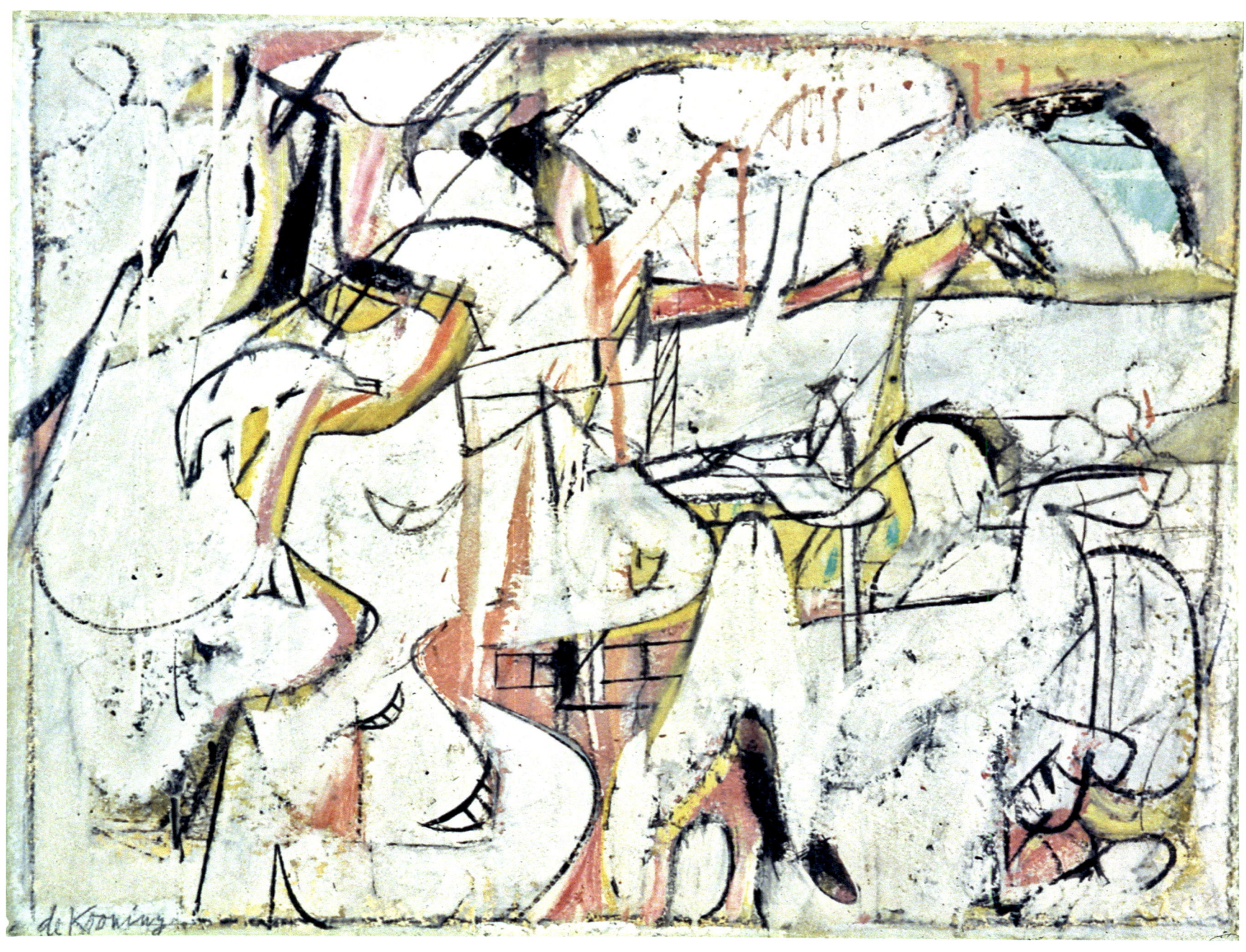

Figure 20

Willem de Kooning, *Valentine,* **1947**

Oil and enamel on paper on board, 92.2 × 61.5 cm. The Museum of Modern Art, New York. Gift of Mr. and Mrs. Gifford Phillips (1093.1969)

Figure 21

Willem de Kooning, *Mailbox,* **1948**

Oil, enamel, and charcoal on paper on composition board, 58.7 × 76.2 cm. Collection of Bettina Bryant

Following pages:

Figure 22

Willem de Kooning, *Noon,* **ca. 1947**

Oil and enamel on Masonite, 121.9 × 86.4 cm. Philadelphia Museum of Art. The Albert M. Greenfield and Elizabeth M. Greenfield Collection, 1974 (1974-178-24)

Figure 23

Willem de Kooning, *Zurich,* **1947**

Oil and enamel on paper mounted on fiberboard, 91.4 × 61.3 cm. Hirshhorn Museum and Sculpture Garden, Smithsonian Institution, Washington, DC. The Joseph H. Hirshhorn Bequest, 1981

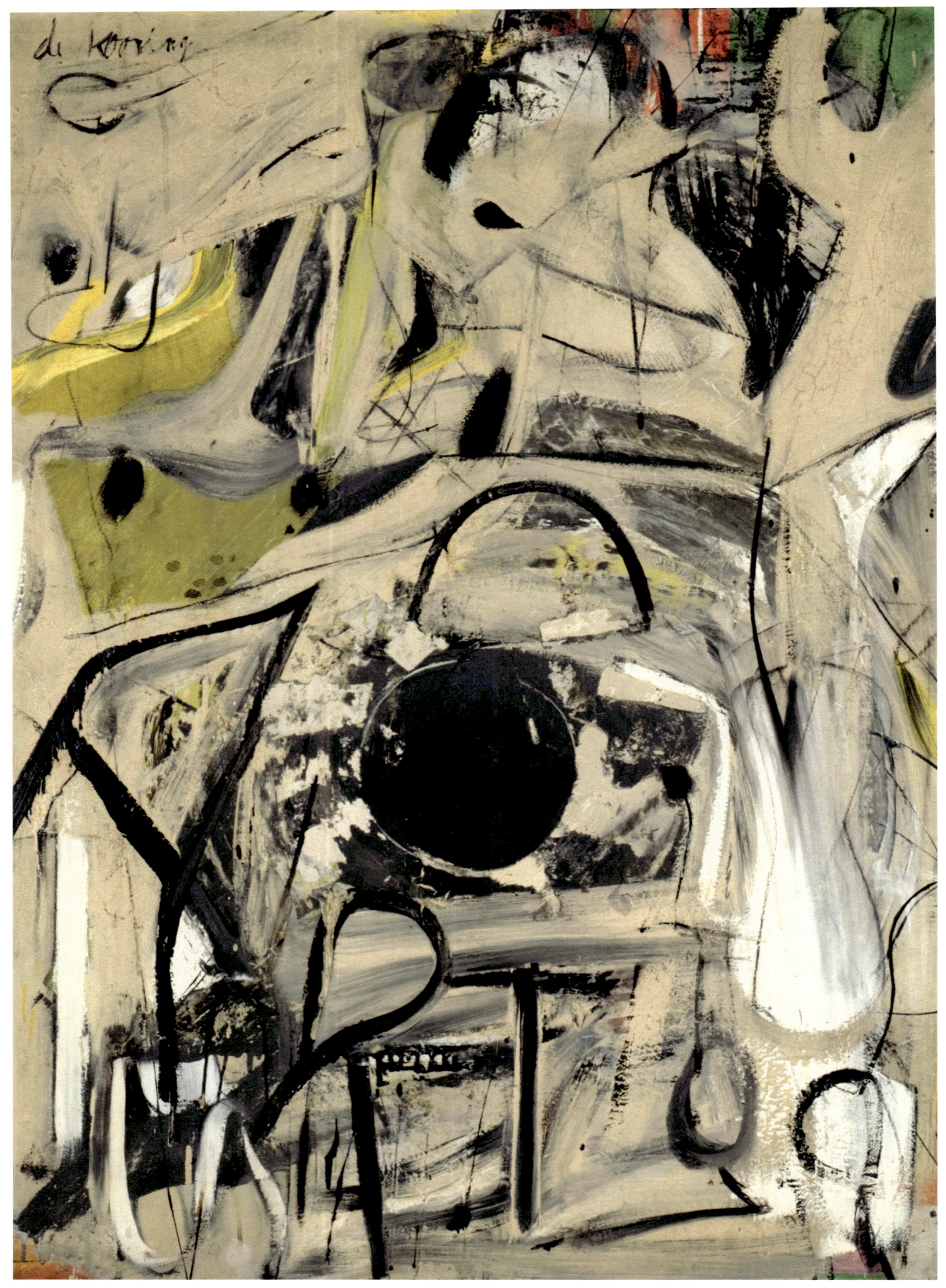

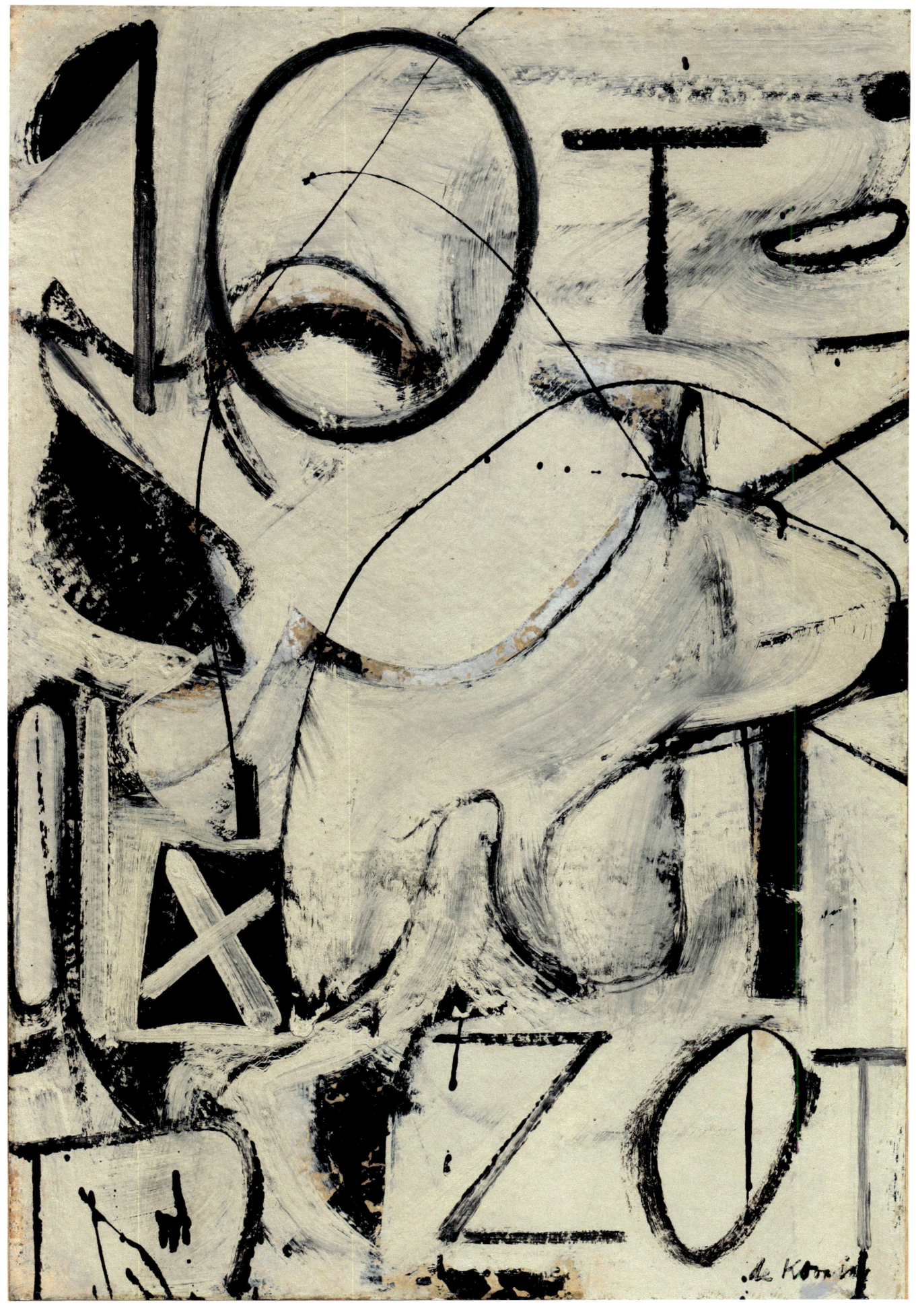

mythology, its publishers, the Stephans, "named a painting of Bill's . . . Orestes. It was not inappropriate. The painting did have this sense of possibly of the furies and so on, but Bill was in no way thinking about Orestes or Greek mythology with which he is not acquainted. So they just kind of imposed it."[57] Nonetheless, the Stephans maintained they would not have done so without de Kooning's approval.[58] Those acquainted with Greek mythology know that Orestes killed his mother, Clytemnestra, but what are we to make of the serious suggestion that de Kooning's *Orestes* alludes to his loathing of his own mother?[59]

As for *Black Friday*, the titular phrase is an alternative name for Good Friday. This being the case, how are we to understand one writer's assertion that de Kooning's painting alludes to the Crucifixion of Christ?[60]

Stuckey has shown that *Light in August* (fig. 18) shares the title of William Faulkner's 1932 novel and has been said to reflect passages in that story of a partly Black and partly white rootless, disinherited man, Joe Christmas, whose surname links up with *Black Friday*, and in whose rootlessness the author recognized his own.[61] Stuckey also tells us that de Kooning was deeply impressed by Faulkner's novels and especially admired *Light in August*, whose melodramatic sex-and-violence aspects associate it with the lurid tabloids the artist enjoyed. Alvin Lustig's dramatic black-and-white dust jacket for the New Directions edition of the novel (fig. 19), published in 1947, is very much in keeping with de Kooning's black-and-white paintings.

I think we have to ask: In such cases, was de Kooning alerting his viewers to allusions that he acknowledged and hoped they would recognize? "To speak of an allusion is to predicate a source," the literary critic Christopher Ricks reminds us, adding, "[but] a source may not be an allusion, for it may not be called into play; it may be scaffolding such as went to the building but does not constitute any part of the building." We have to decide whether we think de Kooning, in voting to adopt these particular titles, did recognize them as now "being part not only of the making of the painting but of its meaning" as well?[62]

Not Black and White

Greenberg's glowing review of de Kooning's first solo exhibition, at the Charles Egan Gallery in the spring of 1948, devoted a considerable amount of space to the artist's use of black.[63] The review was not illustrated, but two paintings in the exhibition were reproduced in the February 1948 issue of the *Magazine of Art,* and four more in the April issue of *Partisan Review*—in black and white in both cases, and without commentary.[64] This allowed those who had not seen the exhibition—as the California painter Richard Diebenkorn told me—to conclude that the works on view were black-and-white paintings. And the exhibition was continually referred to as a "black-and-white exhibition" of abstract paintings, although that characterization is supported by only about half of its ten or eleven works. The remainder comprised one multicolored composition; one that suggested an interior; another that advanced the series of grotesque interiors; two works with conspicuous lettering on a painterly white ground; and one brown-and-white and another brown-and-black canvas that do bear obvious comparison to the black-and-white paintings. Let me take them in this order, which may well not be the sequence in which they were made.

The multicolored work was the canvas now titled *Bill-Lee's Delight* (see fig. 16), completed to display bright-green biomorphic and anthropomorphic forms set against a red-orange ground. It is unclear whether the picture was unique in the Egan exhibition. There may have been more like it: As we saw earlier, Renée Arb's short review in *Art News* speaks of "brilliant hues" as well as black and white, but no such others appear to have survived—that they were painted over seems a very plausible explanation. I think all we can reasonably conclude from this single anomalous canvas is that de Kooning had chosen to work with not only the tonal polarities of black and white, but also the chromatic polarities of red and green, which he had exploited in earlier figure paintings.[65]

He engaged two polarities in the larger *Valentine* (fig. 20). The black-and-white contrast in this composition is clearly more vivid than the pink-and-white one, both intrinsically so and enhanced by the reflectance of the slick black enamel. De Kooning thereby draws attention to their use: While the pair of pink shapes and the single red form seem unspecific, not especially worthy of our notice, the black shapes suggest a figure seated upon a chair in the bottom-right corner, and a window in the opposite corner. Yet, he associates the areas of black enamel and pink oil paint that, while set flatly separately on the canvas, hardly overlapping, nonetheless appear to be floating, mutually attracted on the white substrate.

Mailbox, with its grinning mouths (fig. 21), follows the sequence of grotesque interiors begun at midcentury but differs in no longer seeming to paste its imagery flat on the surface as they did, and as *Valentine* does. Rather, de Kooning disposed the larger forms so they all lie more or less in plane, forming the proximate layer of the depicted incident; have open spaces around them that reveal an essentially continuous drawn layer beneath them; and feature a ground plane beneath that. There is some overlapping of these layers, but not to such a degree as to negate the effect of foreground and background. Whereas Pollock painted in layers, the layers cannot be distinguished in the viewing of his canvases. De Kooning is often said to have painted wet-in-wet, a common technique in oil painting that allows blending of subsequent layers, and that is largely true of his work in the 1950s and 1960s. However, as the essay on *Black Friday* in this volume explains (see p. 130), he did not employ a true wet-in-wet technique in the later 1940s, but used solvent to work lower layers up to the surface. And in works like *Mailbox* and *Valentine*, he painted in layers and let the layers show. In effect, de Kooning followed the embrace of stratification in Paul Cézanne's paintings of rocks and quarries—that is, interest in parallel layers of material one upon another.[66]

Painting by layering—Cézanne's gift to modern painting—lived on in the layering of early Cubist collages before they became the flat, jigsaw-like unities, their space squeezed out of them, that shaped the airless abstractions de Kooning inherited in the 1930s. *Mailbox* shows him engaging the art of adjustment to pry open the space in his paintings. His pursuit of this goal is seen

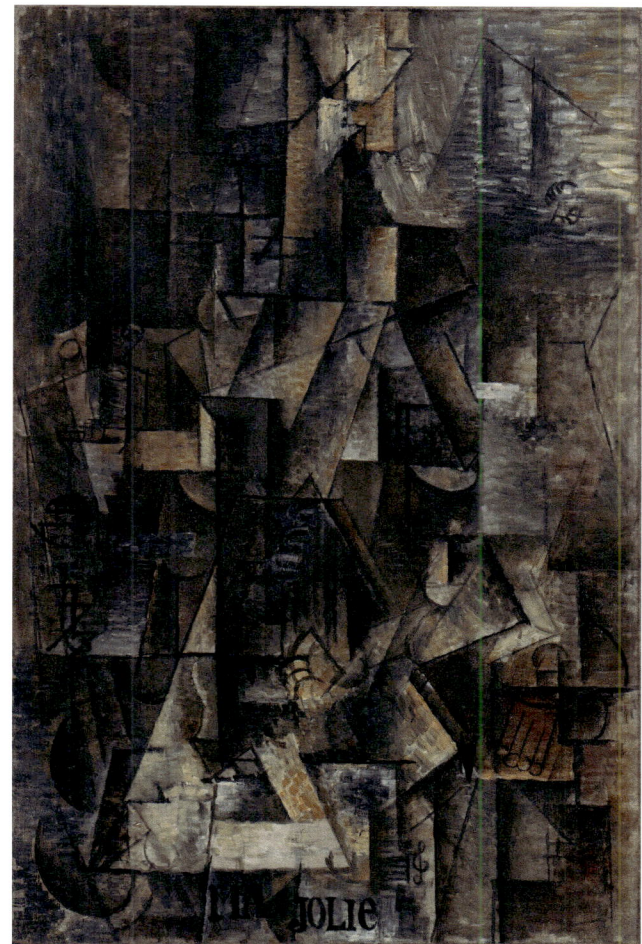

Figure 24
Pablo Picasso (1881–1973; born Málaga, Spain; died Mougins, France), ***Ma Jolie*, 1911–12**
Oil on canvas, 100 × 64.5 cm. The Museum of Modern Art, New York. Acquired through the Lillie P. Bliss Bequest (by exchange) (176.1945)

in the firm manner in which he drew the edges of the planes, along with their sheer multiplicity and density within a composition. Both challenges, each a matter of surface composition, were affected by—and influenced—how de Kooning managed the planes so that they appear to be layered.

A pair of works in the Egan exhibition with lettering on a mainly white painterly ground, *Noon* (fig. 22) and *Zurich* (fig. 23), the former less certainly in the Egan show than the latter, convey the impression of having been conceived as contrasting versions of the canvas as a page. The former—ironically—has the word "Art" "hastily scrawled . . . using the greatest possible muscular freedom of shoulder or arm," as Elaine de Kooning remembered such a work.[67] The latter includes a carefully composed but largely unintelligible text focused on the word "Zot." The writing comprises the proximate zone of each painting, set more independently upon the canvas in the former work than in the latter. For, in the case of *Zurich*, the narrow letters belong equally with linear markings that are not letters, akin to Analytic Cubist paintings with stenciled lettering, the most prominent example for de Kooning being Picasso's *Ma Jolie* (fig. 24).[68]

In neither *Noon* nor *Zurich* does the writing form the matrix for the entire composition, as it perhaps had with *The Wave* (see fig. 3). But it did in one of the black-and-white paintings, *Orestes* (see fig. 17), which brings us to the four black-and-white paintings and the two related brown-and-black paintings that were the most radical works in the Egan exhibition.

The Color Black

While Greenberg did not identify any of the works in the Egan exhibition, it was to the black-and-white paintings that he explicitly referred. The critic not only emphasized de Kooning's use of black, associating him in this respect with Gorky, Adolph Gottlieb, and Pollock, but also applauded his unique method of employing it:

> **For de Kooning black becomes a color—not the indifferent schema of drawing, but a hue with all the resonance, ambiguity, and variability of the prismatic scale. Spread smoothly in heavy somatic shapes on an uncrowded canvas, this black identifies the physical picture plane with an emphasis other painters achieve only by clotted pigment. De Kooning's insistence on a smooth, thin surface is a concomitant of his desire for purity, for an art that makes demands only on the optical imagination.[69]**

Greenberg's first two points are uncontroversial. For de Kooning, black became a color, functioning on the prismatic, not merely the tonal, scale. And black paint spread thinly on the canvas makes us as much aware of the flat picture plane as does the thick paint used by other artists. But the critic's ascribing to de Kooning a "desire for purity" would have amused the artist, who in 1951 spoke disparagingly of painters for whom "the "pure form of comfort became the comfort of pure form," adding, "Art never seems to make me peaceful or pure. I always seem to be wrapped in the melodrama of vulgarity."[70]

This is not the place to offer a history of the use of the color black prior to de Kooning's use of it, commonly viewed as beginning in modern art with the work of Édouard Manet. Nor is it even the place to begin recounting its later history, in which African American artists played an increasingly important role. But we do need to be cognizant of the milieu in which de Kooning's black-and-white paintings were produced.[71] Greenberg mentioned a trio of American artists besides de Kooning. I take it that neither he nor de Kooning knew that European painters were also making such paintings. It is likely, however, that the Galerie des Deux Îles in Paris was aware of the response to the Egan exhibition, since it opened its own presentation of nine such painters some three months later, *Blanc et neige* (in English, *White and Black*), on July 19, 1948.[72]

In New York itself, there were four important examples of black or black-and-white paintings of which de Kooning was certainly aware. Most notably, although clearly hard to assimilate with what he was doing, was Picasso's *Guernica*, which had returned to the Museum of Modern Art in 1942 after touring the United States for two years. (The artist had a postcard of the work in his studio.)[73] A second was Gorky's *Charred Beloved* paintings of 1946, mentioned above. Less obvious, but well received by Greenberg, was the Albert Pinkham Ryder exhibition at the Whitney Museum of American Art in the autumn of 1947 (fig. 25). The Pinkham retrospective coincided with the news, in September 1947, that MoMA had foolishly sold twenty-six early modernist works to the Metropolitan Museum of Art in order to obtain funds to buy recent art. Matisse's *Gourds* (fig. 26) was among the three Matisses in the group of works that MoMA gave up.[74]

Judging from what de Kooning exhibited the following year, it seems fair to say that it was the

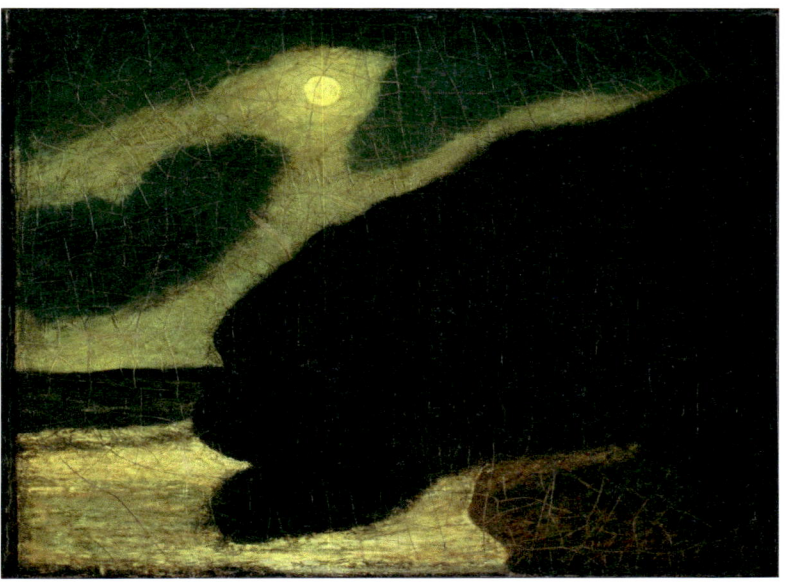

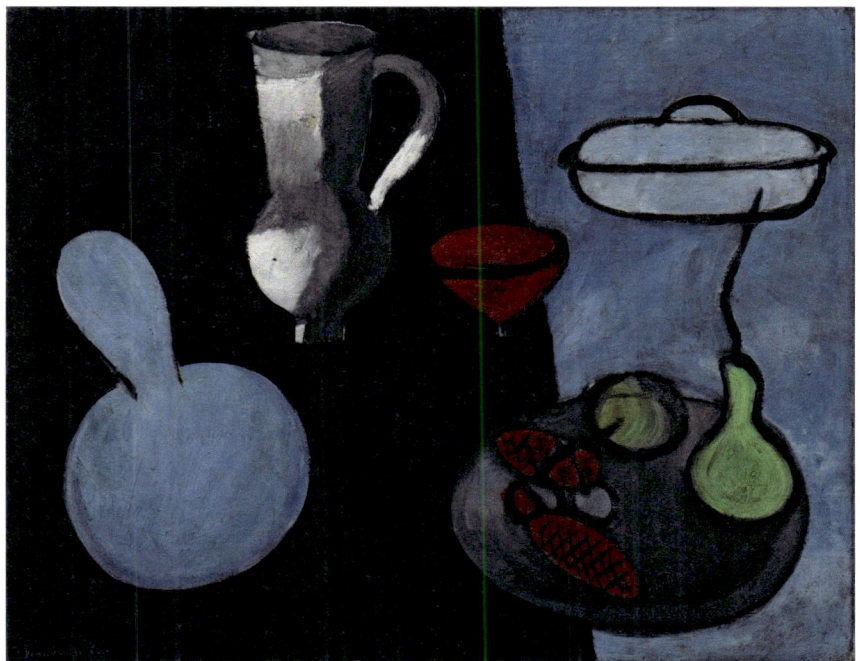

Matisse that attracted his particular attention. Whereas his chiaroscuro *Night* (see fig. 13) is of a type with the Gorky paintings, and *The Moraine* (see fig. 14) with the heavily impastoed Ryders, his black-and-white paintings in the Egan exhibition are akin to the Matisse in being composed "on a smooth, thin surface," as Greenberg put it—whereas not always comprising one, but often heavily marked by evidence of de Kooning's revisions. Nonethless, his blacks do not seem to break the continuity of the surface. When Matisse visited the aged Pierre-Auguste Renoir in 1918 to show him some paintings, Renoir said that one thing prevented him from telling Matisse that he was not a good painter: "When you put on some black, it stays in its plane. All my life I thought that you couldn't use it without breaking the chromatic unity of the surface. . . . As for you, using a colored vocabulary, you introduce a black, and it holds."[75] That is precisely what de Kooning started doing with the works in the Egan exhibition.

The artist admitted that he began using black and white paints because they were inexpensive: "I did not have any money, I did not have any particular aesthetic idea or theory, but I could go to a store and buy a gallon of white and a gallon of black and be in business, I wanted to be free of the material. . . . and out of that came some idea about black-and-white pictures."[76]

Figure 25
Albert Pinkham Ryder (1847–1917; born New Bedford, MA; died Elmhurst, NY), ***Moonlit Cove*, 1880s**
Oil on canvas, 35.9 × 43.5 cm. The Phillips Collection, Washington, DC. Acquired 1924 (1708)

Figure 26
Henri Matisse (1869–1954; born Le Cateau-Cambrésis, France; died Nice, France), ***Gourds*, 1916**
Oil on canvas, 65.1 × 80.9 cm. The Museum of Modern Art, New York. Mrs. Simon Guggenheim Fund (109.1935)

These were gallons of "black and white household enamels."[77] They were mainly Ripolin, the first branded version of enamel paint, which was produced by the merger of Briegleb, a Dutch company, and LeFranc, a French manufacturer of artists' materials. The white version was popularized by the architect Le Corbusier's "la loi du ripolin" (Law of Ripolin) in his book *L'Art décoratif d'aujourd'hui* (1925), which argued that Ripolin could invest buildings with the "eye of truth," since any blemishes would stand out against such pristine surfaces, and against such cleanliness the accumulated soot of a building would obscure its constructive essence.[78] It is doubtful that de Kooning was aware of this history, but he was familiar with enamels from his early days as a sign- and housepainter and presumably reasoned that, since they were designed for outside use, they should be particularly durable. One problem with Ripolin is that

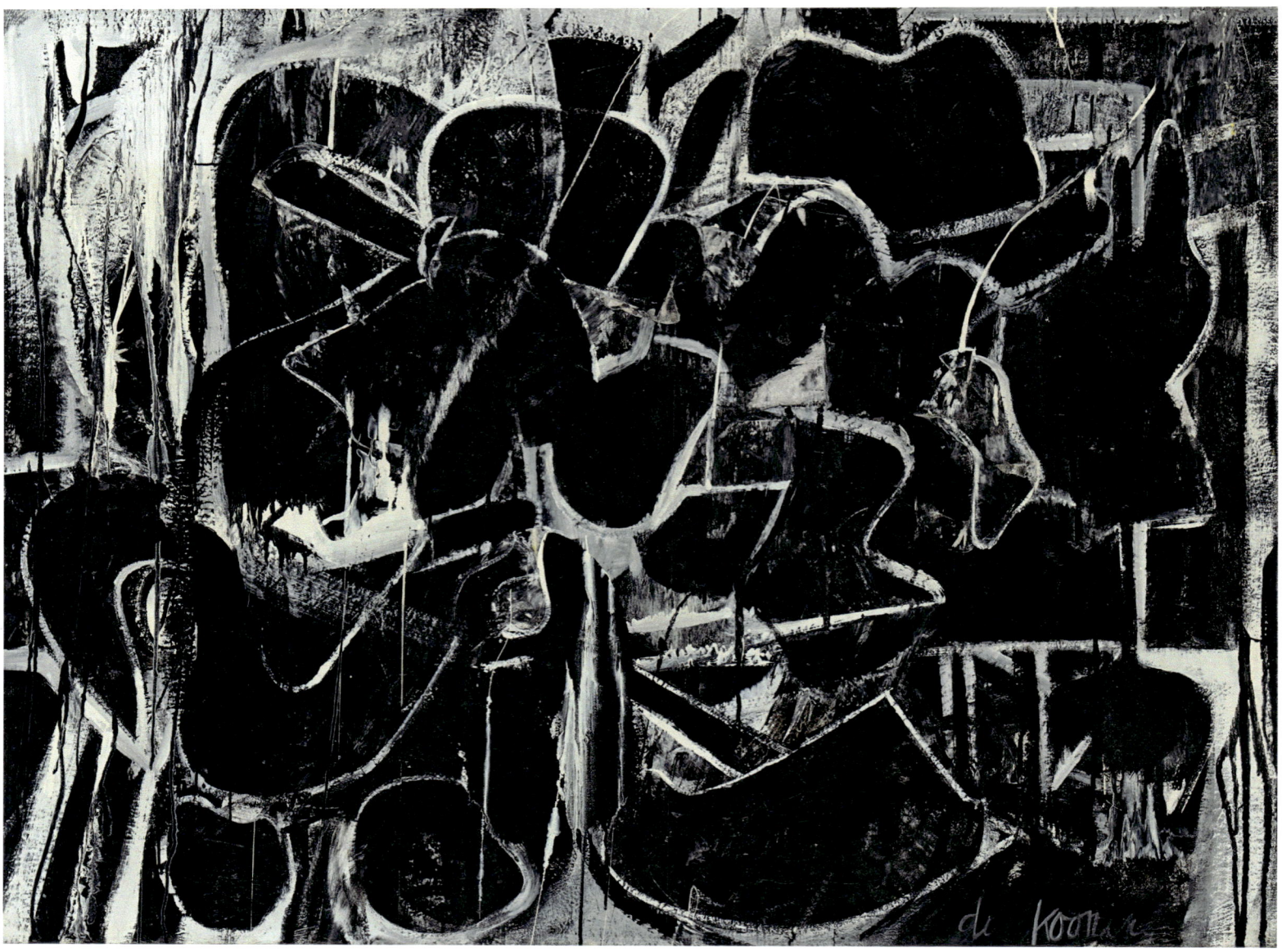

Figure 27
Willem de Kooning, *Painting*, 1948
Enamel and oil on canvas, 108.3 × 142.5 cm. The Museum of Modern Art, New York. Purchase, 1948 (238.1948)

it could become very brittle and, as de Kooning himself explained, the paper had to be pasted onto a wooden panel: "It would not be sufficient for it to be supported by so flexible a material as canvas, since the slightest dent or twist could make it chip or crack like glass."[79]

Moreover, de Kooning did not utilize these enamels solely because they were cheap. Much has been made of his use of black as reflecting de Kooning's poverty and attendant anxieties—even that there "was an element of rapture, an undeniable joy, in de Kooning's confrontation with his own darkness. In the lush, volca-nic blacks he found a metaphysical grandeur in his private despair."[80] Unexpectedly, Greenberg would not go along with so hyperbolic an assessment. Speaking of *Painting* (fig. 27) in 1948, he conceded that "Mr. De Kooning was wrestling with his fears," yet "this over-tone of foreboding and anxiety was not the most important aspect of the picture."[81] And a fellow artist, Barnett Newman, was more to the point when he said that "[going] to black" was "a way of clearing the table—of getting to new ideas."[82]

In any event, de Kooning's friend Hess wrote, "If he wanted the best (and only the best) tube colors, he always found a way to get them."[83] Because the Ripolin enamels, both black and white, dried slowly, he could work directly wet-in-wet as he painted if he wished. Moreover, while

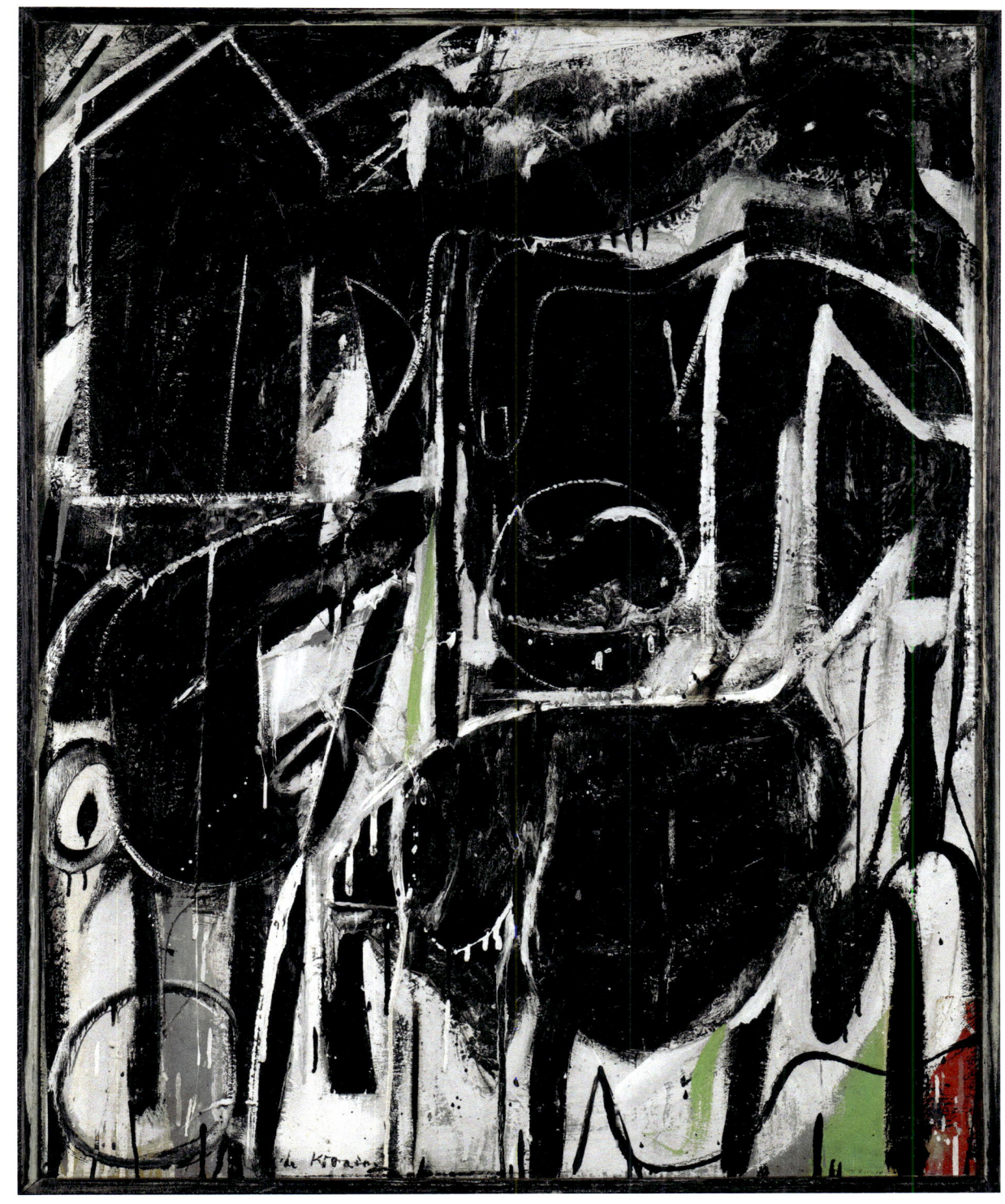

matte black (often called "ultrablack") absorbs nearly all visible (ultraviolet) light, Ripolin enamels had a slick, somewhat glossy surface that reflected some light, producing a livelier effect. And de Kooning could use them together with Ronan's quick-dry lettering enamel as well as with oil paint, which had a different degree of resistance and speed of drying. Moreover, he could include in the mix additional materials like charcoal, plaster, sand, and even

Figure 28
Willem de Kooning, _Black Friday_, 1948
Enamel and oil over paper collage on fiberboard in painted wood frame; 125 × 99 cm, 128.3 × 102.2 × 7.3 cm (frame). Princeton University Art Museum. Gift of H. Gates Lloyd, Class of 1923, and Mrs. Lloyd in honor of the Class of 1923 (y1976-44)

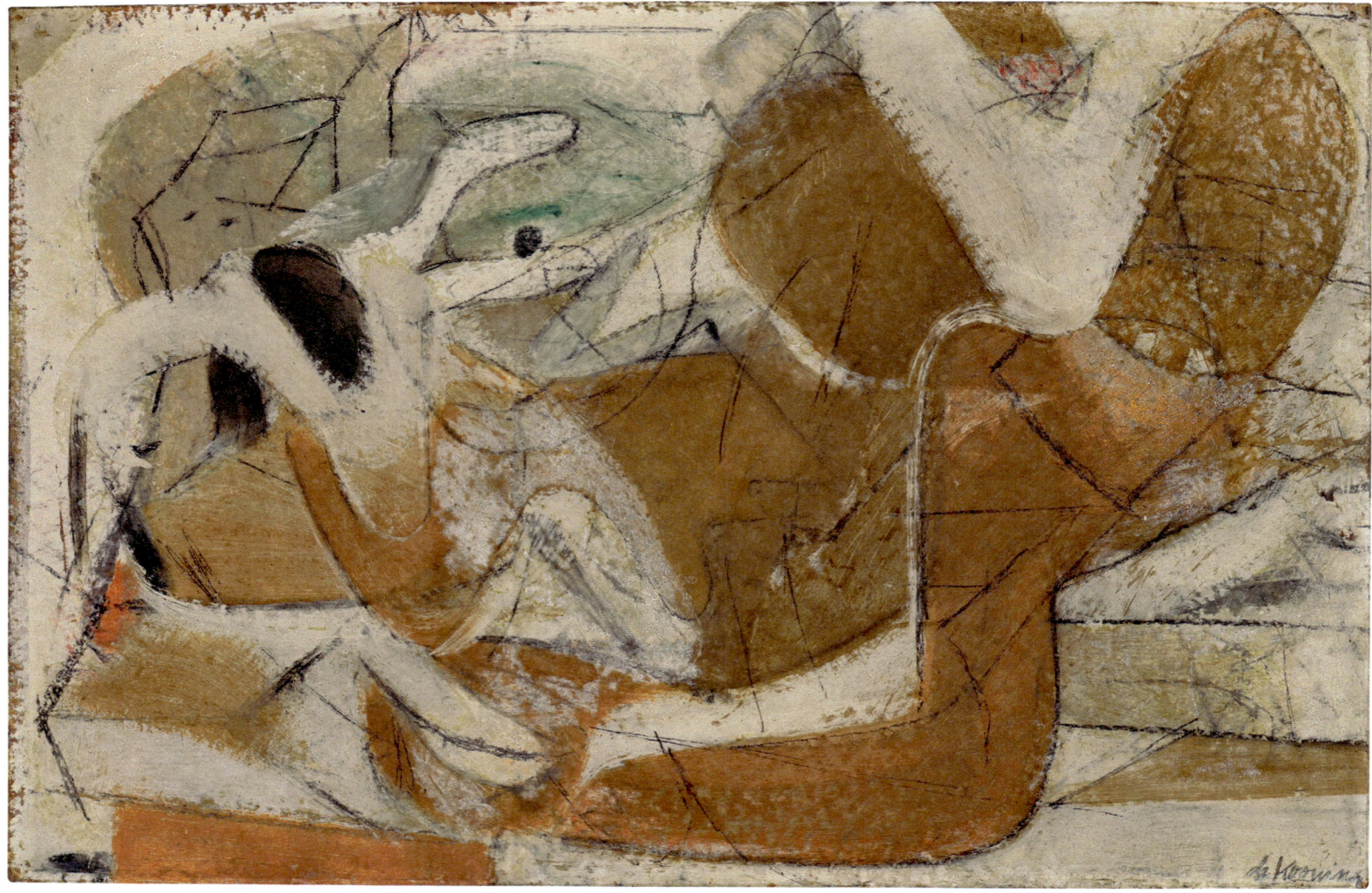

Figure 29
Willem de Kooning, *Brown and White*, ca. 1947
Oil and charcoal on paper mounted on canvas, 63.5 × 94 cm.
Private collection

powdered glass, thereby further modifing the reflectance of parts of the surface.[84] But whatever the mix in any particular work, the common factor was that the black stayed, to paraphrase de Kooning, "right there on the canvas"—and the white did, too.[85]

This is not to say that the black, or the white, always *reads* flatly on the canvas surface. In 1941–42, the German émigré art historian Max Raphael was spending days at the Metropolitan Museum of Art analyzing black as a constituent element of paintings in the museum's collection.[86] His *Die Farbe Schwarz: Zur materiellen Konstituierung der Form* (The Color Black: On the Material Construction of Form) was only published posthumously in 1984, but sets forth a brilliant analysis of the issues

that de Kooning and his contemporaries were very soon addressing. Among its many insights, the following aids appreciation of de Kooning's utilization of black.

For Raphael, black and white, like the use of gold in icons of saints, are distinguished from all other colors in being free of "earthly" influences, except that black and white connote, respectively, darkness and light. He insisted, however, "that one has to make a very sharp distinction between the emotive value of the color as such, and the emotive value of *the material* of color.[87] Especially influential on the materiality of black paint is its relative thickness on the surface—thick or thin, heavy or light—which will itself influence its emotive value. Like any color, black can fulfill three spatial functions: it can advance, recede, or hold a plane.

Whereas the chiaroscuro tonality of de Kooning's *Night* recedes and loses the plane, his heavily impastoed *The Moraine* so firmly holds the plane that, as

Raphael writes of a painting by Francisco Goya at the Metropolitan Museum of Art, it pushes "its capacity to cohere to the point where it becomes impenetrable, so hard and unporous, so resistant, that it seems less a color and more a petrification of color."[88] He continues: "Almost forcibly this gives rise to a predominance of smooth and structureless surfaces."[89] This was de Kooning's response as well.

Only what Greenberg termed "a smooth, thin surface" provided the means for black to fulfill the three spatial functions: advancing, receding, and holding the plane. To this end, what was necessary was creating what Raphael describes as a "vibration of color tones in a constant state of oscillation between minute gradations of color and the various qualities of the material surface, such as rough or smooth, warm or cold . . . moistness and dryness, softness and hardness."[90] This meant—as he said of Goya—working with several layers of color, not all necessarily intended to be perceived directly, but still infusing the black with such cohesion and firmness that it acquires a definite materiality. The result, he proposed in words that also apply to de Kooning's use of black, is a distancing and objectification of the pigment so that it affords a sense of opening and closing, pressing forward and bowing backward.[91]

Black and White

Of the four black-and-white paintings in the Egan exhibition, *Light in August* (see fig. 18) is an outlier. First, for its size; it is about 4½ feet tall, by far the largest of the group. Second, insofar as it comprises one tightly filled surface of black organic shapes interwoven with bands and strands of white and cream pigment. The work has been sequestered for decades in the Tehran Museum of Contemporary Art, and it is difficult to tell from a reproduction how uniformly black are the shapes, or the extent to which they are either outlined or overlapped by the white or cream drawing. Moreover, while some drawn lines appear to have been set down broadly, others clearly roam sporadically, achieving a filigree effect. This second kind of drawing associates the work with a group of likely

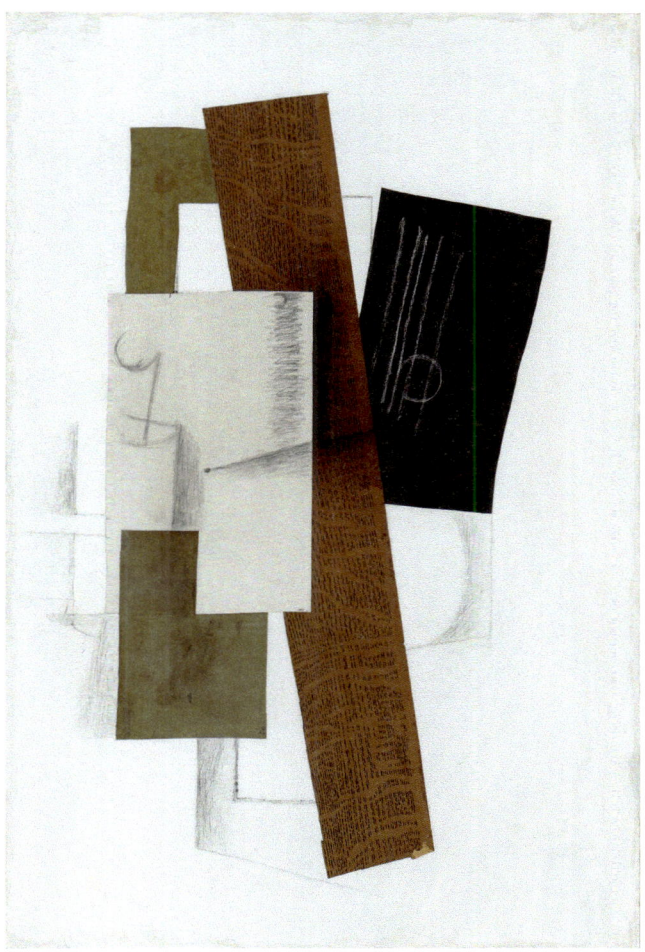

Figure 30
Georges Braque (1882–1963; born Argenteuil, France; died Paris, France), ***Guitar,* 1913**
Cut-and-pasted printed and painted paper, charcoal, pencil, and gouache or gessoed canvas, 99.7 × 65.1 cm. The Museum of Modern Art, New York. Acquired through the Lillie P. Bliss Bequest (by exchange) (304.1947)

later paintings that I shall consider in due course, which use it exclusively to shape a plane in advance of the black surface. Here, the two kinds of drawing and the variety of black shapes create a single, variegated surface that covers the whole rectangle, akin to Raphael's impenetrable Goya, as an unporous carapace to a richly ornamental but somewhat claustrophobic effect. In contrast, each of the remaining three black-and-white paintings in the Egan exhibition imply at least two surfaces—one composed of seemingly proximate black shapes, the other of white interstices between and seemingly mainly behind them.

But only *seemingly* in both cases. Again, it is Hess who explains: De Kooning had studied lettering at the Rotterdam Academy, and his jobs in the 1930s

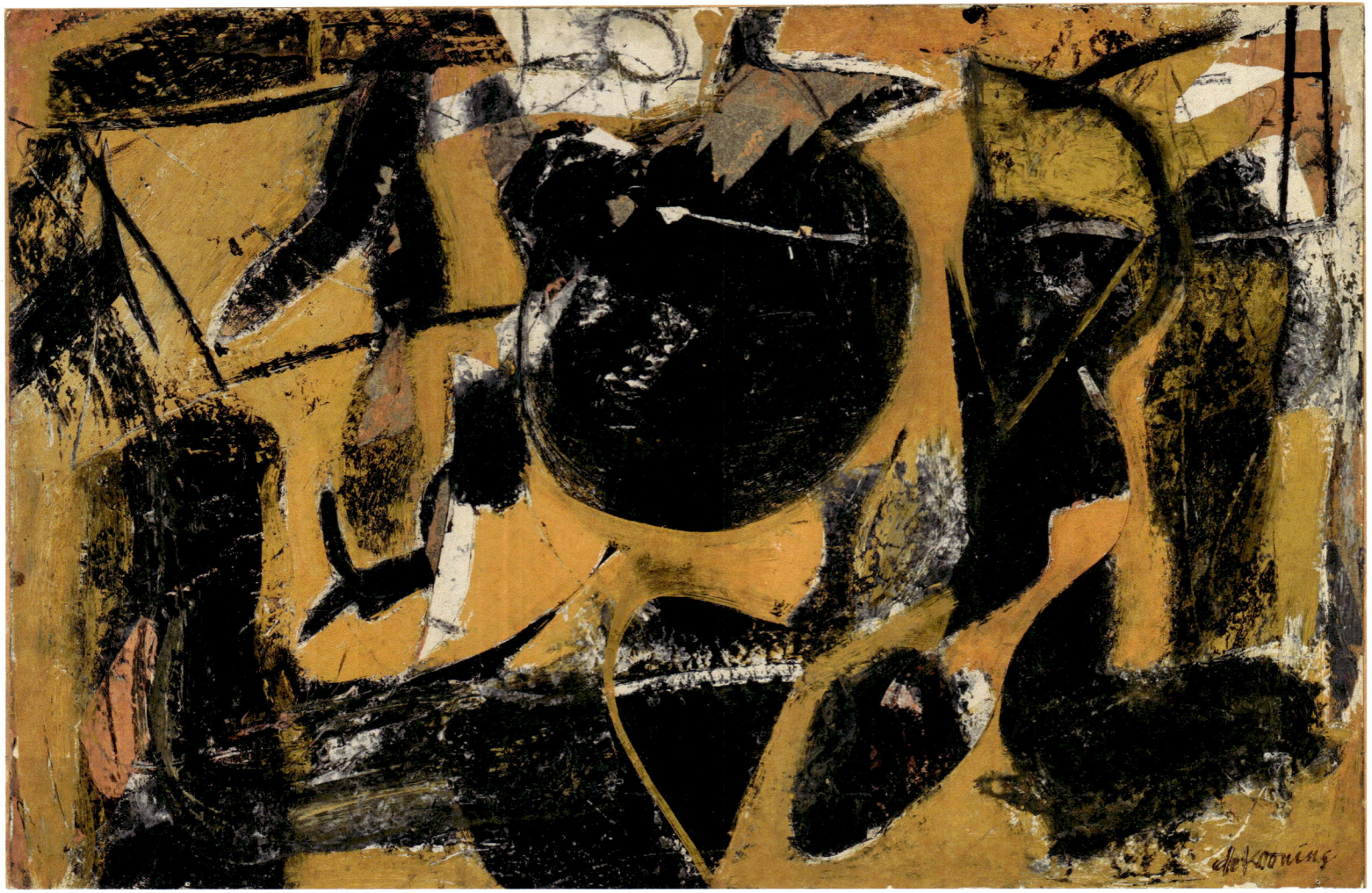

Figure 31
Willem de Kooning, *Abstraction*, 1948
Oil, charcoal, enamel, and paper collage on paper mounted on
board, 61.6 × 91.8 cm. Private collection

included sign painting. The technique for painting letters
he had learned was to lay a rough quadrangle of color
over outlined letters, then paint the background up to
these outlines, not touching the letters. While the letters
were literally behind their surrounding background, they
appeared to be in front of it. Similarly, Hess observes
that, in de Kooning's black-and-white paintings, "it is
impossible to tell what is 'on top' of what."[92] In the case
of *Orestes* (see fig. 17), white voids enclosed by black
may be read as positive shapes in front of the black
surroundings; and a basic law of tonal contrast is that
the smaller a white shape is within a black surround,
the brighter, and therefore nearer, it seems. De Kooning
would certainly have noticed how the roughly painted

white pitcher in Matisse's *Gourds* thus appears almost
incandescent, hovering in space above its large, surrounding black zone.

At the left of *Black Friday* (fig. 28), a tiny black
oval within a white one leaves us wondering which one
seems more proximate. But this painting is full of such
puzzles, as whites invade areas of black, either overlapping or dividing them. While an area of black will
usually seem to be heavier than one of white, such is
not the case with this predominantly black composition,
which seems to float over a largely white base. *Painting*
(see fig. 27) suggests a three-part stratification: small,
peripheral areas of white modified to gray form a shallow
space; the black shapes appear to rest on top of the
space; and the stronger whites that outline these shapes
appear optically to come forward of them.

Orestes (see fig. 17) is descended from
de Kooning's earlier possibly word-based paintings

like *The Wave*, but is unique in affording a primary role to wide, flat lettering, which composes the nonsensical word "ORAPT," with the hint of an "E" beneath the "O" and of an "A" between the "P" and the "T." These letters hover above and around a strange, winged form that may derive from the head of an abstracted reclining figure, which we will again encounter (see fig. 54). Here, this shape, the lettering, and a smattering of small black lines and dashes sit on a white-gray ground that, we see from the lower-right and lower-left margins, itself sits on an ocher-to-reddish substrate that warms the upper two layers. Within this busy, mobile composition, de Kooning set down the black of the frontal forms—as Raphael put it regarding a Goya, "with such cohesion and firmness that it acquires a definite materiality and presses forward."

The same is true of the far more complex *Black Friday*. It is impossible to know how this painting began. It is clear that some features had been laid in, then overpainted; but all that remains recognizable are a schematic roof form, a looping finger, and a table-like form with a ball resting on it. The visible fragments of green and brown substrate in the right corner may be thought to evoke a foreground. But de Kooning chose not to complete this area of the painting in the palette of the rest, recognizing, in Delacroix's words I quoted earlier, that he would "never seek after an empty perfection," and that "some things which the vulgar call faults, often give vitality to a work."[93] In any event, this is hardly a painting of known things. "Instead of painting objects, he paints situations," de Kooning's friend the painter Louis Finkelstein proposed in 1950, while Hess spoke of "no environment" in which proximate and distant things mix and merge.[94] More epigrammatically, de Kooning himself, explained his friend Edwin Denby, "talked about how a masterpiece made the figures active and the voids around them active as well, as active as possible."[95] Denby added that this "squeezed everything dramatically, but somehow the picture opened itself way out, changing the center and the frame. He thought perhaps it opened where the eye believed it saw one thing, but

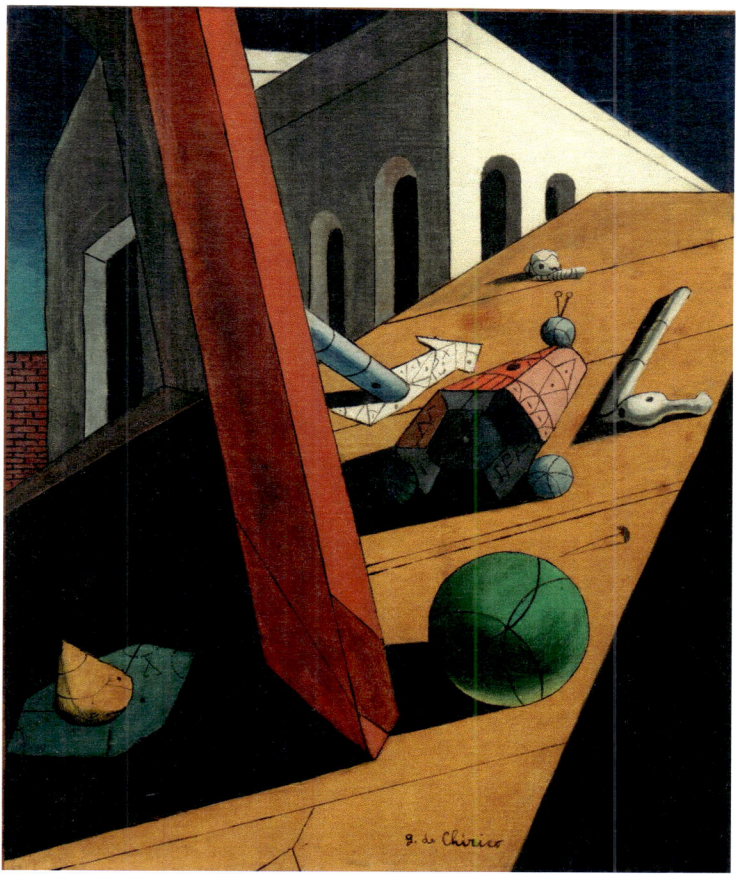

Figure 32
Giorgio de Chirico (1888–1978; born Vólos, Greece; died Rome, Italy), ***The Evil Genius of a King,*** **1914–15**
Oil on canvas, 61 × 50.2 cm. The Museum of Modern Art, New York. Purchase (112.1936)

knew it saw another, like near and far, resemblance and form, [. . .] as in a primitive."[96]

If *Orestes* is the final and most resolved of de Kooning's letter paintings, *Black Friday* is the final and wonderfully least resolved of his ludicrous rather than fearful grotesque compositions. The final canvas in his great trio of black-and-white canvases, simply titled *Painting* (see fig. 27), is without precedent in his art in being an almost modular composition of like and unlike black shapes outlined in white, sometimes in gray, that jostle together above a streaky gray ground. *Mailbox* anticipated its layering of similar elements, except they are anthropomorphized there, whereas those in *Painting* are generically organic. This use of nearly—but not entirely—standardized components marks a major development in de Kooning's work, which he would advance through the end of the decade.

Writing in the early nineteenth century, the poet William Wordsworth commended "the perception of similitude in dissimilitude" as "the great spring of the activity of our minds and their chief feeder."[97] However, he also stressed "the accuracy with which [both] similitude in dissimilitude and dissimilitude in similitude are perceived."[98] In *Painting*, as art historian Richard Shiff writes of Cézanne's canvases, "the general principle at work in his art is analogy; one thing is made to look like, or somehow be like, another, despite the differences that otherwise obtain."[99] The common blackness and clustered composition of the shapes, along with the sense that they belong to an organic species, akin to leaves on a plant, makes them alike while also inviting us to notice their differences. De Kooning would speak of what he called "fitting-in," the creation of a tightly interwoven surface that, as he saw it, was "where modern art came from," referring to Cubism and its source in Cézanne.[100] He was now moving in this direction, yet not completely fitting-in everything tightly and precisely.

Even more than in *Orestes*, each black shape in *Painting* is outlined by a white or sometimes gray contour. The density and color of the nominally white lines vary enormously so that confusion abounds, engendering variously reasonable and improbable readings ranging from what appears to be legs of a table in the lower right to what looks like a sock hanging on a long strand above it. On occasion, two such outlines are abutted to show two adjacent shapes. More often, though, a single white outline does not tell us whether we are seeing two shapes meeting in the same plane or a division within a single shape. As a result, the eye hesitates in deciding to which of the two tangential black areas, or portions of black areas, the white contour belongs. And, as the eye moves across the boundaries between areas of black and white, an optical flicker occurs. De Kooning admired that effect in the work of an artist rarely associated with him, saying: "I'm crazy about Mondrian. I'm always spellbound by him. Something happens in the painting that I cannot take my eyes off. It shakes itself there. It has terrific tension. The optical illusion in Mondrian is that where the lines cross

they make a little light. Mondrian didn't like that, but he couldn't prevent it. The eye couldn't take it, and where the black lines cross they flicker."[101]

John Ruskin, whom we encountered earlier in regard to the Grotesque, wrote, "There is no proportion between equal things. . . . Any succession of equal things is agreeable; but to compose is to arrange equal things, and the first thing to be done in beginning a composition is to determine which is to be the principal thing."[102] In all three of these great compositions, de Kooning clearly wanted to create something more than agreeable but not to determine what would be the principal thing. He knew that his task of composition was to arrange unequal things—and to keep them sufficiently unequal.

Two remaining paintings have unequally recognizable components and are outliers in their different ways. And one unverifiable reason for their unexpected appearances is that they may have been influenced by de Kooning having seen elements to reuse in works at the Museum of Modern Art.

Brown and White (fig. 29) contains what resembles a reclining figure resting against a geometric shelf surrounded by unspecific forms. The unexpectedly brown, paper-thin figure set against the white ground, perhaps unique in de Kooning's art, could have been prompted by his seeing the overlapping strips of brown and white paper in Georges Braque's 1913 collage *Guitar* (fig. 30), acquired by MoMA in 1947.

Abstraction (fig. 31), an exterior view, is the only exception to de Kooning's recent sequence of abstracted interiors, with the only partial exception of *Black Friday*, which hardly describes anything exterior except the house in the background. It is also an early example of what de Kooning would much later call a "slipping glimpse" of someone crossing a a street.[103] It does show a figure crossing a street at the left of the background, with a ladder at the right, between a puzzling central, circular motif and subsidiary unspecific forms that circulate around it. It raises the question whether, given the translation of de Kooning's own name, he may have been attracted to the strange cluster of circular, conical, and linear forms set

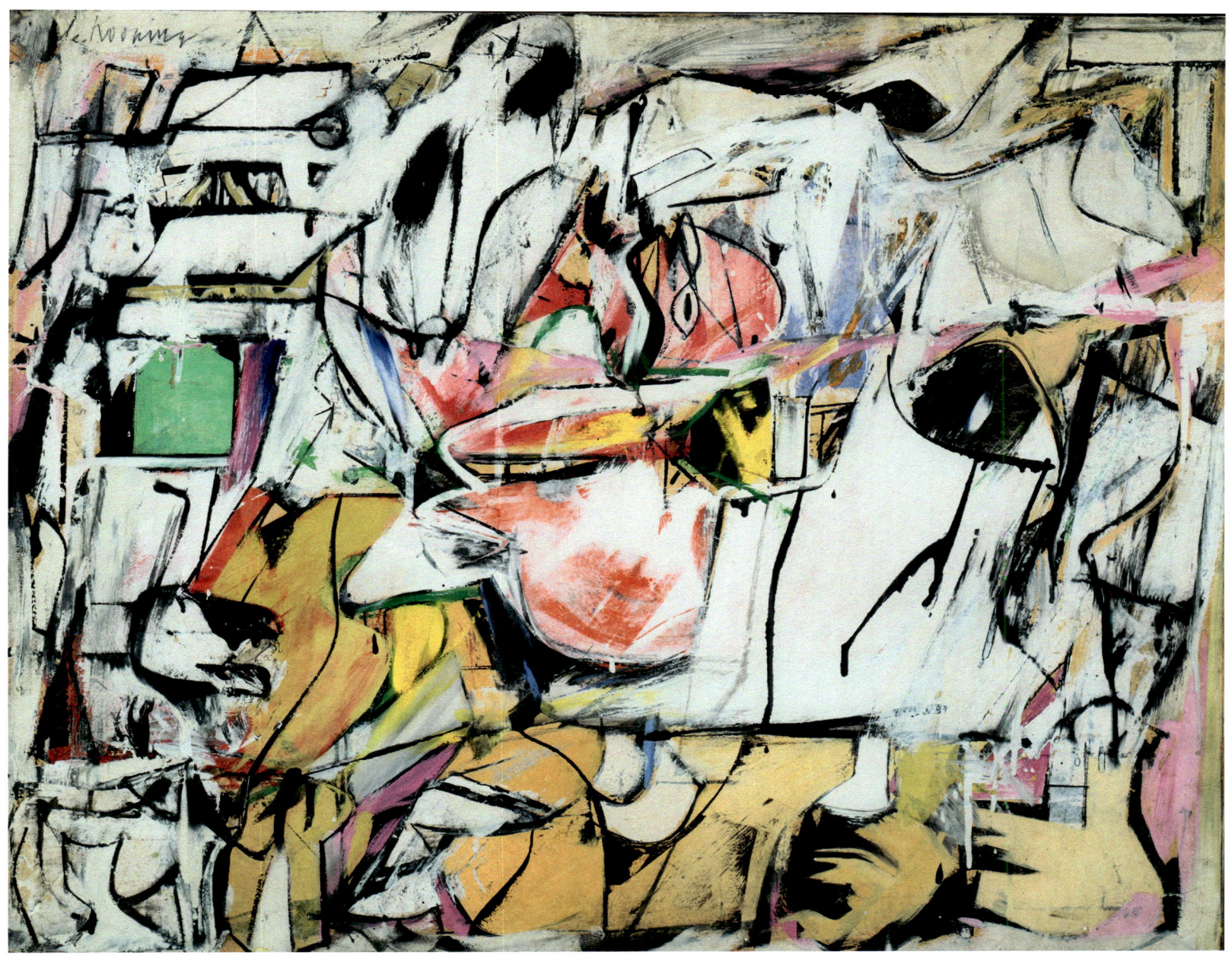

against the dense orange-brown background of Giorgio de Chirico's *The Evil Genius of a King* of 1914–15 (fig. 32), long in the MoMA collection.

As we shall see, there would be more exterior views the following year. But the immediate future lay elsewhere. Renée Arb's *Art News* review of the 1948 Egan exhibition, which employed that phrase, prompted Josef Albers to invite de Kooning to teach at Black Mountain College near Asheville, North Carolina.[104] In late June, he and Elaine went there for the summer.

Figure 33
Willem de Kooning, *Asheville*, 1948
Oil and enamel paint on cardboard, 64.9 × 81 cm. The Phillips Collection, Washington, DC. Acquired 1952 (0484)

ASHEVILLE TO EXCAVATION
Cézanne and the Color of Veronese

According to Elaine, de Kooning instructed his students to work on only one composition for the entire summer session. He himself did the same, focusing on *Asheville* (fig. 33), although additionally making drawings in black enamel and working with pastels, a new medium for him.[105] Whether *Asheville* was actually made there is uncertain, and what became of the pastels is unknown.[106]

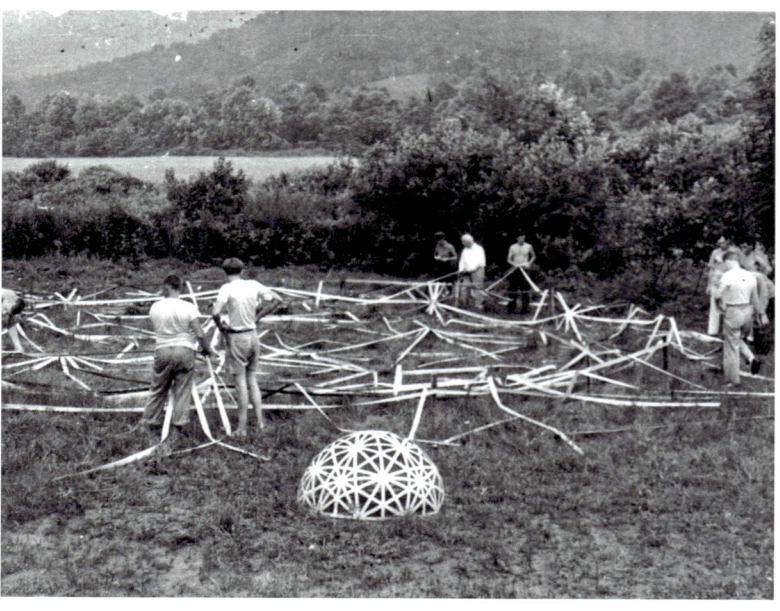

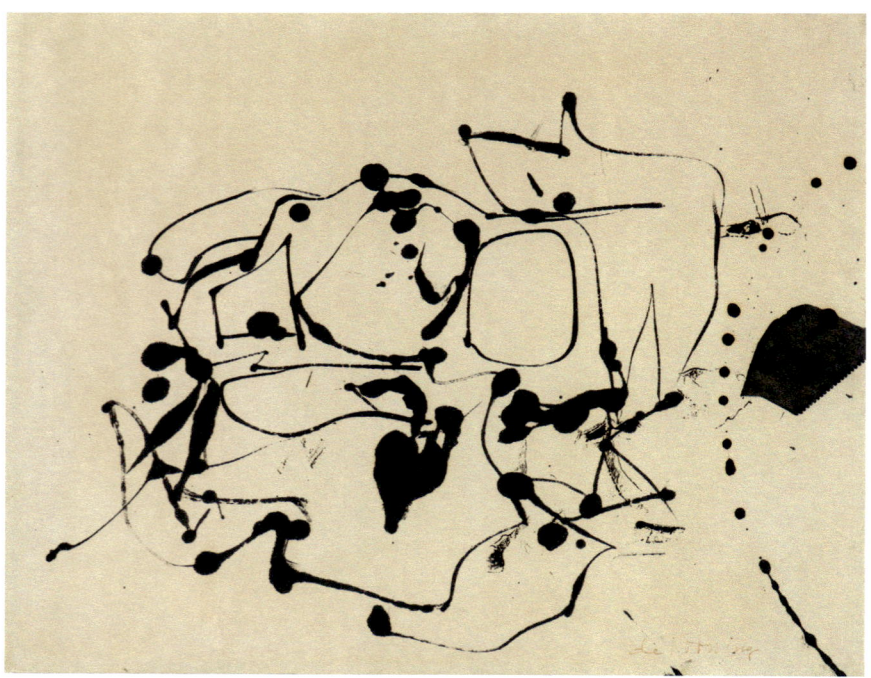

Figure 34
Beaumont Newhall (1908–1993; born Lynn, MA; died Santa Fe, NM), **Students attempting to assemble with long strips of venetian blind one of Buckminster Fuller's geodesic domes in a field at Black Mountain College, 1948.**
Photographic print. Western Regional Archives, State Archives of North Carolina

Figure 35
Willem de Kooning, *Asheville*, 1948
Enamel on paper, 48.4 × 61 cm. Saint Louis Art Museum. Museum Purchase (150:1966)

Moreover, what happened when de Kooning returned to New York is particularly difficult to place in sequence.

It is often said that de Kooning embarked on his second series of Woman paintings in the autumn of 1948.[107] As noted earlier, one of these started out as a black-and-white composition, presumably like those in the Egan exhibition with which it shares similar shapes, to which color and anatomical elements were later added. (Since these paintings depart somewhat from the increasing abstraction of his work in the final years of the decade and have been widely discussed, I shall not linger on them here.) Perhaps simultaneously with, or after, creating the Woman paintings, de Kooning made the new set of white-on-black compositions to which I also referred earlier, which develop the filigree drawing of *Light in August* (see fig. 18) to an allover effect. Pat

Passlof, a student of de Kooning's at Black Mountain College, remembers de Kooning that summer making "a lot of paintings on paper . . . the black and white enamel things on paper."[108] However, at present only one black-and-white work on paper has been firmly attributed to that visit, albeit with possibly an intriguing source of inspiration.

Also on the Black Mountain faculty that summer was Buckminster Fuller, who had arrived with an aluminum trailer filled with what he termed his "magical world of mathematical models."[109] Chief among these was a model of the geodesic dome that he had made famous: a thin, shelled lattice composed exclusively of multiple triangular elements, because they were stronger than rectangular ones, distributing stress equally throughout the structure. Seeing the linear components of a geodesic dome laid out on the ground (fig. 34) would likely have been of great interest to de Kooning, and the one drawing we know he made at Black Mountain (fig. 35) may be a response.[110] And this drawing, in turn, is akin to *Asheville*'s drawn lattice within which the artist disposed his patches of color.

The color of *Asheville* is unexpected, and may owe something to his working there in pastels. Elaine de Kooning said that he was "working feverishly on one after the other for a couple of weeks until the walls were covered with them."[111] Making a pastel is not like making a drawing with a pencil or pen. It involves working with

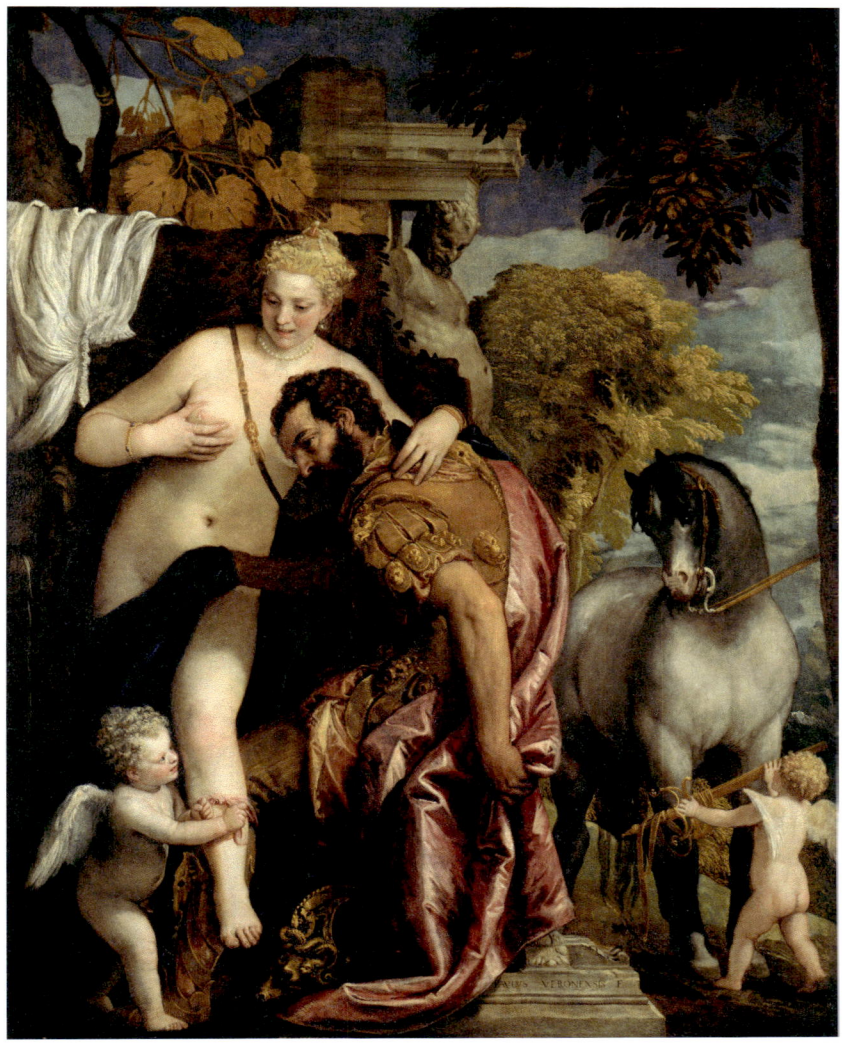

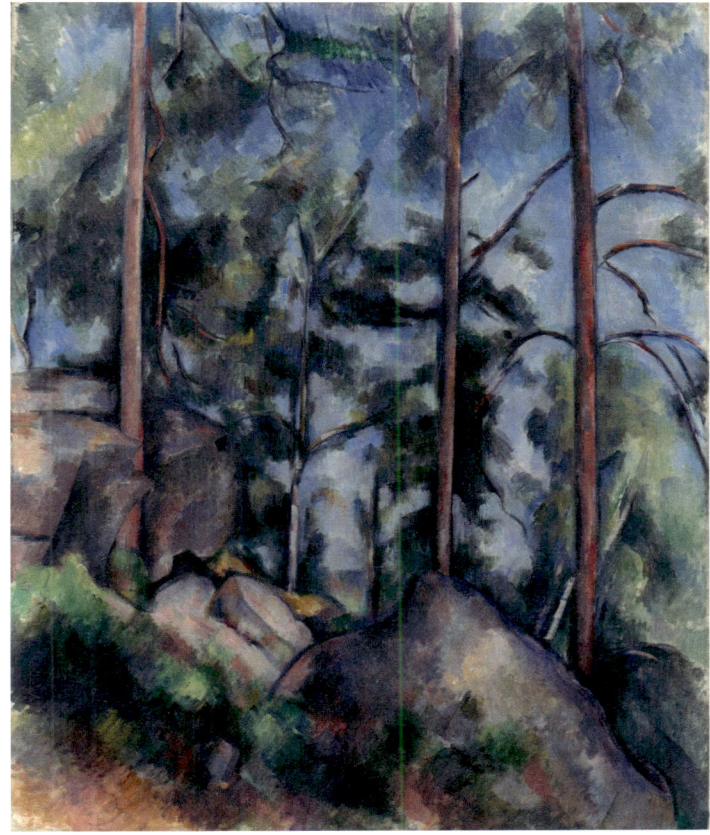

color, with a wide array of powdered hues compressed into individual sticks. Of course, de Kooning could have worked in color using turpentine to thin his oil paint, but not without loss of color sensation. Yet there is virtually no binding medium in pastels; they are almost pure pigment. So, when an artist applies pastel to white paper, color seems to be lit up not only from behind—by light reflected forward from the paper—but also from within the powdered pastel itself. The color is very much there, but there is also a sense of insubstantiality because it is less dense than a covering layer of colored oil paint. Color and light are interdependent. Such would have been the lesson de Kooning learned from making pastels.[112]

At Black Mountain, de Kooning gave a talk entitled "Cézanne and the Color of Veronese."[113] This is not the odd contrast it is sometimes taken to be, for Cézanne was in fact a great admirer of Paolo Veronese. On February 3, 1902, he wrote to a young artist friend, "Since

you are now in Paris, and you are drawn to the masters in the Louvre, make studies from the great decorative masters, Veronese and Rubens if you like."[114] De Kooning would have known Veronese's *Mars and Venus United by Love* (fig. 36), from the 1570s, at the Metropolitan Museum of Art, likely seeing in it what Cézanne would have seen in the Veroneses in the Louvre. It is a construction not of tonalities, but of color—of mid-tone color set down by the associated gray rocks and horse to which all the other hues are matched: on one side by the brown clothes and the flesh color of the two figures; on the other by the mid-blue sky. There is nothing vivid—no reds and yellows—to break the coherent color envelope. The result is what Cézanne termed "decorative," and what we see—and presumably what de Kooning then saw—in Cézanne's landscapes at MoMA as well (fig. 37): something not "*merely* decorative," but praiseworthy for renouncing what is commonly understood to be vividly expressive storytelling as a distraction—in favor of giving each color a weight, which itself shapes the movement of each compositional part, even while contributing to the overall color sensation and also remaining itself.[115]

It is, naturally, pure speculation on my part to suggest that this is what de Kooning said in his talk, but I do take his title for granted in proposing that he must have associated the work of Cézanne with the Venetian color-space of Veronese's paintings. If he did, he would certainly have observed the extraordinary lengths to which Cézanne had transformed it, often maintaining an overall mid-color tonality but arriving at it from the modulation of hues at high intensity as well as those at their most somber. Additionally, of course, the components of Cézanne's paintings are color patches—small, parallel strokes of almost uniform weight—often describing sharply fractured planes that shape movement between near and far, while maintaining the Venetian standard of color as depth as well as surface.

The color of de Kooning's *Asheville* is not specifically associable with that of either a Veronese or a Cézanne, but it shows an awareness of construction via color that is new to his art. To compare the painting with what may well have been his previous full-color composition, *Secretary* (see fig. 12), is to see that it takes an enormous step forward. It reads as a full-color composition without actually employing many colors: the line of pale orange-to-yellow shapes that resembles a line of ducks running along the bottom edge; the adjacent scumbled light-red areas that partly fill and surround two grotesque heads, with a few flashes at each side of the composition; and the audacious mid-green rectangle without which all

else would seem labored, perhaps a door set in the middle of a pile of architectural rectangles. Passlof recorded that de Kooning had said he wanted to produce "leap[s] of space," and "the paint to appear as if it had materialized there magically all at once as if it was 'blown' on."[116] But as prominent as the vocabulary of shapes is the black-line drawing—cursive and rectilinear; thick and thin; firm and dripping; abstract and descriptive, notably of a staring eye—that must have been applied late in its composition and associates the painting with works in the Egan show, while pointing it toward new directions.

New Directions

A trio of paintings composed with color that de Kooning made back in New York reveal him exploring new directions. *Collage* (fig. 38) has even more of the windswept, "blown on" look of *Asheville*, although composed almost entirely of collaged cut-out shapes, mainly yellow with a few red and green, attached by pushpins. *Painting* (fig. 39) has a palette close to *Asheville*'s, including the critical green focal point, but is dominated by packed, splintery white triangles and rectangles outlined in black. It is far more indebted to Cézanne than to Veronese and belongs with de Kooning's summative compositions at the end of the decade, to which I will presently turn.

The surface of *Gansevoort Street* (fig. 40), aside from its simpler black-line drawing and some exposed underpainting, eventually was almost completely covered with red. The actual Gansevoort Street, located on the Lower West Side of Manhattan, was famous in de Kooning's time for its slaughterhouses. His choice of title for a not-actually bloodred painting was, at best, a joke for those who knew their Downtown geography. The color appears to reflect de Kooning's study of the work of artist Henri Matisse. It may well have been painted in 1949. That year, Matisse's *The Red Studio* (1911) was acquired by MoMA, and the Pierre Matisse Gallery held the first postwar exhibition of Matisse's work in New York. The exhibition featured the artist's recent paintings, shown without frames, along with drawings and—not seen before—paper cutouts. De Kooning had to have been impressed.

Nonetheless, the composition of *Gansevoort Street* is strikingly similar to that of *Dark Pond* (fig. 41), which is effectively its monochrome companion, with white drawing on a black ground, suggesting that the two works may have been made around the same time.

Dark Pond belongs to the series of black-on-white compositions, some of which were possibly made at Black Mountain, which develop the filigree drawing of *Light in August* to an allover effect. They are more radical and complete in their abstraction than the works in the Egan show—indeed, of anything the artist had done thus far—de Kooning having all but eliminated enclosed black shapes and large areas of white. Instead, lines of varying width, opacity, tonality, velocity, and manner of application skitter around the surface, throwing up shapes to either side of them. Being the most fluidly drawn, patently allover works that de Kooning had made to date, these paintings invite obvious comparison with Jackson Pollock, who had exhibited his first "drip paintings" at the Betty Parsons Gallery in January 1948. But de Kooning's are far tauter, far more on and of the surface than Pollock's aerated webs. Moreover, close inspection reveals that some of these shapes invoke identifiable elements of figuration, ranging from fragments of human anatomy to architectural elements and automobiles. The movement of the lines is such that the eye is constantly finding and losing images in a flash, unable to settle on any one for very long.

With Pollock in mind, Greenberg wrote that "often we cannot distinguish centers of interest within the abstract picture's field and have to take the whole of it as one single, continuous center of interest, which in turn compels us to feel and judge it in terms of its over-all unity to the exclusion of everything else."[117] De Kooning wanted it both ways. His method of composition was designed precisely to accommodate distinguishable centers of interest as well as to take the whole of the picture as a single, continuous center of interest.

The same is true of complementary works that de Kooning had been making by April of 1949, consisting of dense black drawing set against a white ground—or, rather, embedded within it.[118] This is the case with *Zot*

(fig. 42). As noted earlier, de Kooning had inscribed that word, among other lettering, on the surface of *Zurich*. With *Zot* and other works of this type, among them *Town Square* (fig. 43), black and white—sometimes gray and cream—interact to shape the surface. Even more so than *Zurich*, they engage with Analytic Cubism.[119]

While critics have largely, and correctly, seen an indebtedness to Picasso in de Kooning's more expressive, figurative works, he himself stressed the importance of a very different quality. In 1951, he would write, "Of all movements, I like Cubism most. It had that wonderful unsure atmosphere of reflection—a poetic frame where something could be possible, where an artist could practise his intuition."[120] This group of paintings especially bears comparison with Analytic Cubist canvases, sharing with them qualities of investigative care and patient thoughtfulness in the shaping, placing, and spacing of forms, guided by the articulation of their drawing. De Kooning would have known such canvases, among them *Ma Jolie* (see fig. 24), from the walls of MoMA, and, even more, from the pages of Alfred H. Barr Jr.'s *Picasso: Fifty Years of His Art* (1946), with its compelling set of illustrations of Analytic Cubist paintings—in black and white, naturally.[121]

Despite their modest size, these paintings represent a great step forward for de Kooning even as they harken back to Analytic Cubism. They do so in comprising compositions of more or less independent planes, depictive of parts of not easily identifiable objects, set flatly in parallel to the picture plane; with shading relegated to the outlined boundaries of these planes; and with a minimal degree of spatial illusionism separating their flatness from the literal flatness of the surface itself.[122] But whereas the planes that fill Cubist paintings such as *Ma Jolie* resemble the facing surfaces of solid, boxlike volumes, many folded flat, those in de Kooning's *Zot* and *Town Square* are decal-thin and layered one above the other.

Pollock's allover paintings were also made in layers but do not reveal their layering. De Kooning's black-on-white paintings such as this pair allow us to infer that they were painted in layers, but we cannot disentangle them in our viewing. Looking back to earlier in the 1940s,

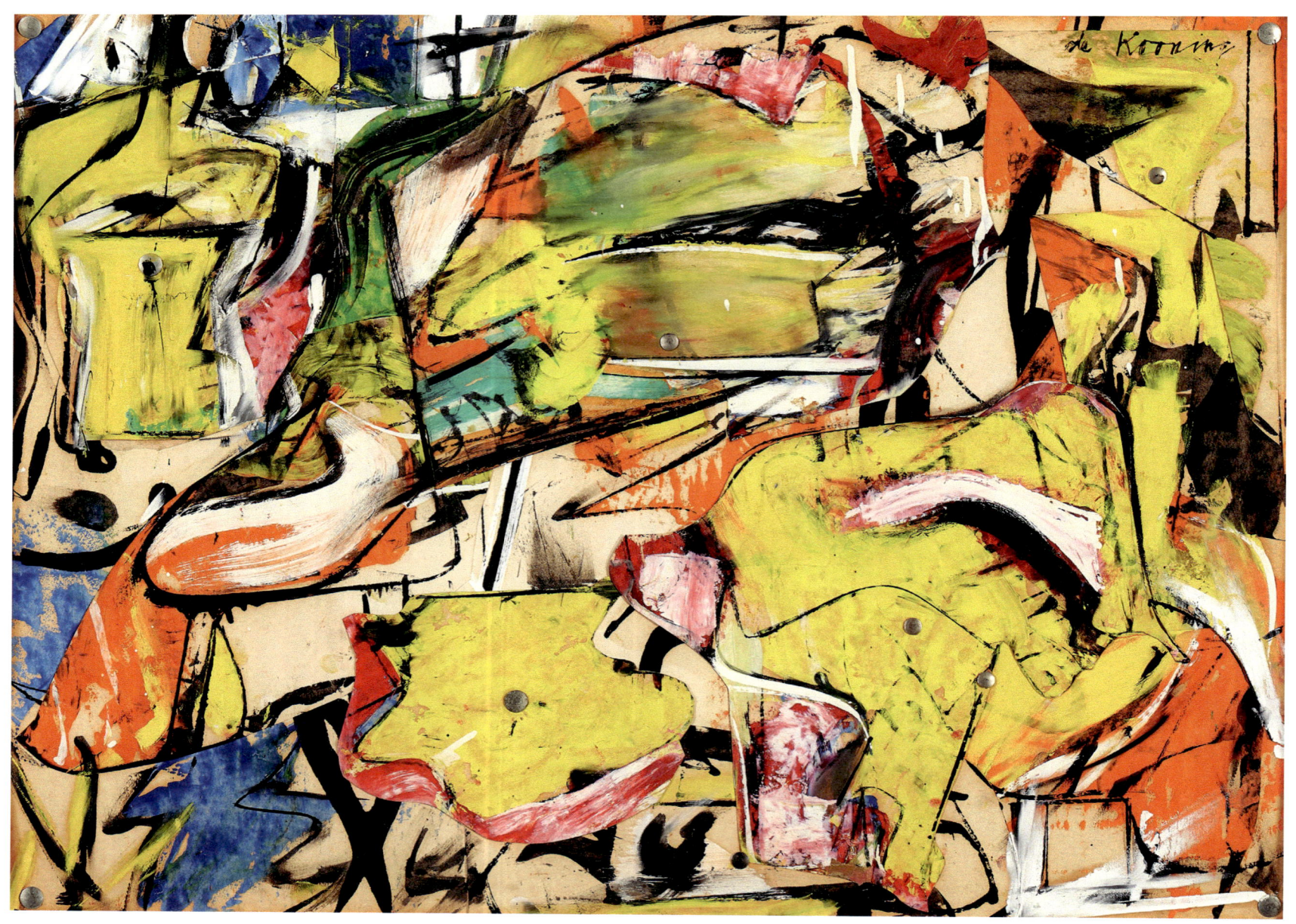

Figure 38
Willem de Kooning, *Collage*, 1950
Oil and lacquer with thumbtacks on paper, 55.9 × 76.2 cm.
Private collection

Figure 39
Willem de Kooning, *Painting*, 1949–50
Oil and enamel on board, 75.9 × 101.9 cm. Collection of David
Geffen, Los Angeles

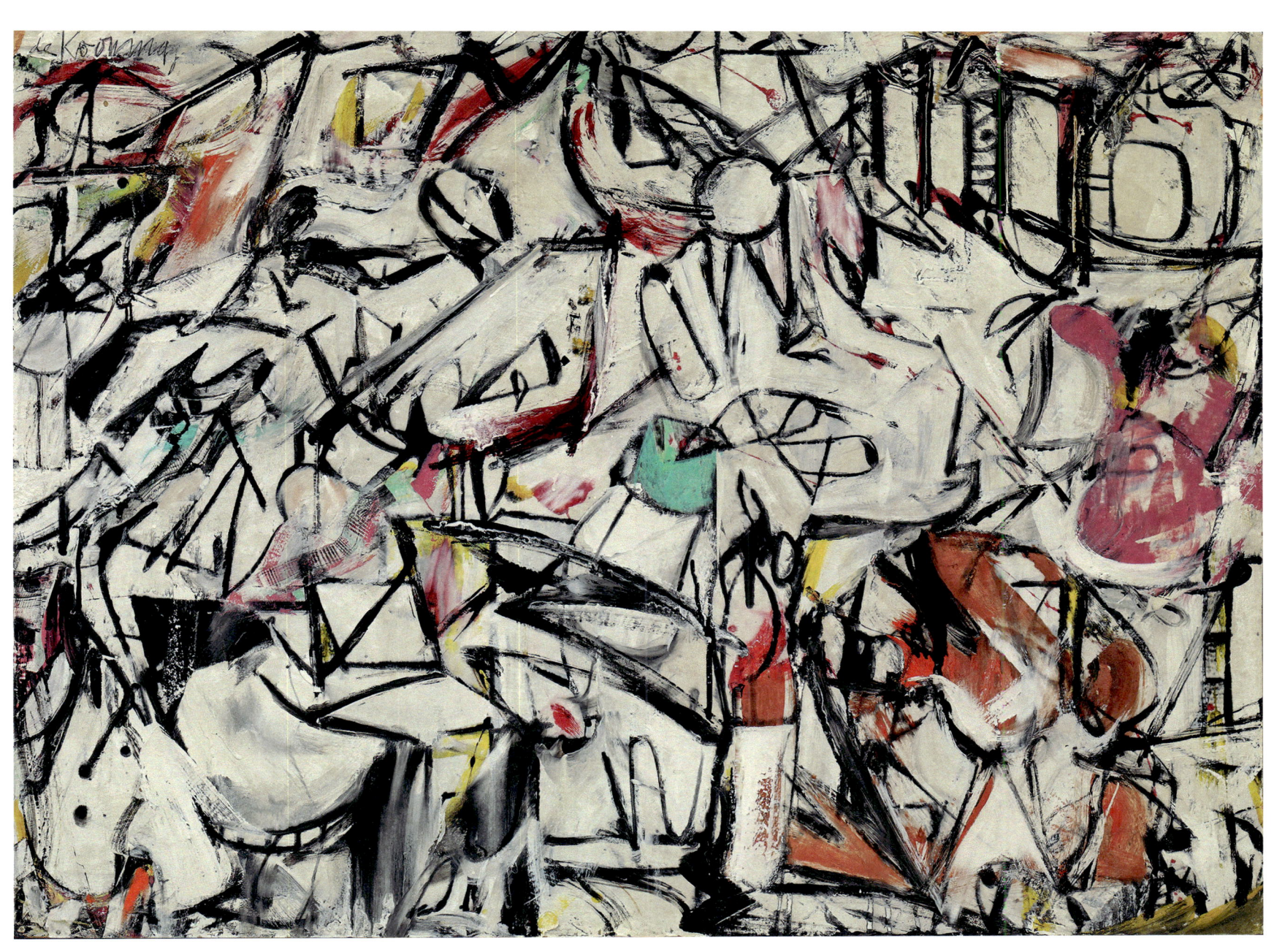

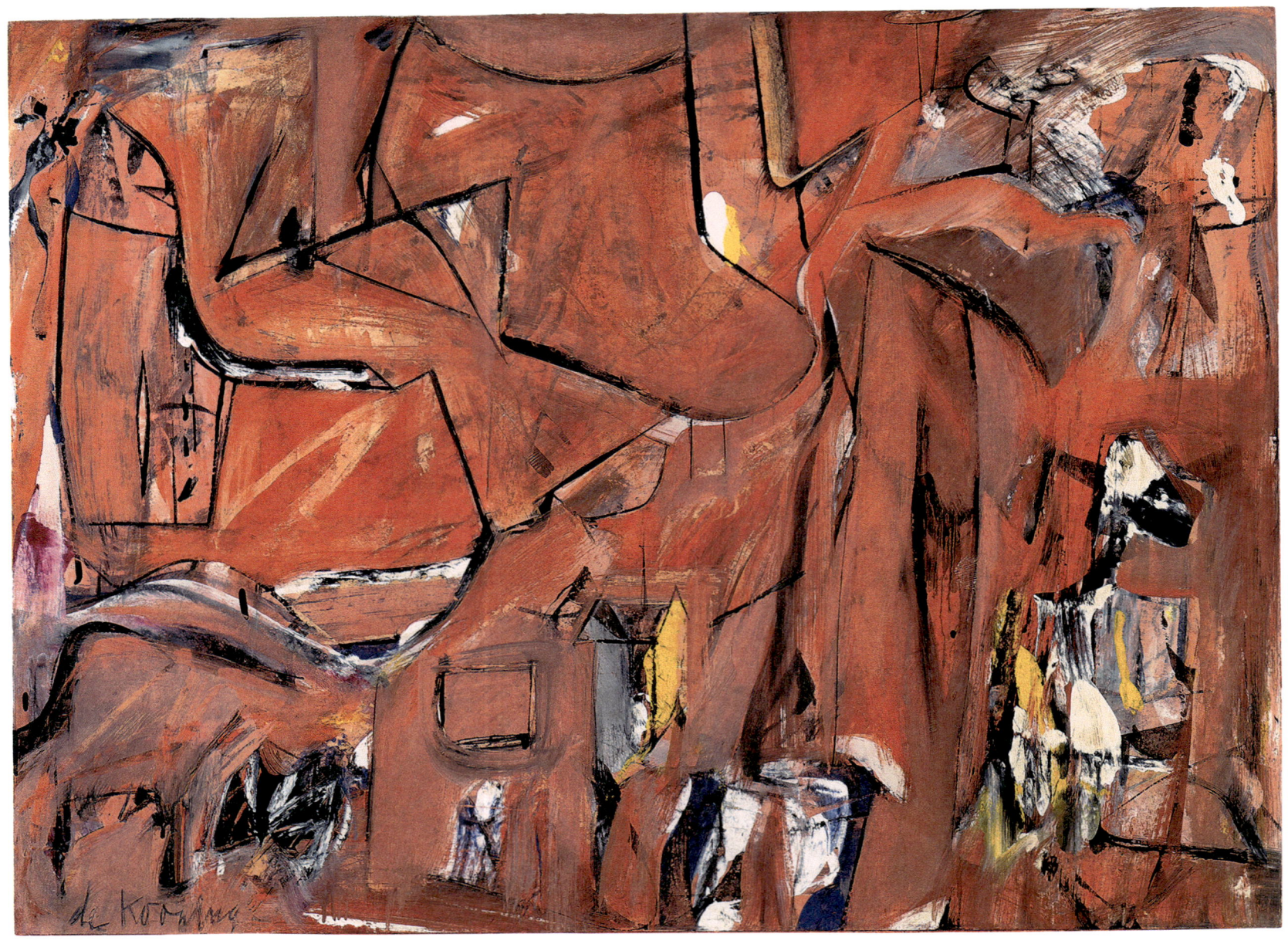

Figure 40
Willem de Kooning, *Gansevoort Street*, ca. 1949
Oil on cardboard, 76.2 × 101.6 cm. Anderson Collection at Stanford
University. Gift of Mary Margaret Anderson (2019.1.1)

Figure 41
Willem de Kooning, *Dark Pond*, 1948
Enamel on composition board, 118.7 × 141.6 cm. Frederick R.
Weisman Art Foundation, Los Angeles

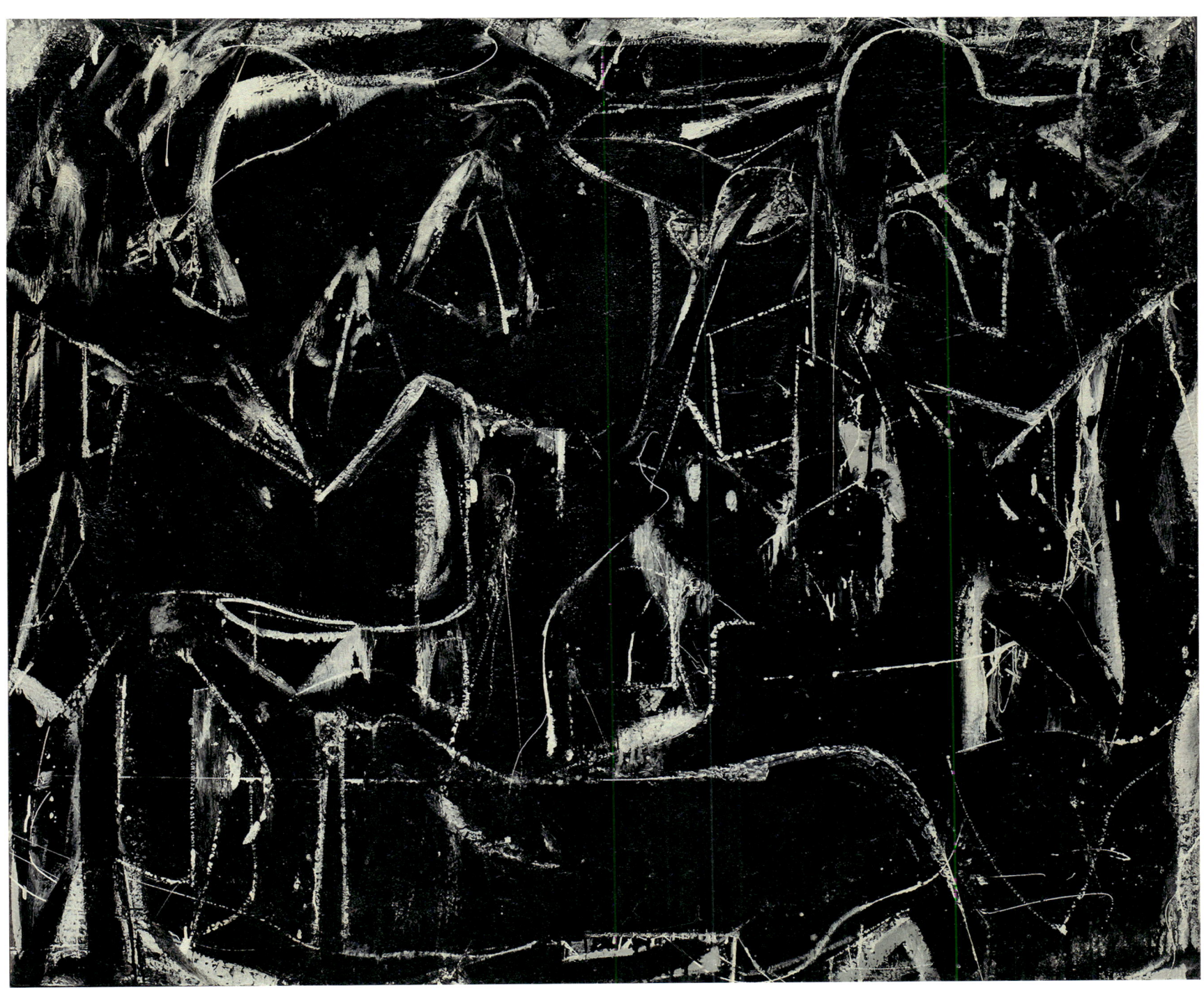

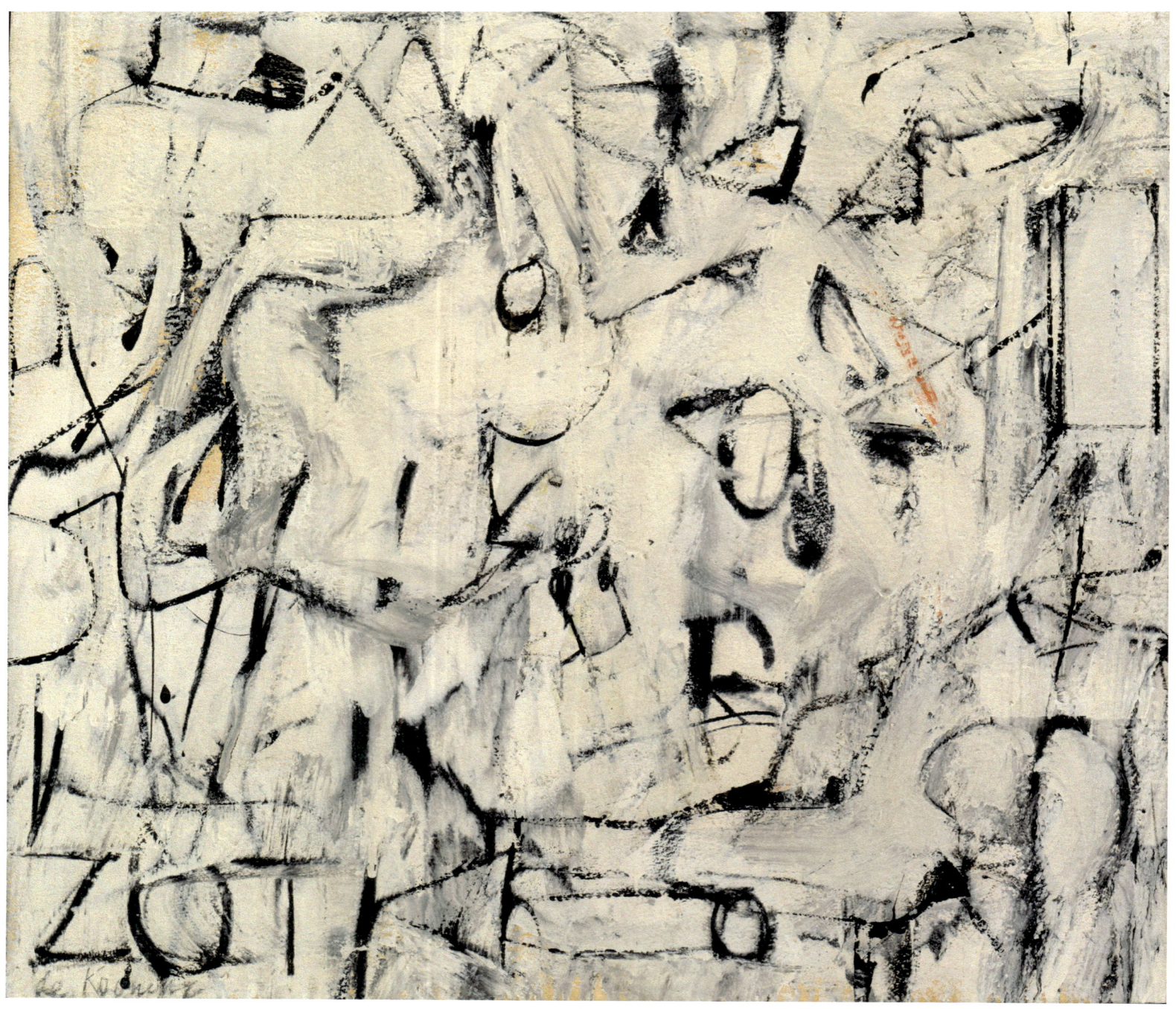

Figure 42

Willem de Kooning, *Zot*, 1949

Oil on paper, mounted on wood, 45.7 × 51.4 cm. The Metropolitan Museum of Art, New York. From the Collection of Thomas B. Hess, Purchase, Rogers, Louis V. Bell and Harris Brisbane Dick Funds and Joseph Pulitzer Bequest, and Gift of the heirs of Thomas B. Hess, 1984 (1984.611)

we can see that he was continually working with the relative density of planar components and the extent to which they seem to be layering: In paintings including *The Wave* and *Valentine*, he had set down flat shapes so that they seem to comprise a layer on the surface but not filling it. In *Judgment Day*, he had completely filled the surface to the extent of not showing it was layered; and in *Mailbox* had disposed large shapes so that they form its proximate layer, with open spaces around them that reveal a largely continuous drawn layer beneath them, and a ground plane beneath that. It is clear that de Kooning painted *Zot* and *Town Square* in layers, but he did not let the painting read as layers; the fore-ground–background effect of *Mailbox* has gone.

In order to do so, de Kooning drew the black lines at varying speeds and densities to orchestrate movement within, around, and between the forms they describe. And he wiped and smeared areas of paint to break boundaries of forms, joining solid to solid, space to space, and space to solid. He would make an individual plane overlap another as often—or as well—as resting upon another, but there are so many places where it is uncertain whether a plane is a solid or a space. They so infiltrate one another, even as they jostle with and deform one another, that our only certainty is awareness of the ground layer as having been brought forward flat on the surface. There is nothing imaginable behind or around the frontal array of such a painting except its literal support.

The same is true of de Kooning's contemporane-ous white-on-black paintings, like *Night Square* (fig. 44), which share a similar iconography. Writing in 1960, Harriet Janis and Rudi Blesh distinguished between these two kinds of paintings through the language of photography, calling them respectively "positives" and "negatives" and also observed, "To look rapidly back and forth at these two pictures creates an effect like that of a dark landscape upon which a searchlight flashed on and off."[123] This com-parison not only applies to looking rapidly from *Town Square* to *Night Square*, but also nicely responds to de Kooning's frequently quoted remark about his painting what he called a "slipping glimpse" or "frozen glimpse," and illustrates his most often-quoted examples of such glimpses: "It is like crossing the street. You want to cross the street fast, so you run across"; "I have a little glimpse of something . . . I want to give somebody else something of that glimpse"[124]; [c]ontent, if you want to say, is a glimpse of something, an encounter, you know, like a flash."[125]

This pair of paintings advances the urban motif of *Abstraction* (see fig. 31), discussed earlier. The upper-left corner of *Night Square* depicts what appears to be the edge of a square with a doorway in an adjacent line of buildings. *Town Square* does not offer anything

similar, although the piled-up, rectangular forms down the left margin may be thought to be architectural, imply-ing a bird's-eye view of an urban square. However, we know that de Kooning often rotated his canvases as he worked.[125] Seen upside down in the direction at which it may well have been begun, the incident in *Town Square* slides in diagonally beside a windowed building at the left, as it does in *Night Square*, and is disposed across a register line just short of the then-bottom of the canvas, on which stands one and probably more prominent fig-ures, with additional figures behind, some with prominent strips of shadow giving them depth. Seen in the painting's completed orientation, these dark zones disengage and flatten to the surface, no longer serving an illusionistic role but comprising an interplay of lights and darks within a composition that is now at once suspended from that register line while also thrusting diagonally up and across from the bottom-left corner. The activity is arrested by details that invite identification—eyes and orifices; win-dow or door shapes; what is perhaps a ladder at the left; a puzzling shield-like element beside it—but identification is as often thwarted as satisfied. "Even abstract shapes must have a likeness," de Kooning insisted.[127]

Fitting-in: Jigsaws and Tiling

Abstract shapes whose likeness de Kooning invites us to discover had long been part of his artistic vocabulary. Among those whose oddity draws our attention because of their resemblance to animated beings is the likely reclining figure in the bottom-left corner of *Special Delivery* (see fig. 9) and the possible but implausible winged creature at the center of *Orestes* (see fig. 17), relatives of which appear in *Town Square*. In a later, small painting, possibly from 1949, that has been called *Attic Study* (fig. 45), de Kooning floats a pair of shapes, facing in opposite directions, that defy description amid a swarm of smaller, similar shapes. They somewhat resemble teeth, hats, or small animals but are in fact repurposed, reversed iterations of the figure in *D* from 1946 (fig. 46). They also bear comparison to the way in which de Kooning represented the exposed body as an

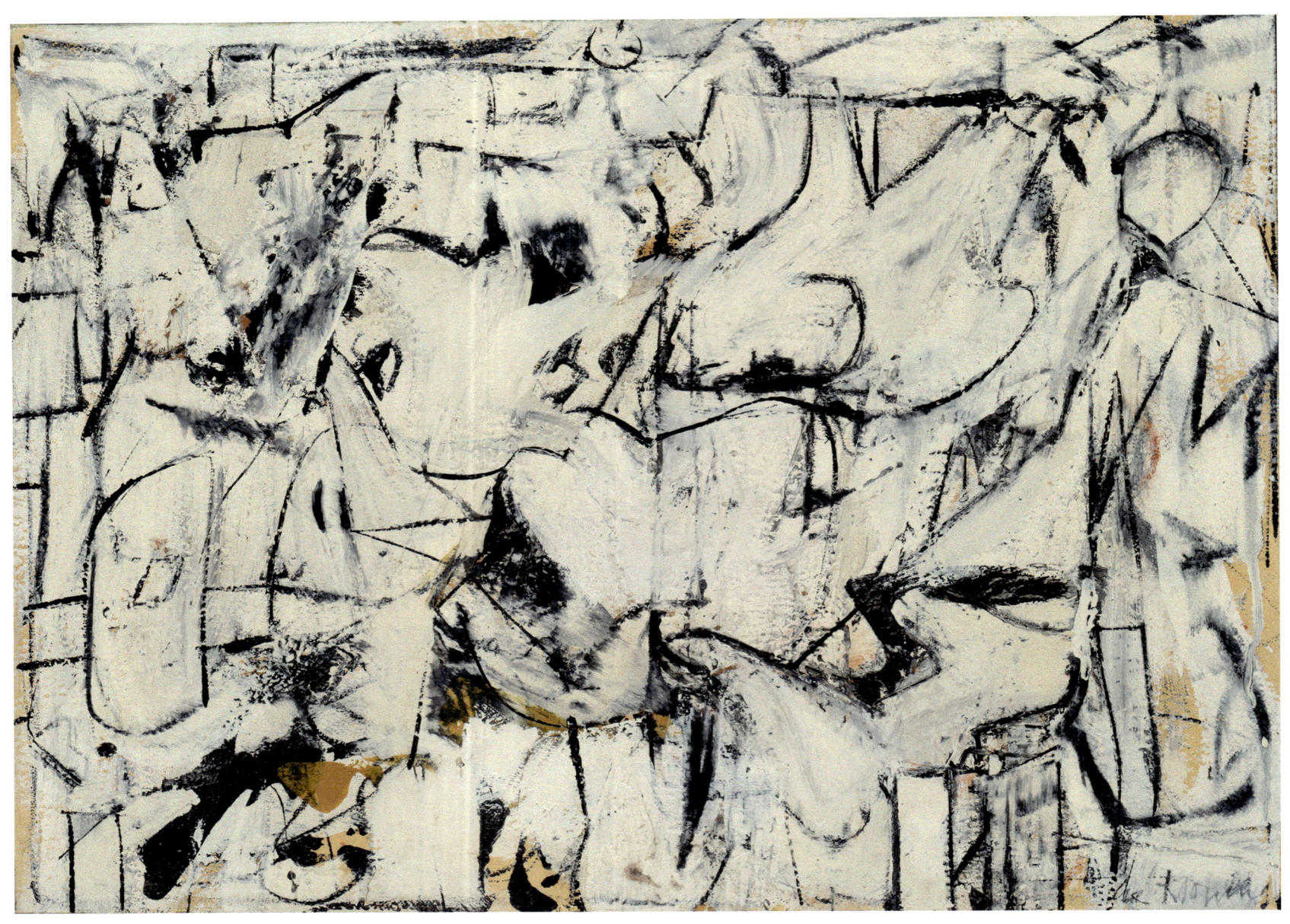

Figure 43
Willem de Kooning, *Town Square*, 1949
Oil on paper mounted on Masonite, 44.2 × 60.3 cm. Seattle Art
Museum. Gift of the Friday Foundation in honor of Richard E. Lang
and Jane Lang Davis (2020.14.2)

Figure 44
Willem de Kooning, *Night Square*, ca. 1949
Enamel on cardboard on composition board, 75.6 × 101 cm.
Collection of David Geffen, Los Angeles

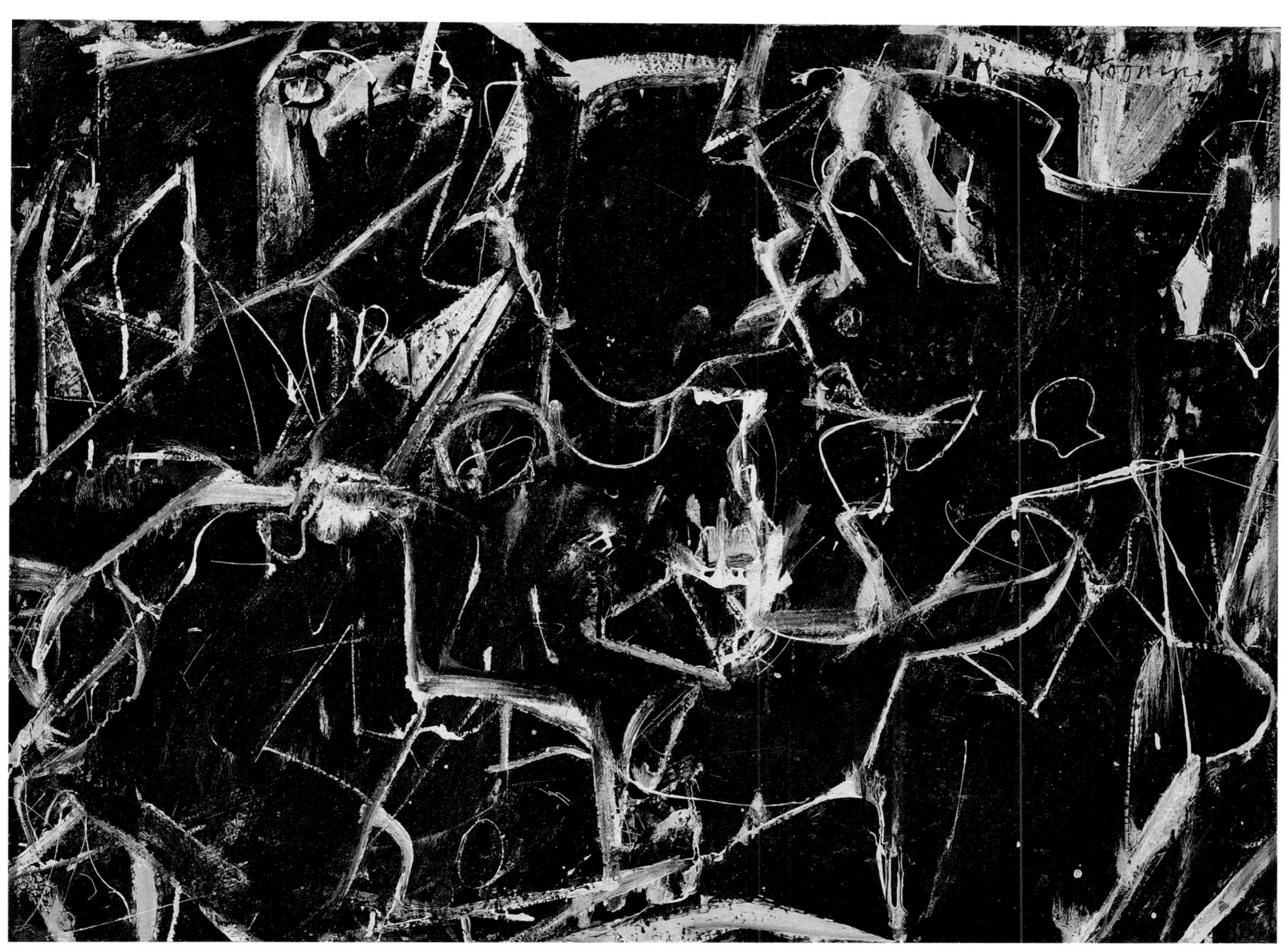

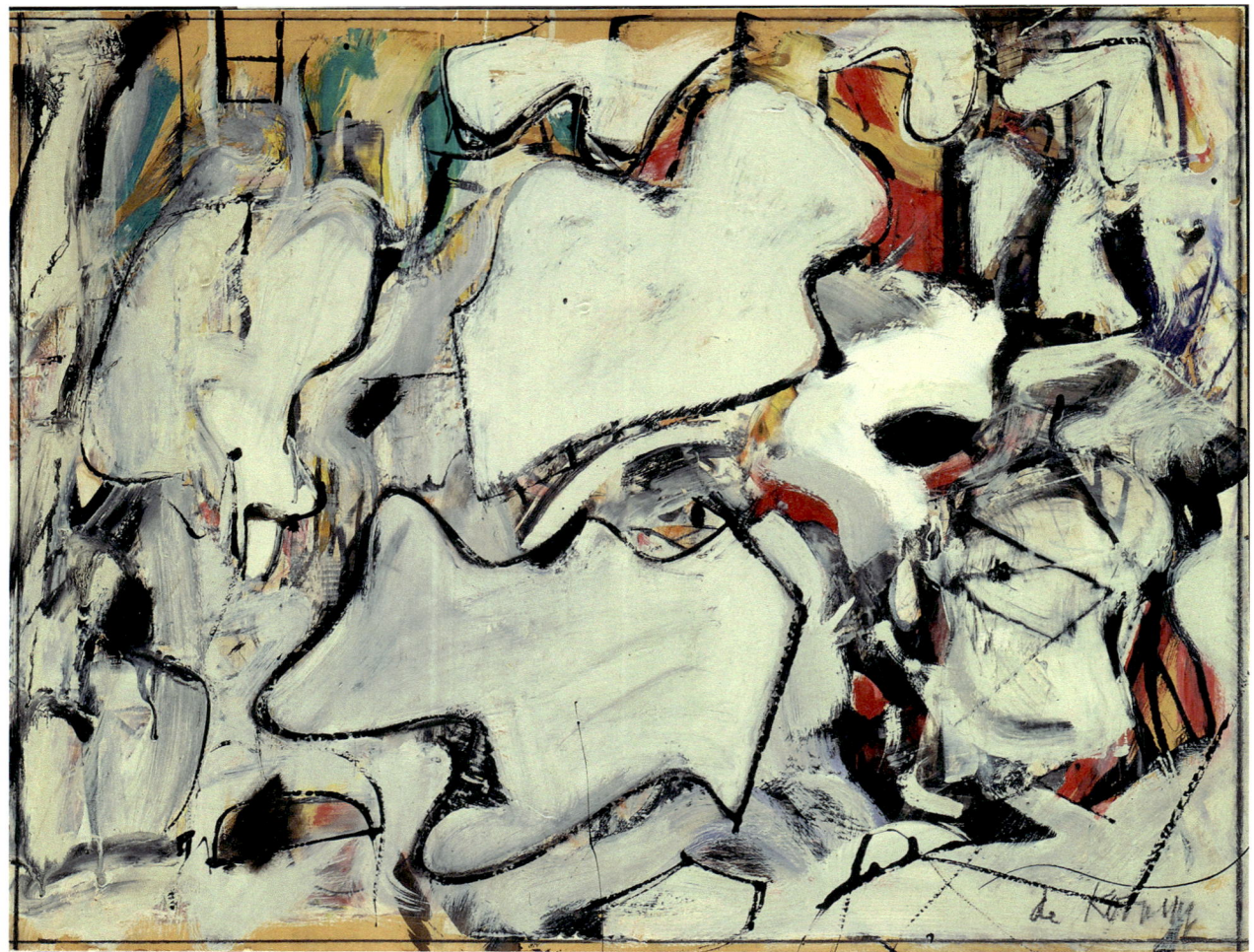

Figure 45
Willem de Kooning, *Attic Study*, 1949
Oil, enamel, and graphite on paperboard mounted on hardboard,
47.9 × 60.6 cm. The Menil Collection, Houston (X 422)

irregular, splayed plane in one of his 1949 Woman paintings (fig. 47). De Kooning appears now to have been thinking about shapes that could mutate or be jigsawed together. Contemporaneous drawings with black enamel paint on white paper (figs. 48, 49) show him trying to avoid interstitial gaps by weaving together such forms as positive and negative areas. But clearly that would have been too difficult to achieve, or too flimsy in effect, for large surfaces.

The contemporaneous composition *Painting*, discussed above, avoids interstitial spaces by featuring more geometric shapes than biomorphic ones, in an extremely dense composition, mainly black and white with added color, everything "fitted-in" in a Cézannist manner. But it is clear that de Kooning's main thrust was to work again solely with black and white, which led him

to make a pair of paintings larger than any he had previously attempted: *Attic* (fig. 50), at five feet tall and almost seven feet wide, which was followed in 1950 by the even more ambitious *Excavation* (fig. 51), measuring nearly seven feet tall and over eight feet wide.

In the course of making *Attic*, de Kooning had learned from the smaller paintings that he could not manage *tight* fitting-in while using elements with irregularly curved boundaries; he had to leave space between them. The best he could manage was to set the elements in tall columns, and, even then, tight fitting-in was impossible. It was also hindered by de Kooning having used elements with such different appearances. But, as Elaine de Kooning reported, he said he titled it *Attic* "because you put everything in it."[128] For simplicity's sake, we might think of *Attic* as composed on the *jigsaw* principle of fitting together elements with irregularly curved boundaries, and *Excavation* on the *tile-like* principle of fitting together elements with geometric contours.

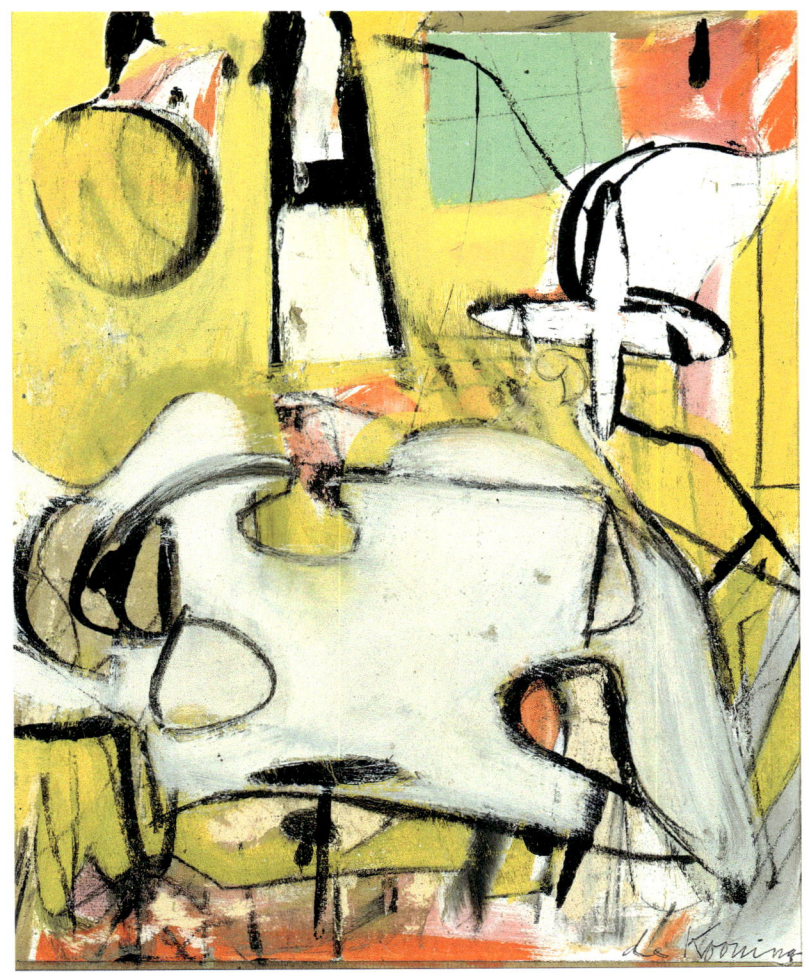

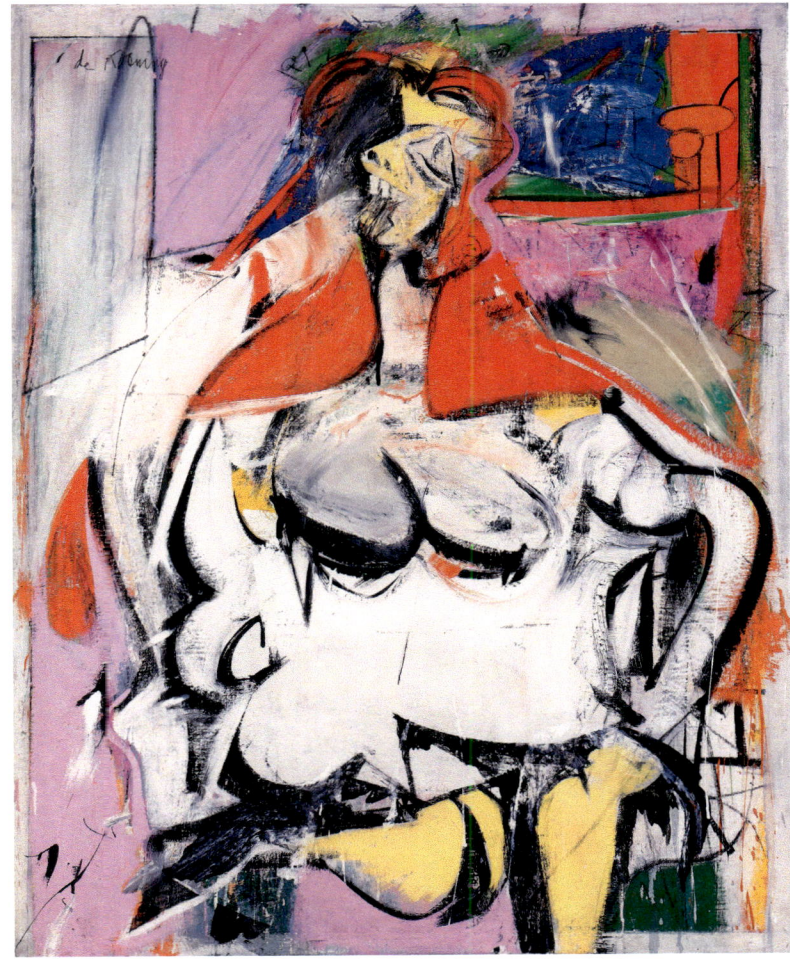

Of course, de Kooning never wanted to produce a pictorial surface that resembled a floor composed of identical tiles.[129] *Excavation* is composed of tiles of different shapes and sizes. Since the work was begun as a figurative composition, and the finished painting features discernible body parts, a connection is often made between it and the Italian Neorealist film *Bitter Rice* (1949), directed by Giuseppe De Santis.[130] It is unlikely that de Kooning saw the film while painting *Excavation*, but he could have seen a still from it showing six scantily clad women standing in a flooded rice field. Nonetheless, the figural fragments that remain in the painting are far removed from that image, recalling instead his interest in Bruegel that informed *Pink Angels* (see fig. 8) and the grotesque in his subsequent works. And this is one of the occasions when we need to pay attention to a painting's title, for the work mainly presents itself as an aggregation of unspecific shards and fragments tumbled together as might be found in an excavation.

Figure 46
Willem de Kooning, *D*, 1946
Oil on paper, 35.6 × 29.2 cm. Private collection

Figure 47
Willem de Kooning, *Woman*, 1949
Oil, enamel, and charcoal on canvas, 152.4 × 121.6 cm.
Private collection

We know that in this period de Kooning enjoyed roaming the New York streets at night, looking at the many construction sites in a city witnessing a postwar building boom. And, inevitably, thoughts of that site of excavation outside Aix-en-Provence, the Bibémus Quarry, famously painted by Cézanne, come to mind. As we have heard, de Kooning said that "fitting-in" was "where modern art came from" in the work of Cézanne and in Cubism, adding: "The way I do it, it's not like Cubism, it's like Cézannism, almost."[131] In its fitting-in of generically similar shapes into a crystalline surface, *Excavation* reaches back to the birthplace of modernism

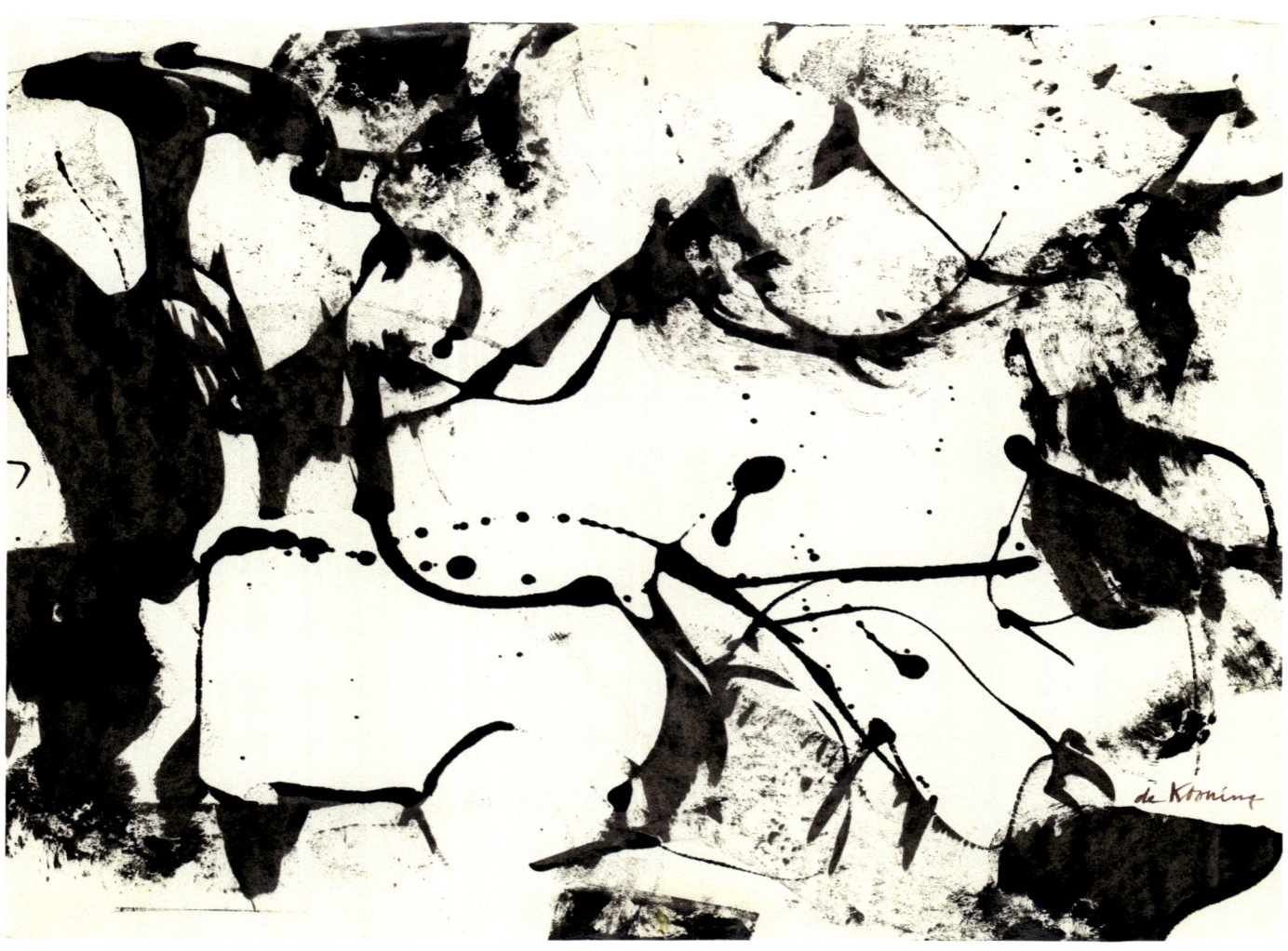

Figure 48
Willem de Kooning, *Landscape, Abstract*, ca. 1949
Enamel on paper, 48.9 × 64.9 cm. Whitney Museum of American
Art, New York. Gift of Mr. and Mrs. Alan H. Temple (68.96)

Figure 49
Willem de Kooning, *Black Untitled*, 1948
Oil and enamel on paper, mounted on wood, 75.9 × 101.6 cm.
The Metropolitan Museum of Art, New York. From the Collection
of Thomas B. Hess, Gift of the heirs of Thomas B. Hess, 1984
(1984.613.7)

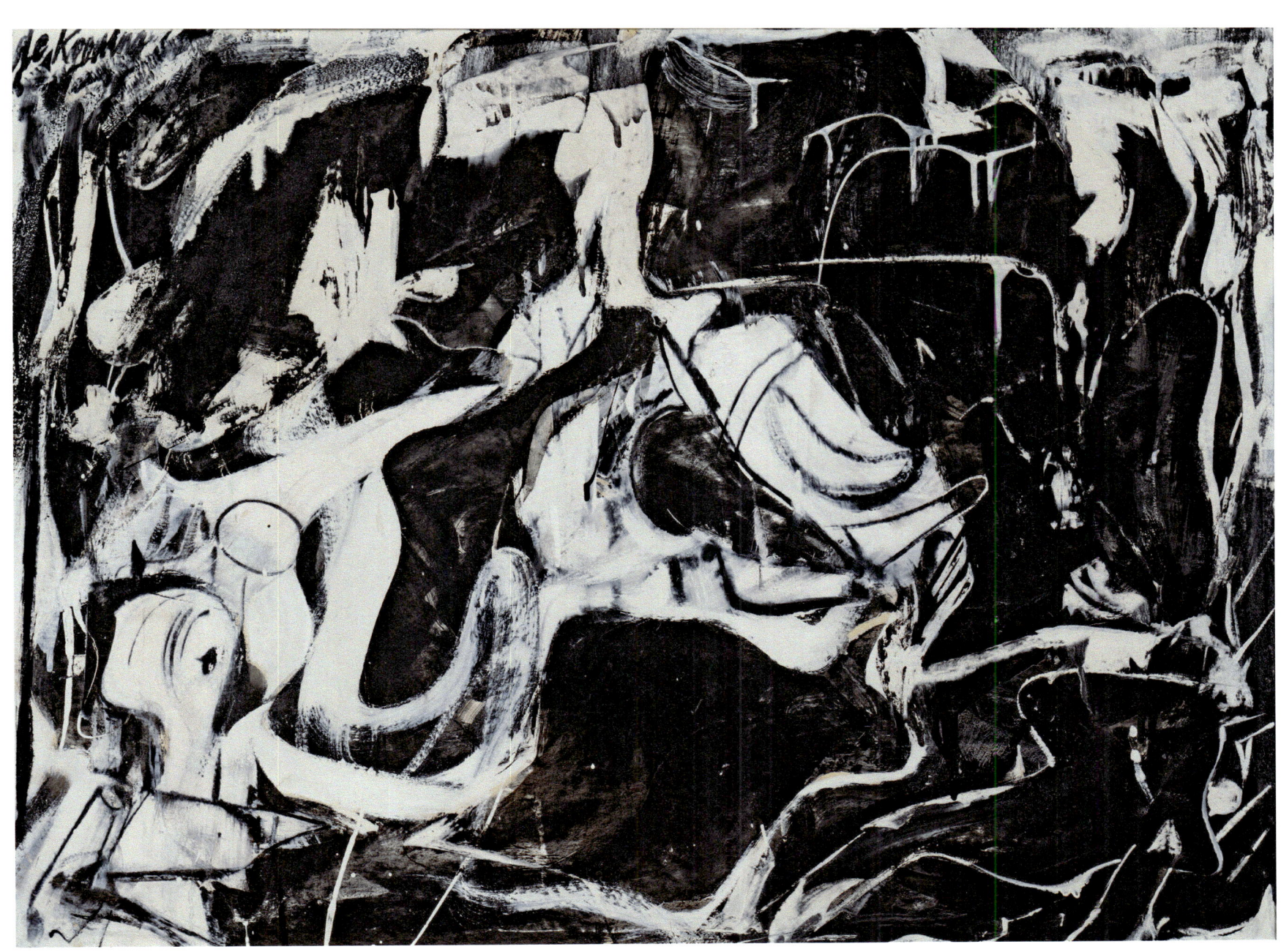

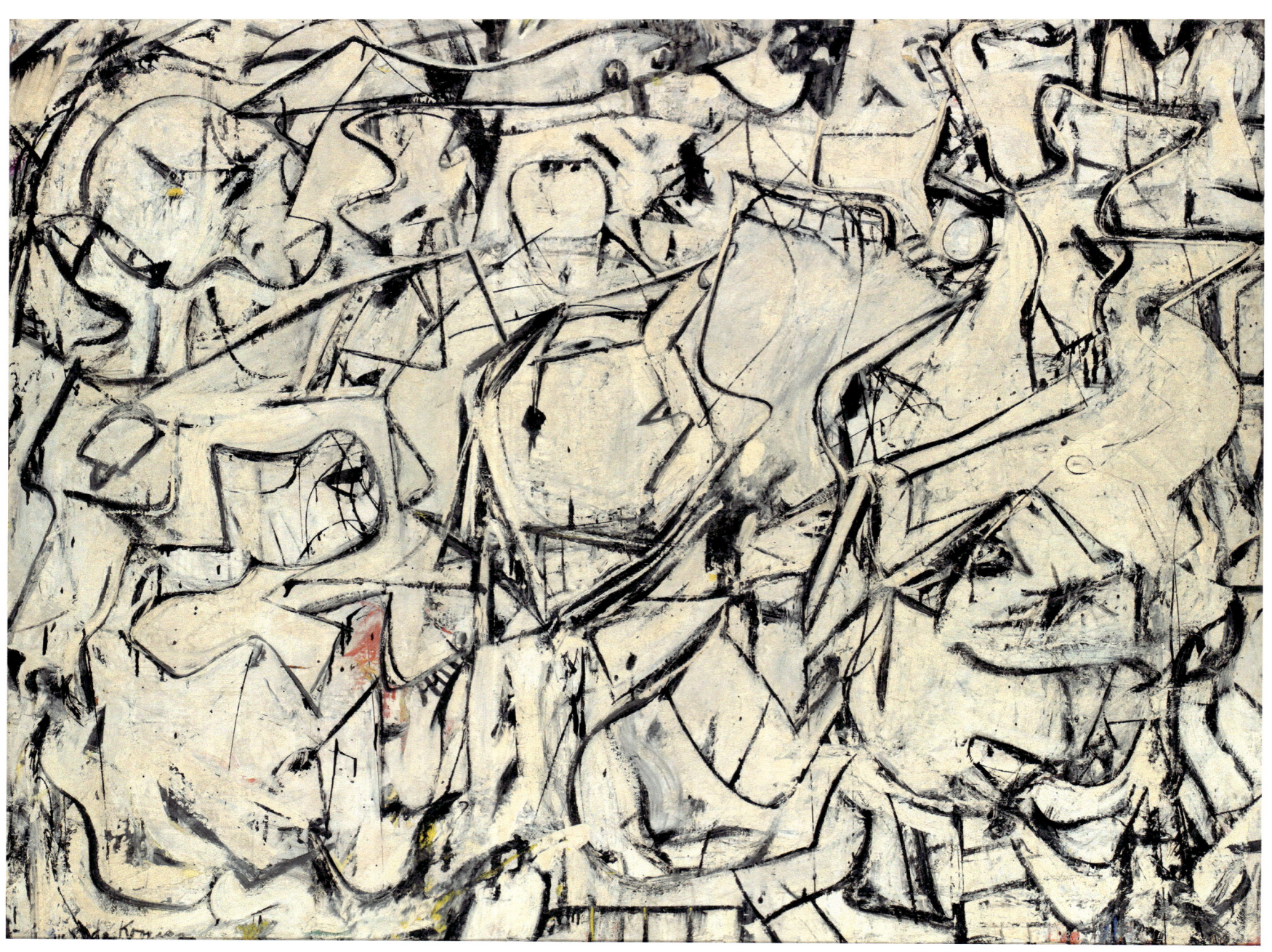

Figure 50
Willem de Kooning, *Attic*, 1949
Oil, enamel, and newspaper transfer on canvas, 157.2 × 205.7 cm.
The Metropolitan Museum of Art, New York. The Muriel Kallis
Steinberg Newman Collection, Gift of Muriel Kallis Newman, in
honor of her son, Glenn David Steinberg, 1982 (1982.16.3)

Figure 51
Willem de Kooning, *Excavation*, 1950
Oil on canvas, 205.7 × 254.6 cm. The Art Institute of Chicago.
Mr. and Mrs. Frank G. Logan Purchase Prize Fund; purchased with
funds provided by Edgar J. Kaufmann Jr. and Mr. and Mrs. Noah
Goldowsky (1952.1)

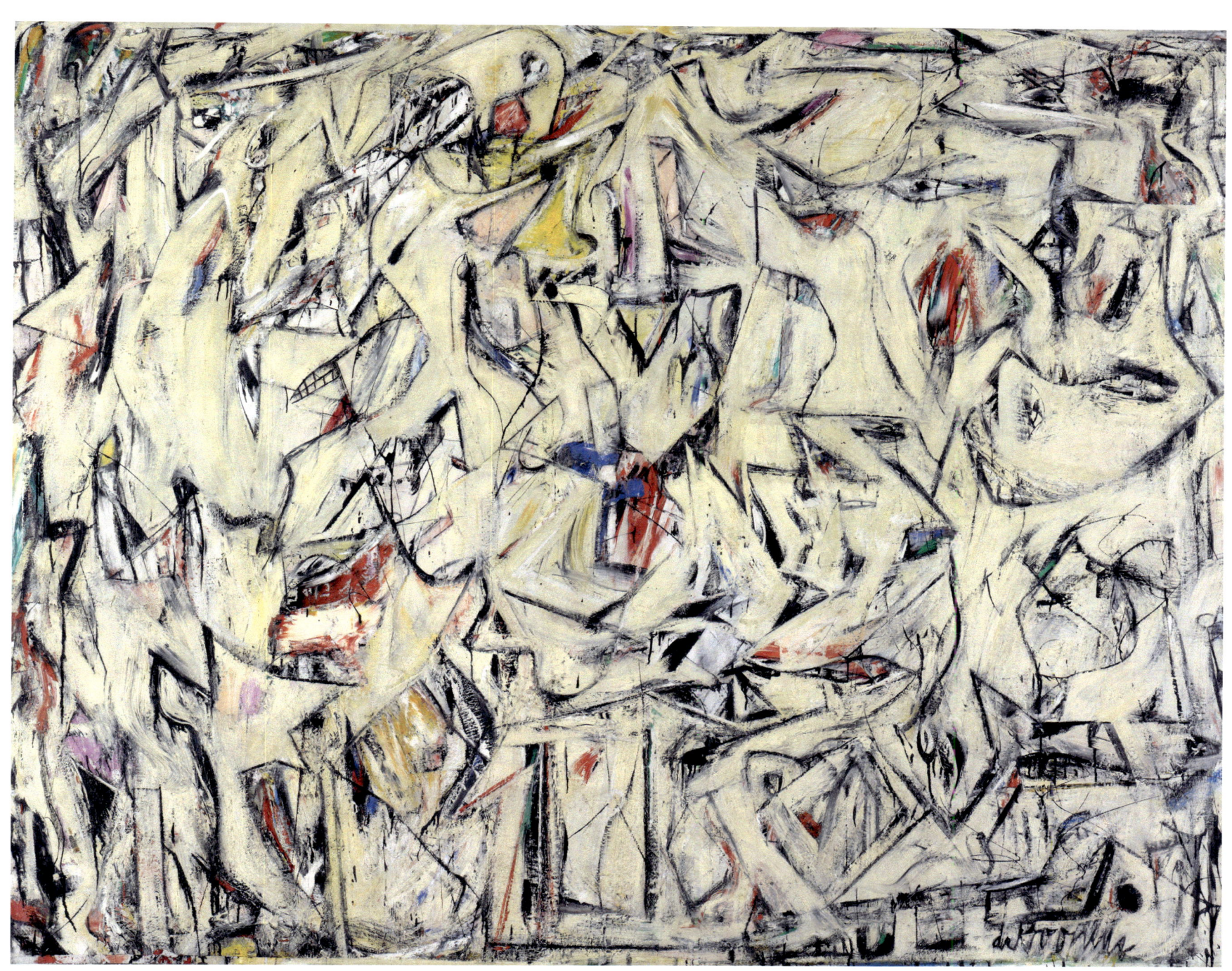

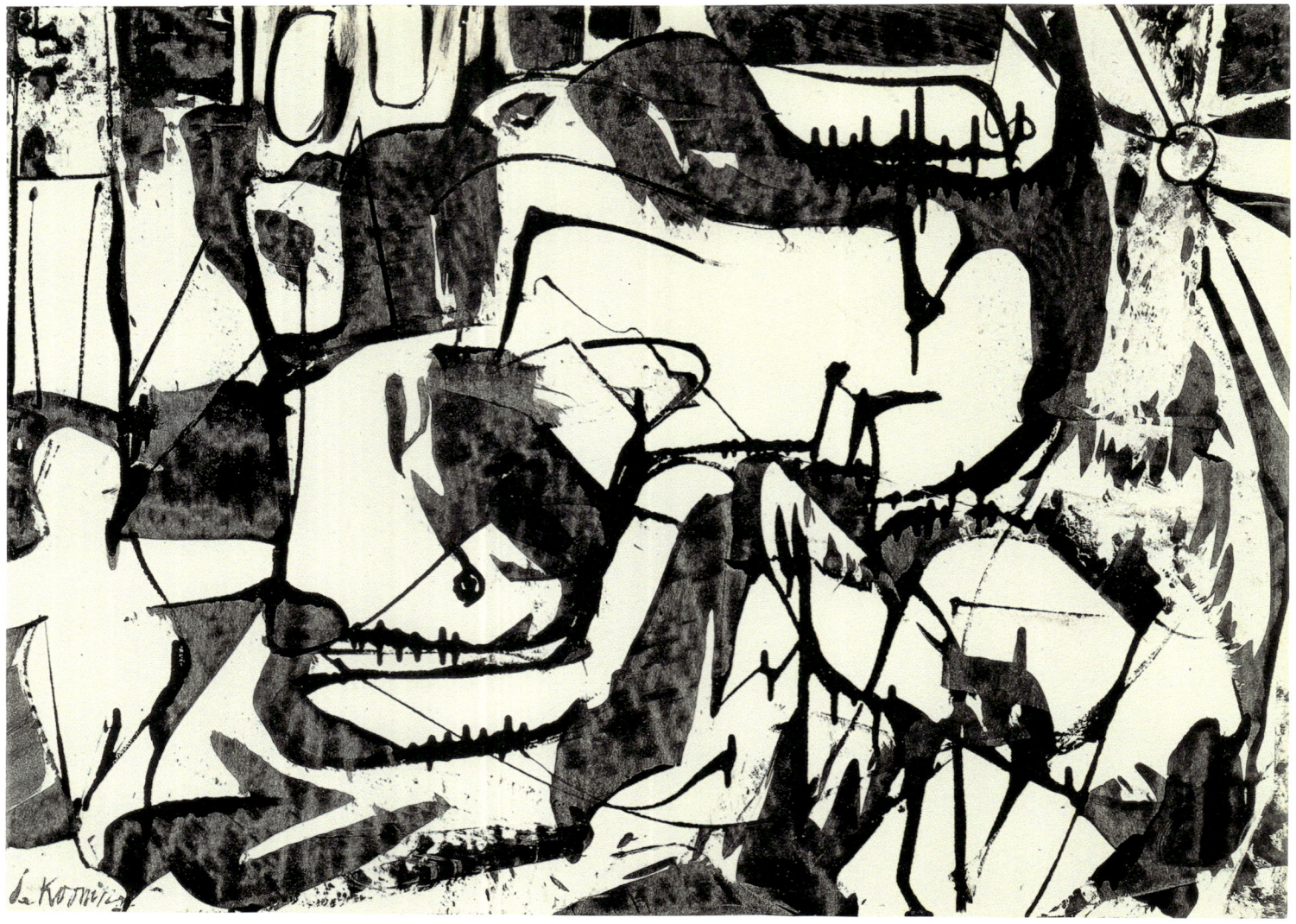

Figure 52
Willem de Kooning, *Untitled (Black and White Abstraction)*, 1950
Sapolin enamel on paper, 55.9 × 76.2 cm. Private collection

and is arguably the last great picture painted in the Cézannist tradition. It was also the largest and most ambitious composition de Kooning had ever painted.

Excavation was celebrated even as it was being painted, with artists and critics coming to de Kooning's studio to view its progress. One of the critics, Harold Rosenberg, called it "a classical painting, distant and majestic."[132] Classical in the sense of being reminiscent of the order of the classical past; distant in the sense of formal and reserved; majestic in the sense of dignified and grand. And it is all of these things, but it is also an atavistic painting: distant in terms of alluding to what is remote; majestic in the sense of awesome. Its reception

was extraordinary: the painting was exhibited at the Venice Biennale in 1950 and at MoMA in 1951; it won the top prize in the Art Institute of Chicago's annual exhibition of American painting and sculpture in 1951, entering its collection the following year; and was later called "the most distinguished modern American work of art to be acquired that year by any museum in the country."[133]

De Kooning's biographers describe *Excavation* as "one of the greatest paintings of the twentieth century and a work that even his harshest critics usually call a masterpiece."[134] While correctly saying that masterpiece-making was not how he commonly proceeded, these writers argue that with the beginning of a new decade and the attention that Pollock received, the urge to paint a masterpiece was not to be resisted. Specifically, the *Life* magazine headline of its August 1949 article on Pollock—"Is He the Greatest Living

Painter in the United States?"—must have caught de Kooning's attention. The only previous time de Kooning had surrendered to the urge to create a masterpiece was when painting *Judgment Day* and *Backdrop for "Labyrinth,"* which ushered in the development we have been following. Then, I argued early in this essay, he appears to have deliberately set out to create a summative, hopefully not boring, perfected composition. Now he seems to have done precisely that.

Excavation may be the only work for which de Kooning described how he had painted it. He did so in 1983, while looking at a reproduction of it:

> **I think I started here [pointing to the upper left-hand corner]. I said, "Well, I'll make a stab at it here." I wasn't thinking about any method or manner that had realities. So you do a little bit, and you feel comfortable with it. Then you say, "I'll make it open here and closed here," and that way you go around and around it, a little bit at a time. It's always coming out nice, because you can keep on going with what's connected to it. Because if you keep a section you're comfortable with, you can build out from it, little by little. Maybe if it doesn't go too well, you put it aside and come back the next day to start up again.[135]**

To what end? We might remember Delacroix's admonition, "Never seek after an empty perfection." The question needs to be asked: Was—and is—the summative *Excavation* so widely praised because it is so perfected? And if so, how does this square with de Kooning's saying of a painting in general, that he worked "[n]ot with the idea of perfection but to see how far one could go, you know—but not with the idea of really doing it"? The critical phrase, I think, is "to see how far one could go." That was what he learned in continually revising *Excavation*. Delacroix also said, "Experience ought to teach us two things; first that we should do a great deal of correcting; secondly, that we must not correct too much."[136] It may be argued that de Kooning did a great deal of correcting

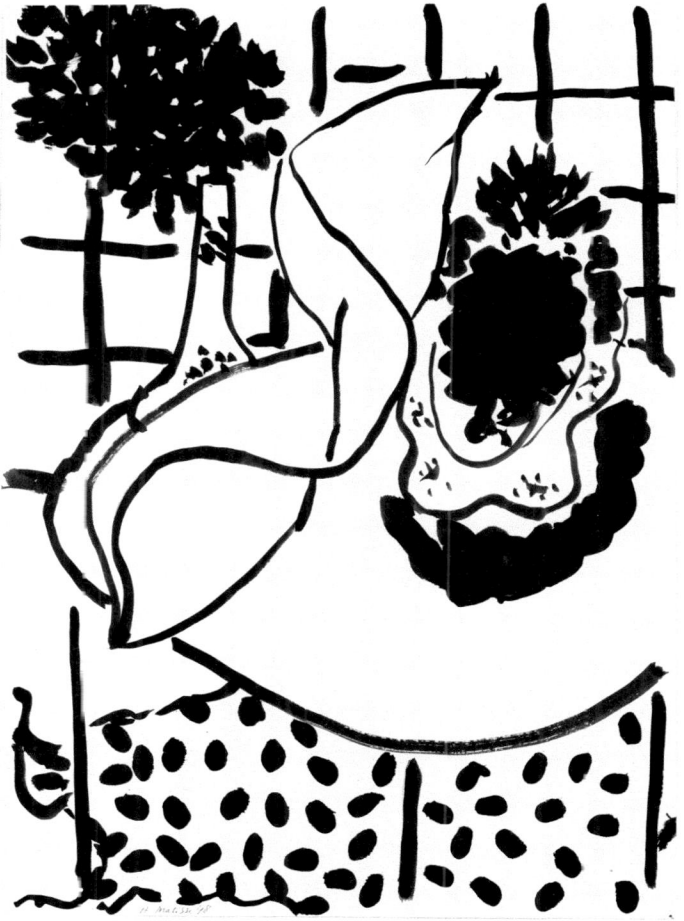

Figure 53
Henri Matisse, *The Black Pineapple*, 1948
Private collection

without correcting too much to see how far he could go—not only with *Excavation* itself, but also with the path he had been following that led up to it.

By correcting so much to bring all the parts together, he learned that nothing more could be done except to go far in a different direction; and even while *Excavation* was receiving its accolades, de Kooning had moved on. Concurrent with the large canvases were paintings on paper made with black Sapolin enamel, revisiting the medium of works in the April 1948 Egan exhibition in a second Egan show, in April 1951 (fig. 52). These images of abstracted figures in imagined interiors are no longer grotesque like their early-1940s precursors, nor are they densely packed, graphic compositions like most of Pollock's contemporaneous black-and-white drawings. Rather, they are crisp, bold,

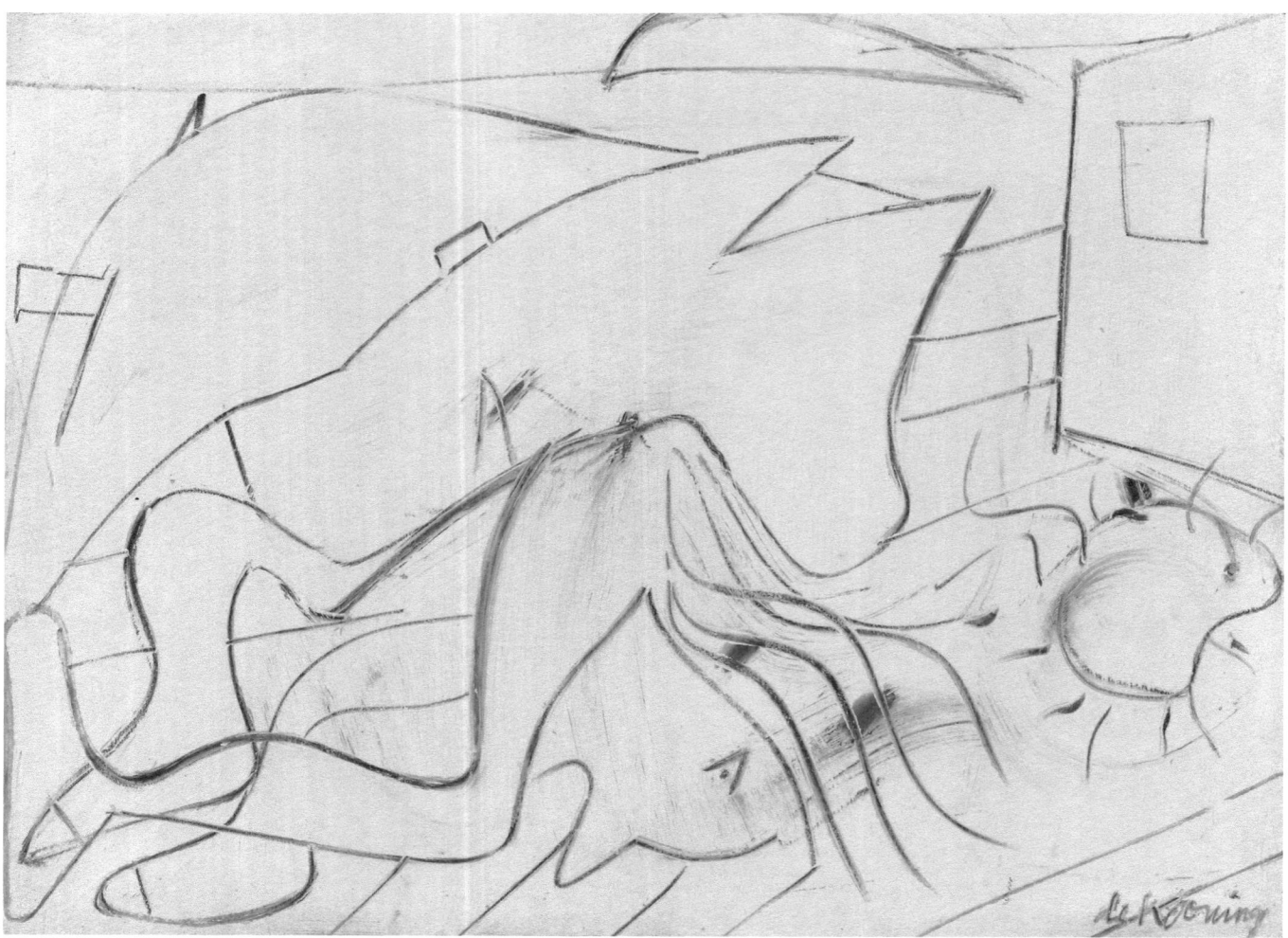

Figure 54
Willem de Kooning, *Untitled (Reclining Figure)*, ca. 1945
Oil and charcoal on Masonite, 38.1 × 50.5 cm. Collection of
Gene and Sueyun Locks

Figure 55
Willem de Kooning, *Untitled XIX*, 1983
Oil on canvas, 195.6 × 223.5 cm. San Francisco Museum of Modern
Art. The Doris and Donald Fisher Collection at the San Francisco
Museum of Modern Art

extremely open compositions as vivid as Matisse's recent black brush-and-ink drawings such as the 1948 *The Black Pineapple* (fig. 53), which de Kooning could have seen in the 1949 Pierre Matisse exhibition and reproduced in the journal *Transition*.[137]

Simultaneously, though, de Kooning had moved on to what would prove to be his most controversial paintings to date. In 1950, he had begun the first of the Woman paintings that would be exhibited in 1953. De Kooning had made a small series of Woman pictures in 1949, but the adverse reaction to the new canvases was not solely about the works themselves. It was also a product of a sense of betrayal, as Pollock put it.[138] Like the outraged reaction to Bob Dylan going electric at the 1965 Newport Folk Festival, it was precisely because an artist who had shaped an esteemed identity had drastically changed.[139] As he had.

Nonetheless, remembrances of the earlier works reappear in a number of de Kooning's late canvases of the 1980s. He still had some drawings he had made in the 1940s in the process of composing paintings and clearly used them again (figs. 54, 55).[140] So, nothing was forgotten, but long remembered—very long remembered. And looking beyond these particular works to the range of late paintings that de Kooning made forty years after those I have been discussing, T. S. Eliot's words on the recovery and revision of this past seem very much to the point: "We shall not cease from exploration / And the end of all our exploring / Will be to arrive from where we started / And know the place for the first time."[141]

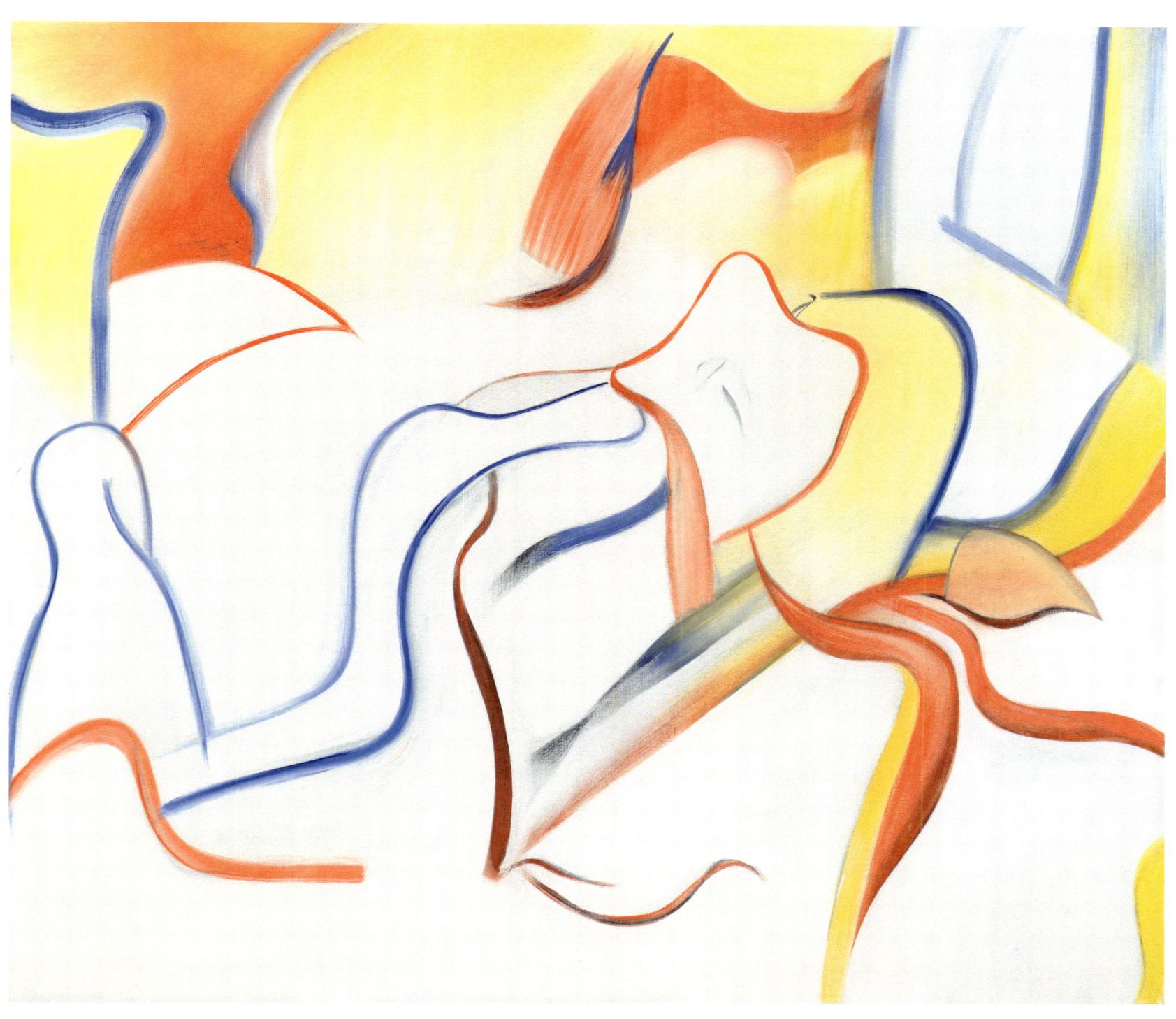

I am, as always, indebted to Jeanne Collins for her editorial review.

1. Clement Greenberg, "Review of an Exhibition of Willem de Kooning," *Nation* 166, no. 17 (April 24, 1948): 448; reprinted in *Clement Greenberg: The Collected Essays and Criticism*, vol. 2, *Arrogant Purpose, 1945–1949*, ed. John O'Brian (Chicago and London: University of Chicago Press, 1988), 228.

2. The account of de Kooning's 1945–50 development that follows is indebted to, but significantly revised from, the more detailed version in John Elderfield, ed., *De Kooning: A Retrospective*, exh. cat. (New York: Museum of Modern Art, 2011), specifically to parts of my introduction, 9–46; my chapter 3 on the years 1946–48, 120–87; Lauren Mahony's on 1948–50, "Around Excavation," 188–237; and, within these two chapters, the chronologies by Delphine Huisinga and the "Methods and Materials" analyses by Susan F. Lake and Jim Coddington. Works by de Kooning mentioned but not illustrated in the present text may be found illustrated there.

3. *Woman* (1948) was initially conceived as a black-and-white abstraction to which anatomical elements were subsequently added. See Lake, "Methods and Materials," 205, where the three large, and one smaller, Woman paintings of 1948–50 are discussed by Mahony, "Second Woman Series," 197–204.

4. See note 1, above.

5. Renée Arb, "Spotlight on de Kooning," *Art News* 47, no. 2 (April 1948): 33.

6. Edvard Lieber, *Willem de Kooning: Reflections in the Studio* (New York: Harry N. Abrams, 2000), 123.

7. Paul Valéry, *The Collected Works of Paul Valéry: Degas Manet Morisot*, Bollingen Series 45 (Princeton, NJ: Princeton University Press, 1989), 12:50.

8. Valéry, *The Collected Works*, 12:50; emphasis in the original.

9. Allan Stone, "Preface," in *De Kooning: Liquefying Cubism*, exh. cat. (New York: Allan Stone Gallery, 1994), v.

10. Thomas B. Hess, *Willem de Kooning* (New York: George Braziller, 1959), 32.

11. Hess, *Willem de Kooning* (1959), 32.

12. James Boswell, *The Life of Samuel Johnson LL. D.*, 2 vols. (Oxford, 1791), 1:155.

13. Thomas B. Hess, *Willem de Kooning* (New York: Museum of Modern Art, 1968), 40.

14. Hess, *Willem de Kooning* (1959), 20.

15. And, to complicate matters, de Kooning made an untitled painting of roughly the same size and very close in composition to *The Wave* (see fig. 3), which Hess in 1959 reasonably dated to the same year. Here, which canvas was painted—or completed—first hardly seems to matter.

16. Edward J. Stafford to Donna Carlson, June 11, 1992; quoted in Mahony, "WPA and Related Works," in Elderfield, *De Kooning: A Retrospective*, 75.

17. See Mark Stevens and Annalyn Swan, *De Kooning: An American Master* (New York: Knopf, 2004), 29.

18. Rudy Burckhardt, quoted in Stevens and Swan, *De Kooning*, 180.

19. Clement Greenberg, "Review of Exhibitions of Joan Miró and André Masson," *Nation* 166, no. 17 (May 20, 1944); reprinted in *Clement Greenberg: The Collected Essays and Criticism*, vol. 1, *Perceptions and Judgments, 1939–1944*, ed. John O'Brian (Chicago and London: University of Chicago Press, 1986), 207.

20. The first Surrealist manifesto, written by Breton in 1924 and published that year as a booklet (Paris: Éditions du Sagittaire, 1924), is widely available.

21. Elaine de Kooning, quoted in Harriet Janis and Rudi Blesh, *De Kooning* (New York: Grove, 1960), 16.

22. Joop Sanders, quoted in Stevens and Swan, *De Kooning*, 186

23. Hess, *Willem de Kooning* (1968), 47.

24. Willem de Kooning, quoted in Stevens and Swan, *De Kooning*, 341.

25. John Ruskin, *The Stones of Venice* (London: Smith, Elder & Co., 1853), vol. 3, chapter 3; quoted and discussed in Clement Greenberg, *Joan Miró* (New York: Quadrangle, 1969), 42.

26. These sources are discussed in Elderfield, "Pink Angels," in Elderfield, *De Kooning: A Retrospective*, 129.

27. How *Judgment Day* and *Labyrinth* were made is discussed in Lake, "Methods and Materials," 143–44, and their sources by Elderfield, "De Kooning's First Solo Exhibition," in Elderfield, *De Kooning: A Retrospective*, 131–38. See also Chronology in this volume for 1946, p. 79.

28. Sally Yard, *Willem de Kooning: The First Twenty-Six Years in New York* (New York and London: Garland, 1986), 146, quoting from her interview with Hess on December 5, 1977.

29. Willem de Kooning, "What Abstract Art Means to Me," *Bulletin of the Museum of Modern Art* 18, no. 3 (Spring 1951): 7; reprinted in Hess, *Willem de Kooning* (1968) and elsewhere.

30. Clement Greenberg, "Abstract, Representational, and So Forth," *Arts* 48, no. 7 (April 1974): 50–51; reprinted in *Clement Greenberg: Late Writings*, ed. Robert C. Morgan (Minneapolis and London: University of Minnesota Press, 2003), 62; emphasis in the original.

31. Greenberg, "Abstract, Representational, and So Forth," 60.

32. Eugène Delacroix, entry of May 7, 1824, in *The Journal of Eugène Delacroix*, ed. Hubert Wellington, trans. Lucy Norton (London and New York: Phaidon, 2001), 39.

33. Delacroix, entry of January 25, 1857, in *Journal of Eugène Delacroix*, 370.

34. David Sylvester, *Interviews with American Artists* (New Haven, CT: Yale University Press, 2001), 52.

35. Clement Greenberg, "Review of an Exhibition," 228.

36. T. S. Eliot, "Tradition and the Individual Talent" (1917), in T. S. Eliot, *Selected Essays, 1917–1932* (New York: Harcourt, Brace, 1932), 10–11.

37. Gus Falk, quoted in Stevens and Swan, *De Kooning*, 294; emphasis in the original.

38. Pierre Schneider, "Through the Louvre with Barnett Newman," *Art News* 68, no. 4 (Summer 1969): 34–39, 70–72. See also the brief discussion of Ingres in Jim Coddington and Bart J. C. Devolder's essay in this volume, p. 127.

39. Harold Rosenberg, "The American Action Painters," *Art News* 51, no. 8 (December 1952): 22.

40. Hess, *Willem de Kooning* (1959), 15

41. Stone, "Preface," iii.

42. Willem de Kooning, quoted in Judith L. Wolfe, "Glimpses of a Master," in *Willem de Kooning: Works from 1951–1981*, exh. cat. (East Hampton, NY: Guild Hall of East Hampton, 1981), 16.

43. See Elderfield, "The Grotesque, Ludicrous and Fearful," in Elderfield, *De Kooning: A Retrospective*, 157.

44. Elaine de Kooning, "De Kooning Memories," in Mervin Lane, *Black Mountain College: Sprouted Seeds; An Anthology of Personal Accounts* (Knoxville: University of Tennessee Press, 1990), 243.

45. Charles Egan Gallery, exhibition announcement with handwritten closing date. James Thrall Soby Papers, 1.80, The Museum of Modern Art Archives, New York.

46. The Museum of Modern Art's acquisition of *Painting* is recorded in Alfred Barr, "Painting and Sculpture Acquisitions from January 1, 1948, to July 1, 1949," *Bulletin of the Museum of Modern Art* 17, nos. 2–3 (1949): 21.

47. Greenberg, "Review of an Exhibition," 228.

48. Charles F. Stuckey, "Bill de Kooning and Joe Christmas," *Art in America* 68, no. 3 (March 1980): 71–79. The full article is on pages 66–79. This account of the contents and titles of works in the Egan exhibition draws upon the fuller one in my "De Kooning's First Solo Exhibition," in Elderfield, *De Kooning: A Retrospective*, 163–73.

49. Ad Reinhardt, "How to Look at a Gallery," *P.M.* (December 1, 1946): M13; illustrated in *Ad Reinhardt: How to Look* (New York: David Zwirner; Ostfildern: Katje Cantz, 2013), 61.

50. "William [*sic*] DeKooning, Lee Gatch," *Magazine of Art* 41, no. 2 (February 2, 1948): 54.

51. Paul V. Buckley, "Art Exhibition Notes: Non-Objective Art," *New York Herald Tribune,* April 20, 1948, 27.

52. See note 48, above.

53. An undated letter from Egan to Hess, probably from when Hess was preparing his 1959 monograph, lists the works he had sold. Thomas Hess Papers, 1939–1978, Box 5, Folder 26, Archives of American Art, Smithsonian Institution, Washington, DC. Among those in the first, 1948, exhibition is *Abstraction (tan)*, which he said he sold to Lawrence Heller from Bethesda, Maryland. I take this to be the work now commonly known as *Abstraction* (fig. 31). Stephen Mack, project manager of the Willem de Kooning Catalogue Raisonné, informs me that Heller had loaned a painting titled *Event in a Barn* to the exhibition *Willem de Kooning: 1937–1953* at the Workshop Art Center, Washington, DC, June 14–July 3, 1953, and that may have been the *Abstraction (tan)* that Egan remembered from his 1948 show. (If so, it would have been a curious choice, being the only work in the 1953 exhibition that had been shown in 1948.) *Event in a Barn* was acquired by Allan Stone in the early 1960s and illustrated in *Liquefying Cubism*, 24. I did ask Stone if he knew which of the works he had acquired had been exhibited before, and he said *Orestes* was in de Kooning's first show, but none of the others. I find it difficult to see how de Kooning would have chosen to exhibit *Event in a Barn* in his first solo show, from which he excluded works like *Secretary*, *Night*, and *The Moraine*, and significant that Hess did not include it in his 1959 monograph.

54. John Stephan and Ruth Stephan, *The Tiger's Eye* (1948; repr. New York: Kraus Reprint, 1977), 78. See Elderfield, *De Kooning: A Retrospective*, 187n36.

55. Cathy Curtis, *A Generous Vision: The Creative Life of Elaine de Kooning* (New York: Oxford University Press, 2017), 39. However, she misremembered, naming *Easter Monday* and *Saturday Night*, neither of which were in the exhibition.

56. I discuss this subject in Elderfield, "De Kooning's First Solo Exhibition," 173, 187nn29–36.

57. Oral history interview with Elaine de Kooning, conducted by Phyllis Tuchman, August 21, 1981, Archives of American Art, Smithsonian Institution, Washington, DC. See also Stuckey, "Bill de Kooning and Joe Christmas," 77.

58. Stevens and Swan, *De Kooning*, 656.

59. Sally Yard, "The Angel and the Demoiselle: Willem de Kooning's *Black Friday*," *Record of the Art Museum, Princeton University* 50, no. 2 (1991): 15–16. Stevens and Swan, *De Kooning*, 251.

60. Yard, "The Angel and the Demoiselle," 15.

61. Stuckey, "Bill de Kooning and Joe Christmas," 71–74, for this and following information, which has been further discussed by others and summarized in my "De Kooning's First Solo Exhibition," 187nn30–34.

62. I borrow this phrasing from Christopher Ricks, speaking of poems, not paintings, in *Allusion to the Poets* (Oxford: Oxford University Press, 2002), 3–4.

63. Greenberg, "Review of an Exhibition," 228.

64. For documentation of the responses to this exhibition, see the Chronology, pp. 85–88.

65. Notably, *Pink Lady*, ca. 1944 (Elderfield, *De Kooning: A Retrospective*, plate 29).

66. I discuss this subject in detail in my "Excavations," in *Cézanne: The Rock and Quarry Paintings*, ed. John Elderfield, exh. cat. (Princeton, NJ: Princeton University Art Museum, 2020), 1–39.

67. See note 21, above.

68. *Ma Jolie* (1911–12) was acquired by MoMA in 1945. De Kooning would also almost certainly have seen the short-lived exhibition heralded in the *New York Times* of January 23, 1947, as "New Phase in Art Noted at Display: 'Ideographic Picture' Is the Title of a Provocative Group Exhibition at Betty Parsons Gallery." Among the eight artists featured were Hans Hofmann, Barnett Newman, Ad Reinhardt, and Mark Rothko.

69. See note 1, above.

70. De Kooning, "What Abstract Art Means to Me," 7.

71. An excellent short account is "Black and White," in Katy Siegel, *Since '45: America and the Making of Contemporary Art* (London: Reaktion Books, 2011), 47–91.

72. At the time, de Kooning was at Black Mountain College for the summer and thus unlikely to have heard of the exhibition. It is discussed in Lawrence Alloway, "Sign and Surface: Notes on Black and White Painting in New York," *Quadrum*, no. 9 (1960): 49–62. Details of the exhibition may be found at tobeart.com/FichierInvitations/WhiteBlack-ParisGalerieDeuxIles48.html.

73. Selden Rodman, *Conversations with Artists* (New York: Devin-Adair, 1957), 101.

74. MoMA repurchased it in 1952.

75. *Henri Matisse: Écrits et propos sur l'art*, ed. Dominique Fourcade (Paris: Hermann, 1972), 202n64.

76. Willem de Kooning, "Inner Monologue" (Summer 1959), unpublished transcript of a conversation between de Kooning, Michael Sonnabend, and Kenneth Snelson, transcribed by Marie-Anne Sichère. Courtesy The Willem de Kooning Foundation.

77. De Kooning, "Inner Monologue."

78. Le Corbusier, *L'Art décoratif d'aujourd'hui* (Paris: G. Grès et Cie, 1925); discussed in Mohsen Mostafavi, "The Color Black in Architecture," in Mohsen Mostafavi and Max Raphael, *The Color Black: Antinomies of a Color in Art* (London: Mack, 2024), 79.

79. Willem de Kooning to Virginia Pearson, Department of Circulating Exhibitions, Museum of Modern Art, January 20, 1953, The Museum of Modern Art Archives, II.1.74.11.2. He uses the term "Sapolin," which was another trade brand, whereas "Ripolin" became the widely used generic name.

80. Stevens and Swan, *De Kooning*, 47.

81. "A Life Round Table on Modern Art: Fifteen Distinguished Critics and Connoisseurs Undertake to Clarify the Strange Art of Today," *Life* 25, no. 15 (October 11, 1948): 62.

82. Thomas B. Hess, *Barnett Newman* (New York: Museum of Modern Art, 1971), 61.

83. Hess, *Willem de Kooning* (1968), 50–51.

84. See Lake, "Methods and Materials," 143–44.

85. See David Sylvester, "Flesh Was the Reason," in David Sylvester et al., *Willem de Kooning: Paintings* (Washington, DC: National Gallery of Art, 1994), 16.

86. Max Raphael, "The Color Black: On the Material Constitution of Form," in Mostafavi and Raphael, *The Color Black*, 126–225; introduced by Mostafavi, "Max Raphael's Point of View," 102–22.

87. Mostafavi, "Max Raphael's Point of View," 109; author's emphasis.

88. Raphael, "The Color Black," 151.

89. Raphael, "The Color Black," 151.

90. Mostafavi, "Max Raphael's Point of View," 110, 115,

91. Raphael, "The Color Black," 163–64.

92. Hess, *Willem de Kooning* (1959), 23–24.

93. There is a possibly contemporaneous drawing that depicts a pitch-roofed house, floating body parts, a row of matches, and the top of a safety pin: *Untitled* (ca. 1945–48), in *Willem de Kooning: Drawings, 1920s–1970s*, exh. cat. (New York: Allan Stone Gallery, 2007), n.p. But whether *Black Friday* began in such a complex manner, we do not know. For the Delacroix quote, see Delacroix, entry of May 7, 1824, in *Journal of Eugène Delacroix*, 39.

94. Louis Finkelstein, "Marin and de Kooning," *Magazine of Art* 43, no. 6 (October 1950): 205; Hess, *Willem de Kooning* (1959), 18.

95. Edwin Denby, "My Friend de Kooning," *Art News Annual* 29 (1964): 91.

96. Denby, "My Friend de Kooning," 91.

97. Preface to *Lyrical Ballads* (1800), in *The Prose Works of William Wordsworth*, ed. W. J. B. Owen and Jane Worthington Smyser (Oxford: Oxford University Press, 1974), 1:148.

98. Preface to *Lyrical Ballads*, 1:148.

99. See Richard Shiff, "Cézanne's Physicality: The Politics of Touch," in *The Language of Art History*, ed. Salim Kemal and Ivan Gaskell (New York: Cambridge University Press, 1991), 14–44.

100. Willem de Kooning, quoted in Wolfe, "Glimpses of a Master," 16.

101. Willem de Kooning, quoted in Harold Rosenberg, *De Kooning* (New York: Harry N. Abrams, 1973), 43.

102. John Ruskin discussing "Proportion in Architecture" in *The Seven Lamps of Architecture*, in *The Works of John Ruskin*, ed. E. T. Cook and Alexander Wedderburn (London: George Allen; New York: Longmans, Green, 1903), 8:168.

103. See de Kooning, "Inner Monologue."

104. Arb, "Spotlight on de Kooning," 33. See also Chronology in this volume, p. 85.

105. Elaine de Kooning, "De Kooning Memories," *Vogue* 173, no. 12 (December 1983): 394. Hess, *Willem de Kooning* (1968), 32, says that his plate 82 (*Stenographer*) was painted at Black Mountain College, which seems unlikely. He may have miswritten "plate 84" (an untitled painting on paper, now in the Phillips Collection), illustrated below it, which a note in his archives indicates was painted there. Thomas Hess Papers, 1939–1978, Box 6, Folder 3. Although the image is unusual (it somewhat resembles a chicken), this is possible.

106. Pat Passlof suggests that *Asheville* "must have come right afterwards, when he got back to New York, because that was on canvas," whereas she remembers that everything he painted at Black Mountain was on paper. Mary Emma Harris and Pat Passlof, January 11, 1997, New York City, Oral History Collection, Special Collections Research Center, Appalachian State University, Boone, North Carolina, 2.

107. See Mahony, "Second Woman Series," 197–204.

108. Mary Emma Harris and Patricia Passlof, January 11, 1997, New York City, Oral History Collection, 12.

109. Stevens and Swan, *Willem de Kooning*, 258.

110. Emily Rauh, a curator at the Saint Louis Art Museum, which was considering the purchase of the drawing, wrote to de Kooning on April 18, 1966, to say that on the back of the frame was a notation stating that the drawing is a study for *Asheville*. The museum records indicate that in a subsequent phone call de Kooning told her that he made the drawing at Black Mountain College at the same time he painted *Asheville*. I am indebted to Pat Boulware, Collections Documentation Assistant at the Saint Louis Art Museum, for this information.

111. Elaine de Kooning, "De Kooning Memories" (1983), 394.

112. My comments on pastels are indebted to those of another painter: John Golding, "Interview with Richard Wollheim," in *Visions of the Modern* (London: Thames & Hudson, 1994), 350–51, which also includes some remarks on Veronese.

113. Stevens and Swan, *Willem de Kooning*, 257.

114. Paul Cézanne to Charles Camoin, February 3, 1902, in *The Letters of Paul Cézanne*, ed. Alex Danchev (London: Thames & Hudson, 2013), 313.

115. These comments on Veronese are indebted to yet another painter, Bridget Riley. See *The Eye's Mind: Bridget Riley; Collected Writings 1965–2009*, ed. Robert Kudielka (London: Ridinghouse, 2009), 197–202, 229–30.

116. Pat Passlof, "1948: The Author's Studies with Willem de Kooning," *Art Journal* 48, no. 3 (Fall 1989): 229.

117. Clement Greenberg, "Abstract and Representational," *Art Digest* 29, no. 3 (November 1, 1954): 7; reprinted in *Clement Greenberg: The Collected Essays and Criticism*, vol. 3, *Affirmations and Refusals 1950–1956*, ed. John O'Brian (Chicago and London: University of Chicago Press, 1993), 191.

118. And we know that, certainly by April of 1949, he was making complementary works comprising allover black drawing set against a white ground, since one of them was exhibited that month in an exhibition at the Peridot Gallery in downtown Manhattan.

119. Here, I draw upon my "Willem de Kooning, *Town Square*," in *Frisson: The Richard E. Lang and Jane Lang Davis Collection*, ed. Catharina Manchanda, exh. cat. (Seattle: Seattle Art Museum, 2021), 58–65.

120. De Kooning, "What Abstract Art Means to Me," 7. The most extended discussion of de Kooning's (and Pollock's) indebtedness to Picasso appears in Michael Fitzgerald, *Picasso and American Art* (New York: Whitney Museum of American Art, 2006), 169–237, a fine account although, concentrating on expressive works, it does not address Analytic Cubism.

121. Details of the handful of such works by Picasso that de Kooning could actually have seen may be found in Julia May Boddewyn's remarkable chronology in Fitzgerald, *Picasso and American Art*, 328–83.

122. The classic account of this means of composition is in "Collage," in Clement Greenberg, *Art and Culture* (Boston: Beacon, 1961), 71–72.

123. Harriet Janis and Rudi Blesh, *De Kooning* (New York: Grove, 1960), 27, 29–30, comparing *Town Square* with *Painting* (fig. 27), which in fact seems more a still life than a townscape; quoted by Mahony, "An Enormous Deed," 209.

124. De Kooning, "Inner Monologue."

125. Willem de Kooning, quoted in David Sylvester, *Interviews with American Artists* (New Haven, CT: Yale University Press, 2001): 43–57. The interview with David Sylvester was conducted in March 1960.

126. This is evidenced by various technical devices he employed—for example, using the direction of drips of paint as lines of drawing, and creating interactions between areas of fresh, fluid paint moved onto dry or drying paint to produce seemingly transient effects.

127. Willem de Kooning, quoted in Hess, *Willem de Kooning* (1968), 47.

128. Elaine de Kooning, statement regarding Willem de Kooning's *Attic*, September 9, 1988, Archives, Department of Nineteenth-Century, Modern, and Contemporary Art, The Metropolitan Museum of Art, New York.

129. Mathematicians who have studied topology have long sought to find an aperiodic monotile: that is, a single shape that could entirely tile a plane but never periodically, never producing a simple repeating pattern. The solution was found in November 2022: a so-called polykite shape with thirteen sides that the discoverer named a "hat," and that resembles the shapes that de Kooning was using. A web search for "polykite" is replete with examples.

130. Stevens and Swan, *De Kooning*, 294, see the film in the painting. The evidence is discussed in Mahony, "An Enormous Deed," 222.

131. Wolfe, "Glimpses of a Master," 10, 16.

132. Harold Rosenberg, *The Anxious Object: Art Today and Its Audience* (New York: Horizon, 1964), 118.

133. James Thrall Soby, quoted in Katharine Kuh, "The Story of a Picture," *Saturday Review* (March 29, 1969): 38. See Mahony, "An Enormous Deed," 221.

134. Stevens and Swan, *De Kooning*, 293.

135. Curtis Bill Pepper, "The Indomitable de Kooning," *New York Times Magazine* (November 20, 1983): 88.

136. Eugène Delacroix, entry of March 8, 1860, in *Journal of Eugène Delacroix*, 430–31.

137. See Mahony, "Around Excavation," 234.

138. Jackson Pollock, quoted in Steven Niafeh and Gregory White Smith, *Jackson Pollock: An American Saga* (New York: Clarkson N. Potter, 1939), 715. The superscript is at the end of the sentence 'It was also a product of a sense of betrayal, as Pollock put it."

139. It was particularly fitting that, upon seeing a wall of the Woman paintings at MoMA's 2011 de Kooning retrospective, Bob Dylan said, "I guess that's when de Kooning went electric."

140. Although figure 54 was not in de Kooning's possession in the 1980s, we may surmise that he still had the drawing that served as the matrix for this work and for figure 55.

141. T. S. Eliot, "Four Quartets: Little Gidding," in *The Poems of T. S. Eliot*, ed. Christopher Ricks and Jim McCue (Baltimore, MD: Johns Hopkins University Press, 2015), 1:208.

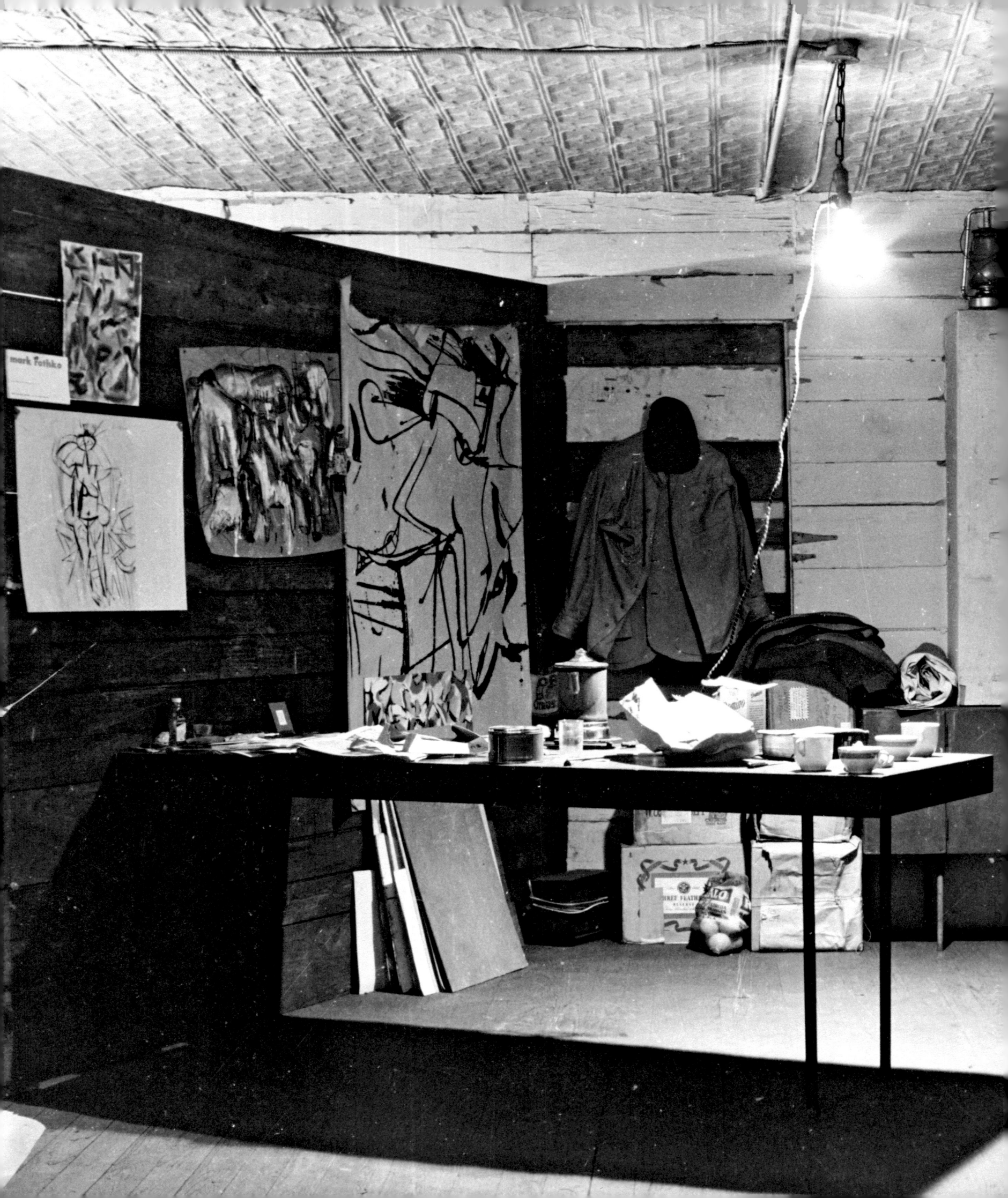

Chronology

LEE COLÓN

1945

Willem de Kooning, forty years old, lives on the top floor of 156 West 22nd Street in Manhattan's Chelsea neighborhood The loft, which the artist has renovated extensively, is spacious; it was once part of a small factory. He paints in front of large windows facing the street on the north side of the building while his wife, the artist Elaine de Kooning, works facing the south, in a space situated in the back of the apartment.[1]

January *Fortune* magazine publishes a large color image of *The Netherlands* (1945) in an advertisement for the Container Corporation of America. The composition is part of Container's *United Nations* series (1944–46), for which an artist represented each of the Allied forces fighting against the Axis powers. Fernand Léger represents France; Henry Moore, Britain; Rufino Tamayo, Mexico; and Paul Rand, the United States.[2]

Mid-January Jean-Paul Sartre visits the US for the first time and stays for five months. He is part of a group of French journalists invited by the Office of War Information, representing the journal *Combat* at Albert Camus's request.[3]

February Opening of *A Painting Prophecy—1950* at David Porter Gallery, Washington, DC. De Kooning exhibits *Pink Landscape* (ca. 1942) alongside works by William Baziotes, Louise Bourgeois, Jimmy Ernst, Adolph Gottlieb, Robert Motherwell, Jackson Pollock, Richard Pousette-Dart, and Mark Rothko.[4]

March 13 The Whitney Museum of American Art opens *European Artists in America*, featuring many artists who sought refuge during the war, and breaking with the museum's usual program of showing American art exclusively.

April Samuel Kootz opens a gallery at 15 East 57th Street. His inaugural exhibition is devoted to works by Fernand Léger. Kootz would become one among a few gallerists—along with Betty Parsons and Charles Egan, both setting up galleries the following year—to exhibit the new American abstract artists. Kootz represents William Baziotes and Robert Motherwell, taking over from Peggy Guggenheim the previous year.

April 27 De Kooning attends the opening of *Modern Art in Advertising: Designs for Container Corporation of America* at the Art Institute of Chicago. *The Netherlands* hangs in a special installation designed by Herbert Bayer (figs. 56, 57).[5]

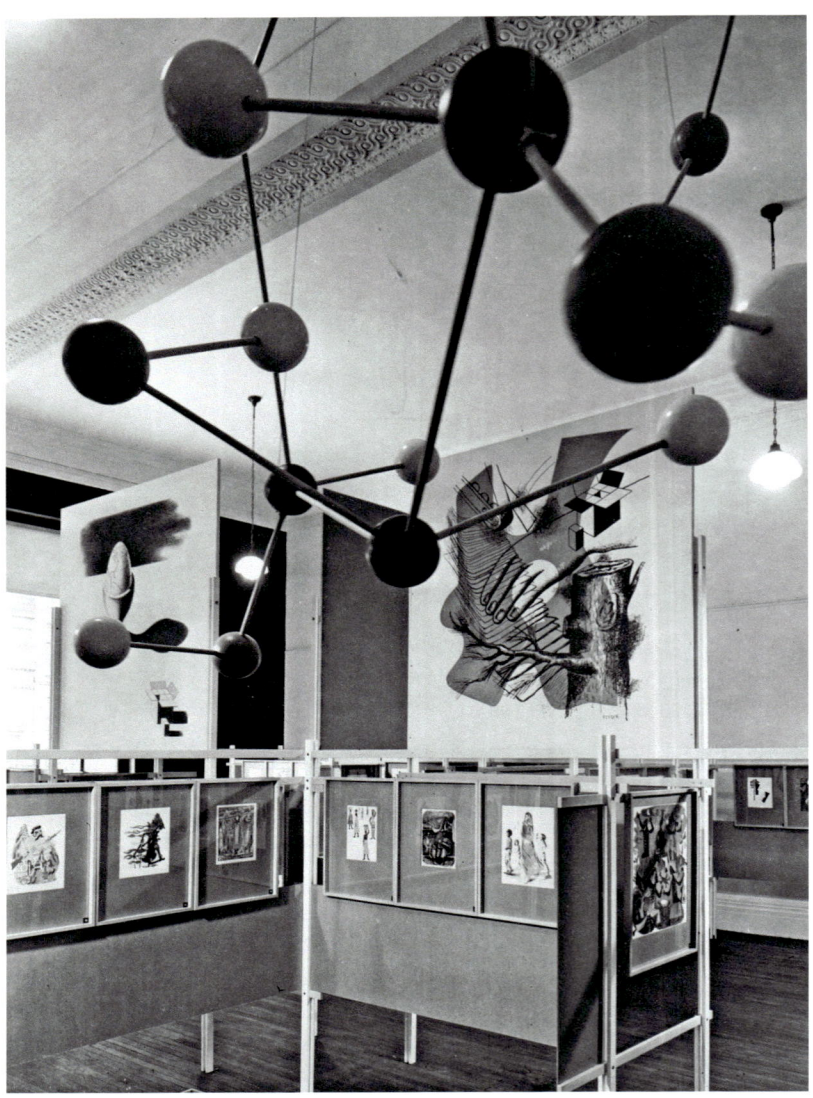

Figure 56
Modern Art in Advertising: Designs for Container Corporation of America, Art Institute of Chicago, April–June 1945. Artists of the work shown, from left: Tibor Gergely, Yugoslavia, December 1944; Leonard Leonni, East Indies, February 1945; Willem de Kooning, Netherlands, January 1945; David Mill, Union of South Africa, May 1945; Henry Moore, Great Britain, September 1944; Zdzisław Czermański, Poland, April 1945; Mario Carreño, Cuba, November 1945; Leonard Leonni, photomontages, February 1945, June 1943, November 1941. Overhead, from left: Herbert Bayer, October 1943; Fernand Léger, October 1941. Photo: Torkel Korling

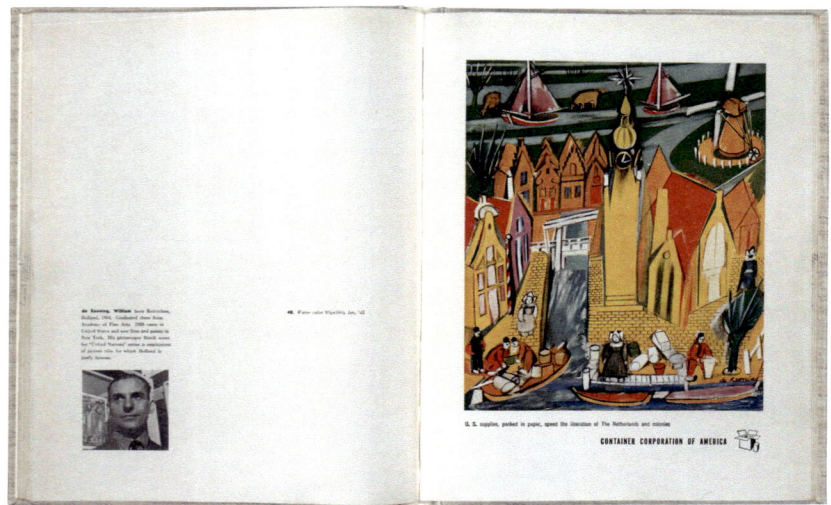

Figure 57
Willem de Kooning (1904–1997; born Rotterdam, Netherlands; died East Hampton, NY), ***The Netherlands* (1945)**, in an advertisement for Container Corporation of America. Printed in the exhibition catalogue *Modern Art in Advertising: Designs for Container Corporation of America* (Chicago: Paul Theobald, 1946)

May 7 V-E (Victory in Europe) Day; Germany surrenders to the Allies, ending World War II in Europe.

August 6/9 US drops atomic bombs on Hiroshima and Nagasaki, Japan.

August 14 V-J (Victory in Japan) Day; Japan surrenders, ending World War II.

Fall Elaine leaves New York and sails to Provincetown, Massachusetts, with a friend, remaining there until December. De Kooning visits occasionally.[6]

October 6 Peggy Guggenheim's Art of This Century's *Autumn Salon* opens with *The Wave* (see fig. 3) on display, de Kooning's only appearance at the gallery.[7] Open since 1941, the gallery has primarily exhibited European artists associated with Surrealism, many of whom have settled in New York since the beginning of the war, as well as a few Americans, including William Baziotes, Robert Motherwell, Jackson Pollock, and Mark Rothko.

December The building at 156 West 22nd Street where Willem and Elaine de Kooning live is sold, and they move into a cold-water flat at 63 Carmine Street in Greenwich Village. The apartment is significantly smaller than their loft in Chelsea, forcing the couple to set up their easels in opposite corners of a modest-size room.[8]

1946

De Kooning rents a separate studio at 85 4th Avenue, between East 10th and East 11th Streets, before November.[9] At first, he returns to Carmine Street at night. Elaine remembers, "Bill would come to my place—on Carmine Street—to sleep. We held to a kind of schedule. We'd like to get up late in the day, go to our studios, and work until about eleven at night. Then we'd be beat and we'd stroll up 42nd Street. We'd walk up and down that street and then go to a movie and come out around three or four in the morning. Then we'd walk back home."[10] Soon, he will spend more time in the studio and at neighborhood cafeterias with other artists in the area, including Franz Kline, Conrad Marca-Relli, Philip Pavia, and Milton Resnick.

January Jean-Paul Sartre visits the US for a second time and lectures at Harvard, Yale, Princeton, and Columbia as well as the French theater at Carnegie Hall, sponsored by the Surrealist magazine *View*, to a crowd including Marcel Duchamp and other artists and gallerists concentrated around 57th Street.[11] For de Kooning, existentialism "was in the air." "Without knowing too much about it," he recalled of the 1940s, "we were in touch with the mood. I read the books, but if I hadn't I would probably be the same kind of painter. I live in my world."[12]

January 16 A fire in Arshile Gorky's Sherman, Connecticut, studio destroys many of his paintings. He is also diagnosed with cancer this year and enters New York's Mount Sinai Hospital in March, where he undergoes surgery.

Figure 58
Harry Bowden (1907–1965; born Los Angeles, CA; died Sausalito. CA), **Willem de Kooning's studio, 1950.** Photographic print. Harry Bowden Papers, Archives of American Art, Smithsonian Institution, Washington, DC

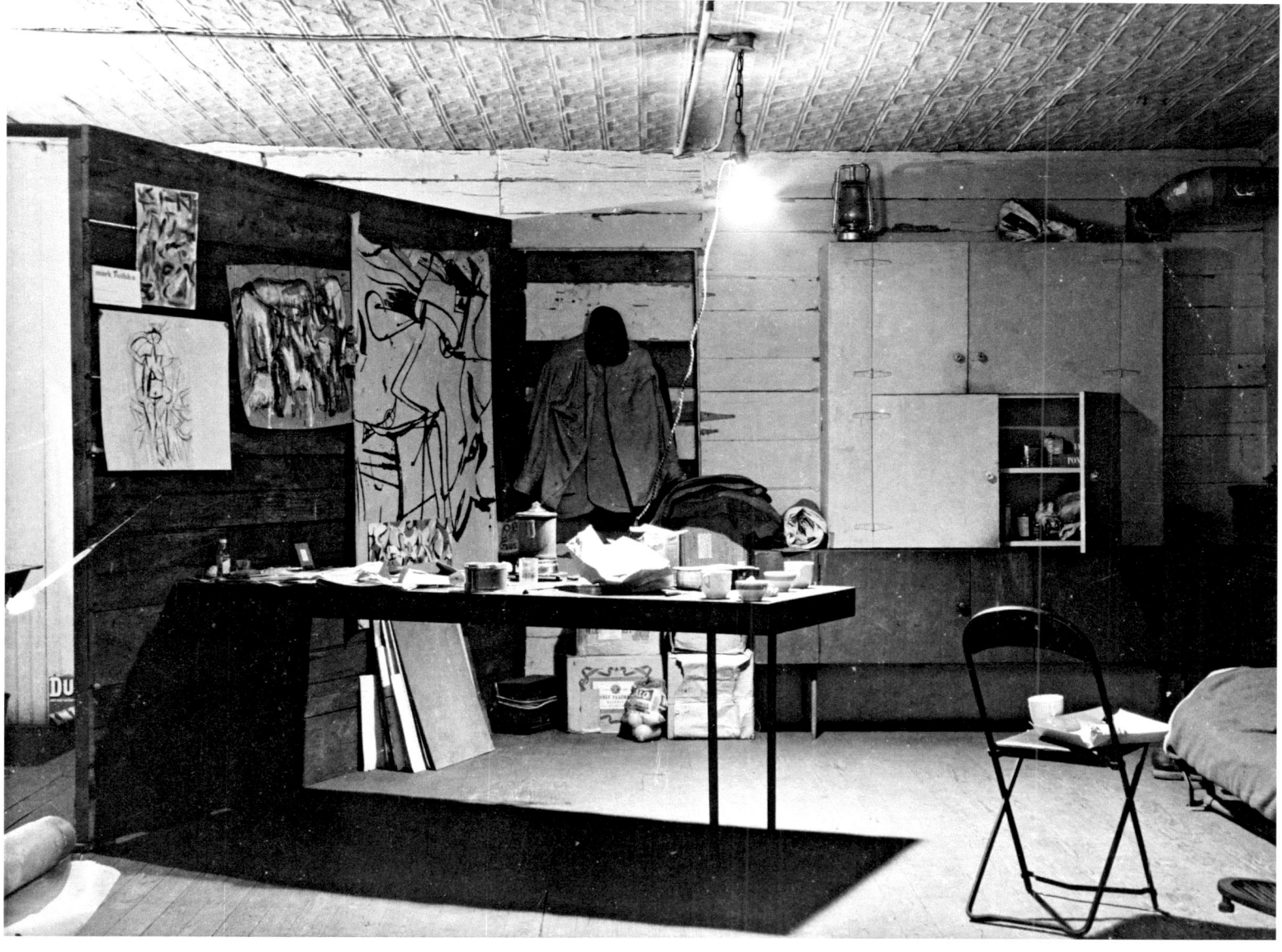

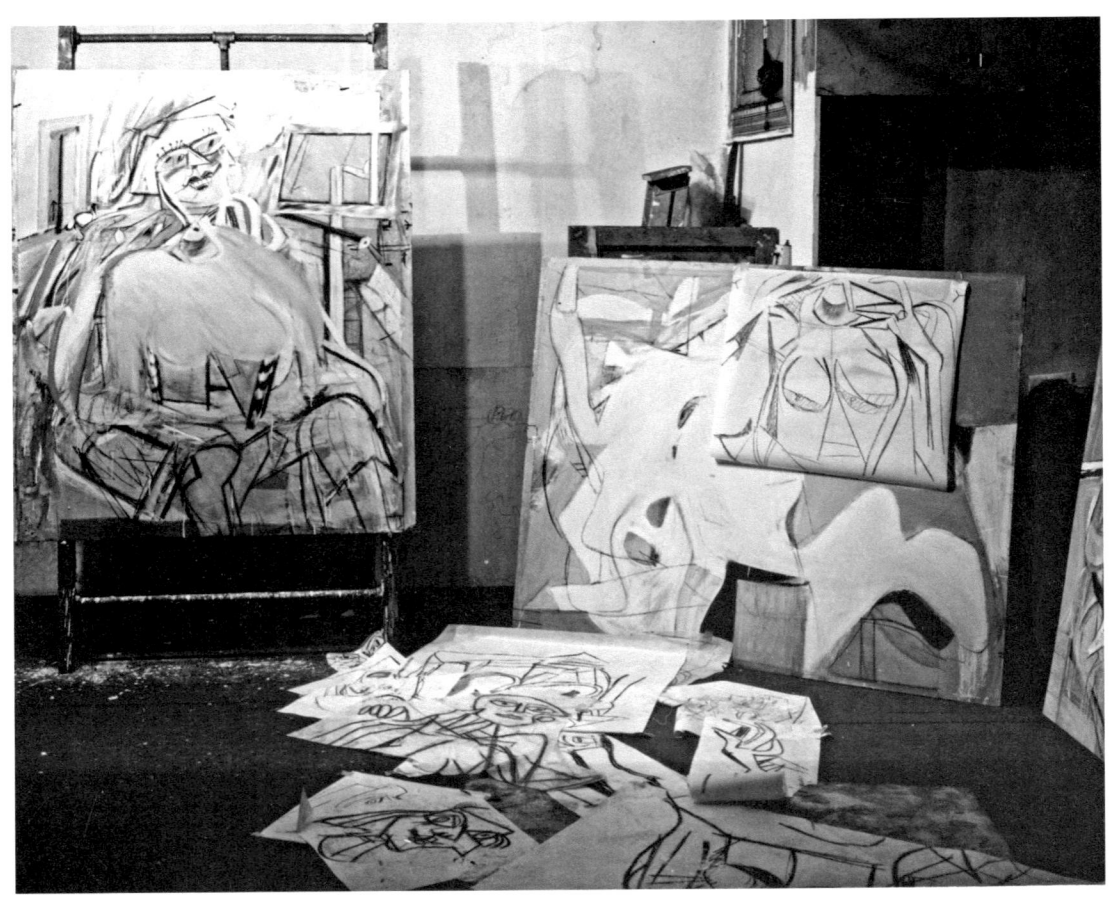

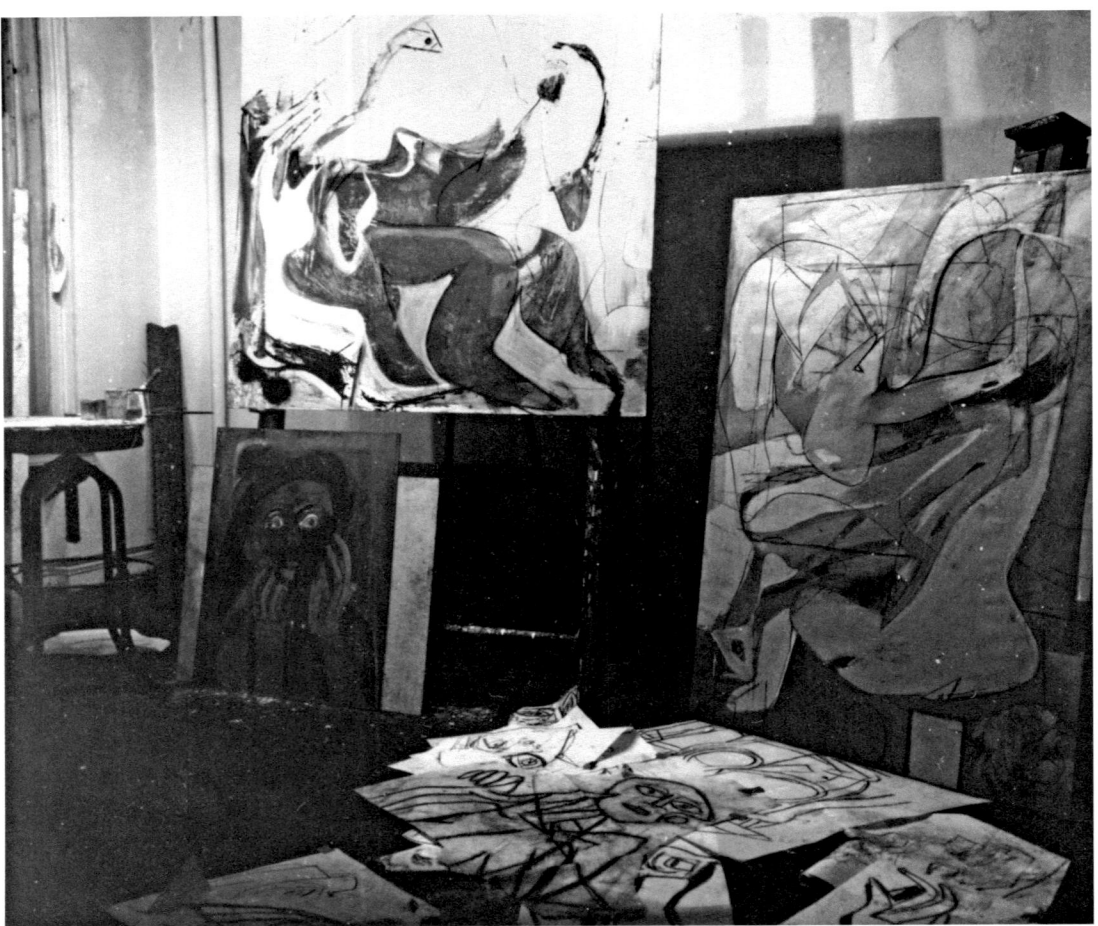

Figures 59 and 60
Harry Bowden, Willem de Kooning's studio, ca. 1946.
Photographic prints. Harry Bowden Papers, Archives of
American Art, Smithsonian Institution, Washington, DC

January 27 Samuel Kootz Gallery opens an exhibition devoted to paintings by Pablo Picasso, the first to take place in New York in several years.[13]

Ad Reinhardt introduces his *How to Look* series, "the beginning of an explanation of modern art," with a cartoon illustrating the "many relative points of view" of Cubist painting in the liberal newspaper *P.M.*[14]

February Thomas Hess and Renée Arb join the editorial staff of *Art News* magazine under the leadership of Alfred Frankfurter.[15] Hess would later reflect, in the role of editor in chief, "the magazine was tepid in its appreciation of avant-garde American art" until March 1946, when "a sympathetic attempt was made in these pages to define the new kind of abstract painting."[16]

February 11 Charles Egan presents his first exhibition at the new Charles Egan Gallery, located on the top floor of 63 East 57th Street. The show is dedicated to gouaches and small oil paintings by the Swiss artist Otto Botto. Egan's friends support this venture; de Kooning and Franz Kline paint the gallery walls, and Isamu Noguchi helps with interior lighting. Egan will champion their work after his first shows of relatively conservative selections, which he thought were more likely to sell.[17]

March Robert Coates, in the *New Yorker*, uses the term "Abstract Expressionism" to describe works by Hans Hofmann in a show at Mortimer Brandt Gallery, dubbing the artist a representative "of what some people call the spatter-and-daub school of painting and I, more politely, have christened abstract Expressionism."[18] This is considered the first published use of the term.

Charles Egan Gallery presents an exhibition of paintings by Leon Polk Smith.

March 5 British statesman Winston Churchill delivers his "Sinews of Peace" speech (also known as the "Iron Curtain Speech") at Westminster College in Fulton, Missouri, solidifying the prevalent idea of a Europe divided into capitalist and communist zones.

April 1 Charles Egan Gallery opens an exhibition of small paintings by Joseph Stella.

April 5 The dancer Maria Marchowsky performs *Labyrinth*, the finale to her choreographic debut, in front of a backdrop by de Kooning, with a score by David Diamond and set pieces by the sculptor Martin Craig. Marchowsky enacts the role of a dreamer with three other dancers in the roles of The Wish, The Represser, and The Mediator. The recital also includes *Foreboding*, with a score by John Cage.[19] To create the design for his backdrop, de Kooning had enlarged the composition of

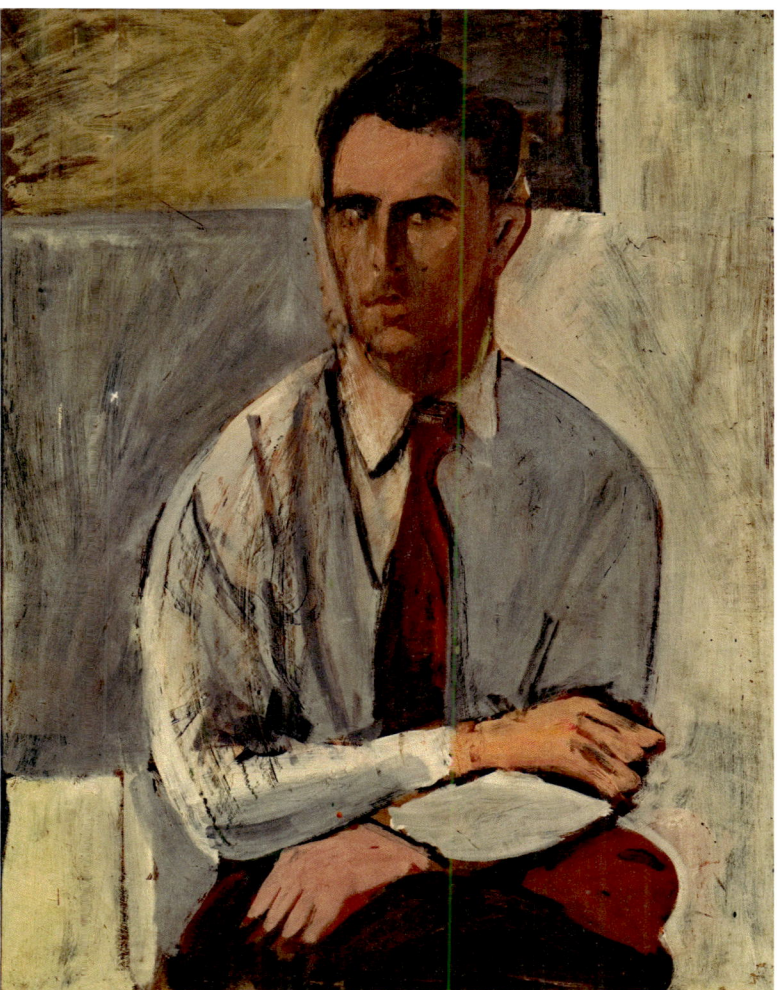

Figure 61
Elaine de Kooning (1918–1989; born Brooklyn, NY; died Southampton, NY), ***Charles Egan*, 1946.** Oil on canvas. Private collection

Judgment Day (fig. 10), a painting completed earlier that year, over the course of several days, with assistance from Milton Resnick.[20]

May De Kooning shows "a figure composition with surrealist overtone" in *12 Works of Distinction* at Charles Egan Gallery. The exhibition also includes works by Charles Demuth, Marsden Hartley, Lee Gatch, Paul Klee, Fernard Léger, Joseph Stella, Mark Rothko, Josef Albers, Georges Braque, and Eric Hesketh Hubbard,[21] and appears alongside "a continuous showing of Joseph Stella."[22]

June 2 *P.M.* runs a cartoon by Ad Reinhardt, "How to Look at Modern Art in America," illustrating a tree of contemporary art with de Kooning's name inscribed on a leaf among those of other abstract painters "hardest to understand." Braque, Matisse, and Picasso dominate the trunk of the tree, and Cézanne, Seurat, Gauguin, and Van Gogh occupy its roots.[23]

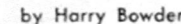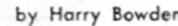

HOW TO LOOK AT A GALLERY ✳

Starting a series on galleries which are interested in aesthetics before they are interested in "business volume or merchandising techniques."

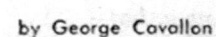
The only way to get behind that iron-curtain-camouflage of "picture-subject-matter," and become "literate" about the special language of painting, is to go "see" what painters "do." To enjoy or judge a work of art one should be able to trace its train of thought. No blind-alley of non-thinking-pot-boiling is the Egan gallery, 63 East 57th Street, run by ex-veteran Charles Egan. Below four paintings which may be seen there.

by William de Kooning   by Harry Bowden   by Joseph Krause   by George Cavallon

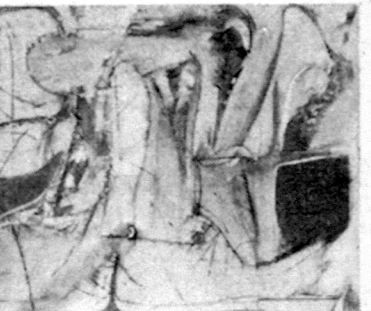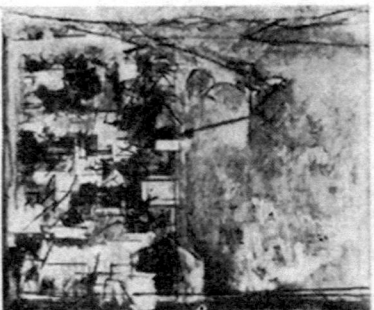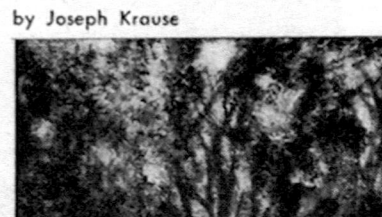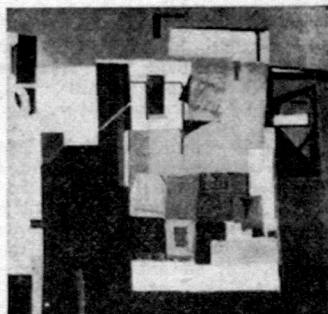

Like in much modern painting, we see in the work of de Kooning and Bowden what may seem to be a "sketchiness" and "unfinishedness" which not only shows the actual process of creation but asks the onlooker to "complete" and "finish" the painting in the looking-act. These are not (bad) neat, finished buck-eye-pictures to "appreciate" "passively" (and exhaust and dismiss with one glance), or picture-puzzles to "figure-out" (in two glances) but (good) painting-experiences which can stand a lot of looking.

A modern painting is not "planned" (like a "picture") and a painter "finds" his meanings while he "works." The meaning of Krause's paintings lies in the intense broken-color-glow through a surface of piled-up-pigment, which are "real, concrete" qualities of paint and canvas. Cavallon's paintings show the "total-working" of an abstract-painting-structure, where no color-area can be changed without its affecting every other area. Cavallon's work is Egan's current show.   ✳what is YOUR theory of looking?

Figure 62
Ad Reinhardt, "How to Look at a Gallery," *P.M.*, December 1, 1946.
Ad Reinhardt Foundation

September Charles Egan Gallery opens a group exhibition at the beginning of the fall art season, including Ben Benn, de Kooning, Eric Hesketh Hubbard, David Smith, and Joseph Stella.

September 30 Betty Parsons opens a gallery at 15 East 57th Street with an exhibition of Northwest Coast Indigenous painting organized by Barnett Newman. Parsons represents about a dozen artists, including Hans Hofmann, Ad Reinhardt, Hedda Sterne, and Alfonso Ossorio.

October 1 Charles Egan Gallery presents black-and-white drawings and colored prints by Josef Albers.

October 4 The Metropolitan Museum of Art opens *Advancing American Art*, an exhibition organized by the US State Department under the aegis of the newly established Office of International Information and Cultural Affairs (OIC). Selections are made by Joseph LeRoy Davidson, a former curator at the Walker Art Center, Minneapolis. The show will travel abroad to regions where there is a perceived communist threat.[24] Clement Greenberg favorably reviews the show in *The Nation*, even though it excluded non-objective abstraction, writing, "Mr. Davidson's exhibition is in a way a remarkable accomplishment, and its moral should be taken to heart by others who control the public destiny of art in our country."[25] However, the conservative media deems the collection of works radical, and the controversy eventually leads to a suspension of the project.

Mid-October Charles Egan Gallery presents *The Cities* by Herman Rose, a series depicting Brooklyn and Manhattan, and the show of graphic works by Josef Albers continues.

October 28 Charles Egan Gallery opens an exhibition of paintings by Joseph Krause with help from Joseph Stella, who will die of heart failure in November.

November Charles Egan Gallery presents paintings by Giorgio Cavallon.

November 21 De Kooning writes to his father, Leendert de Kooning, in Rotterdam, for the first time in twenty years. They begin to correspond occasionally.[26]

December 1 Ad Reinhardt publishes "How to Look at a Gallery" in *P.M.*, illustrating examples of paintings seen at Charles Egan Gallery, including one by de Kooning later titled *Bill-Lee's Delight* (see fig. 16) and compositions by Harry Bowden, Joseph Krause, and Giorgio Cavallon (fig. 62).[27] Reinhardt writes, the work "asks the onlooker to 'complete' and 'finish' the painting in the looking-act."[28]

1947

Charles Egan sets a date for an exhibition at his gallery—spring 1948—so that de Kooning can work toward completing a set of pictures for display. The artist begins a series of largely black-and-white paintings, likely late this year.[29] He uses commercial house paints, selected in part for their affordability, along with higher-quality colored oils.[30]

January Charles Egan Gallery presents abstract works by Abraham Walkowitz.

January 25 The Whitney Museum of American Art opens *Painting in France, 1939–1946*, an exhibition selected by French museum officials. Works by young artists hang alongside paintings by Henri Matisse, Pablo Picasso, and Pierre Bonnard. The Whitney's director, Juliana Force, comments in the catalogue on the museum's break from its usual program of showing American art exclusively, as they had in 1945: "It seems fitting that an American museum should be the first to renew relations in art that have been almost severed for six years, and in a small way to return the hospitality accorded American artists in the happier days before the war when the spirit of liberality and freedom made France an international proving ground for new ideas in art," indicating a shift in the art world's center.[31]

January 27 Samuel Kootz Gallery opens *The First Post-War Showing in America of Recent Paintings by Picasso*, a show of ten paintings obtained directly from the artist.[32]

February 8–28 Charles Egan Gallery presents paintings by Louis Harris and four drawings by Abraham Walkowitz.

March Charles Egan Gallery presents collages by Landès Lewitin.

March 12 In a speech to Congress, President Truman announces the Truman Doctrine, which commits military and economic aid to prevent communist expansion.

March 21 Truman issues Executive Order 9835, calling for an investigation into the loyalty of all federal employees and forbidding communists and communist sympathizers from holding federal employment.

Figure 63
Walter Auerbach (1908–1966; born Dortmund, Germany; died Mallorca, Spain), **Willem de Kooning in his studio, ca. 1947.** Photographic print. Courtesy Robert Mann Gallery

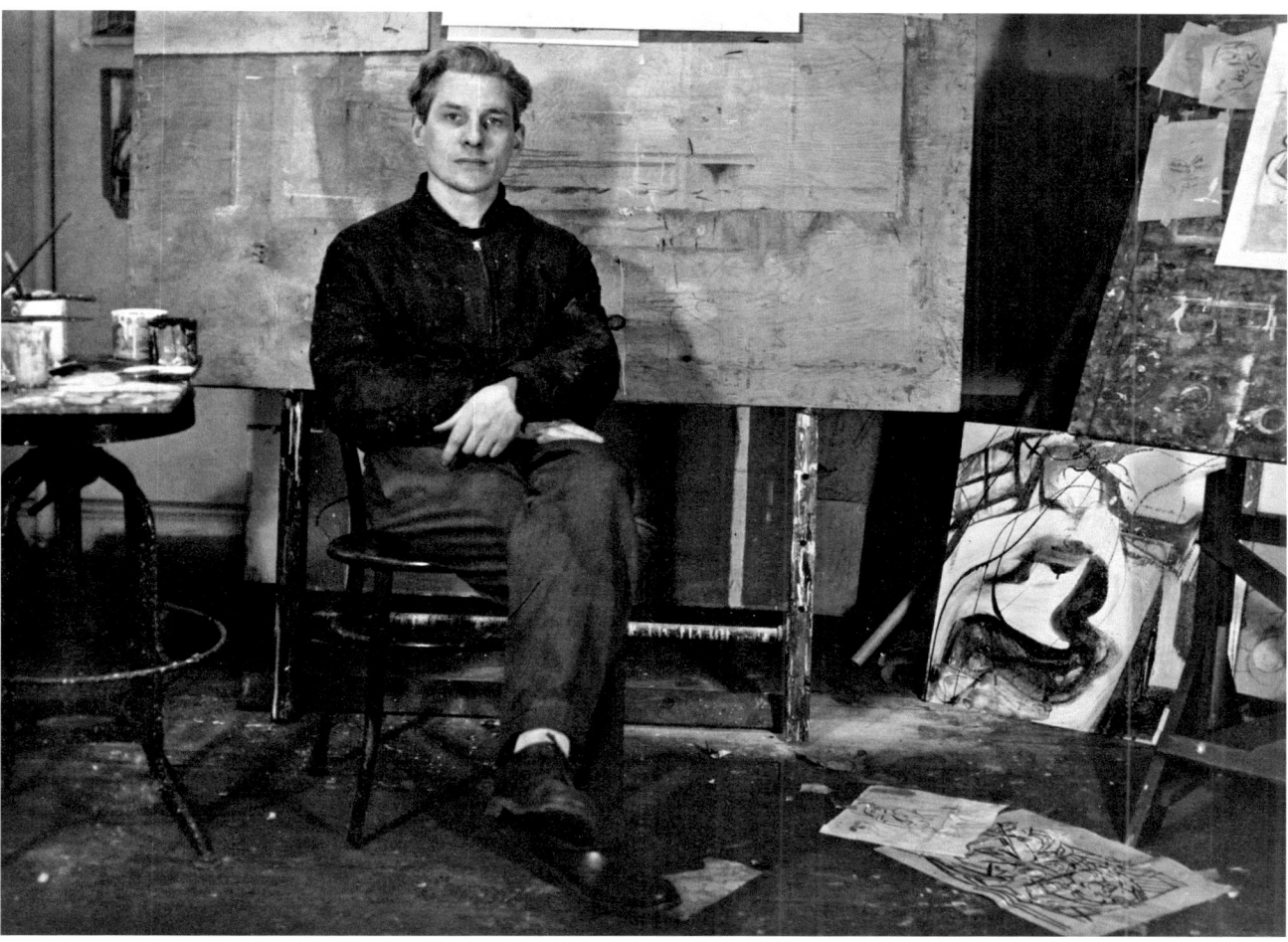

March 28 Galerie Maeght in Paris opens *Introduction à la peinture moderne Américaine*, the first exhibition of new American abstraction to take place in Europe. Organized by Samuel Kootz, it includes works by William Baziotes, Romare Bearden, Byron Browne, Adolph Gottlieb, Carl Holty, and Robert Motherwell. In the catalogue, Harold Rosenberg writes, "From the four corners of their vast land they have come to plunge themselves into the anonymity of New York, annihilation of their past being not the least compelling project of these aesthetic Légionnaires."[33]

April 1 Charles Egan Gallery presents an exhibition of paintings by Ben Benn.

The Museum of Modern Art (MoMA) opens *Large-Scale Modern Paintings*, an exhibition of mural-size paintings including Jackson Pollock's *Mural* (1943), lent by Art of This Century, and works by Ben Shahn and Joseph Stella, as well as Max Beckmann, Fernand Léger, Pablo Picasso, Henri Matisse, David Alfaro Siquieros, and others.

April 28 Charles Egan Gallery presents an exhibition of thirty recent photographs by Aaron Siskind.

April 29 Art of This Century opens its last exhibition, the first American retrospective for Theo van Doesburg. Guggenheim closes the gallery at the end of May and returns to Europe, moving to Venice, Italy. Betty Parsons begins representing several of Guggenheim's artists, including Jackson Pollock, Mark Rothko, Barnett Newman, and Clyfford Still.

June Charles Egan Gallery presents collages by Landès Lewitin (for a second time that year). During the summer, Egan repeats shows from earlier that year, replacing purchased works with alternatives.

June 5 In a speech at Harvard University, US Secretary of State George C. Marshall announces what becomes known as the Marshall Plan, an economic aid program to rebuild Western Europe following the destruction of World War II. One purpose of the Marshall Plan is to counteract the influence of communist parties in Western Europe.

July 14 An exhibition of paintings by Herman Rose opens at Charles Egan Gallery (for a second time that year).

July 26 Truman signs the National Security Act, which establishes the Department of Defense, the Central Intelligence Agency (CIA), and the National Security Council (NSC).

September MoMA and the Metropolitan Museum of Art sign an agreement to establish a cooperative relationship. MoMA agrees to give the Met an option to buy paintings and sculptures from its collection "as they come of age," and to use the money for new purchases.[34]

October Charles Egan Gallery presents a still-life series by Jack Tworkov.

October 18 The House Un-American Activities Committee (HUAC) begins an investigation of communism and the movie industry in Hollywood.

December Charles Egan Gallery opens a group show including works by Elaine de Kooning, Aaron Siskind, Jack Tworkov, and others.

1948

Remembering a visit to de Kooning this year, the writer George Dennison describes the artist seated in "the simplest sort of workshop, cared for but decrepit, with no amenities of any kind beyond a hot plate for coffee, chipped cups, and sugar in a blue Maxwell House can," engaged in a discussion about Cézanne and Picasso.[35] De Kooning borrows a Bell-Opticon projector probably this year that he uses to enlarge sketches on the wall of his studio.[36] The artist meets Thomas Hess, now the managing editor of *Art News*, either in the spring, on the occasion of his first exhibition, or in the fall, following the opening of the Whitney Annual.[37]

The Greek Floor (1944; now destroyed) serves as the frontispiece of dance critic Edwin Denby's book of poetry *In Public, In Private* (figs. 64 and 65). Two poems make reference to de Kooning. "The Silence at Night" describes "designs on the sidewalk Bill pointed out." Of "The Shoulder," de Kooning recalled, "This dumb shape here—I had terrific trouble with it. Denby used to giggle always."[38]

January 5 Betty Parsons Gallery presents to the public Pollock's first drip paintings.

Mid-January: Charles Egan Gallery presents landscape paintings by Elias Goldberg.

The *Partisan Review* becomes a monthly publication (previously bimonthly) and adds a relatively conservative advisory board (James Burnham, Allan Dowling, Sidney Hook, James Johnson Sweeney, Lionel Trilling).[39] The first issue under this new advisory board contains a contribution from Jean-Paul Sartre and reproductions of two paintings by Jackson Pollock owned by Clement Greenberg.[40]

January 19 Pierre Matisse Gallery presents an exhibition of sculptures, paintings, and drawings by Alberto Giacometti, the first to feature the attenuated figures that characterize the artist's post-Surrealist works. De Kooning is deeply moved by what he sees.[41] "We all felt that it was so important," Mercedes Matter recalls, effecting "a change of epoch."[42]

January 26 Samuel Kootz Gallery opens an exhibition of paintings by Picasso completed over the previous year.

Late winter/early spring: Josef Albers organizes an exhibition of photographs by Aaron Siskind at Black Mountain College in Asheville, North Carolina.[43]

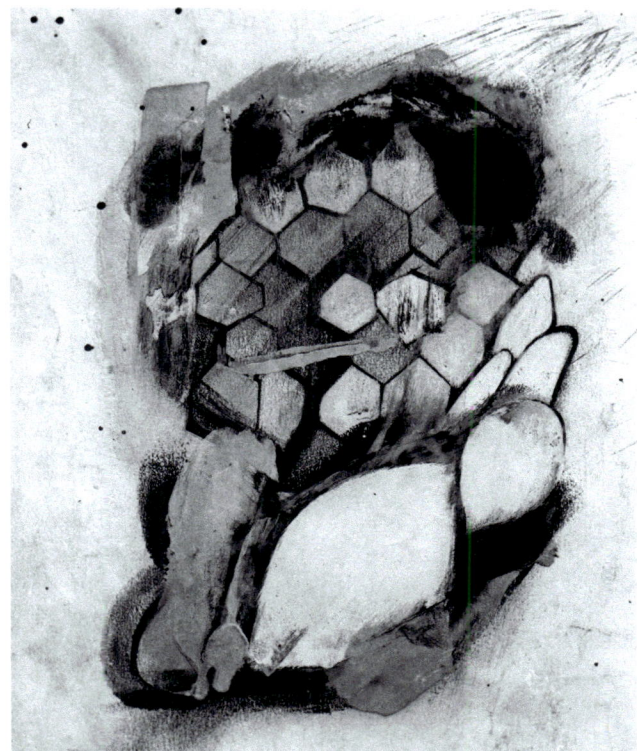

Figure 64
Willem de Kooning, *The Greek Floor*, 1944
Oil on canvas, 25.4 × 20.3 cm. Destroyed. Reproduced as the frontispiece of Edwin Denby's poetry collection *In Public, In Private* (1948). Estate of Rudy Burckhardt

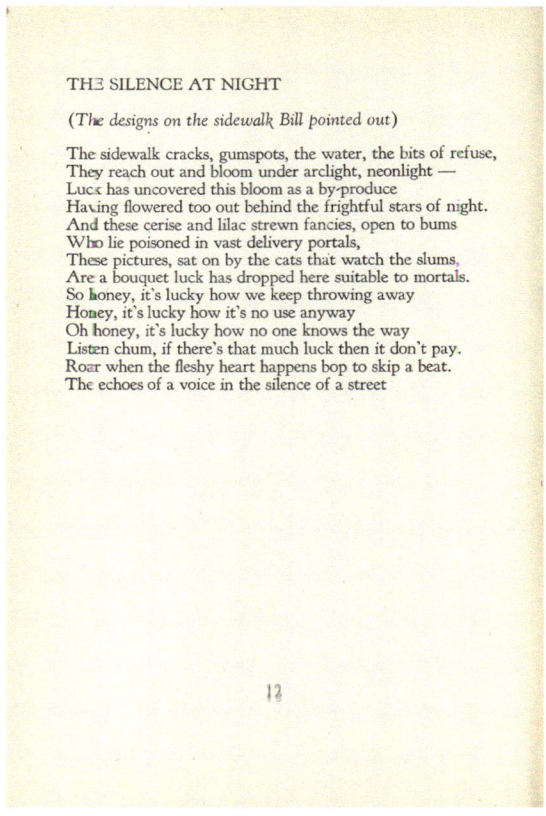

Figure 65
Edwin Denby, "The Silence at Night," in *In Public, In Private* (Prairie City, IL: Decker, 1948). The Henry W. and Albert A. Berg Collection of English and American Literature, The New York Public Library, Astor, Lenox and Tilden Foundations

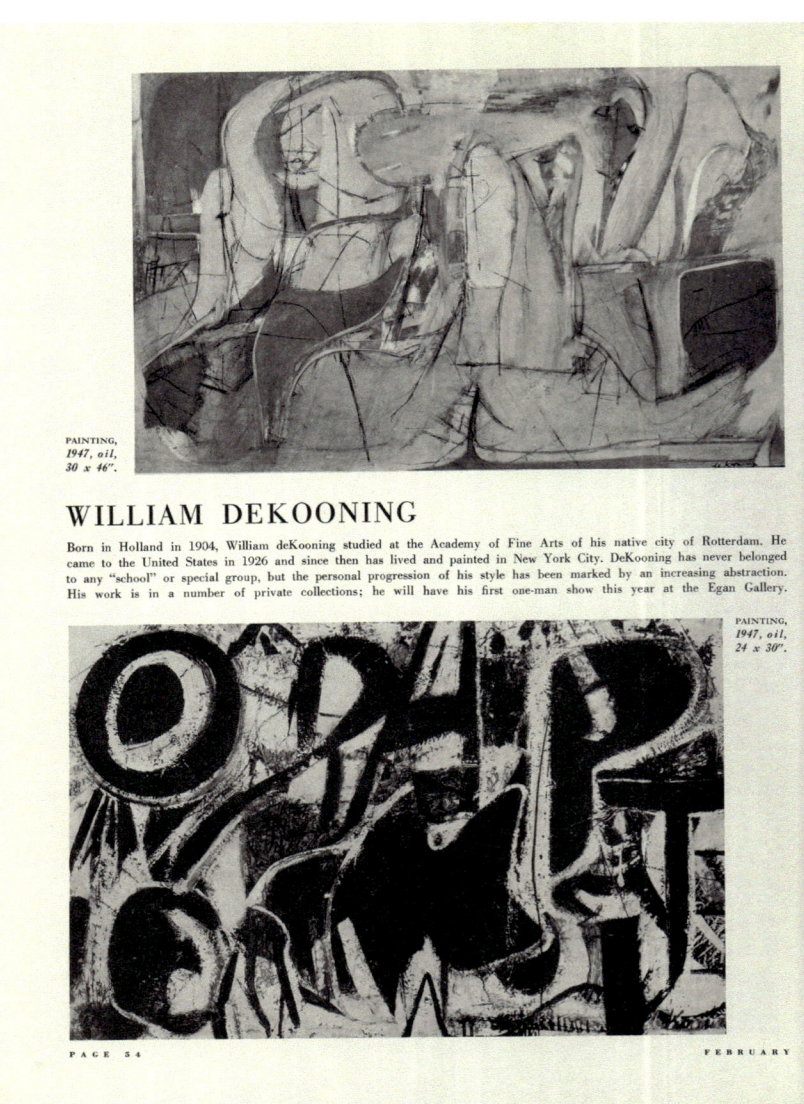

Figure 66
Lee Gatch, "Biographical Sketch: Willem de Kooning," *Magazine of Art* 41, no. 2 (February 1948): 54

February 2 *Magazine of Art* publishes a "biographical sketch" (fig. 66) of de Kooning with illustrations of two works called *Painting*, later titled *Orestes* (see fig. 17) and *Bill-Lee's Delight* (see fig. 16).[44]

Biographical Sketch
WILLIAM DEKOONING
Born in Holland in 1904, William deKooning studied at the Academy of Fine Arts of his native city of Rotterdam. He came to the United States in 1926 and since then has lived and painted in New York City. DeKooning has never belonged to any "school" or special group, but the personal progression of his style has been marked by an increasing abstraction. His work is in a number of private collections; he will have his first one-man show this year at the Egan Gallery.

February 17 The Institute of Modern Art in Boston announces that its name has been changed to the Institute of Contemporary Art. In a statement issued on the thirty-fifth anniversary of the 1913 Armory Show in New York, the institution's director, James S. Plaut, writes, "Now that a full generation has passed since its inception, it has become imperative to re-appraise the [modern art] movement." Since that time, "Modern art failed to speak clearly," he continues, describing "a private, often secret, language" used by artists, requiring interpretation and remaining "unintelligible, even meaningless" to the public.[45]

February 23 Charles Egan Gallery presents abstract paintings by de Kooning, Josef Albers, and Giorgio Cavallon.

February 29–March 20 Julien Levy Gallery presents its fourth exhibition of paintings by Gorky. Greenberg writes in *The Nation*, "Gorky at last arrives at himself and takes his place . . . among the very few contemporary American painters whose work is of more than national importance."[46] The exhibition would be the artist's last before his premature death in June. De Kooning will see him for the last time either at the opening or shortly after.[47]

March A black-and-white reproduction of *Orestes* runs in the third issue of *The Tiger's Eye*. The magazine's art editor, John Stephan, is the owner of the painting.[48]

March 17 Charles Egan Gallery presents photographs by Aaron Siskind.

March 21 Artists in Boston form the Modern Artist Group and stage protests in response to Plaut's statement regarding the Boston Institute's name change. On March 25 they organize a panel and subsequently issue a report stating, "The Institute's highly sensational manifesto is a fatuous declaration which misinforms and misleads the public concerning the integrity and intention of the modern artist."[49]

April *Art News* hires Elaine in the role of "editorial associate" to write freelance reviews. Elaine recalls complaining to Renée Arb that the graduate-student reviewers didn't know anything about art. Arb then mentioned this to Thomas Hess, prompting Hess to invite Elaine to his office. Elaine, like all reviewers, is instructed to visit an artist's studio a month before a gallery opening. The magazine had a two-hundred-word limit for reviews and paid a $2 fee.[50]

De Kooning makes his first trip to East Hampton, Long Island, sometime in the spring, with Elaine, Franz Kline, and Charles Egan, and likely visits Jackson Pollock and Lee Krasner.[51]

De Kooning, Elaine, and Charles Egan meet at the apartment on Carmine Street to plan for the upcoming exhibition at Egan Gallery. They agree on titles for the works to be exhibited by unanimous vote.[52]

April 12 Charles Egan Gallery presents de Kooning's first solo exhibition (fig. 67).

Renée Arb's review (fig. 68) runs in *Art News* with an illustration of *Painting* (see fig. 27).[53]

April 20 Paul V. Beckley's review runs in the *New York Herald Tribune*.[54]

Willem de Kooning is holding a one-man show at the Egan gallery through May 12. The Holland-born artist paints non-objectively—almost completely so. Although some of his forms hint at reality; close study reveals him as inscrutable as ever. There is a liveliness in these canvases, however, and one feels a creative personality behind them. Certain color passages—in "Brown and White" [see fig. 29], for instance, are delightful.

April 24 Clement Greenberg's review runs in *The Nation*. He opens, "Decidedly, the past year has been a remarkable one for American art. Now, as if suddenly, we are introduced . . . to one of the four or five most important painters in the country."[55]

April 25 Sam Hunter's review runs in the *New York Times*.[56]

One of the stronger currents of abstract art today has become an obsession with the medium of paint itself for its internal dramatic possibilities. Characteristic are the paintings by William de Kooning, holding his first American show at the Egan Gallery. His canvases are scarred, kneaded, dragged with amorphous squibs of paint that bear testimony to the violence and anguish of the struggle of his forms from their raw estate [sic] as possibilities upward toward realization. Curiously enough the artist seems to controvert his own aims by withholding life from these forms at the crucial moment when they are about

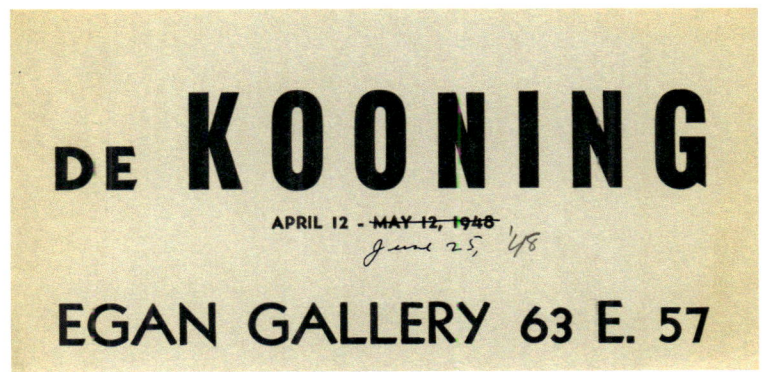

Figure 67
James Thrall Soby's announcement for the exhibition *de Kooning* at the Egan Gallery, 1948. Offset with black ink and pencil, 22.6 × 44.7 cm. James Thrall Soby Papers, I.80. The Museum of Modern Art Archives

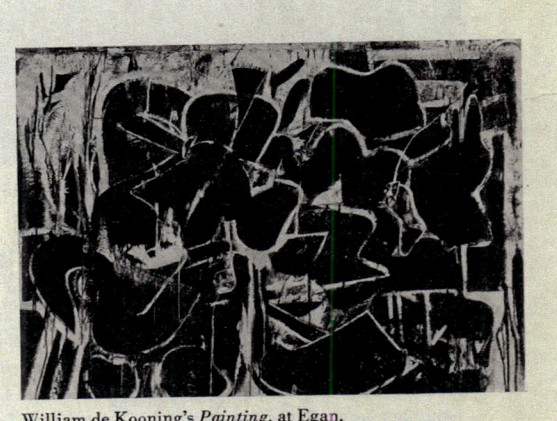

De Kooning

To his New York debut, William de Kooning [Egan; to Apr. 30], Dutch-born artist who has devoted twenty years exclusively to painting in New York City, brings a singular concentration of passion and technique. His abstractions with their fierce energy are the result of months of sketching and alteration, and they reveal a new, self-contained personality. For here is virtuosity disguised by voluptuousness—the process of painting becomes the end. Technique is lavish and versatile; draftsmanship elegant and concise; the range of color seems as rich in black and white as in the brilliant hues. In the compositions, there is constant tension as space envelopes and then releases these ambiguous forms. Indeed, his subject seems to be the crucial intensity of the creative process itself, which De Kooning has translated into a new and purely pictorial idiom. $300-$2,000.   R.A.

William de Kooning's *Painting*, at Egan.

Figure 68
Renée Arb, "Spotlight on de Kooning," *Art News* 47, no. 2
(April 1948): 33

Our box score of the critics

Artist & Gallery and where to find ARTNEWS review of each exhibition	New York Times Howard Devree: H. D. Aline B. Louchheim: A. B. L. Sam Hunter: S. H.	Herald Tribune Carlyle Burrows: C. D. Paul V. Beckley: P. V. B.	Sun Henry McBride, H. McB. Helen Carlson; H. C.	World-Telegram Emily Genauer: E. G.
Arnest, Kraushaar See ARTNEWS, May, p. 37	. . . one of the most authoritative first one-man shows this season . . . satisfies mind and senses equally . . . S. H.	. . . beautifully brushed on the canvases . . . betraying a sure alliance between seeing and feeling. C. B.	. . . has the genuine painter's touch . . . exceedingly promising show. . . . H. McB.	. . . have a fluency (and) romanticism . . . which is always saved from sentimentality by his unerring taste . . . E. G.
Ben-Zion, Schaefer See ARTNEWS, May, p. 47	. . . his work is certainly uneven, part of the time inept and groping, but its best . . . bears comparison in some respects with work by Rouault . . . S. H.	Employs heavy color to furnish warmth and give these large and dignified themes a human quality. P. V. B.	. . . the largeness of manner, the exalted fervor, and the implacable challenge of the symbols he employs are most impressive. H. McB.	. . . takes for his material familiar Biblical episodes and casts them in an expressionist mold. E. G.
Berman, Knoedler See ARTNEWS, May, p. 36	. . . seem largely stage sets (with) . . . surrealist touch of mystery, and . . . an air of antiquity. Prevalence of blues and pinks add to the artificiality of the work . . . H. D.	. . . depicts an unrealistic world . . . enormously clever . . . (but) less sensational than Dali . . . C. B.		
Le Corbusier, Rosenberg See ARTNEWS, April, p. 52	. . . seem to date more than most work by well-known modernists. . . . Most of the paintings seem coldly objective exercises. H. D.			. . . they make a very satisfying combination of precisely balanced form and lyrical line and color. E. G.
Delaney, Artists' Gallery See ARTNEWS, May, p. 47	. . . work seems pervaded by the physical vitality and overtones of melancholy of the racial subjects depicted. S. H.	Painted with a heavy impasto and in a high key, most of his works are characterized by a jaggedness of composition . . . P. V. B.		One can see, now . . . why (the collectors) have found (his work) agreeable. E. G.
Hare, Kootz See ARTNEWS, May, p. 47	More plastic than his previous work, his sculpture still seems personally unresolved.	. . . at his best in his subtle recreating of the African primitive form. C. B.	. . . realism is not (his) game, (but) delivering the emotion, for it is the associated idea you get each time . . .	
De Kooning, Egan See ARTNEWS, April, p. 33	. . . either adds up to an impression of imprisonment with possible contemporary spiritual implications, or one of lugubrious vacillation . . . S. H.	Although some of his forms hint at reality, close study reveals him as inscrutable as ever . . . P. V. B.		. . . loose, arbitrary, unconventional, and curiously anguished expressions . . . What exactly he is trying to get at is not entirely clear . . . E. G.
Lam, Matisse See ARTNEWS, May, p. 37	His figures seem to be masked and in the spell of incantations. . . . Finds primitive terror in our life today . . . H. D.	Sometimes the elements are well placed in the canvases . . . but usually they are as arbitrary in a creative sense as any Picasso canvas. C. B.	. . . bolder abstract paintings than ever and more gruesome. . . . They have a curious kind of authority. H. McB.	. . . a strange, complex, symbolic expression superbly designed, and ominously powerful. E. G.
Lamba, Passedoit See ARTNEWS, May, p. 47	. . . employs barbarous shapes . . . but usually manages to transform them into pictorial and plastic ideas. S. H.	Rather bizarre but romantic oils, representing highly abstracted phantasies of the world about her . . . P. V. B.	at her best . . . daring yet sensitive, fanciful yet credible. . . . But can also be impetuous and overly ambitious . . . H. C.	. . . Impress one first as being disconcertingly monotonous. . . . Yet . . . cannot help but appreciate its extremely sensitive color . . . E. G.
Leech, Pepsi-Cola See ARTNEWS, Summer, p. 54	. . . reveals a typically artificial, shiny paint quality and leans toward a rather cramped romantic expressionism . . .	. . . is natural but motivated by a realist's sense of the mystic forces governing man and nature. C. B.		. . . proficient, agreeable . . . (but) communicates no singular emotional depth or freshness of vision. E. G.
Levine, Downtown See ARTNEWS, May, p. 36	. . . the intensity of his convictions has led him to overstatement and bitterness of satire, but (his) growing maturity . . . has led to a diminution of his tendency. H. D.	. . . has gone far in an expressive way toward making his pictures more dynamic . . . (but) explicitness, in particular, has been crowded out . . .	. . . have the expected exuberance of spirit and instinctive cleverness in the use of pigment . . . H. McB.	. . . even the least successful of them are so vital and so imaginative as to make his earlier works suffer in comparison. E. G.
Lipton, Parsons See ARTNEWS, May, p. 54	. . . very grim and uncompromising . . . So many pieces seen at once, however, become monotonous . . . H. D.	. . . making a conscious effort to create original and atavistic forms . . . (in which) there is a savage, primitive quality. P. V. B.	. . . they suggest a sense of the fearful dangers confronting us all. The drawback is a tendency toward repetition. H. McB.	This is hardly decorative stuff, but it reveals great integrity and intensity of purpose plus superior technique . . . E. G.
Morrison, Grand Central See ARTNEWS, April, p. 50	Echoes of Rouault and Tamayo in these bone forms and tortured figure compositions.	. . . solemnly expressive, and rely on the power of form and its color complement to invest the themes with superior richness and feeling. C. B.	. . . an excellent draftsman and an exciting colorist. By virtue of these likely qualifications he can speak acceptably and authoritatively. H. C.	. . . all rugged power. . . . Brings something of his racial (Indian) heritage . . . and over all there is a brooding emotional quality . . . E. G.
M. Phillips, Bignou See ARTNEWS, May, p. 47	. . . pleasing landscapes, portraits, and, best of all, poetically envisioned flower pieces.	. . . paints thinly and with somewhat bland technique, but has a fine breadth of style . . . P. V. B.	. . . a good colorist . . . an instinctive feeling for landscape. . . . What is new is an increased emphasis upon design . . . H. McB.	. . . nothing complicated . . . paints serene landscapes, decorative still-lifes, ancient trees, using a cool silvery palette . . . E. G.
Weisenborn, Levitt See ARTNEWS, May, p. 49	Somewhat mechanical non-objective arrangements with accent on bold outline and rugged textures.	. . . somewhat rigid, despite the warmth of the coloring. A cool intellectuality pervades most of them. . . . P. V. B.	. . . compounded of power, more power and speed, alarming speed. That (his) intention is so outstandingly clear is really remarkable . . . H. McB.	. . . sharp and clear in color, precise and somewhat mechanical in form, and electric in movement . . . but there is also little originality and less poetry . . . E. G.

52

Figure 69
"Our Box Score of the Critics," *Art News* 47, no. 4 (Summer 1948): 52

to emerge from their dense, seething web of automatic activity. This method of canceling out, contradiction, of maintaining an interminable fluidity either adds up to an impression of imprisonment with possible contemporary spiritual implications, or one of lugubrious vacillation and paucity of motifs and content, according to your point of view.

The Partisan Review illustrates *Valentine* (see fig. 20), *Zurich* (see fig. 23), *Brown and White* (see fig. 29), and *Painting* (see fig. 27), in that order. Clement Greenberg's essay "The Crisis of the Easel Picture" follows the latter two.[57]

May 4 Emily Genauer's review runs in the *New York World-Telegram*.[58]

Although William de Kooning has been painting 25 years, his current exhibition in the Egan Gallery is his first solo show in New York. It would have been a more revealing and provocative occasion if the gallery had chosen to hang, along with his late abstractions, some earlier work, so we might know through what stages de Kooning has traveled before evolving these loose, arbitrary, unconventional and curiously anguished recent expressions. That he is a skilled draftsman (in the sense that he makes line perform his bidding) is evident, I think, in even the most abstract of them. What exactly he is trying to get at, however, is not entirely clear, unless it's to paint constructions of form, color and line that will be satisfying per se or, what is more likely, will entirely without reliance on recognizable symbols or shapes, suggest various specific moods.

May 5 The Museum of Modern Art hosts "The Modern Artist Speaks," an independent forum organized in response to the mid-February announcement by the Boston Institute of Modern Art that it would change its name, and the subsequent fallout in the press.[59] Thirty-six artists respond to Paul Burlin's call to voice opposition to "a journalistic and pseudo intellectual wave of animosity directed against the spirit and name of Modern Art."[60] De Kooning receives the notice but does not reply.[61] Speakers accuse specific art critics of censorship, including Robert Coates, Howard Devree, Emily Genauer, and Aline Louchheim, and criticize publications across the political spectrum, from the *New York Times* and the *New York World-Telegram* to the communist magazine *Masses & Mainstream*. "The black sheep," Adolph Gottlieb cautions in his speech, "are neither white nor red enough, and that is very dangerous from either point of view. Why? Because even a few black sheep in the large flock might contaminate the others. The pure white and pure red might then become grey or maroon. With the cry of unintelligibility the critics attack whatever is out of line with the status quo of art." More than two hundred people attend the event.[62]

June 30 First day of the summer session at Black Mountain College in Asheville, North Carolina. De Kooning will teach painting at the invitation of Josef Albers, replacing the better-known painter Mark Tobey, who is ill.[63] The summer program this year focuses on art, bringing to the campus artists John Cage, Merce Cunningham, Peter Grippe, and Richard Lippold, art historians Winslow Ames and Beaumont Newhall, and architects Charles Burchard and Buckminster Fuller. Soon after arriving, de Kooning delivers a lecture, "Cézanne and the Color of Veronese." Pat Passlof, one of his students, is deeply affected by his praise of figurative works from the past, in contrast with the strictures of "the doctrinaire abstractionists of the period."[64]

A total of seventeen students, with a range of experience, complete de Kooning's course.[65] V. V. Rankine (then known as Elvine Magruder), Gorky's sister-in-law, drops the course before the end of the summer but remembers de Kooning's teaching style: "[He] really just wanted to lead with his gut and . . . tell you something about what he thought about painting, but he's not going to tell you all at once. He'd only tell you by talking about your work to you."[66] Passlof recalls, "In my horse-stall studio, I painted black-and-white abstractions with immoderate encouragement from Bill."[67]

De Kooning works in the living room of his assigned cottage, which he "fill[s] with pastels," according to Elaine,[68] and displays his new work in one or two exhibitions held in the dining hall's interior and covered porch. Students recall works of black and white enamel painted on newsprint, collage, and both small and large studies for the painting *Asheville* (see fig. 33).[69] That important work may have been completed in Asheville or painted in New York using the studies.[70]

July 20 American Communist Party leaders are arrested under the Smith Act on charges of conspiring to overthrow the US government. They are later convicted during the Foley Square Trial in 1949.

July 21 Gorky dies by suicide three weeks after a car accident breaks his neck and leaves his painting arm temporarily paralyzed.[71] De Kooning receives news of Gorky's death at Black Mountain.

August 14 John Cage culminates a summerlong series of scores by Erik Satie with the performance of a play, *The Ruse of the Medusa* (figs. 75 and 76).[72] Buckminster Fuller acts in the role of the Baron Medusa; Merce Cunningham, a dancing mechanical monkey; and Elaine de Kooning, the female lead, Medusa's daughter; with Cage on piano. De Kooning and Elaine work on the set, de Kooning applying a veneer of faux pink and gray marble onto an oversize desk[73] and painting a woman's head on a pedestal above a closet-like shrine or tomb for "Mother Medusa."[74] Ruth Asawa makes a large bell prop and Fuller a hat for his character, constructed out of the venetian-blind strips he brought for his geodesic dome.[75]

WEDNESDAY, June 30 - Sometime between 9 a.m. and 5 p.m. report
to the business office, check to make sure all financial
arrangements are taken care of, and get a card from CHARLIE
BLOOMSTEIN permitting you to register. Go across the office
lobby to the registrar's office and get your registration card
from CORA BURGHARD. (You will need this card at the Thursday
morning meeting)

THURSDAY, July 1 - first meeting, faculty and students, time to
be announced.

MEAL TIMES:
weekdays:
  breakfast 7:30 to 8 a.m.
  lunch   12.45 p.m.
  *dinner   6:15 p.m.

Sundays:
  breakfast 8 - 9 a.m.
  lunch   1 p.m.
  **supper   5:15 p.m.

*informal dress for breakfast and lunch; something a little more
 formal,but not too much so, for dinner

**Sunday night supper is picnic style in paper bag style; come to
 the dining hall at 5:15 p.m. and get your share of what is there
 and take it out

STORE: The store is open for about a half hour after meals

COMMISSARY: the kitchen has provisions to sell fruit,margarine,
            lettuce, and packaged goods not sold in the store--
            DOROTHY ALBERS is in charge and will post a price
            list on Friday

            beginning Friday night, immediately after dinner, the
            commissary will be open on Friday nights, Sunday
            afternoons (during picnic supper), and Tuesday nights

SHEETS,TOWELS,ETC. On Saturday afternoon,immediately after lunch,
            take your own sheets,towels,etc. to RUTH ASAWA in
            the linen room, South Lodge, turn them in and get a
            receipt

            if they are plainly marked, they can be sent with the
            college laundry free of charge, if not plainly marked,
            we cannot be responsible for their safe return at the
            end of the summer session

DRY CLEANING: Dry cleaning is sent out every Tuesday. Take your
            dry cleaning to RUTH ASAWA immediately after lunch on
            Mondays - to the dry cleaning closet in North Lodge.
            It is returned the Tuesday of the following week.

            if you wish to send laundry out,it can be at the same
            time

WASHING: There is a college washing machine underneath South Lodgge,
Personal:also an ironing board. PLEASE learn HOW to use the
            MACHINE before you try it out - see Chris Noland, nurse,
            she knows all the ailments of the machine and the procedure
            of signing up for time,etc.,etc.

BED LINEN: Clean bed linen is put out in South Lodge on Saturday
            at noon. Each community member is entitled to ONE sheet,
            two towels, 1 pillow case

            take your soiled sheet,towels,and pillow case to the
            BIN near the washing and ironing room under South Lodge

Figure 70
Introduction to summer session at Black Mountain College, June
1948. Western Regional Archives, State Archives of North Carolina

Arthur Penn, still a student, directs the play. A few days later, the sets and costumes travel with the cast to New York. The group hopes to restage the play, perhaps on Broadway, but lack the money, connections, and organization to realize the project.[76]

August 20 Cunningham performs several dances at Black Mountain, including one titled *Orestes*, with accompaniment by Cage. The dance shows Orestes grappling with the decision of whether or not to kill his mother.[77]

August 25 Last day of the summer session. Albers questions de Kooning about his students, Elaine recounts, capturing perhaps a broader truth: "Six of them are leaving the college to go to New York City this September. Do you know anything about it?" "Sure," de Kooning responds, in Elaine's memory, "I told them if they wanted to be artists, they should quit school and come to New York and get a studio and start painting."[78] Students Gustave Falk and Pat Passlof confirm that he helped them find studios; Etta Mandelbaum that he procured free tubes of oil paint for her, back in Manhattan.[79]

September 20 Collector and writer Sidney Janis opens Sidney Janis Gallery (15 East 57th Street) with an exhibition of works by Fernand Léger, taking over the space previously occupied by Samuel Kootz Gallery. Kootz has closed his gallery in order to work as a private dealer, primarily for Picasso, operating out of his home at 470 Park Avenue.[80]

Fall De Kooning probably begins his second series of Woman paintings.[81] He divides his studio in half and sublets space to Jack Tworkov.[82]

October MoMA purchases *Painting* (see fig. 27).

Alfred H. Barr Jr. has been away since the spring, missing de Kooning's exhibition, and brokers the purchase upon his return.[83]

Life magazine's October issue features "A Life Round Table on Modern Art," on an event that took place at MoMA in a room hung with paintings. The article reports on the discussion among fifteen "critics and connoisseurs," including Alfred Frankfurter, Aldous Huxley, Meyer Schapiro, and the Met's director, Francis Henry Taylor, all invited to answer the question "Is modern art, considered as a whole, a good or a bad development?" MoMA curator James Thrall Soby and Clement Greenberg praise

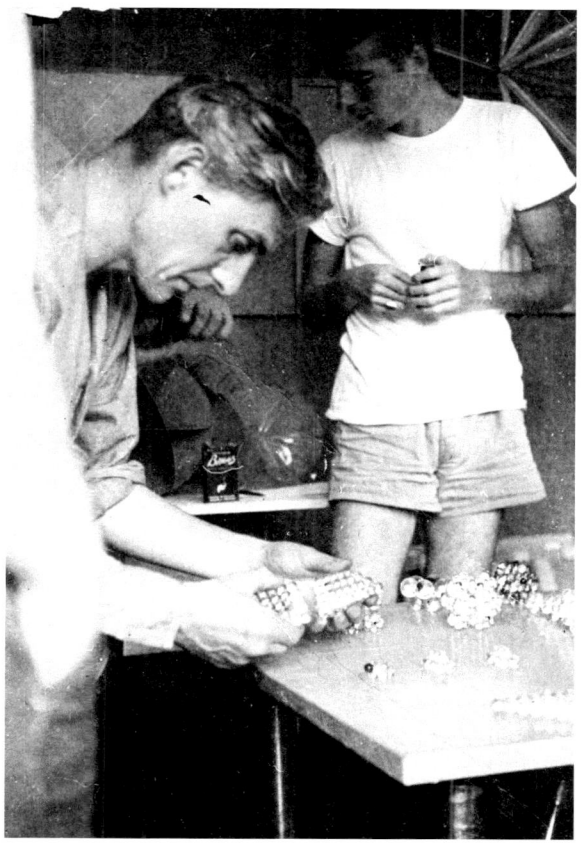

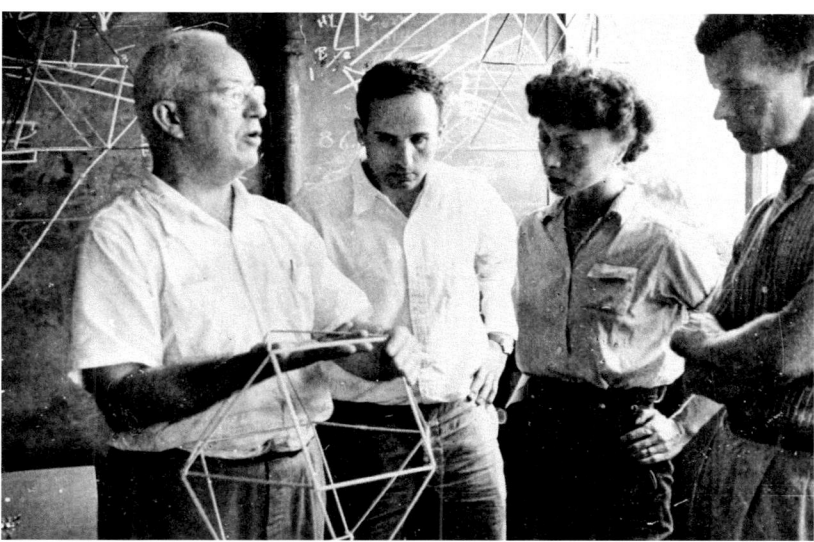

Figures 71 and 72
Kenneth Snelson (1927–2016; born Pendelton, OR; died New York, NY) **Willem (above) and Elaine (below) de Kooning in Buckminster Fuller's architecture class at Black Mountain College, 1948.** Photographic prints. Western Regional Archives, State Archives of North Carolina

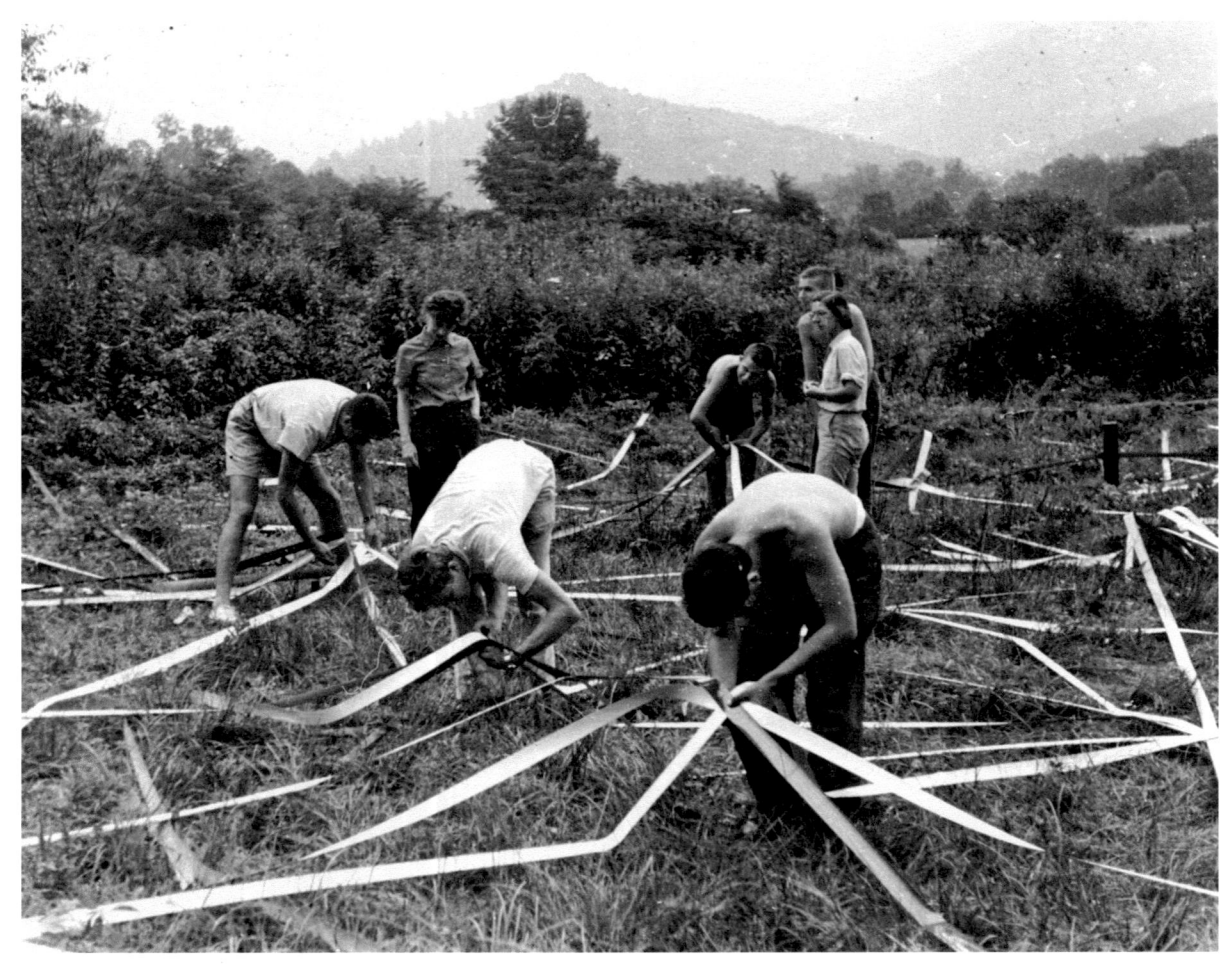

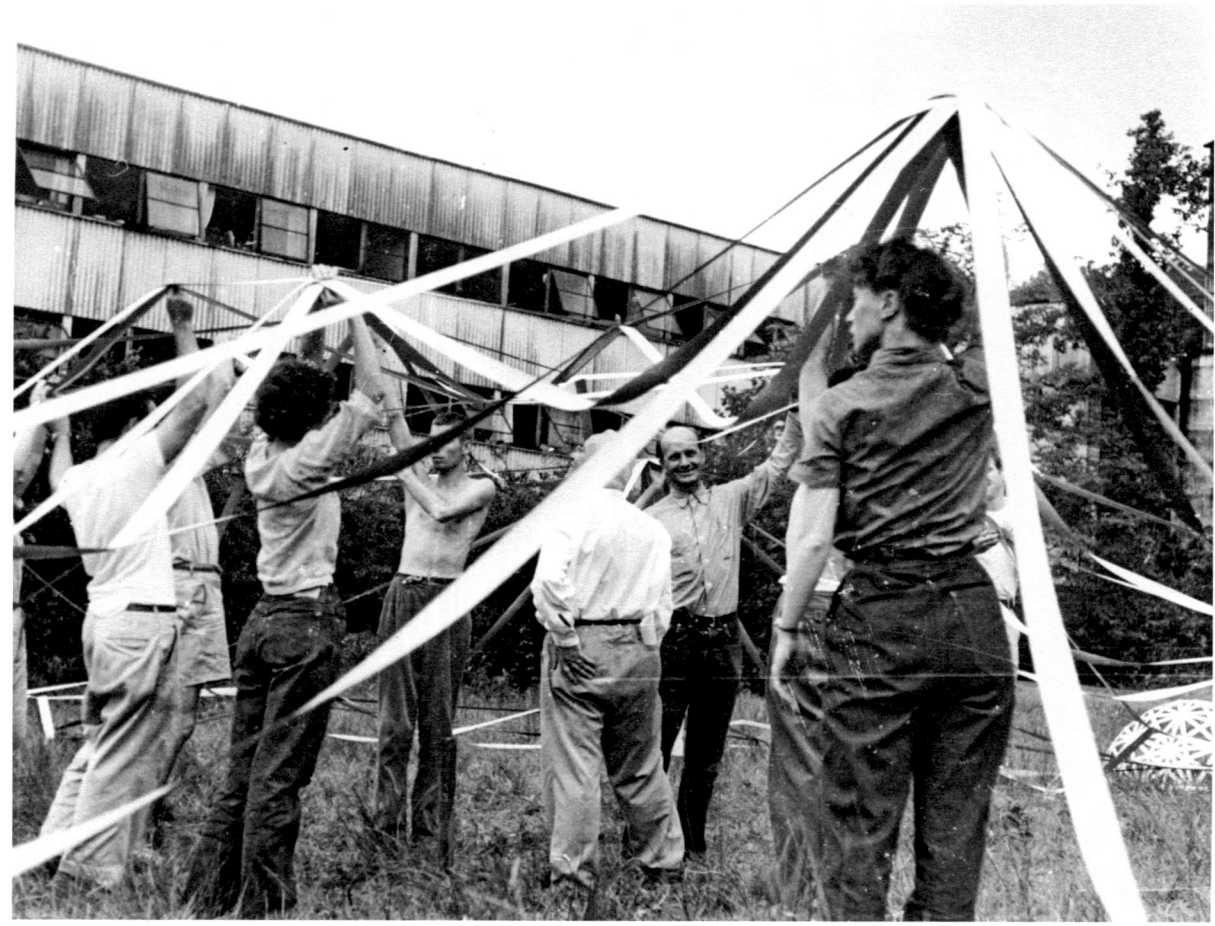

Figure 73
Beaumont Newhall (1908–1993; born Lynn, MA; died Santa Fe, NM), **Students working on Buckminster Fuller's venetian blind dome at Black Mountain College, 1948.** From left: Elaine de Kooning, Albert Lanier, Sewell Sillman. Photographic print. Western Regional Archives, State Archives of North Carolina

Figure 74
Beaumont Newhall, Students working on Buckminster Fuller's venetian blind dome at Black Mountain College, 1948. Photographic print. Western Regional Archives, State Archives of North Carolina

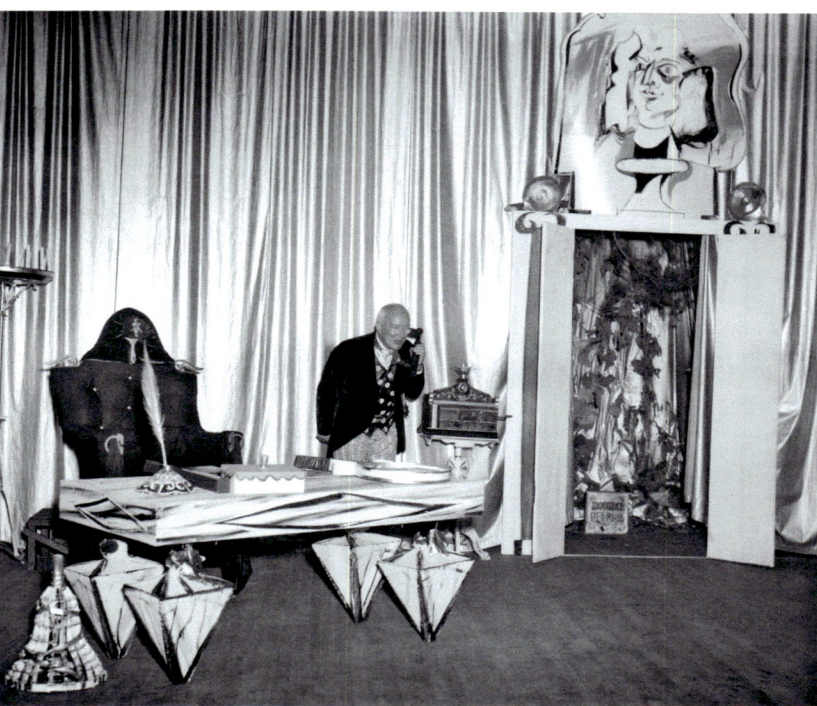

Figure 75
Hazel Larsen Archer (1921–2001; born Milwaukee, WI; died Tucson, AZ), **Buckminster Fuller in *The Ruse of the Medusa* at Black Mountain College, 1948.** Set designed by Willem and Elaine de Kooning with a painting of a woman's head by Willem de Kooning and bell prop by Ruth Asawa. Photographic print. Courtesy Black Mountain College Museum + Arts Center

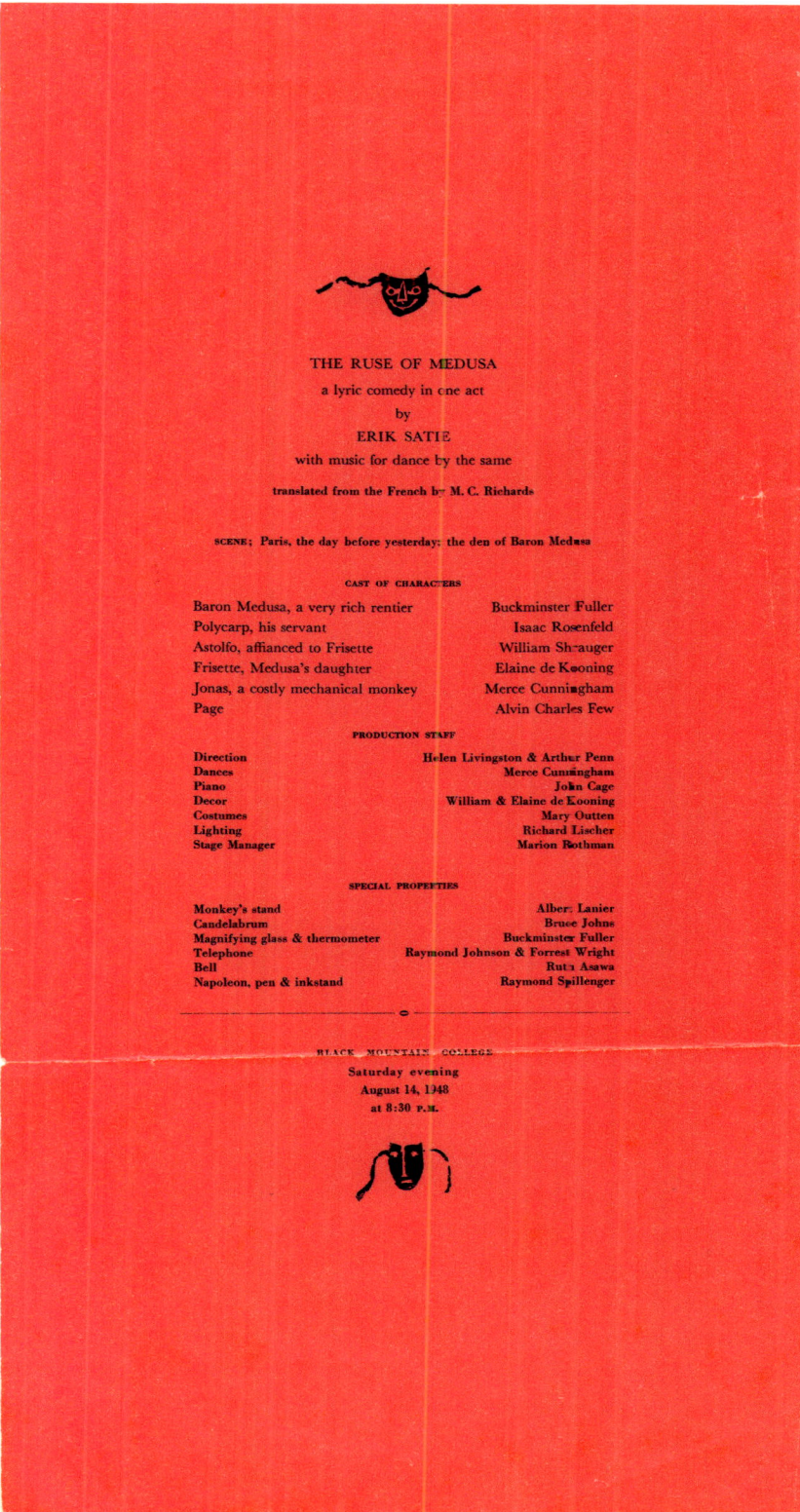

Figure 76
Program for *The Ruse of the Medusa*, performed August 14, 1948. Mimeograph on pink paper. Western Regional Archives, State Archives of North Carolina

de Kooning's *Painting*, hung alongside works by William Baziotes, Adolph Gottlieb, and Jackson Pollock, though the report is suffused with a subtext of caution.[84]

November Charles Egan Gallery presents paintings by Giorgio Cavallon.

René d'Harnoncourt, then curatorial director at the Museum of Modern Art, publishes an essay, "Challenge and Promise: Modern Art and Modern Society," in *Magazine of Art*. "During the past few years," he writes, summarizing recent local and international events, the function of art in society "has become the direct concern of governments, of their ministries of education and propaganda and sometimes of their police; and here it has given rise to discussion, controversy and occasionally to violent polemics in popular magazines and the daily press." He implores readers to embrace pluralism in the arts, across the spectrum of "a more or less abstract rendering of subject matter."[85]

November 2 Harry S. Truman narrowly wins reelection over Republican challenger Thomas E. Dewey. Progressive Party candidate Henry Wallace receives slightly more than a million votes.

November 13 The Whitney Annual opens with *Mailbox* (see fig. 21) on display, the first time its jury has selected a work by de Kooning for inclusion. In his review for *Art News*, Thomas Hess comments on the "freedom of forms," asking, "Are these ovals grinning mouths; are these wings, breasts, tusks or legs that seem to bob up among the moving curves?" In his first printed discussion of de Kooning's work, Hess critiques an essential ambiguity that he would later champion.[86]

Late Fall William Baziotes, Robert Motherwell, Mark Rothko, and David Hare found the Subjects of the Artist School at 35 East 8th Street. Motherwell organizes public talks on Friday evenings, filling the loft to capacity with students and visitors eager to hear guest artists speak, including John Cage, de Kooning (February 1949), Adolph Gottlieb, and Ad Reinhardt.[87]

December *The Atlantic* publishes an essay by Francis Henry Taylor, director of the Met, titled "Modern Art and the Dignity of Man." He defends modern art but criticizes artists for "their insistence on avoiding living forms."[88]

Charles Egan Gallery presents paintings by Herman Rose.

December 22: MoMA opens *American Painting from the Museum Collection*, with de Kooning's *Painting* among approximately 150 works, including those by William Baziotes, Stuart Davis, Arshile Gorky, Adolph Gottlieb, Karl Knaths, Jacob Lawrence, Jackson Pollock, Ben Shahn, and Mark Tobey.

1949

January De Kooning writes to *Art News* to refute the idea that he was influential on Gorky.[89]

In a piece on Arshile Gorky's memorial show—and it was a very little piece indeed—it was mentioned that I was one of his influences. Now that is plain silly. When, about fifteen years ago, I walked into Arshile's studio for the first time, the atmosphere was so beautiful that I got a little dizzy and when I came to, I was bright enough to take the hint immediately. If the bookkeepers think it necessary continuously to make sure of where things and people come from, well then, I come from 36 Union Square. It is incredible to me that other people live there now. I am glad that it is about impossible to get away from his powerful influence. As long as I keep it with myself I'll be doing all right. Sweet Arshile, bless your dear heart.

Charles Egan Gallery presents an exhibition of photographs by Aaron Siskind.

January 24 Charles Egan Gallery presents an exhibition of paintings in black, gray, and white by Josef Albers in collaboration with Sidney Janis Gallery, which displays "color and optical variations."[90]

February 1 Pierre Matisse Gallery opens an exhibition of recent paintings and drawings by Henri Matisse where his paper cutouts can be seen for the first time.

February 18 The Subjects of the Artist School hosts de Kooning on a Friday evening as a guest lecturer, his first public presentation. The talk, titled "A Desperate View," discusses the relationship of art of the past with the activities of a working artist. "Whatever an artist's personal feelings are," he observes, "as soon as an artist fills a certain area on the canvas or circumscribes it, he becomes historical. He acts from or upon other artists. . . . The idea of space is given to him to change it if he can. The subject matter in the abstract is space. He fills it with an attitude. The attitude never comes from himself alone. You are with a group or movement because you cannot help it."[91]

February 21 *Life* magazine publishes a six-page spread on the widespread critical controversy that has followed the announcement by Boston's Institute of Modern Art that it would become the Institute of Contemporary Art. The article includes an excerpt from John Hay Whitney's introduction to the catalogue of *Painting and Sculpture in the Museum of Modern Art*, positioning it as a "countermanifesto" to Boston's statement, in which he states, "The word 'modern' is valuable."[92]

March Charles Egan Gallery presents twelve sculptural works by Isamu Noguchi.

April Peridot Gallery presents an exhibition of non-objective art by nine painters and one sculptor, including Louise Bourgeois, de Kooning, and Hans Hofmann. De Kooning exhibits *Little Attic* (1949; private collection) under the title *Light of the Borough*.[93]

April 4 The North Atlantic Treaty Organization (NATO) is formed to contain communist expansion in Europe.

April 5 Charles Egan Gallery presents an exhibition of paintings by Fannie Hillsmith.

April 8–10 The San Francisco Museum of Art convenes a "Western Round Table on Modern Art" and mounts an exhibition of modern art. De Kooning exhibits *Painting* (see fig. 27) with works by Fernand Léger, Henri Matisse, Piet Mondrian, Wifredo Lam, Pablo Picasso, Clyfford Still, and Mark Tobey. The discussion, organized by Douglas MacAgy, then the director of the California School of Fine Arts, includes the anthropologist Gregory Bateson, Marcel Duchamp, Robert Goldwater, Mark Tobey, and Frank Lloyd Wright.[94]

Charles Egan Gallery presents an exhibition of sculpture by Reuben Nakian.

May The Subjects of the Artist School closes for financial reasons.[95]

July The de Koonings rent a cottage in Provincetown, Massachusetts.

July 3 Forum 49 opens at Gallery 200, a new art space in Provincetown, with an exhibition of approximately one hundred works by fifty artists and a panel discussion devoted to the question "What Is an Artist?" The local news reports that many were turned away at the door due to the popularity of the event.[96] De Kooning does not arrive in time or possibly declines an invitation to speak on the opening panel.[97] Weldon Kees, one of the organizers, is confident at the end of June that, "through a complicated interlocking network of phone calls and telegrams," he has secured a painting by de Kooning to include in the exhibition, but the work never arrives. De Kooning has already been advertised as among the "widely-publicized leaders in the modern movement" to be shown.[98] A total of ten events continues on Thursday evenings through July and August. At some point, de Kooning travels to East Hampton and returns with Robert Motherwell in time for the latter to speak on the controversial panel "French Art vs. U.S. Art Today," which takes place on August 11.[99] Elaine speaks at a closing event on Labor Day in a group of fifteen artists and writers.[100]

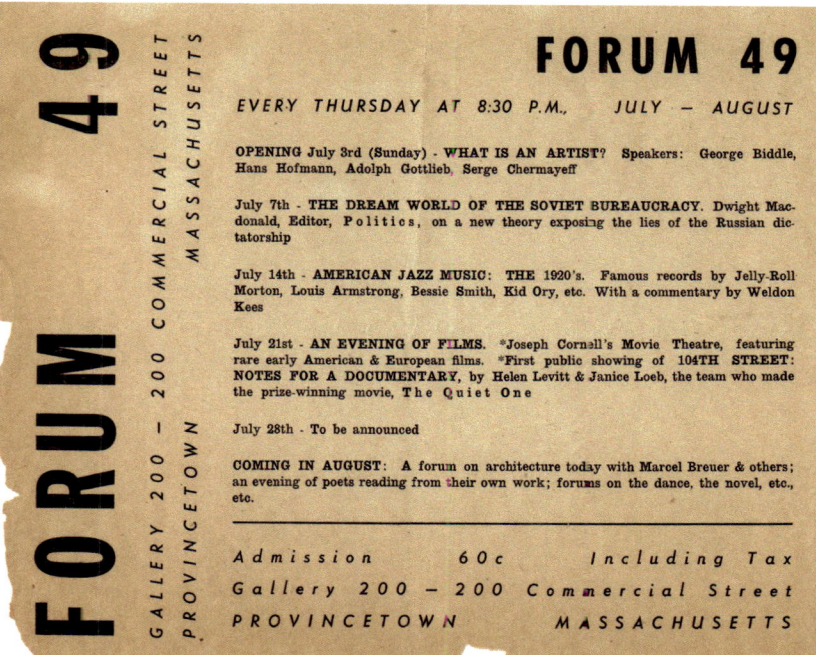

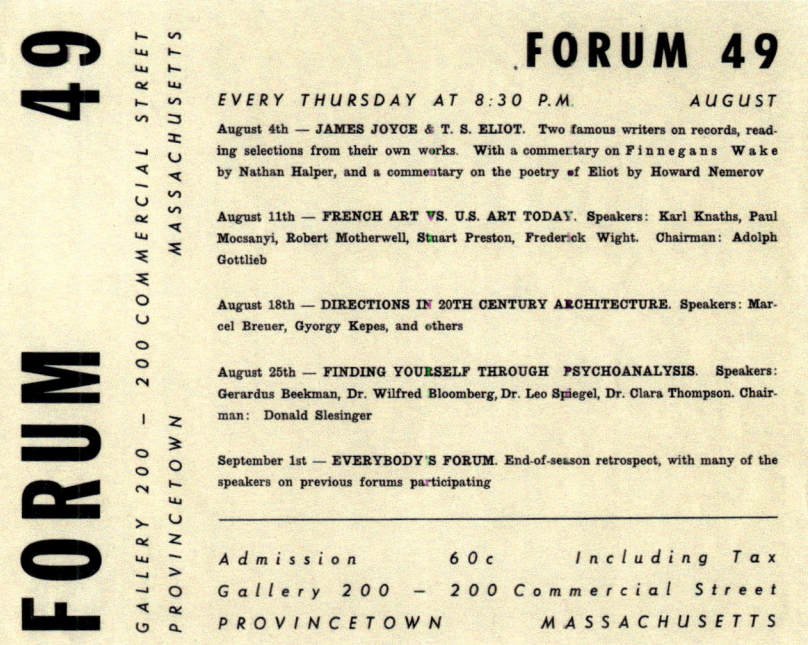

Figures 77 and 78
Schedule of events and advertisements for Forum 49, Provincetown, MA, summer 1949. Adolph and Esther Gottlieb Foundation Archives, New York

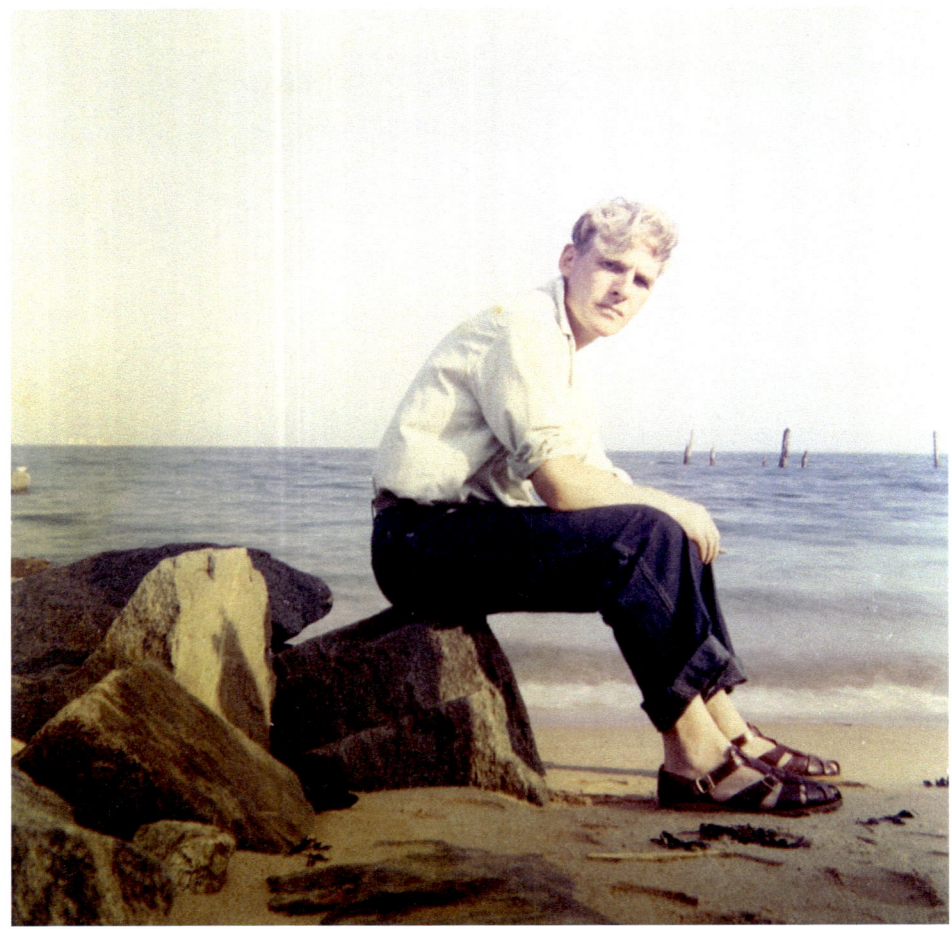

Figure 79
Willem de Kooning on the beach in Provincetown, MA, Summer
1949. Photographic print. Ibram Lassaw Archives

August 8 *Life* magazine publishes a feature article titled "Jackson Pollock: Is He the Greatest Living Painter in the United States?" At Forum 49, where two of Pollock's works are on display, a poll is circulated repeating this question (figs. 77 and 78).[101]

August 29 The Soviet Union conducts its first atomic bomb test. The US no longer has a monopoly on nuclear weapons.

September Emily Genauer reports in *Harper's* following an interview with George Dondero, a congressman who has accused the organizers of a traveling art show for a Long Island hospital of spreading communist propaganda. The list of artists exhibited overlaps with that of the State Department show that was dismantled on similar charges. Genauer writes, "So far there has been little lightning with Dondero's thunder, but the clouds seem to be gathering."[102]

Fall New York University instructors Robert Iglehart, Tony Smith, and Hale Woodruff launch Studio 35, taking over the space at 35 East 8th Street previously occupied by the Subjects of the Artists School. They continue orga-

nizing Friday-night public lectures and provide students with studio and exhibition spaces.

The sculptor Philip Pavia rents a loft on the top floor of 39 East 8th Street, two doors down from Studio 35, as a gathering place for artists, referred to as The Club.[103] Pavia soon begins organizing talks and panels on Friday nights, and artists meet informally on other nights, each member holding their own key. Key holders include de Kooning, Franz Kline, Ibram Lassaw, Conrad Marca-Relli, Herbert and Mercedes Matter, Ad Reinhardt, Milton Resnick, Joop Sanders, and others.[104] Admission grows from twenty members to sixty by 1950.[105]

September 14 Samuel Kootz reopens his gallery at 600 Madison Avenue after a one-year hiatus with a group show. Organized by Kootz and Harold Rosenberg, the show, called *The Intrasubjectives*, refers to an essay by José Ortega y Gasset published the previous month in the *Partisan Review*.[106] "After Cézanne," Ortega y Gasset writes, "painting only paints ideas—which, certainly, are also objects, but ideal objects, immanent to the subject or intrasubjective." "Intrasubjectivism," Kootz explains in the catalogue, "is a point of view in painting rather than an identical painting style. Note, in the varied person-alities here, the lyricism of Pollock . . . Motherwell's felt images, Gottlieb's inventive recall of ancient and modern myths, de Kooning's love of paint; these, and the others included, have a joint passion for ideas and for a subtler, surer way of expressing them." De Kooning exhibits *Attic* (see fig. 50).

September 19 Sidney Janis Gallery opens *Man and Wife*, a group exhibition featuring the work of artists in romantic pairs. Elaine and Willem de Kooning show side by side as a couple. Others include Jean (Hans) Arp and Sophie Taeuber-Arp, Robert and Sonia Delaunay, Max Ernst and Dorothea Tanning, David Hare and Jacqueline Lamba, Stanley William Hayter and Helen Phillips, Ben Nicholson and Barbara Hepworth, Pablo Picasso and Françoise Gilot, and Jackson Pollock and Lee Krasner.[107]

October 10 Betty Parsons Gallery presents *European and American Painters*, organized by the French art dealer Louis Carré.

October 17 Charles Egan Gallery presents an exhibition of paintings by Jack Tworkov.

November 14 Charles Egan Gallery opens an exhibition of crayon drawings by Landès Lewitin.

November 21 Betty Parsons Gallery presents Jackson Pollock's third solo show with the gallery, the first since he was featured in *Life* magazine. Milton Resnick finds the crowd changed, full of well-dressed people he has never seen, shaking hands. He remembers de Kooning commenting, "Jackson has finally broken the ice."[108]

Charles Egan Gallery presents an exhibition of Joseph Cornell's *Aviary* boxes.

December 16 The Whitney Annual opens. De Kooning's *Attic* hangs in the first gallery with works by Jackson Pollock and John Marin. Thomas Hess, reviewing the show in *Art News,* classifies them as examples of "three of the most important styles in modern American art." In contrast to his 1948 Whitney Annual review, Hess finds strength in the ambiguity of de Kooning's "all but unrecognizable figures—whose sections interchange with the marvelously confusing rapidity of images."[109]

1950

In January, de Kooning likely begins working on *Excavation* (see fig. 51), the largest painting of his career. He will labor over this composition until April or May of 1950, when the work will leave his studio to travel to Venice. There, it will represent the US in the American Pavilion at the Venice Biennale.[110]

De Kooning is invited to speak at Studio 35, his second public presentation. The lecture, titled "The Renaissance and Order," considers the subjectivity of the Renaissance painter, whom he imagines "on the inside of his picture."[111] Hess remembers that it was Motherwell who read de Kooning's talk aloud, delivering it twice, after which de Kooning answered questions.[112]

January 23 Betty Parsons Gallery opens Barnett Newman's first solo exhibition.

February *Vogue* features "53 Living American Artists" with de Kooning's *Little Attic*, then called *Light of the Borough*, among a group of works arranged and photo-graphed by Herbert Matter (fig. 81).[113]

Charles Egan Gallery presents an exhibition of paintings by George McNeil.

February 9 Joseph McCarthy delivers "Enemies from Within" speech in Wheeling, West Virginia. He claims to have a list of 205 communists working within Truman's State Department.

February 28 Samuel Kootz Gallery opens *Black or White: Paintings by European and American Artists* (fig. 82). De Kooning exhibits *Dark Pond* (see fig. 41).[114] The show also includes work by William Baziotes, Georges Braque, Fritz Bultman, Jean Dubuffet, Adolph Gottlieb, Hans Hofmann, Weldon Kees, Joan Miró, Piet Mondrian, Robert Motherwell, Pablo Picasso, Mark Tobey, and Bradley Walker Tomlin. Thomas Hess suggests Henri Matisse, Jean (Hans) Arp, and Diego Velázquez are conspicuously missing in his review in *Art News.*[115]

March *Magazine of Art* publishes responses from sixteen critics to a questionnaire distributed by Robert Goldwater on American art. Clement Greenberg's response identifies nine artists "under forty-five years old," including de Kooning, Arshile Gorky, Adolph Gottlieb, Robert Motherwell, Jackson Pollock, and David Smith, who have made "an original contribution to the mainstream" in helping to develop an American abstract painting.[116]

March 22 Max Margulis visits de Kooning's studio with a stereoscopic camera and captures images of *Excavation* (see fig. 51) in progress, including images with the artist and visitors Harold Rosenberg and Landès Lewitin (figs. 83 and 84).[117]

March 27 The Institute of Contemporary Art, the Museum of Modern Art, and the Whitney Museum of American Art issue a joint statement in support of modern art, declaring, "We believe that the so-called 'unintelligibility' of some modern art is an inevitable result of its exploration of new frontiers." Emily Genauer affirmatively comments, "The stand which opposes a narrowly chauvinistic approach to art and one which rejects the notion that all esthetic innovations are somehow politically subversive and 'un-American,' is particularly welcome in the face of recent confused and often reckless attacks."[118] Critic Aline Louchheim wonders whether Boston "were not intending to take back its maiden name."[119]

March 28 Charles Egan Gallery opens an exhibition of sculpture by Reuben Nakian.

April Alfred Barr Jr. chooses *Excavation*, *Mailbox* (see fig. 21), *Light in August* (see fig. 18), and *The Mirror* (probably *Dark Pond*; see fig. 41) for the American Pavilion at the upcoming Venice Biennale, serving as co-commissioner alongside *Art News* editor Alfred Frankfurter.[120] The works begin transit to Venice in early May, with *Excavation* leaving from de Kooning's studio.[121]

The Dutch artist Martha Bourdrez visits de Kooning in his studio for an interview, published in May.[122]

April 21–23 Studio 35 holds a roundtable discussion over three days before it closes permanently in May. De Kooning is among twenty-five participants moderated by Alfred Barr Jr., Richard Lippold, and Robert Motherwell (figs. 85–87). The conference proceedings are published in *Modern Artists in America*, a single-issue journal edited by Motherwell, Reinhardt, and Bernard Karpel in 1951 covering the two previous art seasons.[123]

Figure 80
Walter Auerbach, Willem de Kooning's studio, looking onto 4th Avenue, ca. 1950. Photographic print. Courtesy Robert Mann Gallery

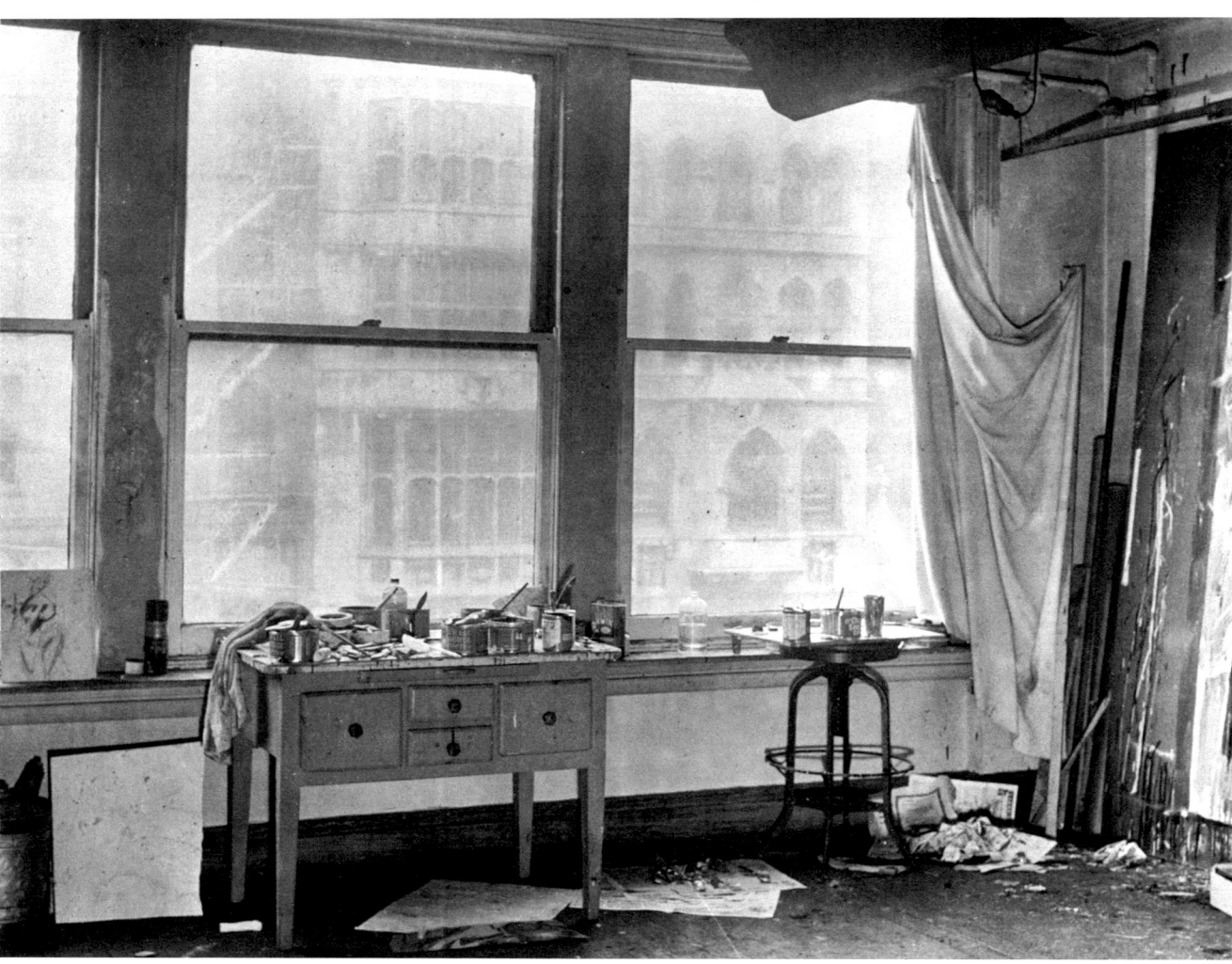

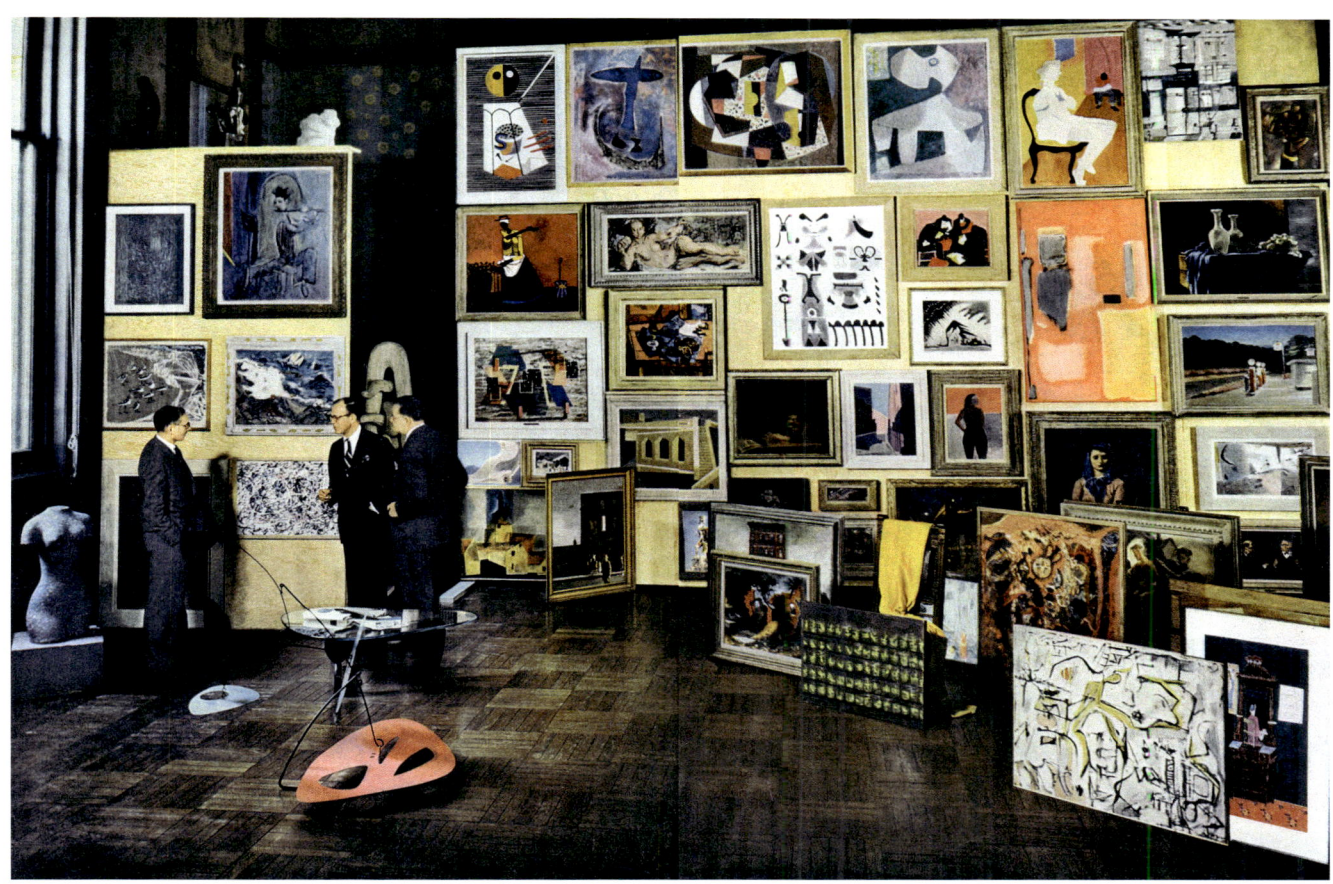

Figure 81
Illustration accompanying the article "Vogue Presents 53 Living American Artists," *Vogue* 115, no. 2 (February 1950). *Little Attic* appears, in an unfinished state, near the lower-right corner. Photo: Herbert Matter

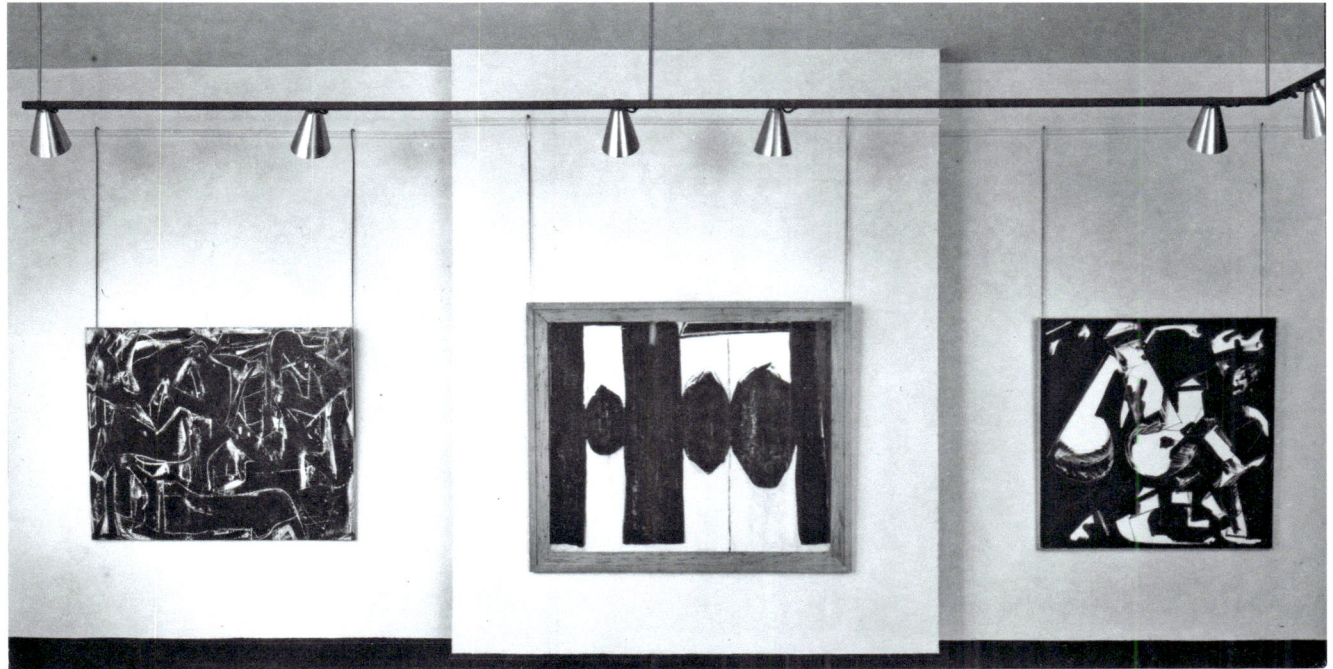

Figure 82
Aaron Siskind (1903–1991; born New York, NY; died Providence, RI), **Installation view of *Black or White: Paintings by European and American Artists*, Kootz Gallery, 1950.** Paintings shown, from left: Willem de Kooning, *Dark Pond*, 1948; Robert Motherwell, *Granada*, 1948–49; Hans Hofmann, *Germania II*, 1949. Kootz Gallery Records, 1923–1966, Photographic print. Archives of American Art, Smithsonian Institution, Washington, DC

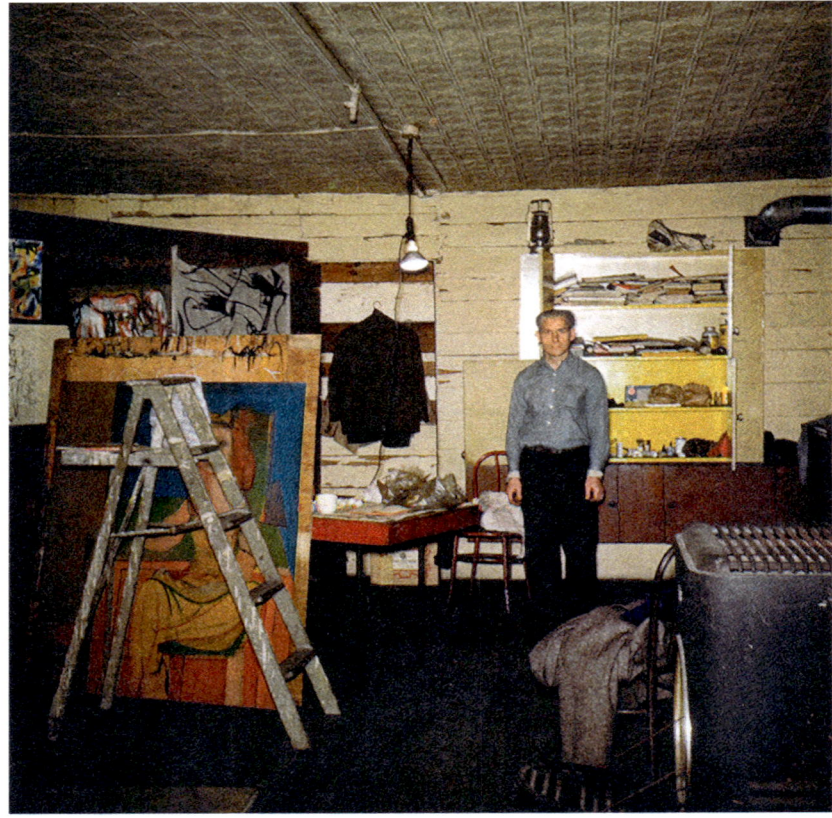

Figure 83
Max Margulis, Willem de Kooning in his studio, March 22, 1950, with *Seated Woman* (ca. 1940) visible behind the ladder. One photograph of a pair taken simultaneously with a stereoscopic camera. Courtesy The Willem de Kooning Foundation

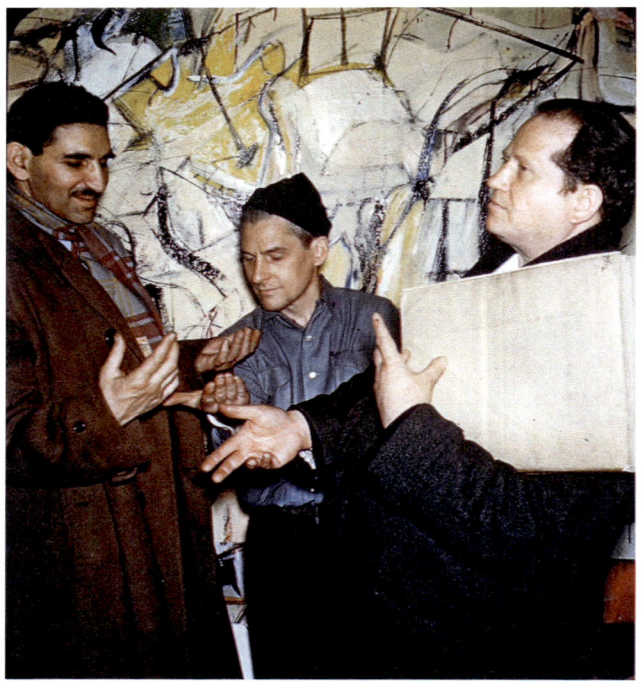

Figure 84
Max Margulis, Willem de Kooning in his studio, March 22, 1950, standing in front of a state of *Excavation* (see fig. 51) with Harold Rosenberg and Landès Lewitin. One photograph of a pair taken simultaneously with a stereoscopic camera. Lawrence Lewitin / The Landès Lewitin Foundation

April 22 Opening of *American Painting, 1950* at the Virginia Museum of Fine Arts. De Kooning shows *Attic* (see fig. 50), chosen by James Johnson Sweeney on a one-person jury.

May 15 Charles Egan Gallery opens a group exhibition, including an "expressionistic nonfigurative" work by de Kooning, with Josef Albers, Giorgio Cavallon, Joseph Cornell, Robert De Niro, Fannie Hillsmith, George McNeil, and Jack Tworkov.[124]

May 20 Eighteen painters, including de Kooning, and ten sculptors issue an open letter to Roland L. Redmond, president of the Metropolitan Museum of Art, stating that they "reject the monster national exhibition" to be held in December with works selected by "a jury notoriously hostile to advanced art."[125] Gottlieb had proposed the letter in April, at the roundtable discussion at Studio 35, and wrote it in consultation with the other artists, especially Barnett Newman and Ad Reinhardt.[126] *Life* magazine would publish a photograph of the group by Nina Leen, taken in November, after the Metropolitan show's opening with the caption "Irascible Group of Advanced Artists Led Fight Against Show,"[127] drawing on the *New York Herald Tribune* editorial "The Irascible Eighteen" (see fig. 94).[128]

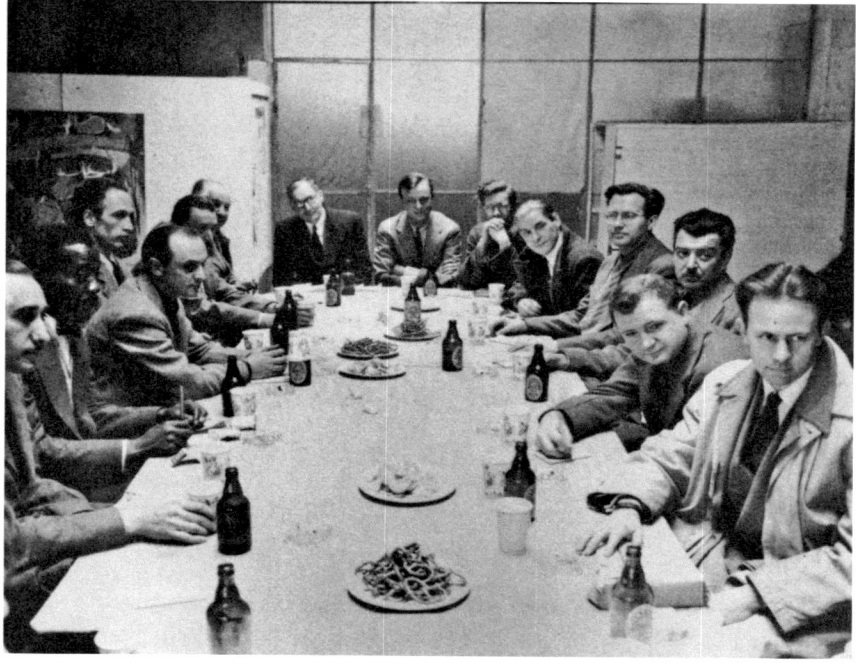

Figure 85
Max Yavno (1911–1985; born New York, NY; died Los Angeles, CA),
Artists' session at Studio 35, April 1950. From left: Seymour
Lipton, Norman Lewis, Jimmy Ernst, Peter Grippe, Adolph Gottlieb,
Hans Hofmann, Alfred H. Barr Jr., Robert Motherwell, Richard Lippold,
Willem de Kooning, Ibram Lassaw, James Brooks, Ad Reinhardt, and
Richard Pousette-Dart. Photographic print. The Museum of Modern
Art Archives

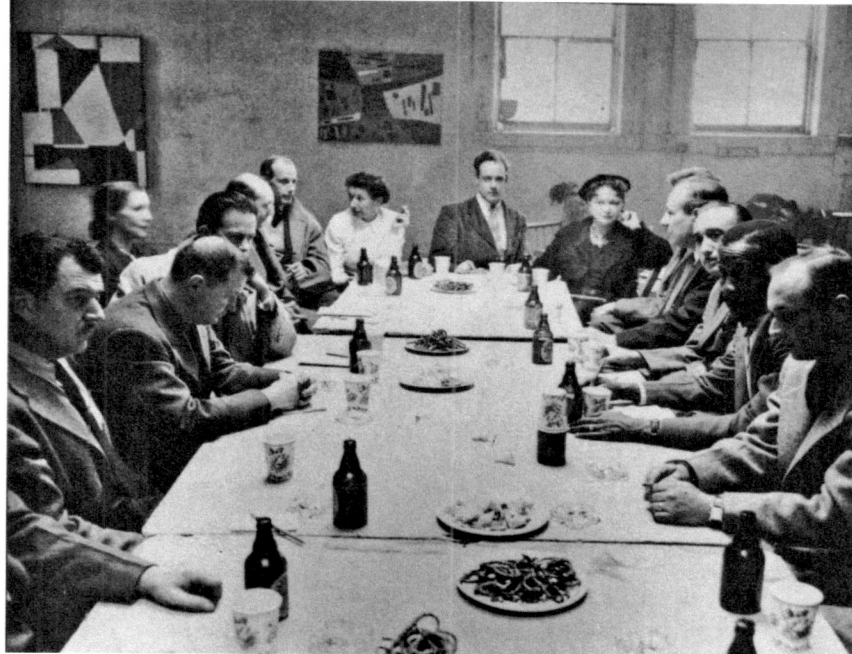

Figure 86
Max Yavno, Artists' session at Studio 35, April 1950. From
left: James Brooks, Ad Reinhardt, Richard Pousette-Dart, Louise
Bourgeois, Herbert Ferber, Bradley Walker Tomlin, Janice Biala,
Robert Goodnough, Hedda Sterne, David Hare, Barnett Newman,
Seymour Lipton, Norman Lewis, and Jimmy Ernst. Photographic print.
The Museum of Modern Art Archives

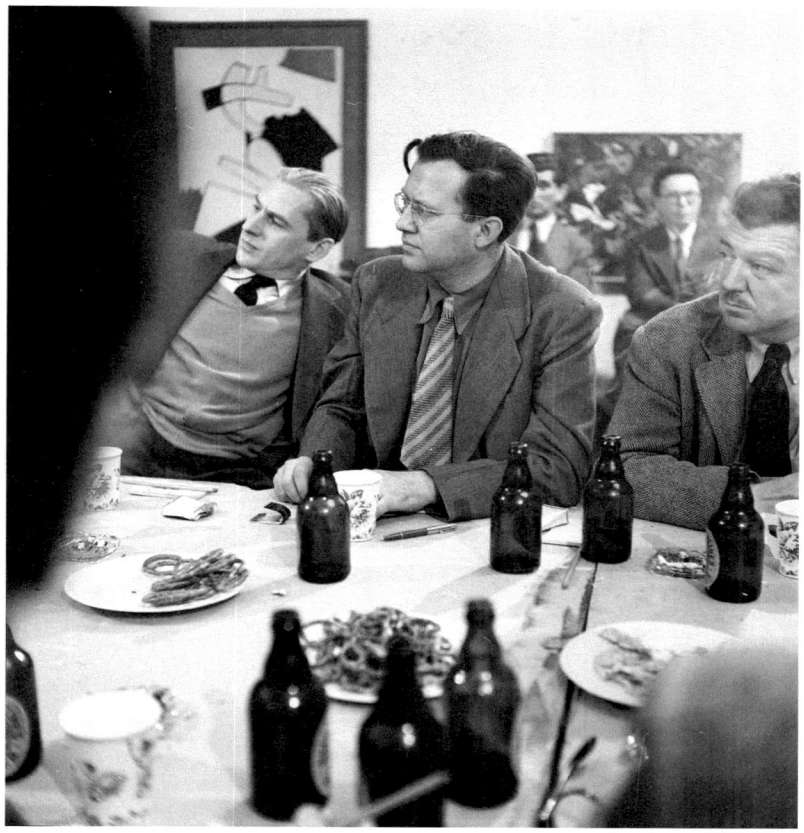

Figure 87
Aaron Siskind, Artists' session at Studio 35, April 1950.
Front row, from left: Willem de Kooning, Ibram Lassaw, James
Brooks; back row, from left: Weldon Kees and possibly Alfonso
Ossorio. Photographic print. Courtesy Ad Reinhardt Foundation

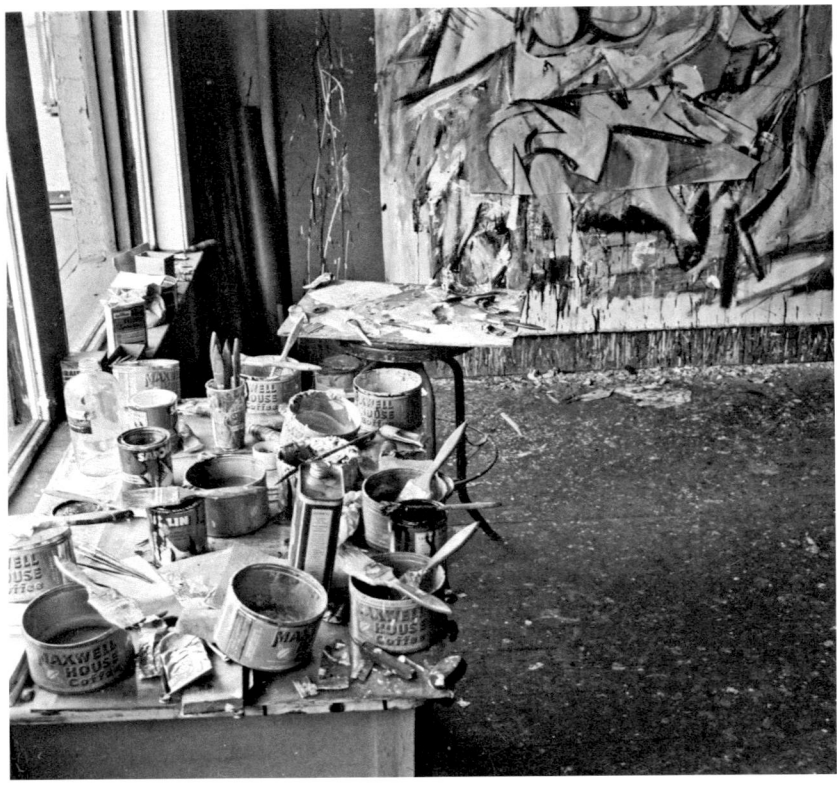

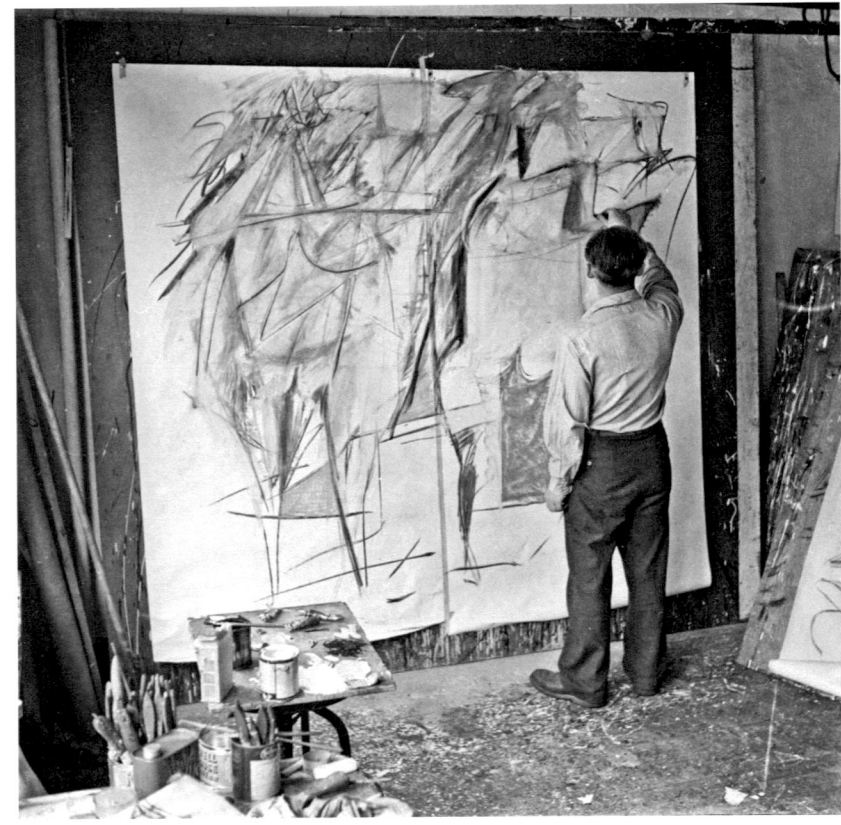

Figures 88–90
Rudolph (Rudy) Burckhardt (1914–1999; born Basel, Switzerland; died Searsmont, ME), **Willem de Kooning's studio with a box of rainbow plaster of Paris on the window-sill and artists' tube paints and cans of paint with the Sapolin label on the worktable, 1950. De Kooning working on drawings preliminary to** *Woman I***, 1950. De Kooning's studio looking out onto 4th Avenue, 1950.** Photographic prints. Estate of Rudy Burckhardt

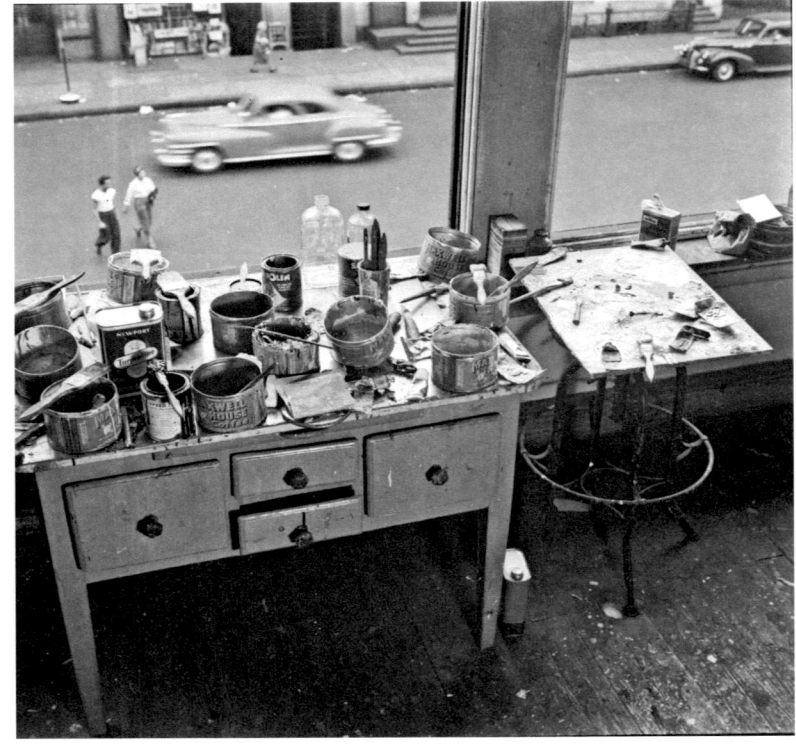

May 28 Emily Genauer publishes an essay that is critical of Barr's selection for the Venice Biennale on the basis that the artists—Gorky, de Kooning, and Pollock—have become the "official" representatives of advanced art at the exclusion of others.[129]

Early June De Kooning begins his third Woman series with *Woman I* (1950–52). He would continue to work on this composition for over two years.[130]

June Charles Egan Gallery presents an exhibition of new works by Isadore Levy.

June 8 Opening of the 25th Venice Biennale (figs. 91 and 92). Two of the American Pavilion's four rooms are dedicated to a retrospective of John Marin; one to abstract paintings by de Kooning, Gorky, and Pollock, selected by Alfred Barr Jr.; and another to "expressionist" paintings by Hyman Bloom, Lee Gatch, and Rico Lebrun, selected by Alfred Frankfurter.[131] In previous years, the US was represented by a large group of around eighty artists, with this being the first year to feature a focused selection. Germany participates for the first time since 1940, when Nazi officials had overseen its display.

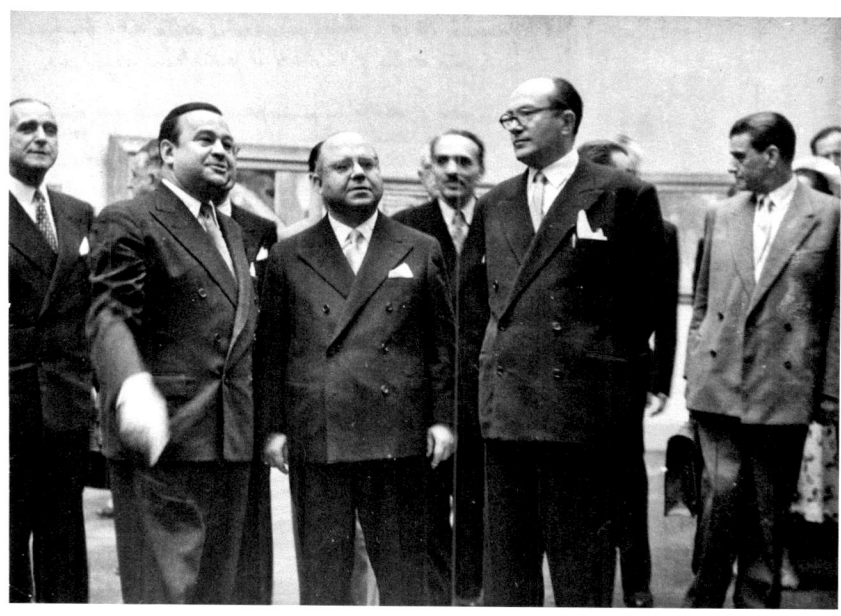

Figure 91

Mario Giacomelli (1925–2000; born Senigallia, Italy), **Visitors at the opening of the Venice Biennale in the American Pavilion, June 8, 1950.** From left: Alfred Frankfurter; Guido Gonella, Italian minister of public education; and Giovanni Ponti, president of the Biennale. Photographic print. Courtesy Archivio Storico della Biennale di Venezia, ASAC

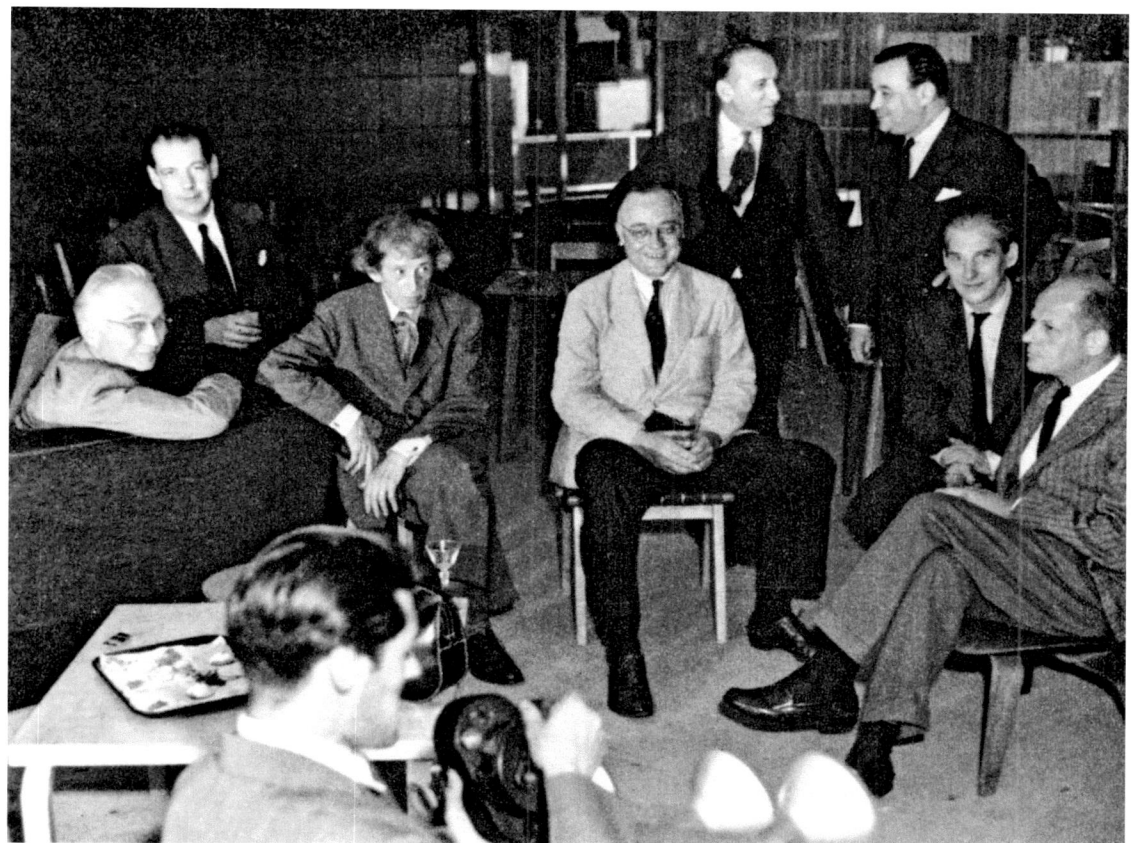

Figure 92

Jack Calderwood, Reception in the penthouse of the Museum of Modern Art, June 27, 1950, for American artists in the Venice Biennale. From left: Edward Steichen, René d'Harnoncourt, John Marin, Andrew Carnduff Ritchie, Lee Gatch, Alfred Frankfurter, Willem de Kooning, and Jackson Pollock. Photographic print. The Museum of Modern Art Archives

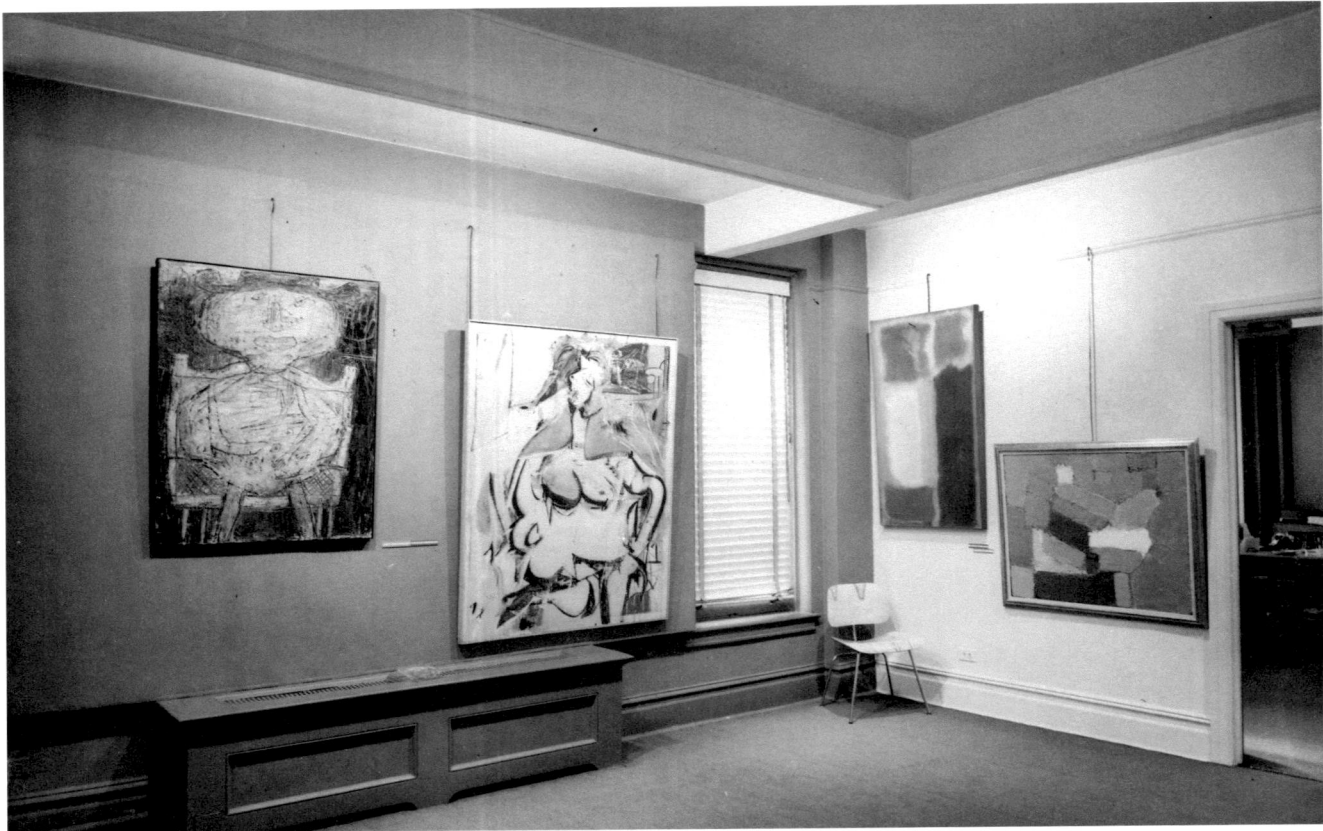

Figure 93
Installation view of *Young Painters in the U.S. and France*, Sidney Janis Gallery, New York, October 22, 1950. Paintings shown, from left: Jean Dubuffet, *L'homme au chapeau bleu*, 1950; Willem de Kooning, *Woman*, 1949; Mark Rothko, *No. 17/No. 15*, 1949; Nicolas de Staël, *Composition (Rouge)*, 1950. Photographic print

Figure 94
Nina Leen (1909–1995), **Portrait of the artists collectively known as "The Irascibles," New York, NY, November 24, 1950.** Front row, from left: Theodoros Stamos, Jimmy Ernst, Barnett Newman, James Brooks, and Mark Rothko. Middle row, from left: Richard Pousette-Dart, William Baziotes, Jackson Pollock, Clyfford Still, Robert Motherwell, and Bradley Walker Tomlin. Back row, from left: Willem de Kooning, Adolph Gottlieb, Ad Reinhardt, and Hedda Sterne. Photographic print. The LIFE Picture Collection / Shutterstock

June 16 The FBI arrests Julius and Ethel Rosenberg on charges that they passed to Soviet agents classified information about the US atomic bomb project.

June 27 De Kooning does not travel to Venice but attends a reception at MoMA for the artists representing the United States in Venice (fig. 92).

August 6 The Provincetown Art Association opens *Post-Abstract Painting 1950—France and America* with most of the "Irascibles" represented. De Kooning exhibits a work called *Black and Tan*, possibly *Event in a Barn* (1947) or *Abstraction* (1948).[132]

September 23 Congress overrides Truman's veto of the McCarran Internal Security Act, which requires communist and communist-dominated organizations to disclose their membership to the federal government. It also empowers the federal government to detain alleged subversives and to construct detention camps for holding them.

September 25 Sidney Janis Gallery opens *Challenge and Defy: Extreme Examples by XX Century Artists, French and American*. De Kooning exhibits *Woman* (see fig. 47).

Fall: De Kooning begins teaching twice a week at Yale University at the invitation of Josef Albers, now the chair of the Department of Design. After two semesters, de Kooning will recommend Franz Kline for the position.[133]

October *Magazine of Art* publishes Louis Finkelstein's "Marin and DeKooning," the first in-depth discussion of de Kooning's body of work beyond the context of an exhibition review. *Mailbox, Attic*, and *Painting* illustrate the essay, along with works by Marin. Finkelstein discusses the two artists as two sides of a "common development" in American art, "the one a man of nature . . . the other a city-dweller, filled with excited activity and a sophisticated, intellectual intricacy revealed in his twisting, writhing line."[134]

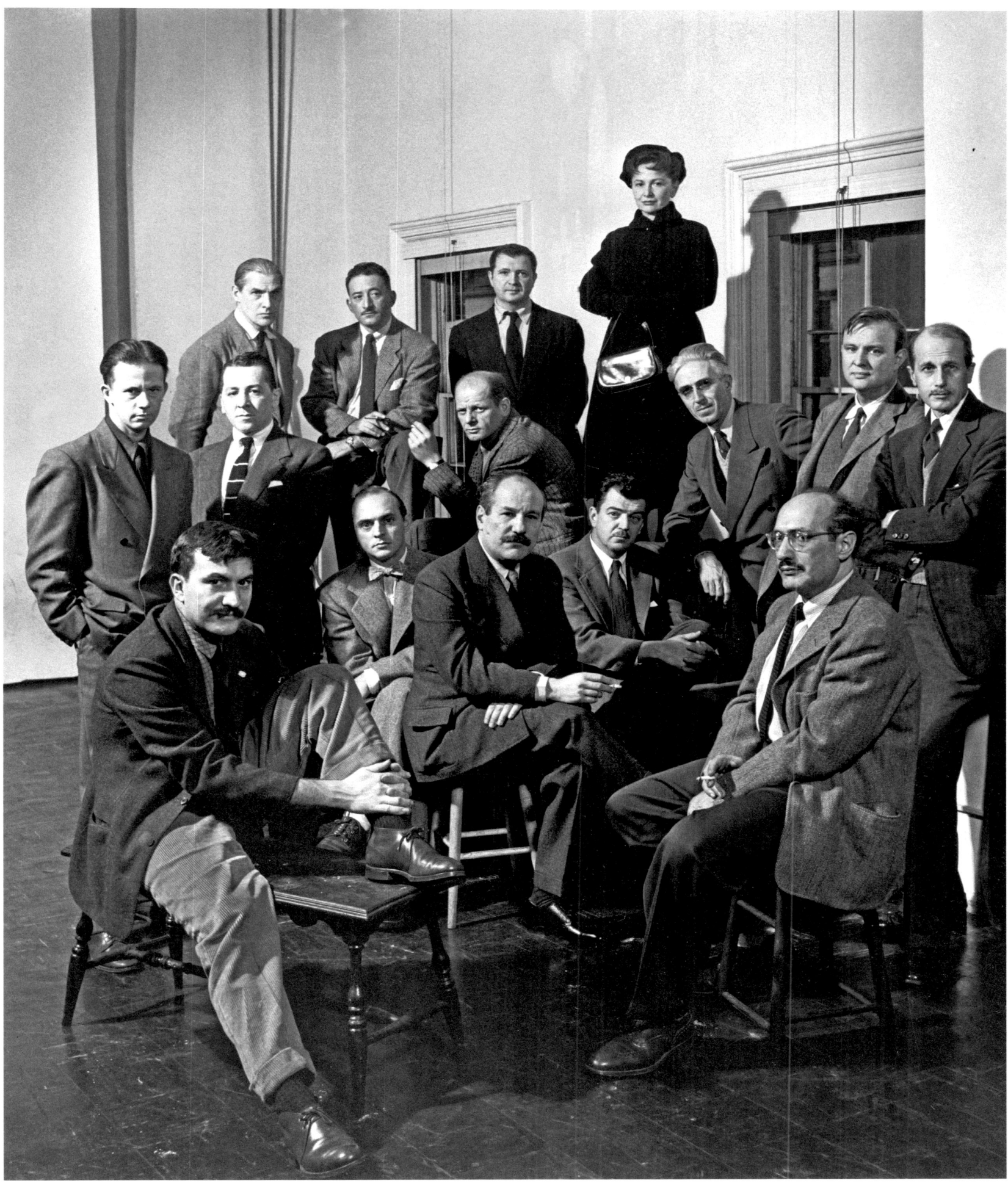

October 16 Charles Egan Gallery opens an exhibition of paintings by Franz Kline, the artist's first solo show.

October 22 Sidney Janis Gallery presents *Young Painters in the U.S. and France*, co-organized with Leo Castelli (fig. 93). The show pairs works by fifteen French and American painters including de Kooning's *Woman* (see fig. 47), a "blonde nude,"[135] and Dubuffet's *L'homme au chapeau bleu* (1950), as well as works by Gorky and Roberto Matta, Kline and Pierre Soulages, Pollock and André Lanskoy, Reinhardt and Nejad Melih Devrim, Rothko and Nicolas de Staël, and Tomlin and Raoul Ubac.

November 10 Opening of the Whitney Annual. De Kooning shows *Woman* (1949).[136]

November 25 The California Palace of the Legion of Honor, San Francisco, opens its *4th Annual Exhibition of Contemporary American Painting*. De Kooning exhibits *Untitled* (1948–49) in a group of works selected based on those discussed in *Life* magazine's "Round Table on Modern Art" in October 1948.[137]

December The New Gallery (63 West 44th Street) opens a group show with a drawing by de Kooning and works by L. Alcopley, James Forsberg, David Hare, Franz Kline, and Michael Stuart.[138]

Charles Egan Gallery presents an exhibition of boxes by Joseph Cornell.

December 8 The Metropolitan Museum of Art opens *American Painting Today—1950* representing more than three hundred artists from across the US. The so-called "Irascibles" are not among this group, having withheld their submissions as a form of protest.

The Charles Egan Gallery program has been reconstructed from advertisements and reviews in the *New York Herald Tribune*, the *New York Times,* and *MKR's Outlook*, a newsletter started by critic Maude Kemper Riley in 1945.

1. Mark Stevens and Annalyn Swan, *De Kooning: An American Master* (New York: Knopf, 2004), 146, 193–96.

2. Advertisement, Container Corporation of America, *Fortune* 31, no. 1 (January 1945): 191. For background on Container's collaborations with modern artists, see Neil Harris and Martina Roudabush Norelli, eds., *Art, Design, and the Modern Corporation* (Washington, DC: Smithsonian Institution Press, 1985). According to Stevens and Swan, *De Kooning*, 185, de Kooning entered the watercolor in an open competition to select works for Container's corporate collection.

3. George Cotkin, *Existential America* (Baltimore, MD: Johns Hopkins University Press, 2003), 112. According to Cotkin, Sartre was better known then as a resistance fighter than an existentialist, had little reputation as a philosopher, and spent little time with American intellectuals, preferring the French exile community, though he did enjoy jazz performances.

4. De Kooning is not mentioned in the exhibition catalogue. On his inclusion in the show, see the Edwin David Porter Papers, N-70-29, Archives of American Art, Smithsonian Institution, Washington, DC; cited in Delphine Huisinga, "Chronology," in *De Kooning: A Retrospective*, ed. John Elderfield, exh. cat. (New York: Museum of Modern Art, 2011), 83, 117n60.

5. Egbert Jacobson, ed., *Modern Art in Advertising: Designs for Container Corporation of America* (Chicago: P. Theobald, 1946), plate 48. The catalogue was published in 1946, and the exhibition toured until May 1949, including stops at Cranbrook Academy of Art, Cincinnati Contemporary Arts Center, Massachusetts Institute of Technology, Los Angeles County Museum of Art, San Francisco Museum of Modern Art, Portland Art Museum, Walker Art Center, and Davenport Municipal Art Gallery.

6. Stevens and Swan, *De Kooning*, 213–14.

7. Melvin Paul Lader, "Peggy Guggenheim's Art of This Century" (PhD diss., University of Delaware, 1981), 414.

8. Stevens and Swan, *De Kooning*, 214–15.

9. Huisinga, "Chronology," citing Harry Bowden's November dating on studio photographs.

10. Elaine de Kooning, quoted in John Gruen, *The Party's Over Now: Reminiscences of the Fifties* (New York: Viking, 1972), 210–11.

11. Cotkin, *Existential America*, 113–14. According to Cotkin, Sartre was celebrated as the leader of existentialism on this trip.

12. Irving Sandler, "Conversations with de Kooning," *Art Journal* 48, no. 3 (Fall 1989): 217.

13. "First Picasso Show in New York in 8 Years," *P.M.*, January 14, 1947, 10.

14. Ad Reinhardt, "How to Look at a Cubist Painting," *P.M.*, January 27, 1946, M5. Published in Ad Reinhardt, *How to Look: Ad Reinhardt Art Comics* (New York: David Zwirner, 2013).

15. Hess and Arb were first included on the masthead in February 1946.

16. Thomas Hess, "Editor's letters," *Art News* 56, no. 5 (September 1957): 58. The 1946 date coincides with Hess's first review in the magazine: Thomas Hess, "The Whitney Draws Slowly to the Left," *Art News* (March 1946): 29, 62.

17. Stevens and Swan, *De Kooning*, 224–25.

18. Robert Coates, *The New Yorker* (March 1950): 83.

19. "Dance Notes," *New York Herald Tribune,* March 31, 1946, D8; Walter Terry, "The Dance," *New York Herald Tribune,* April 6, 1946, 9A.

20. According to Elaine de Kooning, the artist agreed to complete the backdrop for $50 and used paint bought at the hardware store for $5; "Study for Labyrinth," object record sheet, May 30, 1989, Metropolitan Museum of Art. Marchowsky recalls that de Kooning and Resnick worked in her studio and created a system suspended from the ceiling for rolling the backdrop up and down; Judith Zilczer, "Notes of Telephone Interview with Marie Marchowsky," July 14, 1993, Judith K. Zilczer Papers, Archives of American Art, Smithsonian Institution, 96-098.02.50.

21. Howard Devree, "Diverse New Group," *New York Times*, May 26, 1946, X6; "News and Notes of Art," *New York Times,* May 20, 1946, 21; display ad, *New York Times,* May 26, 1946, X6.

22. Display ad, *New York Times,* May 19, 1946, X6.

23. Ad Reinhardt, "How to Look at Modern Art in America," *P.M.*, June 2, 1946, M13.

24. More than half of the paintings were sent to Eastern Europe (Prague, Czech Republic; Brno, Czech Republic; and Bratislava, Slovakia) after a stop in Paris. The rest were directed to locations in the Caribbean and Latin America, including Havana, Cuba, and Port-au-Prince, Haiti. Works on paper were set to travel to China and Southeast Asia but ultimately did not leave New York. See Taylor D. Littleton and Maltby Sykes, *Advancing American Art: Painting, Politics, and Cultural Confrontation at Mid-Century*, 2nd ed. (Tuscaloosa: The University of Alabama Press, 2005). The original exhibition was re-created almost in full for *Art Interrupted: Advancing American Art and the Politics of Cultural Diplomacy* (January 25–April 20, 2014), organized by the Fred Jones Jr. Museum of Art at the University of Oklahoma, Norman, OK; the Jule Collins Smith Museum of Fine Art at Auburn University, Auburn, AL; and the Georgia Museum of Art at the University of Georgia, Athens, GA. These university museums collectively owned 82 of the 117 works sold at auction as "war assets."

25. Clement Greenberg, *Nation* 163, no. 21 (November 26, 1946): 593–94. Other positive reviews ran in *Art News* and the *New Yorker*: Alfred Frankfurter, "American Art Abroad: The State Department's Collection," *Art News* 45, no. 8 (October 1946): 21–30; Robert Coates, "The Art Galleries," *New Yorker* (October 12, 1946): 84–85.

26. Willem de Kooning Academy, *"En terwijl ik naar bed gaat denk ik aan de Zaagmolenstraat": Twee brieven (1946 / 1948) van Willem de Kooning aan zijn vader* (Rotterdam: Willem de Kooning Academy Hogeschol, 2004), 20; cited in Huisinga, "Chronology," 123.

27. Ad Reinhardt, "How to Look at a Gallery," *P.M.,* December 1, 1946, M13; illustrated in *Ad Reinhardt Art Comics*, 61.

28. Reinhardt, "How to Look at a Gallery."

29. Stevens and Swan, *De Kooning*, 250–51, situate the creation of de Kooning's black-and-white paintings and the invitation from Egan in winter of 1947–48, consistent with the account of Betsy Duhrssen who met and married Charles Egan in 1948. Thomas B. Hess, *Willem de Kooning* (New York: George Braziller, 1959), 116, identifies the beginning of the black-and-white series in 1946. Edvard Lieber, *Willem de Kooning: Reflections in the Studio* (New York: Harry N. Abrams, 2000), 31, places Egan's invitation in September 1946.

30. See material analysis of *Black Friday* in this volume (pp. 125–35), and of *Painting* (1948) in Jim Coddington, "Methods and Materials: Painting," in Elderfield, *De Kooning: A Retrospective*, 175–77.

31. *Painting in France, 1939–1946*, exh. cat. (New York: Whitney Museum of American Art, 1947).

32. "Show of New Picassos," *MKR's Art Outlook*, February 3, 1947, 4.

33. Rosenberg's essay is reprinted in Robert Motherwell et al., eds., *Possibilities I: An Occasional Review*, Problems of Contemporary Art 4 (New York: Wittenborn Schultz, 1947).

34. Discussed by Alfred Barr Jr. in *Painting and Sculpture in the Museum of Modern Art* (New York: Museum of Modern Art, 1948), 11–12. The first transaction involved the sale of fourteen nineteenth-century American folk paintings and sculptures, and twenty-six modern European paintings, sculptures, and drawings. Honoré Daumier's *Laundress* was transferred permanently to the Met, which in turn lent MoMA Aristide Maillol's torso and Picasso's *Portrait of Gertrude Stein*.

35. George Dennison, "In Praise of What Persists," *American Poetry Review* 11, no. 6 (November–December 1982): 12.

36. This may have taken place in 1948 or 1949, based on Elaine de Kooning's memory; Harry F. Gaugh, *Franz Kline: The Vital Gesture* (New York: Abbeville, 1985), 170n12.

37. Elaine suggests Hess sought de Kooning out in response to Renée Aro's review; see Judith Zilczer, *Willem de Kooning: From the Hirshhorn Museum Collection* (Washington, DC: Hirshhorn Museum and Sculpture Garden, 1993), 36. In Stevens and Swan, *De Kooning*, 277, Hess met de Kooning after he reviewed the artist's contribution to the Whitney Annual. Hess was first listed on the *Art News* masthead as managing editor in January 1948.

38. Sally Yard, unpublished conversations with de Kooning, October 15, 1976, The Willem de Kooning Foundation. See discussion in Zilczer, *From the Hirshhorn Museum Collection*, 21, 23, 34. Edwin Denby, *In Public, In Private* (Prairie City, IL: Decker, 1948), 6, 12. Denby's own first-edition copy indicates that the last two lines of the poem should be swapped, a change realized in subsequent editions; I thank Jacob Burckhardt for this insight.

39. Serge Guilbaut writes, "the radicalism that had once been central to the magazine's interests gave way to liberalism," in *How New York Stole the Idea of Modern Art: Abstract Expressionism, Freedom, and the Cold War* (Chicago: University of Chicago Press, 1985), 165. He notes the possibility that the CIA played an important role in this change, citing James Burkhart Gilbert, *Writers and Partisans: A History of Radicalism in American* (New York: Wiley, 1968), 274–75, who "implies but does not document" this idea, 240n1.

40. *Partisan Review* 15, no. 1 (January 1948).

41. According to Elaine de Kooning, "[It] knocked him out. . . . It was crucial. It looked like the work of a civilization—not one man," quoted in Sally Yard, *Willem de Kooning: Works, Writings, Interview* (Barcelona: Ediciones Polígrafa, 2007), 43.

42. Mercedes Matter remembers that she intended to write a letter to Giacometti, and that de Kooning and Milton Resnick agreed to sign it, but that the letter was never completed; December 19, 1986, Mercedes Matter, interview by Sigmund Koch, Sigmund Koch collection, Howard Gottlieb Archival Research Center, Boston University, courtesy of The Willem de Kooning Foundation.

43. *Black Mountain College Bulletin* 6, no. 2 (March 1948), Black Mountain College Records, Western Regional Archives, 506.2.26.26. Siskind would teach at Black Mountain in the summer of 1950.

44. "Willem de Kooning," *Magazine of Art* 41, no. 2 (February 1948): 54.

45. James S. Plaut, "'Modern Art' and the American Public: A Statement by The Institute of Contemporary Art," February 17, 1948, The Boston Institute of Contemporary Art. According to J. Pedro Lorente, the ICA took issue with MoMA's preference for Cubism, Surrealism, and abstraction, and sought to include more humanist painting, but was understood as issuing an attack on Abstract Expressionism in favor of Regionalism; J. Pedro Lorente, *The Museums of Contemporary Art: Notion and Development* (London and New York: Routledge, 2016), 190.

46. Clement Greenberg, "Art," *Nation* 166, no. 12 (March 20, 1948): 331.

47. Elaine recalls de Kooning saw Gorky last at the opening in Lieber, *Reflections in the Studio*, 122. Milton Resnick recalls he and de Kooning had a chance encounter with Gorky in the streets in the days following, in Hayden Hererra, *Arshile Gorky: His Life and Work* (New York: Macmillan, 2003), 564.

48. *Tiger's Eye* 3 (March 1948): 101; reproduction credited "Collection John Stephan." Elaine recalls that John and Ruth Stephan titled the painting without de Kooning's approval; Charles Stuckey, "Bill de Kooning and Joe Christmas," *Art in America* 68, no. 3 (March 1980): 77, but the Stephans have maintained they would not have done so; Stevens and Swan, *De Kooning*, 656.

49. Judith Arlene Bookbinder, *Boston Modern: Figurative Expressionism as Alternative Modernism* (Hanover: University of New Hampshire Press, 2005), 227; "Report on the Panel Discussion Sponsored by the Modern Art Group of Boston," March 25, 1948, Alfred H. Barr Papers, The Museum of Modern Art Archives, reel 3263:0824.

50. Cathy Curtis, *A Generous Vision: The Creative Life of Elaine de Kooning* (New York: Oxford University Press, 2017), 53.

51. Zilczer, *From the Hirshhorn Museum Collection*, 190.

52. Stuckey, "Bill de Kooning and Joe Christmas," 70–71; Curtis, *Generous Vision*, 39

53. Renée Arb, "Spotlight on de Kooning," *Art News* 47, no. 2 (April 1948): 33.

54. Paul V. Beckley, "Art Exhibition Notes: Non-Objective Art," *New York Herald Tribune,* April 20, 1948, 27; referenced in "Our Box Score of the Critics," *Art News* 47, no. 4 (Summer 1948): 52.

55. Clement Greenberg, "Art," *Nation* 166, no. 17 (April 24, 1948): 448.

56. Sam Hunter, "By Groups and Singly; French Graphics—Racing—Odets—de Kooning," *New York Times,* April 25, 1948, X11.

57. Clement Greenberg, "The Crisis of the Easel Picture," *Partisan Review* 15, no. 4 (April 1948): 481–84; illustrations inserted between 448 and 449, 480 and 481.

58. Emily Genauer, "De Kooning's First Solo Hard to Pin Down: De Kooning a Puzzle," *New York World-Telegram,* May 4, 1948, 29.

59. See discussion in Guilbaut, *How New York Stole the Idea of Modern Art*, 181.

60. Draft letter from Paul Burlin, Carl Holty, and B. Tomlin, March 12, 1948, Paul Burlin Papers, Archives of American Art, 01.01.20.

61. De Kooning did not respond to the letter but may have been in the audience. No list of attendees has been found.

62. Adolph Gottlieb's statement published in Clifford Ross, *Abstract Expressionism: Creators and Critics* (New York: Harry N. Abrams, 1990), 52–54, quote on 53. Gottlieb was one of five speakers, along with Paul Burlin, Stuart Davis, George L. K. Morris, and James Johnson Sweeney. Speeches by Paul Burlin, Morris, and Stuart Davis printed in "The Modern Artist Speaks," press release, May 6, 1948, Paul Burlin Papers, 01.01.20. The speeches were followed by a roundtable.

63. John Cage remembers recommending de Kooning to Albers; Mary Emma Harris, May 1, 1974, New York City, Oral History Collection, Special Collections Research Center, Appalachian State University, Boone, North Carolina, 23. Martin Duberman also suggests that John Cage and Merce Cunningham influenced the de Koonings' decision to go to Black Mountain in *Black Mountain College: An Exploration in Community* (Garden City, NY: Anchor Books, 1973), 293. Elaine recalls that Renée Arb's review of the Egan exhibition prompted Albers to contact de Kooning; Elaine de Kooning, "De Kooning Memories," *Vogue* 173 (December 1983): 352.

64. Pat Passlof, "1948: The Author's Studies with Willem de Kooning," *Art Journal* 48, no. 3 (Fall 1989): 229.

65. Western Regional Archives, Black Mountain College Records, 02.35.17; Western Regional Archives, Course cards. Full list of de Kooning's students: Stella Balderston, Anne Banks, Gustave Falk, Joseph Fiore, Ruth Goldenberg, Maccabi Greenfield, Bruce Johns, Margaret Jones, Roger Lovelace, Etta Mandelbaum, James Robert Orr, Mary Phelan Outten, Patricia Passlof, Raymond Spillenger, Donald Thrall, Florence Weinstein, and Richard Yonkers.

66. Mary Emma Harris, V. V. Rankine, February 19, 1971, New York City, Western Regional Archives, Asheville, North Carolina, 26. This account echoes that of Donald Thrall; Mary Emma Harrris, Donald Thrall, April 22, 1992, New York City, Oral History Collection, Special Collections Research Center, Appalachian State University, Boone, North Carolina—"I painted with de Kooning. He didn't really teach. We just sort of painted freely. And then observed other people," 3—and Kenneth Noland, who did not study with de Kooning—"I mean he didn't teach really. He said early on that he would come to people's studio and talk with them if they wanted him to come in . . ." (n.p.), Mary Emma Harris and Kenneth Noland, January 29, 1998, North Bennington, Vermont, Oral History Collection, Appalachian State University—as well as Etta Mandelbaum—"He did not give classes that I remember. . . . he more or less said, 'If you need me, I will come,'" Mary Emma Harris, Etta Mandelbaum Deikman, February 24, 1998, Mill Valley, California, Oral History Collection, Appalachian State University, 3.

67. Passlof, "1948," 229.

68. Elaine de Kooning, "De Kooning Memories," 394.

69. Mary Emma Harris, Ruth Asawa, February 17, 1998, San Francisco, Oral History Collection, Appalachian State University. "I remember de Kooning had a show in the dining hall on the walls. We ate on the porch and on the walls were his paintings," 31; Mary Emma Harris, Charles Burchard, October 12, 1971, Blacksburg, Virginia, Western Regional Archives, recalls "several exhibits of his work," 3; Mary Emma Harris, Patricia Passlof, January 11, 1997, New York City, Oral History Collection, Appalachian State University, Boone, "'Asheville' must have come right afterwards, when he got back to New York . . . They were, you know, the black and white enamel things on paper . . . I remember the ones that he had in that show at the school . . . these were really the black and white sort of dripped paintings . . . they were really painted with a brush," 12; Mary Emma Harris, V. V. Rankine, February 19, 1971, "He worked in his house on the floor . . . I can remember a show that he put up in the dining room…Part of it in the dining room and part of it on the porch. . . . And it was mostly collage, some of those great early collage. . . . There were like fifteen works. Small, I think he worked quickly . . . the price of each one of them was fifty dollars. And no one bought them," 27–28; Mary Emma Harris, Kenneth Snelson, February 28, 2000, New York City, Oral History Collection, Appalachian State University, "Bill's were painted on newsprint, I think, as I recall, with house enamel, and they were taped up with masking tape on the corners," 23; Mary Emma Harris, Donald Thrall, April 22, 1992, "I remember he did a number of small studies for it [Asheville], and some the same size. I think he did several variations of this one, as I recall," 12.

70. Elaine de Kooning, "De Kooning Memories," 394; Mary Emma Harris, Patricia Passlof, January 11, 1997, 12.

71. Rudi Blesh, *Modern Art USA: Men, Rebellion, Conquest, 1900–1956* (New York: Knopf, 1956), 259.

72. Cage found a copy of Daniel-Henry Kahnweiler's 1921 edition, with illustrations by Georges Braque, at the New York Public Library in the Rare Books Collection. He then had the play translated by Mary Carolyn (M. C.) Richards. Martin Duberman, "Phone interview with John Cage," April 26, 1969, Western Regional Archives, 6–7.

73. Elaine notes this is a technique he had been taught as a teenager while working in a decorator's shop in Holland; Elaine de Kooning, "De Kooning Memories," 394.

74. Huising, "Chronology," notes the image resembles the Woman paintings photographed in de Kooning's studio in November 1946 and two circa-1947 figure compositions, 190.

75. Mary Emma Harris, Buckminster Fuller, October 3, 1971, oral history interview, Washington, DC, Western Regional Archives, Asheville, North Carolina, 1.

76. Martin Duberman, "Phone interview with John Cage," April 26, 1969, 8.

77. Pat Grant, "Dance Recital Evaluated; Explained by Performers," *Vassar Chronicle* (March 12, 1949): 3; cited in David Wayne Patterson, "Appraising the Catchwords, c. 1942–1959: John Cage's Asian-Derived Rhetoric" (PhD diss., Columbia University, 1996), 301.

78. Elaine de Kooning, "De Kooning Memories," 394.

79. Mary Emma Harris, Gustave Falk, December 15–16, 2002, Provence, France, Oral History Collection, Appalachian State University, 30; Passlof, "1948," 229; Etta Mandelbaum Deikman, February 24, 1998, Mill Valley, California, Oral History Collection, Appalachian State University, 10.

80. Dorothy Seckler, Samuel Kootz, April 13, 1964, Oral history interview, Archives of American Art; "In the Art Galleries," *New York Herald Tribune*, September 19, 1948, C6.

81. See David Sylvester et al., eds., *Willem de Kooning: Paintings*, exh. cat. (Washington, DC: National Gallery of Art, 1994), 97.

82. Tworkov would remain there until 1953, per Huisinga, "Chronology," 190.

83. Charles Egan to Alfred H. Barr Jr., October 19, 1948. Willem de Kooning files, Museum Collection Files, Department of Painting and Sculpture, The Museum of Modern Art.

84. "A Life Round Table on Modern Art," *Life* (October 11, 1948): 56–8, 62.

85. René d'Harnoncourt, "Challenge and Promise: Modern Art and Modern Society," *Magazine of Art* 41 (November 1948): 251–52. The essay expands on a talk the author gave at a meeting of the American Federation of the Arts in May of that year.

86. Thomas Hess, "The Whitney: Exhibit Abstract," *Art News* 47, no. 8 (December 1948): 24–62. Clement Greenberg reviewed the show in *The Nation* 167, no. 24 (December 11, 1948): 675–76, writing that *Mailbox* "is the best thing present and it is not deKooning at his strongest either."

87. Robert Motherwell and Ad Reinhardt, eds., *Modern Artists in America* (New York: Wittenborn Schultz, 1951), 9. Clyfford Still was involved in early planning, and Barnett Newman joined later. Newman took over the planning of Friday-night lectures from Motherwell.

88. Taylor argued that museums should not lower their standards for the art of the present. For context on the antagonism between modern and contemporary art in 1948, see Aline Louchheim, "'Modern Art': Attack and Defense: A Survey of Arguments on an Old Problem During the Year," *New York Times*, December 26, 1948, X11.

89. Willem de Kooning, *Art News* 47, no. 9 (January 1949): 6. According to Elaine de Kooning, there was a misconception that she had written the essay on Gorky, beginning the convention at *Art News* of including authors, initials with reviews, which were previously unattributed; Curtis, *Generous Vision*, 55. In fact, Elaine's initials began appearing in the following issue, published in February 1949.

90. Sam Hunter, "Among the New Shows," *New York Times,* January 30, 1949, X9; Paul V. Beckley, "Art Exhibition Notes," *New York Herald Tribune*, January 25, 1949, 23.

91. De Kooning stated in the introduction to his speech that Motherwell gave the talk its title. Motherwell may have also delivered the lecture itself, using de Kooning's transcript, per Huisinga, "Chronology," 235n18, based on a note written by Annalee Newman related to the typescript held at the Barnett Newman Foundation, New York.

92. "Revolt in Boston: Shootin' Resumes in the Art World," *Life* (February 21, 1949): 84–89; *Painting and Sculpture in the Museum of Modern Art* (New York: Museum of Modern Art, 1948), 6.

93. "Non-Objective Art Shown at Peridot," *New York Times,* April 8, 1949, 23. Elaine de Kooning reviewed the Peridot show in *Art News* 48, no. 2 (April 1949): 56.

94. The session is transcribed and published along with an exhibition checklist in Motherwell and Reinhardt, *Modern Artists in America,* 24–38; reprinted in Ann Eden Gibson, *Issues in Abstract Expressionism: The Artist-Run Periodicals* (Ann Arbor, MI: UMI Research Press, 1990), 345–94.

95. Motherwell and Reinhardt, *Modern Artists in America,* 9.

96. Rosalind Browne, "Art World Eyes Forum 49 Program of Abstract Work and Discussions," *Provincetown Advocate,* July 7, 1949, 2.

97. Weldon Kees to Adolph Gottlieb, June 11, 1949, Tony Vevers Papers, Box 3, Folder 4, Archives of American Art.

98. Weldon Kees to Adolph Gottlieb, June 24, 1949, Tony Vevers Papers, Box 3, Folder 4, Archives of American Art; "Forum 49 Spotlights Early Pioneers In Modern Art Movement In America," *Provincetown Advocate,* June 30, 1949, 1. Elaine de Kooning describes works included in "Record Exhibit of Paintings Shown," *Cape Cod Standard Times,* July 5, 1949, 1–2.

99. "Provincetown and Days Lumberyard: A Memoir," in *Days Lumberyard Studios, Provincetown 1914–1971* (Provincetown, MA: Provincetown Art Association and Museum, 1978), 17–18.

100. "15 Speakers Listed for Last Forum," *Provincetown Advocate,* August 25, 1949, 3.

101. "Shore Studios and Gallery 200 Notes," *Provincetown Advocate,* August 25, 1949, 2.

102. Emily Genauer, "Still Life with Red Herring," *Harper's* (September 1949): 91. She was responding to George A. Dondero, "Communist Art in Government Hospitals," Congressional Record, 81st Congress, 1st session, March 11, 1949, 95: 2317–18. Dondero responded to Genauer in "Letters," *Harper's* (December 1949): 18. The full list of artists is given in "Red Tint Denied in Art Show at Naval Hospital," *New York Herald Tribune,* April 3, 1949, 34.

103. There is disagreement over when The Club was formed. Philip Pavia placed this event in 1948 and in 1949 on different occasions; for example, 1949 in Bruce Hooton, Philip Pavia, January 19, 1965, oral history interview, Archives of American Art, and 1948 in an interview in Emile de Antonio and Mitch Tuchman, eds., *Painters Painting: A Candid History of the Modern Art Scene, 1940–1970* (New York: Abbeville, 1984), 39; and Gruen, *Party's Over Now,* 268–69.

104. De Kooning discusses The Club in James T. Valliere, "De Kooning on Pollock: An Interview," *Partisan Review* 34, no. 4 (Fall 1967): 604. For more information on The Club, see Dore Ashton, *The New York School: A Cultural Reckoning* (New York: Viking, 1973), 193–208; Gruen, *Party's Over Now*; Philip Pavia, *Club Without Walls: Selections from the Journals of Philip Pavia,* ed. Natalie Edgar (New York: Midmarch Arts, 2007); Irving Sandler, "The Club," *Artforum* 4 (September 1965): 27–31; Irving Sandler, *A Sweeper-Up After Artists: A Memoir* (New York: Thames & Hudson, 2003).

105. Ross, *Abstract Expressionism,* 298.

106. José Ortega y Gasset, "On the Point of View of the Arts," *Partisan Review* 16, no. 8 (August 1949): 822–36.

107. Carlyle Burrows, "Art: Two New Abstract Shows," *New York Herald Tribune,* September 25, 1949, C7; Stuart Preston, "By Husband and Wife," *New York Times,* September 25, 1949, X9.

108. Steven Naifeh and Gregory White Smith, *Jackson Pollock: An American Saga* (New York: Clarkson N. Potter, 1989), 598.

109. Thomas Hess, "8 Excellent, 20 Good, 133 Others," *Art News* (January 1950): 34.

110. For a discussion of *Excavation,* see Lauren Mahony, "Around Excavation" and "An Enormous Deed," in Elderfield, *De Kooning: A Retrospective,* 188–89, 208–22.

111. Published in *trans/formation* 1, no. 2 (1951).

112. Thomas Hess, "When Art Talk Was a Fine Art," *New York* 8, no. 1 (December 30, 1974): 82. Huisinga ("Chronology") considers two reasons why de Kooning may not have delivered his own talk: insecurity about his Dutch accent and concern that Elaine had changed it too extensively in revision, 196, 235n36; citing Fairfield Porter, June 6, 1968, oral history interview, Archives of American Art; Annalee Newman remembered that de Kooning refused to read the talk because of Elaine's revisions; see Richard Shiff, "de Kooning Controlling de Kooning," in Cornelia H. Butler et al., *Willem de Kooning: Tracing the Figure* (Los Angeles: Museum of Contemporary Art, 2002), 167n71.

113. "Vogue Presents 53 Living American Artists," *Vogue* 115, no. 2 (February 1950): 150–52. *Little Attic* appears in an unfinished state.

114. March 22, 1950, etched into the stereoscope slide in the collection of Lawrence Lewitin.

115. Thomas Hess, "Black or White," *Art News* 49, no. 1 (March 1950): 45.

116. De Kooning was in fact forty-five years old and would turn forty-six the following month. "A Symposium: The State of American Art," *Magazine of Art* 42, no. 3 (March 1949): 82–102.

117. Date etched onto stereoscopic slides, The Landès Lewitin Foundation.

118. Emily Genauer, "Art and Artists: Questions of Museum Policy Raised by Statement of Three Institutions, *New York Herald Tribune,* April 2, 1950, C5. *Newsday* writes, the "manifesto . . . might touch off a Congressional investigation any day now"; "It's 'Vital'—Is It Art?," *Newsday,* March 29, 1950, 47.

119. Aline Louchheim, *New York Times,* April 2, 1950, 104.

120. Dorothy Miller to Alfred Frankfurter, April 25, 1950. The Museum of Modern Art Archives, AHB.I.546; cited in Huisinga, "Chronology," 193, 235n54. Huisinga notes the dimensions and provenance given for *The Mirror* in the catalogue match those of *Dark Pond. Mailbox* (see fig. 21) was lent by Nelson Rockefeller, *Light in August* (see fig. 18) and *Excavation* (see fig. 51) by Charles Egan, and *The Mirror* (likely *Dark Pond*) (see fig. 41) by Jeanne Reynal. See *XXXV Biennale di Venezia,* exh. cat. (Venice: Alfieri Editore, 1950).

121. Shipping arrangements are discussed in letter from Dorothy Miller to Alfred Frankfurter, April 25, 1950. Alfred H. Barr Papers, The Museum of Modern Art Archives, AHB I.A.601; mf2198:1361.

122. Martha Bourdrez, "De Kooning: Painter of Promise; A Dutch Rebel on His Way to the Top," *Knickerbocker* 12, no. 5 (May 1950): 8.

123. The moderators were Alfred H. Barr Jr., Richard Lippold, and Robert Motherwell. Contributions from de Kooning are featured in Motherwell and Reinhardt, *Modern Artists in America*, 231–22, 323, 325, 327, 328, 329, 336, 337, 338, 340, 341, 343, 344.

124. "New Art Offerings in Galleries Here," *New York Times*, May 15, 1950, 17; Stuart Preston, "Diversely Modern," *New York Times*, May 21, 1950, X6.

125. The *New York Times* and the *New York Herald Tribune* reported on the letter in the days that followed, and *The Nation* reprinted the letter on June 3 with commentary by Weldon Kees—"18 Painters Boycott Metropolitan; Chare 'Hostility to Advanced Art'," *New York Times*, May 22, 1950, 1, 15; "The Irascible Eighteen," *New York Herald Tribune*, May 23, 1950, 18; Weldon Kees, "Art," *Nation* 170, no. 22 (June 3, 1950): 556–57.

126. See Bradford R. Collings et al., eds., *The Irascibles: Painters Against the Museum, New York, 1950* (Madrid: Fondación March, 2020).

127. "Irascible Group of Advanced Artists Led Fight Against Show," *Life* (January 15, 1951): 34.

128. "The Irascible Eighteen," *New York Herald Tribune,* May 23, 1950, 18.

129. Emily Genauer, "Art and Artists: American Selection For Venice Show; Does It Represent Us as It Should?," *New York Herald Tribune*, May 28, 1950, section 5, p. 5.

130. See Thomas Hess, "De Kooning Paints a Picture," *Art News* 52, no. 1 (March 1953): 30–32, 64–67.

131. The gallery layout is described in Aline Louchheim, *New York Times*, May 28, 1950, 55. The catalogue includes introductions written by Alfred Barr Jr., Alfred Frankfurter, and Duncan Phillips discussing their respective selection of artists, in Italian; *XXXV Biennale di Venezia*. *Art News* published these in August, in English: "7 Americans Open in Venice," *Art News* (June–August 1950): 20–25, 59–60.

132. *Post-Abstract Painting 1950—France and America* (Provincetown, MA: Hawthorne Memorial Gallery, Provincetown Art Association, 1950), Provincetown Art Association and Museum archives.

133. De Kooning to Josef Albers, n.d., MS32, Box 1, Folder 5, Josef Albers Papers, Manuscripts and Archives, Yale University Library.

134. Louis Finkelstein, "Marin and DeKooning," *Magazine of Art* (October 1950): 203–6.

135. Manny Farber, "Art," *Nation* 171, no. 20 (November 11, 1950): 445.

136. It was exhibited with the title *Figure*; *1950 Annual Exhibition of Contemporary American Painting*, exh. cat. (New York: Whitney Museum of American Art, 1950). *Woman* (1949) is identified in Sally Yard, *Willem de Kooning: The First Twenty-Six Years in New York* (New York and London: Garland, 1986), 155.

137. It is illustrated in the catalogue with title *Black and White*, lent by Charles Egan Gallery. A letter from Charles Egan to Alfred Barr Jr. indicates the exhibition was conceived "based on the *Life* magazine symposium"; February 14, 1949, Willem de Kooning files, Museum Collection Files, Department of Painting and Sculpture, The Museum of Modern Art.

138. "Some Holiday Art at Galleries Here," *New York Times*, December 8, 1950, 27.

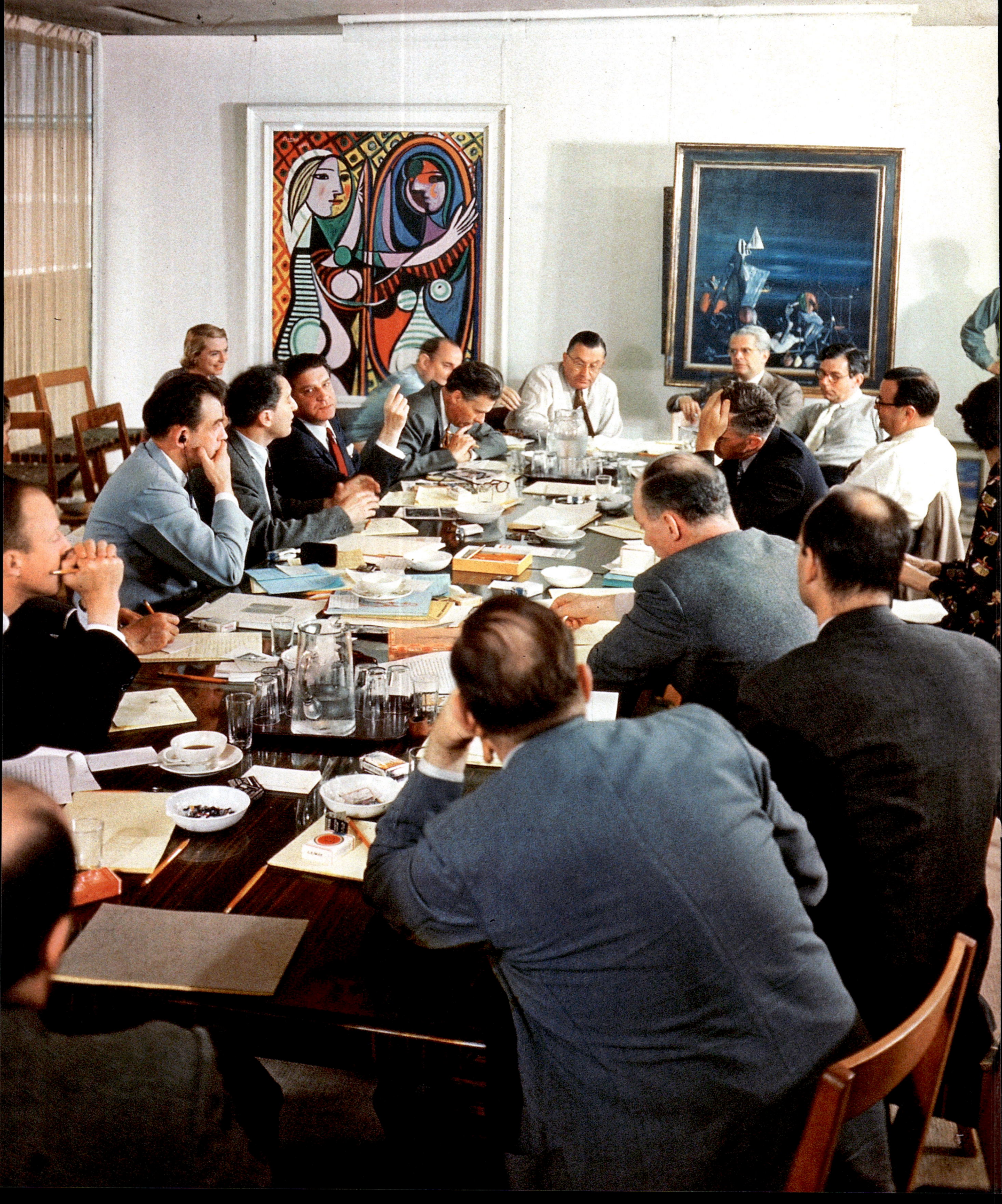

1948:
A Remarkable
Year for the
American
Avant-Garde

MITRA ABBASPOUR

> Decidedly, the past year has been a remarkably good one for American art. Now, as if suddenly, we are introduced by Willem de Kooning's first show. . . . to one of the four or five most important painters in the country.
>
> —Clement Greenberg, April 24, 1948[1]

Clement Greenberg, by now New York's most celebrated art critic, thus proclaimed Willem de Kooning's first solo exhibition, at the Charles Egan Gallery in 1948, a watershed event for both the artist and American art. The preceding October, Greenberg had published the lengthy essay "The Present Prospects of American Painting and Sculpture," in which he addressed the dependency of most American artists on those in Europe, and the promise provided by a few artists, including David Smith and Jackson Pollock, not yet mentioning de Kooning.[2] His first published essay in 1948 had been "The Situation at the Moment," in which he opined: "As dark as the situation still is for us, American painting in its most advanced aspects—that is, American abstract painting—has in the last several years shown here and there a capacity for fresh content that does not seem to be matched either in France or Great Britain."[3]

In characterizing de Kooning's exhibition as a signpost of the state of the nation's avant-garde, Greenberg was both proselytizing his vision of the future and reflecting on the development of an American modernism in relationship to gallery infrastructure, museum representation, and art-critical discourse in New York in the two and a half years since the end of World War II. The previous year, he had written that "it is still downtown that the fate of American art is being decided—by young people, few of them over forty, who live in cold-water flats and exist from hand to mouth. Now they all paint in the abstract vein."[4] Independence from Europe and from representational painting became Greenberg's watchwords, and they carried influence in shaping a rapidly expanding critical conversation and art market for the new painting in the United States. Such was true of the paintings de Kooning selected for presentation at his 1948 exhibition, which came to embody his preeminent place in the artistic avant-garde of his time. The impact of Greenberg's writings was not only in shaping the developments to come but also in his full-throated defense of the new artistic approaches—specifically those that would come to define Abstract Expressionism—approaches that were far from accepted, and indeed were often perceived as threateningly oblique or overly European, both among his fellow art critics and in the popular press.

The paintings de Kooning presented at Egan Gallery were the outcome of a time of intense exploration undertaken by the artist over more than a year preceding the opening.[5] It was a time of enormous transformation not only for de Kooning. In the three years following World War II and through the reelection of Harry Truman as president, the United States' alliances and standing on the world stage were at the center of political discourse. In the wake of the war's overwhelming devastation and with further atrocities coming to light in the press, a determination to defend against another war was widespread; how best to do so, however, was a subject of heated debate. Former political alliances and ideologies (both communism and the value of public art chief among these) were tested, as the Soviet Union consolidated power, annexing the countries that came to be known as the Eastern Bloc, and many European economies lay in ruin. Yet, it was the conditions of this transitional period, writes the art historian Serge Guilbaut, that gave rise to the innovations and figures that established the dominance of postwar American art. He describes the era as "a rare moment in modern American history, a time when there was again diversity in political debate, a brief interval sandwiched between the left-wing uniformity of the New Deal in the thirties and the right-wing uniformity of the fifties. . . . Not only political but also artistic commitments were being questioned: there were battles, splits, shifts, reorganizations, and redefinitions, even as new positions began to solidify."[6] Reflecting on his experiences in the postwar years, the American writer George Dennison echoes these sentiments, describing these years as "a time of grim discoveries. The true extent of the Holocaust was becoming known. . . . The list might go on and on. Anxiety and

doubt were not unreasonable states. At the same time, energy (and pent-up energy) had been released. One felt it especially in the arts. A complex revolution had been underway for years and now entered a period of great success."[7] Centering the dynamism and unsettled mood of this era, this essay aims to consider how these debates that sought to define the character of American art in the postwar years informed the cultural discourse, the emerging contemporary art market, and the community of artists that constituted the milieu in which de Kooning would create the paintings that he presented in his debut exhibition and that would establish him as a leader of American modernism.

1948—"An Outright 'Abstract' Painter"

At his Egan Gallery solo debut, de Kooning decided to feature only nonrepresentational compositions even though in that same period he was painting figurative works as well as abstractions and, indeed, would continue to do so throughout his lifetime. Biographical accounts indicate that the artist's wife, Elaine de Kooning, and gallerist, Charles Egan, played a crucial role in selecting the paintings for inclusion in the exhibition and understood all too clearly the stakes of this solo presentation for the artist's reputation and future.[8] This choice was prophetic: in his review, Greenberg declared de Kooning "an outright 'abstract' painter" even while surrounding the adjective in scare quotes—conceding that the paintings in the show could be called abstract only because they could not be said to be representational.[9]

Greenberg was not alone in taking notice of de Kooning's solo debut; the exhibition received considerable attention in the press. Reviews in *Art News,* the *New York Herald Tribune*, and the *New York Times* called out de Kooning, respectively, for his "singular concentration of passion and technique," for the "liveliness in these canvases," and for the internal drama with which he treated his surfaces, which were described as "one of the stronger currents of abstract art today."[10] Yet, even as these responses underscore the distinctive quality of de Kooning's painterly approach, they also surface the trepidation with which many approached abstract art in the United States at this time. Critic Emily Genauer titled her review of the Egan exhibition in the *New York World-Telegram* "De Kooning's First Solo Hard to Pin Down," then went on to characterize the paintings as "loose, arbitrary, unconventional and curiously anguished recent expressions," remarking that, despite evidence of skill, "what exactly he is trying to get at . . . is not entirely clear."[11] A similarly divided opinion was expressed in the same *Herald Tribune* review that commended the "liveliness" of de Kooning's paintings; it did so as a counterpoint to their elusiveness, explaining that in the Egan show, "although some of his forms hint at reality; close study reveals him as inscrutable as ever."[12] Then, with a tone of simultaneous redemption and apology, the writer, Paul V. Beckley, continued, "There is a liveliness in these canvases, however, and one feels a creative personality behind them."[13] The mix of celebration and apprehension with which critics received de Kooning's presentation speaks to the heightened political and cultural landscape of the year of the artist's debut.

1948—Young American Extremists

In the years following World War II, discussions of art were closely intertwined with questions of culture, nation, and society. Since the late 1930s, Clement Greenberg had been positioning himself as a leading arbiter of the nation's avant-garde, often defining the terms of the conversation, and he was at the height of his influence in 1948.[14] In a series of increasingly strident essays and reviews in the early months of that year, Greenberg built his case that "the main premises of Western art have at last migrated to the United States, along with the center of gravity of industrial production and political power."[15] His commitment to American supremacy in leading the postwar avant-garde was matched by his fierce advocacy for abstraction, and, through his writings, he sought to both merge these two concepts as well as make them synonymous with modernism as well as with the principles of democracy and freedom of expression within the context of the postwar world order. Indeed, this was a moment in which popular, political, and art-critical discourse shared a common investment in defining artistic

value as an articulation of national ideals and interests. Yet, herein lay one of the central philosophical tensions of the era: those who championed abstraction in the United States celebrated its independence from representational art and its attendant ideological resonances, while simultaneously conferring upon certain abstract artists the role of spokesperson for national and international democratic ideals.

The meaning attributed to figurative painting and the position of the avant-garde were not only intellectual questions but ones enmeshed in the remapping of the post–World War II world order. Authoritarian regimes, including those of East Germany and the Soviet Union, embraced many of the same populist themes the left had championed in the United States in the 1930s, along with a style of idealized realism as official state art. Significantly, Greenberg's first published essays, in 1939 and 1940, addressed these very issues.[16] Socialist politics and narrative paintings had now both become associated with the far right. Avant-garde styles, however, continued to be associated with Europe. At the moment of its unprecedented economic and political might, the United States sought to create an identity distinct from that of Europe, but in a context in which the nature of that identity was hotly contested. While Greenberg focused on a formal and material analysis of paintings in his writings, his dedication to young, experimental artists like de Kooning stemmed from an ardent belief that abstract art and the United States were interlinked as the champions of free, democratic thought in a postwar world order.[17]

De Kooning's Egan Gallery exhibition thus opened on April 12, 1948, in the midst of a series of public debates over modern art and the stakes of its cultural and political import in a postwar America focused on asserting its independence from Europe as well as the primacy of democratic governance. The question of what artistic style would not only represent this stance but also resist, equally, the forces of fascism and the Soviet Union's authoritarian approach to communism was at the crux of the critical debates of the era. While critics such as Greenberg and Genauer might agree on the defense of freedom of expression, their differing interpretations of the importance of European modernism or "abstract" compositions reveals just how contested the art of de Kooning and those in his circle could be at this moment.

On February 17, 1948, two months prior to the Egan Gallery opening, the Boston Institute of Modern Art issued a statement announcing its name change to the Institute of Contemporary Art. With this move, the Boston venue sought to distance itself from the term "modern," which it identified with European-derived sociopolitical revolutionary forces. Underscoring the nationalist tenor of the decision, the Institute made the announcement, to the day, on the thirty-fifth anniversary of the opening of the Armory Show in New York in 1913. Officially titled the *International Exhibition of Modern Art*, the Armory Show was (and is) widely credited with introducing European avant-garde art to the United States; thus, while it included many American artists, the Armory Show retained its associations with European cultural values. In announcing the name change, the Boston Institute explained its decision as reflecting a necessary reappraisal of "modern art" a generation after the Armory exhibition, offering a corrective to the "'cult of bewilderment' [that] emerged from the failure of modern art to 'speak clearly.'"[18] The postwar nationalist sentiment driving this effort to distinguish contemporary art in America from that of Europe and to discourage abstraction was made more directly in the four pillars of the mission statement written to accompany this announcement, which included a direct entreaty to the artist: "to exercise his historic role of spiritual leadership, and to forge closer ties with an ever-growing public in terms of common understanding. Nature and mankind remain an inexhaustible source of inspiration. World chaos and social unrest, which prompted many of the excesses of modern art, are still with us, but the artist . . . if he is to help build a culture able to counteract the trend toward world dissolution, he must come forward with a strong, clear affirmation of truth for humanity."[19]

The threat of the "modern" was rhetorically intertwined with the move toward abstraction and away from "nature and mankind" as subjects of art. The risk of the "modern" was, in the absence of a clearly recognizable subject, the possibility that it could be usurped by a political ideology and used to mislead its confused audience. Legibility, or the lack thereof, was the quality that separated abstraction from figurative painting in the discourse, and abstraction's refusal of narrative scenes or symbolism that clearly identified the work's ideological stance was at the center of much anxiety about these compositions.

The rebranding of the Boston Institute was covered widely in the press, with Genauer celebrating the challenge to new art even while cautioning against the prescriptive nature of the treatise: "That's what I like about America. An artist can be as unintelligible as he pleases, feeling no responsibility to budge from his ivory tower, his clouds of hashish, or his insulated laboratory. The museum as a public institution, simply ought not to indorse his stuff by repeatedly exhibiting it to the exclusion of all else, and heaping it with prizes, thereby confusing the public and discouraging those artists who recognize the natural function of art to be communication of ideas and emotions."[20]

The Boston Institute's renaming made explicit the connection between a resistance to artistic approaches perceived as European and the demand for legibility in art among a sector of vocal critics as well as the general public. An expectation that art would deliver an edifying narrative was cemented in popular expectations during the years of the Federal Art Project (FAP, 1935–43), a New Deal initiative that directed government funds to employ artists to create public artworks—murals, easel paintings, prints, and photographs—to serve the public good. While de Kooning and others had made abstract art within the FAP,[21] narrative realism dominated the program and had become strongly associated with progressive-leftist politics. The opening tenet of the Boston Institute's revised mission—a commitment to "narrowing . . . the inevitable gap between artist and public through conscientious and forthright interpretation"—along with the goal of eliminating "double talk, opportunism and chicanery at the public expense," might be read as recalling the principles that had guided the FAP as well as the possibility that large-scale, publicly funded arts initiatives had lost their galvanizing appeal in the postwar years.[22] In any event, the ground had been laid for a series of fiercely contested debates on the nature of contemporary art, as well as its purpose and value for a broad public audience and as a representation of postwar America.

The response to the Boston Institute's newly issued mission statement fittingly came from the United States' institutional anchor of the European avant-garde, the Museum of Modern Art (MoMA). But not everyone at MoMA was happy with the museum's direction. In March 1948, Greenberg wrote of "the murmuring of newspaper critics against the new acquisitions shown by The Museum of Modern Art."[23] Whether influenced or not by the Boston proclamation, MoMA's director, Alfred H. Barr Jr., recalled, "some older members of the Committee on the Museum Collections, encouraged by adverse newspaper criticism, vigorously questioned the validity of certain acquisitions, including paintings called 'abstract expressionist.'"[24] So, boundaries were being drawn around the time of the Boston announcement.

Barr's response included convening that May a forum at MoMA entitled "Modern Artist Speaks," in which artists Paul Burlin, Stuart Davis, Adolph Gottlieb, and George L. K. Morris presented their views on contemporary art.[25] The discussion covered topics such as the role of the artist as cultural critic, the perceived failures of art criticism, and how abstract art was being attacked as a means to control societal attitudes toward artists. The artists did not hesitate to state their positions in contrast to the "infamous episode" at the Boston Institute. Artists likewise spoke out against critics who were seen as antagonistic toward modern art, including Howard Devree of the *New York Times* and Emily Genauer of the *World-Telegram*, whose lack of expertise Morris chided: "Not many people have seen paintings signed 'Devree' or 'Genauer.'"[26] Taking up the central claim of the Boston Institute in its name change, Davis insisted that "art was no exception to the rule that to understand any field of human activity, a certain aptitude, education, and experience are required."[27] Beyond these direct rebuttals, however, the May forum created a

platform for the articulation of a case for the new trends in American painting among artists who did not otherwise belong to a collective or issue aesthetic treatises. Burlin called out those advocating for modern painting as "the bulwark of the individual creative expression, aloof from the political left and its blood brother, the right."[28] Contentious as it was, the MoMA exchange became the cornerstone for official recognition of a new generation of American artists—not only those who spoke, but a whole network of artists determined to develop distinctive approaches. The contest to define a postwar American artistic identity was encapsulated by the responses of critics, artists, and other museums to the renaming of the Boston Institute, and the debates catalyzed a series of further public conversations, striking in the rapid pace of their development.

Thirty-four artists were listed in the roster of attendees at the May gathering, but neither de Kooning nor Pollock were among them. De Kooning's exhibition at Egan had just opened, and its impact had yet to be fully felt, although by that autumn this was no longer the case. In October of that same year, another roundtable was convened at MoMA. This one, titled "A Life Round Table on Modern Art: Fifteen Distinguished Critics and Connoisseurs Undertake to Clarify the Strange Art of Today," was instigated by *Life* magazine with the stated intent to harness the dynamic energy and popular attention surrounding the new American art.[29] Among the fifteen were critic Alfred Frankfurter; writer Aldous Huxley; art historian Meyer Schapiro; Francis Henry Taylor, director of the Metropolitan Museum of Art; Juliana Force, director of the Whitney Museum of American Art; MoMA curator James Thrall Soby; and Clement Greenberg. Watched over by two large canvases, hung side by side, representing the Cubist and Surrealist poles of European modernism—Pablo Picasso's *Girl Before a Mirror* (1932) and Yves Tanguy's *Slowly Toward the North* (1942)—the panel was asked to respond to the question "Is modern art, considered as a whole, a good or a bad development?" (fig. 95). Juliana Force made clear that any effort to "enjoin the artist as to what he should say or how he should say it" would be a threat to artistic freedom.[30]

Soby and Greenberg praised de Kooning's *Painting* (see fig. 27), which was then hanging in the museum's boardroom, discussed along with Pollock's work in a section devoted to "Young American Extremists."

The results of the May roundtable appeared in sixteen illustrated pages in the October 11, 1948, issue of *Life*, consumed in living rooms across the United States. This was the second such forum facilitated by the magazine; the first, appearing in July, addressed the "Pursuit of Happiness." If the initial roundtable took up a question indelibly linked to the United States' Declaration of Independence, the second one was hardly less subtle in framing its topic as one of national import, asking at the outset, "How can a great civilization like ours continue to flourish without the humanizing influence of a living art that is understood and enjoyed by a large public?"[31] What was at risk here was not the vitality of an art of the present, but rather its broad legibility. Viewed generously, *Life* magazine was offering those gathered an opportunity to justify modern art and to articulate the values of this new generation of artists in the most widely distributed American publication of the day.

Both European and United States–based modern artists were taken into consideration: from Picasso's Analytic Cubist work to the five artists deemed "Young American Extremists" including de Kooning, along with Pollock, Adolph Gottlieb, Theodoros Stamos, and William Baziotes. Pointing to de Kooning's *Painting*, the moderator inquired of the group what de Kooning was "trying to say" in his painting. Greenberg apparently replied that he "thought Mr. de Kooning was wrestling with his fears, but that this overtone of foreboding and anxiety was not the most important aspect of the picture."[32]

The published accounts of the conversations encapsulate the discourse of a year in which the new work of a group of New York artists would shift the axis of the art world, anchoring a dominant pole of the avant-garde and modernist innovation in America. Ultimately, the publication of these dynamic exchanges among the artists and institutions in the popular press underscored the growing importance of American art in shaping a national culture on the world stage. The conversation around the leading artists of the day would both buoy and parallel a similarly rapid growth in the galleries supporting the American avant-garde.

1948—Artists and Galleries: The Tide Turns

From 1940 to 1946, the number of galleries in Manhattan more than tripled, and sales likewise multiplied each year.[33] In part this reflected a gradual reemergence of the market from the economic depression of the previous decade, but another key factor in this growth was the influx of artists and other art-world figures who were escaping the rising tide of fascism in Europe. Commercial galleries, with very few exceptions, were uptown, clustered within a few blocks on 57th Street in Midtown Manhattan and predominantly exhibited European art, often of the late nineteenth and early twentieth centuries. There was not yet a viable market for the radical experimentation of local contemporary artists. Reflecting on the period in a 1977 interview, American artist David Hare noted, "There were only three places in New York in the early 1940s: Julien Levy, Pierre Matisse, and Peggy [Guggenheim]. She was the only one who showed contemporary Americans."[34] In 1947, when Guggenheim shuttered her gallery, Art of This Century, to return to Europe, Greenberg underscored her contribution, noting, "She gave first showings to more serious new artists than anyone else in the country."[35] According to Dennison, "A mere handful of galleries then were exhibiting the new art, Betty Parsons was one. . . . Charles Egan was another."[36] The two galleries opened on East 57th Street in 1946, Egan at number 63, Parsons at number 15, later moving to 24 West 57th. For both, 1948 turned out to be a watershed year as well.

In January of 1948, the first exhibition that opened at Betty Parsons was devoted to Jackson Pollock's brand-new allover, dripped and poured paintings (fig. 96); three months later, de Kooning's first solo exhibition opened at Egan—the geographical proximity aiding the critical comparison of the two artists. But neither exhibition was a financial success. Nor was the exhibition of Arshile Gorky's work at the Julien Levy Gallery in March: only one of fourteen paintings, *Soft Night* (fig. 97), sold, even though Gorky had been chosen

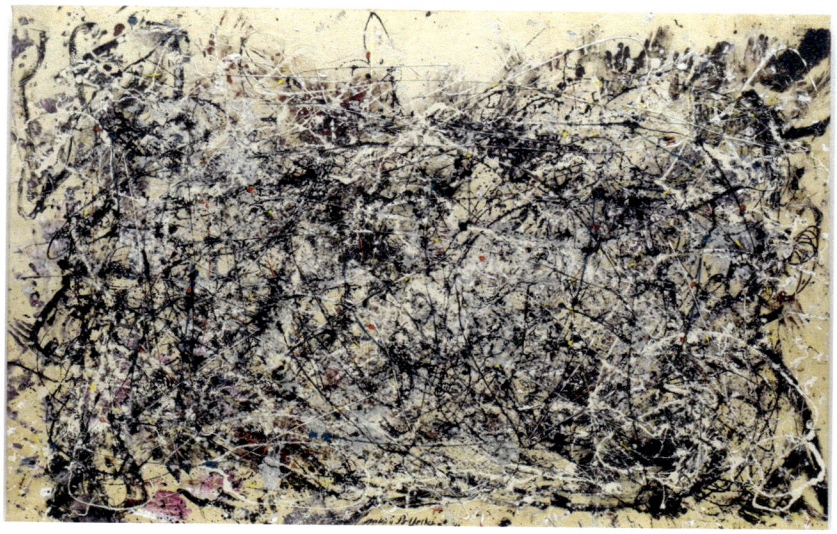

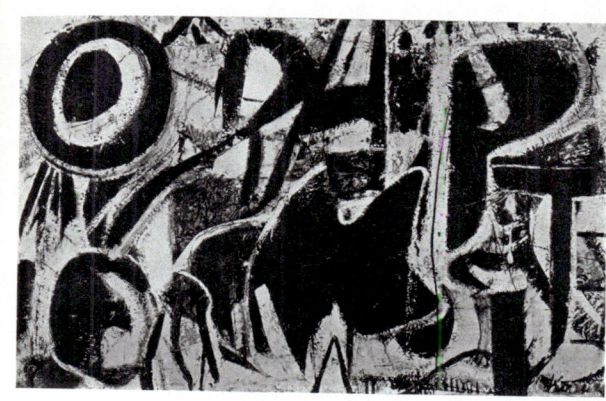

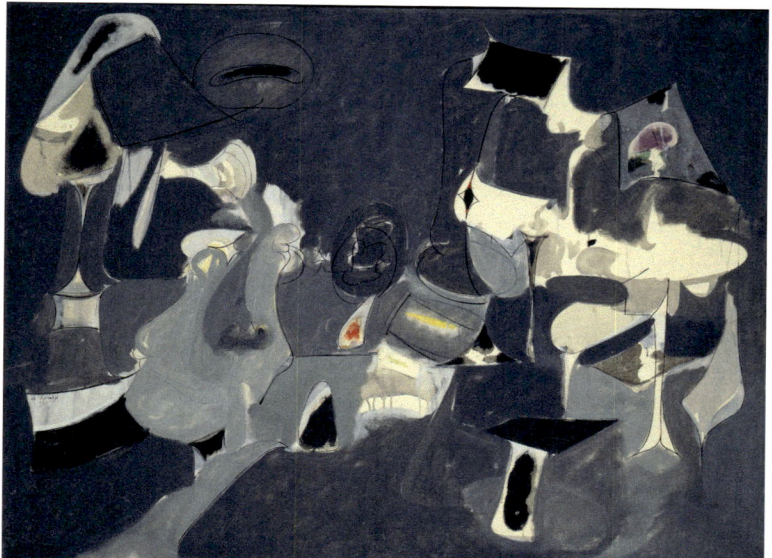

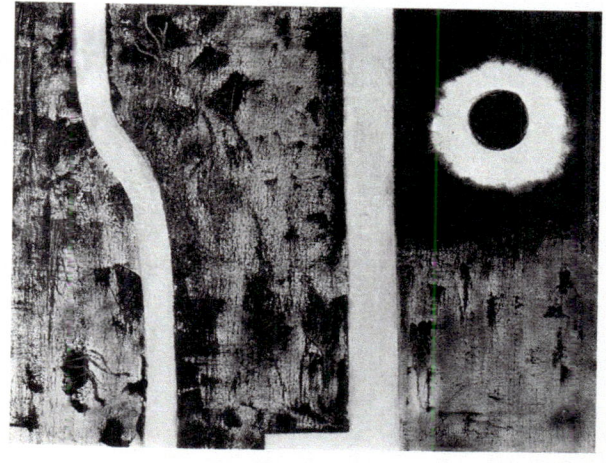

101

as one of the artists representing the United States at the Venice Biennale that summer—the first Biennale since the end of the war. Gorky's painting was purchased by John and Ruth Stephan, editors of the little magazine *Tiger's Eye*, which reproduced de Kooning's *Orestes* (see fig. 17) in the March issue (the month before his exhibition opened) and would later also purchase the painting (fig. 98).

Motivated by the significant attention that de Kooning's exhibition attracted (and the urgency for both artist and gallery to make a sale), Egan extended it through June, thus doubling the length of its run. Yet despite the added weeks and the public notice, there were no sales during the exhibition, and the de Koonings—Willem and Elaine—were left disappointed as well as financially desperate at the show's close.[37]

Figure 96
Jackson Pollock (1912–1956; born Cody, WY; died East Hampton, NY), ***Number 1A, 1948*, 1948**
Oil and enamel paint on canvas, 172.7 × 264.2 cm. The Museum of Modern Art, New York. Purchase (77.1950)

Figure 97
Arshile Gorky (1904–1948; born Dilkaya, Turkey; died Sherman, CT; active New York, NY, and Boston, MA), ***Soft Night*, 1947**
Oil, india ink, and conte crayon on canvas, 96.7 × 127.1 cm. Hirshhorn Museum and Sculpture Garden, Smithsonian Institution, Washington, DC. The Joseph H. Hirshhorn Bequest, 1981 (82.2341)

Figure 98
The Tiger's Eye 1, no. 3 (March 1948): 101
Top: **Willem de Kooning, *Orestes*, 1947** (see fig. 17). Bottom: **Barnett B. Newman** (1905–1970; born New York, NY), ***Death of Euclid*, 1947**

Such an outcome was not unusual for a debut of a new body of work in New York at that time, however, as both Pollock's and Gorky's presentations also attest.

The couple were rescued from their economic straits by a call from Josef Albers (whom Egan had placed in an exhibition with de Kooning earlier that winter). Albers invited Willem to teach in the summer session of the experimental arts program at Black Mountain College—an invitation de Kooning eagerly accepted. When the de Koonings returned to New York that autumn, the tide began to turn for the artist: the Museum of Modern Art acquired a painting that had been in de Kooning's Egan exhibition (see fig. 27); *Mailbox* (see fig. 21) was included in the Whitney Annual; he was featured as one of five "Young American Extremists" in *Life* magazine; and he started teaching Pat Passlof, a young artist he had met at Black Mountain. The speed at which this all transpired is remarkable, unquestionably aided not only by the ascendant US economy and the increasing number of exhibitions of new art, as discussed above, but also by the sheer number of other artists who were inspired by de Kooning's example.

That de Kooning and Passlof met at Black Mountain College in the summer of 1948 was a fortunate happenstance that had also arisen thanks to his solo exhibition at the Egan Gallery. Passlof recounts the experience in her autobiographical essay "1948," which opens, "I was so excited about Bill's first show that I quit college."[38] Seeking to connect with artists in de Kooning's circle, Passlof discovered Black Mountain College and enrolled that summer, not yet knowing that de Kooning would be hired for the season. She recalls his opening lecture, "Cezanne and the Color of Veronese," and the reassurance she felt knowing that, in her words, "the abstract artist I admired most had strong, natural ties to the past," and was not locked into an absolutist dialectic between abstraction and tradition.[39] This outlook would remain consistent in de Kooning's approach to teaching, which, Passlof details, demanded simultaneous work on "the series of painstaking 6H pencil still-life drawings" as well as an abstract still-life painting. It is indeed the biographies and accounts of Passlof and other artists

influenced by de Kooning—and there are many who would cite his influence—that often provide the greatest insight into his studio processes.

An encounter with an earlier de Kooning painting, likewise led painter Edith Schloss to seek out the artist. Schloss recounts that when photographer Rudy Burckhardt (whom she would later marry) took her on her first visit to de Kooning's studio, in 1943, they encountered a gathering of fellow artists, including Elaine de Kooning, Fairfield Porter, and Milton Resnick. Here, in a space Schloss described as "like nothing [she] had ever seen before. Everywhere were surfaces lashed with paint—flows and drips and splatters of paint," these artists who endeavored to work in a new idiom discussed historical techniques of the Renaissance, Peter Paul Rubens, and the Venetians as well as their contemporaries Milton Avery and Arshile Gorky.[40] And Schloss remembers that the conversation into which she entered in de Kooning's studio that day avowed that "painting was about the painting of paintings, not about the needs of people," making explicit the group's desire to step away from the leftist politics that, in many cases, had given rise to their employment in the previous decade. Passlof concurs that de Kooning's interest in historical painters, whether Jean Auguste Dominique Ingres or Paul Cézanne, was his way of introducing her to his primary concerns as a painter—"finding and consolidating the picture plane; the role of movement, speed, and stillness in creating space; what paint does."[41]

Although recounted via anecdotes, these were sustained conversations. In 1944, Schloss moved into a loft on 21st Street near the de Koonings, Burckhardt, and poets Edwin Denby and James Schuyler. By 1948, de Kooning had relocated his studio to 10th Street, where he also found a space for Passlof that autumn. Art critic Harold Rosenberg dubbed this block—10th Street between Third and Fourth Avenues, where he too would live—"the block of artists." The area, he wrote, "was uninteresting and devoid of color, having not even the picturesqueness of a slum." But to the artists, this "no environment" was interesting.[42] Schloss recalls in her memoir:

Denby would make these details of atmospheric space, motion, and surfaces—the same foci that de Kooning would center in his paintings—the subject of poems; Burckhardt would transform the landscape into an abstraction of forms and textures (fig. 99). Burckhardt had his first solo exhibition at the Photo League uptown in September of 1948. His pictures from that year frame the city at an oblique angle, trading the horizon line of a landscape for the layered textures of building facades, pavement, and people, echoing lines from Denby's verses "An adult looks new in the weather's motion / The sky is in the streets with the trucks and us / Stands awhile, then lifts across land and ocean."[44] Photographer Aaron Siskind's second solo show with Egan immediately preceded de Kooning's 1948 debut. His photographs so closely framed the textures, patterns, and graphic signage of the urban landscape they are discussed as "Abstract Expressionist" compositions, a term coined to encapsulate paintings of this period.[45] (Siskind would also work for hire, documenting many of Egan's exhibitions.)

Notwithstanding the genuine friendships among, and the multidisciplinary nature of, this community of artists, de Kooning's statements—whether firsthand or through anecdote—are with a mind to the possibilities of painting. Of his contemporaries, he spoke of his respect for painter Arshile Gorky, whose death by suicide the

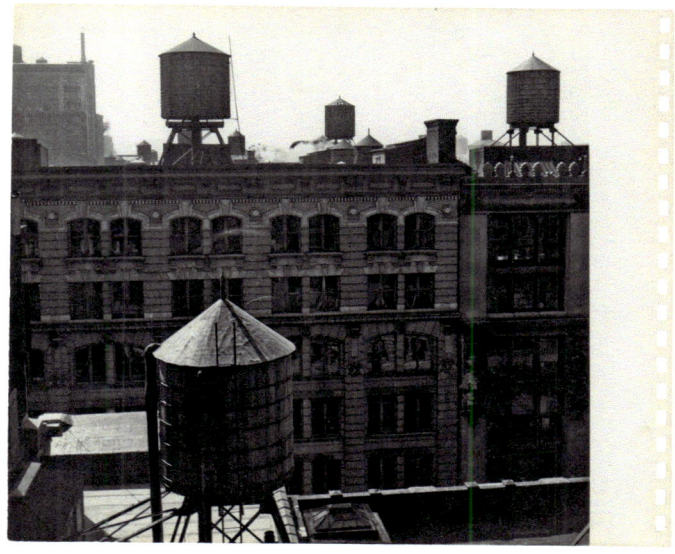

Figure 99
Rudolph (Rudy) Burckhardt (1914–1999; born Basel, Switzerland; died Searsmont, ME), **Untitled photograph from an untitled album with a sonnet by Edwin Denby, 1946–47** Gelatin silver print, 11.7 × 17.4 cm. The Museum of Modern Art, New York. Gift of CameraWorks, Inc. and Purchase (51.1993)

summer of 1948 while de Kooning was at Black Mountain shocked the artist and indeed the entire New York arts community. MoMA had acquired *Soft Night* (see fig. 97) in March from his exhibition at Julien Levy Gallery: a composition of biomorphic forms with soft edges in shades of charcoal, slate, and flashes of light gray. Beyond Gorky's move toward a more monochrome palette, the painting reflects a transition from the crisp figural contour lines and the symbology of the early 1940s toward an approach to layering painted forms—both building up areas of paint and rubbing away others—to embed the composition in the very character of its surface.

Mark Rothko would undertake a similar transition in 1947–48 from the more clearly drawn figures of the mid-1940s to the consolidation of rounded blocks with soft edges and more limited palettes. Another close contemporary of de Kooning (among those whom Schloss met on her first visit to his studio) was Milton Resnick, who had spent 1946–48 in Paris. The two reunited in New York in the autumn of 1948. To create his untitled composition of that year (fig. 100), Resnick poured skeins of paint in loose arcs, cut painted color fields out of paper, and built layers of drawn and collaged elements into a composition that has striking resonance with

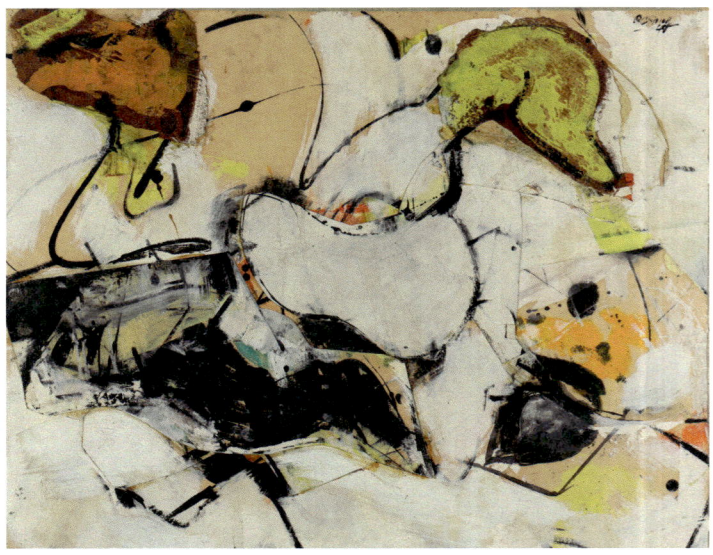

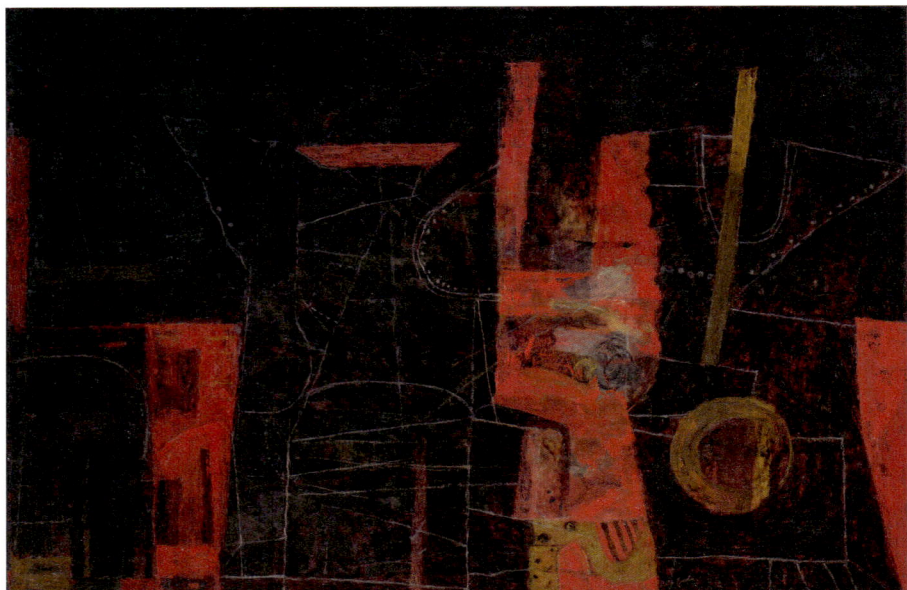

Figure 100
Milton Resnick (1917–2004; born Bratslav, Ukraine; died New York, NY), ***Untitled*, 1948**
Oil and cut-and-pasted paper on paper on board, 45.7 × 57.2 cm. The Museum of Modern Art, New York. Committee on Drawings Funds (36.2011)

Figure 101
Philip Guston (1913–1980; born Montreal, Canada; died Woodstock, NY), ***The Tormentors*, 1947–48**
Oil on canvas, 103.9 × 153.7 cm. San Francisco Museum of Modern Art. Gift of the artist

de Kooning's works of this moment, especially *Valentine* (see fig. 20) and *Secretary* (see fig. 12).

During his Guggenheim Fellowship year in 1947, Philip Guston moved to Woodstock, New York, to be closer to New York City and visited the studios of, and received visits to his own from, Rothko, Pollock, and de Kooning. Guston expressed his need for a breakthrough: "I felt I needed to abandon representational forms and the construction of the picture altogether."[46] The resulting painting, *The Tormentors* (fig. 101), features a heavily worked surface—layered, burnished, and etched—in a dark-brown-black field interrupted with fields of crimson and ocher. Guston developed great admiration for de Kooning, his elder by about a decade, and years later, when Guston returned to figuration and was harshly criticized for his depiction of political subject matter in a style of graphic caricature, de Kooning remained a steadfast supporter, defending the artist's right to move freely

among abstraction, figuration, or whatever stylistic means were of interest and at their disposal.[47]

This lively community of painters, poets, dancers, and writers, in which de Kooning played a central role, was as instrumental to the formation of a new American art as any gallery show, museum roundtable, or formal movement. In writing of the energy and sense of artistic revolution he perceived during the period, George Dennison wrote particularly of de Kooning's first solo exhibition: "It was in this year [1948], at the show of de Kooning at the Egan gallery, that the abiding great pleasure of painting came into my own life; more than a pleasure—an affinity and a second language, a tonic and support."[48]

The pleasure was shared as artists went back and forth between one another's studios, and ideas and initiatives emerged from casual encounters and individuals' own grassroots efforts. Schloss, for example, participated in exhibitions of the Pyramid Group, a collective established by painter Lois Dodd in 1947 to create opportunities—exhibitions, salons, or life-drawing sessions (in which they would pose for one another)—for young, experimental New York City–based artists. And, paralleling the artists' roundtable discussions of 1948–51 was a sequence of exhibitions showcasing still little-known artists, beginning with *Talent 1950* at the Samuel Kootz Gallery at 600 Madison Avenue, organized by Clement Greenberg and Meyer Schapiro, and culminating with the now-famous *9th St. Exhibition of Paintings and*

Sculpture, organized by artists with the gallerist Leo Castelli, in an empty storefront at 60 East 9th Street. The latter overlapped with *The New Generation* at Tibor de Nagy Gallery at 206 East 53rd Street, which introduced five young artists including Helen Frankenthaler and Grace Hartigan.

Even as de Kooning's reputation was cemented following the 1948 Egan exhibition, critics and galleries were beginning to look ahead, and the boundaries between downtown and uptown eroded. De Kooning's appearance in *Life* magazine in October 1948, along with MoMA's purchase of *Painting*, marked the beginning of his increasing prominence among New York artists.

1950–51—The Avant-Garde in Art History

As if to announce that the tide was again turning, and that the "Young Extremists" of just three years prior were now mainstays of the modern era, on the evening of February 5, 1951, MoMA held a symposium on abstract art in connection with the exhibition *Abstract Painting and Sculpture in America* (January 23–March 25, 1951). Six artists, this time including de Kooning, were invited to respond to the prompt "What abstract art means to me."[49] In April of 1950, William Seitz, then a graduate student in art history at Princeton University, put forward a proposal to write his dissertation on the Abstract Expressionist movement. He was not alone among young people interested in Abstract Expressionism, and de Kooning in particular. On March 10, 1950, having read a dozen essays for an art criticism prize offered by MoMA, Alfred Barr wrote to MoMA president Nelson Rockefeller, surprised that de Kooning was written about more than any other artist, and "that all of the writers are around 30 years of age."[50] But an essay is not a dissertation, and MoMA is not Princeton. Seitz's proposal set off a debate at Princeton that would last a year and a half and establish a benchmark for the role of contemporary art in art historical scholarship.

Seitz had enrolled at Princeton to pursue graduate degrees in art history with a focus on modern art. Having arrived with a bachelor's in fine art from the University of Buffalo, he encountered strong resis-tance from the faculty of the Department of Art and Archaeology to his interest in the art of the present. Since this art remained unproven by the test of time, and since the research would be conducted via interviews and the direct study of living artists, Princeton's graduate committee was concerned whether an "objective study" could be possible. Undaunted, Seitz enlisted the support of Barr, a Princeton alumnus, which gave rise to a more-than-yearlong debate by mail among Princeton, Barr, and Seitz concerning the validity of contemporary art as a subject of serious consideration for doctoral studies. In the end, the committee approved the topic.[51]

Seitz developed his foundational study of Abstract Expressionism through an interpretation of, in his words, "the works and thought of six leading painters: Willem de Kooning, Arshile Gorky, Hans Hofmann, Robert Motherwell, Mark Rothko, and Mark Tobey."[52] Having outlined this constellation of figures, Seitz reminded his readers that, absent a treatise or group affiliation, these artists did not constitute a formal movement; nevertheless, "Abstract Expressionism" was a valid rubric to encapsulate the state of American art in 1950. Specifically, Seitz argued, if it could be agreed that the dominant modes of artistic practice in America prior to World War II were a form of native realism or art inspired by the European avant-garde, then Abstract Expressionism marked developments since the war's conclusion that revealed its independence from both pictorial realism and Europe. While Seitz valorized the work of these artists by situating them in the context of art historical precedents, he emphasized their articulation of an American voice.

Submitted in the spring of 1955, Seitz's dissertation was the first doctoral degree from the institution on a modern subject, and the text would unite de Kooning with five contemporaries under the banner of Abstract Expressionism. After earning his doctorate, Seitz joined the Princeton faculty as an assistant professor and then, in 1960, the curatorial body of the Museum of Modern Art. He is best known for *Claude Monet: Seasons and Moments* (March 9–May 15, 1960), exploring the artist's late work and its effect on the New York School, as well as the contemporary exhibitions *The Art of Assemblage*

(October 4–November 12, 1961) and *The Responsive Eye* (February 23–April 25, 1965). He also curated shows on three of the artists he had studied in his dissertation: Mark Tobey (September 12–November 9, 1962), Arshile Gorky (December 19, 1962–February 12, 1963), and Hans Hofmann (September 11–December 1, 1963). And he did ask de Kooning about mounting an exhibition of his work, to which de Kooning responded positively. The show was to occur in 1961, although it was postponed to September 1963; in January of that year, however, Seitz received a letter from de Kooning saying that the artist was indefinitely postponing his MoMA exhibition—which turned out to be permanent.[53] So, Seitz's curatorial presentation of de Kooning never came to pass.

The transformation of de Kooning's profile from the opening of his solo show at Charles Egan Gallery in the spring of 1948 to the spring of 1951, when, well established as a leading artist, he participated in the MoMA roundtable with the statement "What Abstract Art Means to Me," was dramatic.[54] He received the Logan Medal from the Art Institute of Chicago that year, resulting in its purchase of *Excavation* (see fig. 51), a grandly scaled painting that summarizes many of the explorations that characterized the paintings in his Egan show. Along with other American artists, he began spending summers in East Hampton, New York, and would continue to evolve and explore new possibilities in painting.

In his public statements in the spring of 1951, de Kooning maintained an unflagging resistance to categorization and nomenclature.[55] Still, he clearly understood the ways in which he was implicated in the cultural discourse of these first years after the war. Even late in his career, he would express discomfort at having been held up not only as a pillar of modernist abstraction but also as a leader of the American avant-garde. He would describe it as "a certain burden this American-ness [. . .] if you come from a small nation, you don't have that. When I went to the Academy and I was drawing from the nude, I was making the drawing, not Holland [. . .] I feel sometimes as an artist must feel, like a baseball player or something. Members of a team writing American history."[56] While de Kooning's art had come to be synonymous with the postwar American avant-garde, and he was canonized as a cornerstone of Abstract Expressionism, a full understanding of the works that earned him this distinction rests in the much more contested period between the end of World War II and his first Egan exhibition—when a diversity of approaches and debate held center stage.

1. Clement Greenberg, "Review of an Exhibition of Willem de Kooning," *Nation* 166, no. 17 (April 24, 1948): 448; reprinted in *Clement Greenberg: The Collected Essays and Criticism*, vol. 2, *Arrogant Purpose 1945–1949*, ed. John O'Brian (Chicago: University of Chicago Press, 1986), 228.

2. Clement Greenberg, "The Present Prospects of American Painting and Sculpture," *Horizon* (October 1947): 20–30; reprinted in *Clement Greenberg*, 2:160–70.

3. Clement Greenberg, "The Situation at the Moment," *Partisan Review* 15, no. 1 (January 1948): 79–84; reprinted in *Clement Greenberg*, 2:192–96.

4. Greenberg, "Present Prospects," 169.

5. See the essay by John Elderfield in this volume.

6. Serge Guilbaut, *How New York Stole the Idea of Modern Art* (Chicago: University of Chicago Press, 1983), 105.

7. George Dennison, "In Praise of What Persists," *American Poetry Review* 11, no. 6 (November–December 1982): 11.

8. Mark Stevens and Annalyn Swan, *De Kooning: An American Master* (New York: Knopf, 2004), 250–51.

9. Greenberg, "Review of an Exhibition."

10. Renée Arb, "Spotlight on de Kooning," *Art News* 47, no. 2 (April 1948): 33; Paul V. Beckley, "Art Exhibition Notes: Non-Objective Art," *New York Herald Tribune*, April 20, 1948, 27; Sam Hunter, "By Groups and Singly; French Graphics—Racing—Odets—De Kooning," *New York Times*, April 25, 1948, X11. For more on the critical response to this exhibition, see the Chronology in this volume, pp. 85–88.

11. Emily Genauer, "De Kooning's First Solo Hard to Pin Down: De Kooning a Puzzle," *New York World-Telegram*, May 4, 1948.

12. Beckley, "Art Exhibition Notes," 27.

13. Beckley, "Art Exhibition Notes," 27.

14. In 1948, Greenberg was an editor of *Partisan Review*, an associate editor of *Commentary*, and art critic for *The Nation*, in which his appraisal of de Kooning appeared.

15. See Greenberg, "Present Prospects." A fine summary of the issues is in Caroline Jones, *Eyesight Alone: Clement Greenberg's Modernism and the Bureaucratization of the Senses* (Chicago: University of Chicago Press, 2005), 84–95, 247–48. A polemical account is Guilbaut, *How New York Stole the Idea of Modern Art*, 173.

16. See *Clement Greenberg: The Collected Essays and Criticism*, vol. 1, *Perceptions and Judgments, 1939–1944*, ed. John O'Brian (Chicago: University of Chicago Press, 1986), 3–41.

17. Clement Greenberg, "Art," *Nation* 166, no. 17 (April 24, 1948): 448.

18. Nelson W. Aldrich and James S. Platt, "'Modern Art' and the American Public: A Statement by The Institute of Contemporary Art (formerly the Institute of Modern Art)," Boston, February 17, 1948; reprinted in *Dissent: The Issue of Modern Art in Boston* (Boston: Institute of Contemporary Art, 1985), 52. Alfred Barr, *What Is Modern Painting?* (New York: Museum of Modern Art, 1946).

19. Aldrich and Platt, "'Modern Art' and the American Public," 2.

20. Guilbaut, *How New York Stole the Idea of Modern Art*, 181; see Emily Genauer, "Boston Museum Hits 'Cult of Bewilderment': Asks Artists to Affirm the Truth," *New York World-Telegram*, February 17, 1948, 12; "Modern Art Loses Face in Boston as Institute Changes Its Name," *New York Times*, February 17, 1948, 23; "Modern into Contemporary," *Newsweek* 31, no. 9 (March 1, 1948): 73; and "Revolt In Boston: Shootin' Resumes in the Art World," *Life* 6, no. 8 (February 21, 1949): 84–89.

21. See Lauren Mahony, "WPA and Related Works," in *De Kooning: A Retrospective*, ed. John Elderfield, exh. cat. (New York: Museum of Modern Art, 2011), 68–75.

22. Genauer, "Modern Art Loses Face in Boston."

23. Clement Greenberg, "Review of an Exhibition of Mordecai Ardon-Bronstein and a Discussion of the Reaction in America to Abstract Art," in *Clement Greenberg*, 2:216–18.

24. Alfred H. Barr Jr., "Chronicle of the Collection of Painting and Sculpture," in *Painting and Sculpture in the Museum of Modern Art, 1929–1967* (New York: Museum of Modern Art, 1977), 635.

25. "The Modern Artist Speaks," transcript of a forum held at the Museum of Modern Art, New York, May 5, 1948. Paul Burlin Papers, Archives of American Art, Smithsonian Institution, Washington DC.

26. "The Modern Artist Speaks," press release, May 6, 1948, 3. Paul Burlin Papers, 01.01.20.

27. "The Modern Artist Speaks," 6.

28. "The Modern Artist Speaks," 1.

29. "A Life Round Table on Modern Art," *Life* (October 11, 1948): 62

30. "The Modern Artist Speaks," 2.

31. Russell W. Davenport, "A Life Round Table on Modern Art: Fifteen Distinguished Critics and Connoisseurs Undertake to Clarify the Strange Art of Today," *Life* 25, no. 15 (October 11, 1948), 56.

32. "Life Round Table on Modern Art," 62.

33. Stevens and Swan, *De Kooning*, 266.

34. Stevens and Swan, *De Kooning*, 66.

35. Michael Brenson "Betty Parsons, Art Dealer, 82; Pioneer in New York School," *New York Times,* July 24, 1982, section 1, p. 28.

36. Dennison, "In Praise of What Persists," 10–18.

37. See Elderfield, *De Kooning: A Retrospective*, 163; Stevens and Swan, *De Kooning*, 253; and Elaine de Kooning, "De Kooning Memories," *Vogue* 173, no. 12 (December 1983): 352. Elaine writes that their financial problems "were solved" by an invitation from Black Mountain College that provided "$200, room and board, and round-trip railroad tickets." A telegram sent to de Kooning on June 28, 1948, from Theodore Rondthaler, Black Mountain College Treasurer, notifies him that a $100 wire has been sent for travel expenses. Black Mountain College Records, Western Regional Archives, 506.2.35.17.

38. Pat Passlof, "1948: The Author's Studies with Willem de Kooning," *Art Journal* 48, no. 3 (Fall 1989): 229.

39. Passlof, "1948."

40. Edith Schloss, *The Loft Generation: From the De Koonings to Twombly; Portraits and Sketches, 1924–2011* (New York: Farrar, Straus and Giroux, 2021), 9.

41. Passlof, "1948," 229.

42. Harold Rosenberg, "Tenth Street: A Geography of Modern Art," *Art News Annual* (New York: Macmillan, 1954): n.p.; reprinted in Harold Rosenberg, *Discovering the Present: Three Decades in Art, Culture, and Politics* (Chicago: University of Chicago Press, 1973), 100–109.

43. Schloss, *Loft Generation*, 66.

44. Edwin Denby, "The Climate," in *In Public, In Private* (Prairie City, IL: Decker, 1948), 5.

45. For a discussion of Siskind's relationship to abstraction and developments in painting of this era, see, for example, Thomas Hess et al., *Aaron Siskind: Photographer* (Rochester, NY: George Eastman House, 1965); and Keith Davis, *Callahan, Siskind, Sommer: At the Crossroads of American Photography* (Santa Fe, NM: Radius Books, 2009).

46. Philip Guston, "Talk at Yale Summer School of Music and Art," 1973, 215, as cited in *Philip Guston Now*, exh. cat. (Washington, DC: National Gallery of Art, 2020), 43.

47. See Harry Cooper, "Guston, Then: Telling Tales," in *Philip Guston Now*, 87.

48. Dennison, "In Praise of What Persists," 11.

49. Willem de Kooning, "What Abstract Art Means to Me," *Bulletin of the Museum of Modern Art* 18, no. 3 (Spring 1951): 4–8.

50. "Letter from Alfred Barr to Nelson A. Rockefeller," Folder Series XV: Nelson A. Rockefeller, 1945–1971; Alfred H. Barr Papers, The Museum of Modern Art Archives, New York, AHB18.1.A5.

51. A fascinating record of the exchanges appears in "William C. Seitz: Defending the Modern," https://www.moma.org/interactives/exhibitions/2007/seitz/.

52. William Seitz, "Abstract Expressionist Painting in America: An Interpretation Based on the Work and Thought of Six Key Figures" (PhD diss., Princeton University, 1955).

53. Willem de Kooning Letter. William Seitz Papers, Archives of the Museum of Modern Art, New York.

54. Further details may be found in Stevens and Swan, *De Kooning*.

55. Willem de Kooning's statements on his art are included in Aline Louchheim, "Six Abstractionists Defend Their Art," *New York Times*, January 21, 1951, 104; and the published statements of the MoMA symposium "What Abstract Art Means to Me," 4–8.

56. Willem de Kooning, interviewed by David Sylvester, New York City, March 1960; published in David Sylvester, *Interviews with American Artists* (New Haven, CT: Yale University Press, 2001), 48.

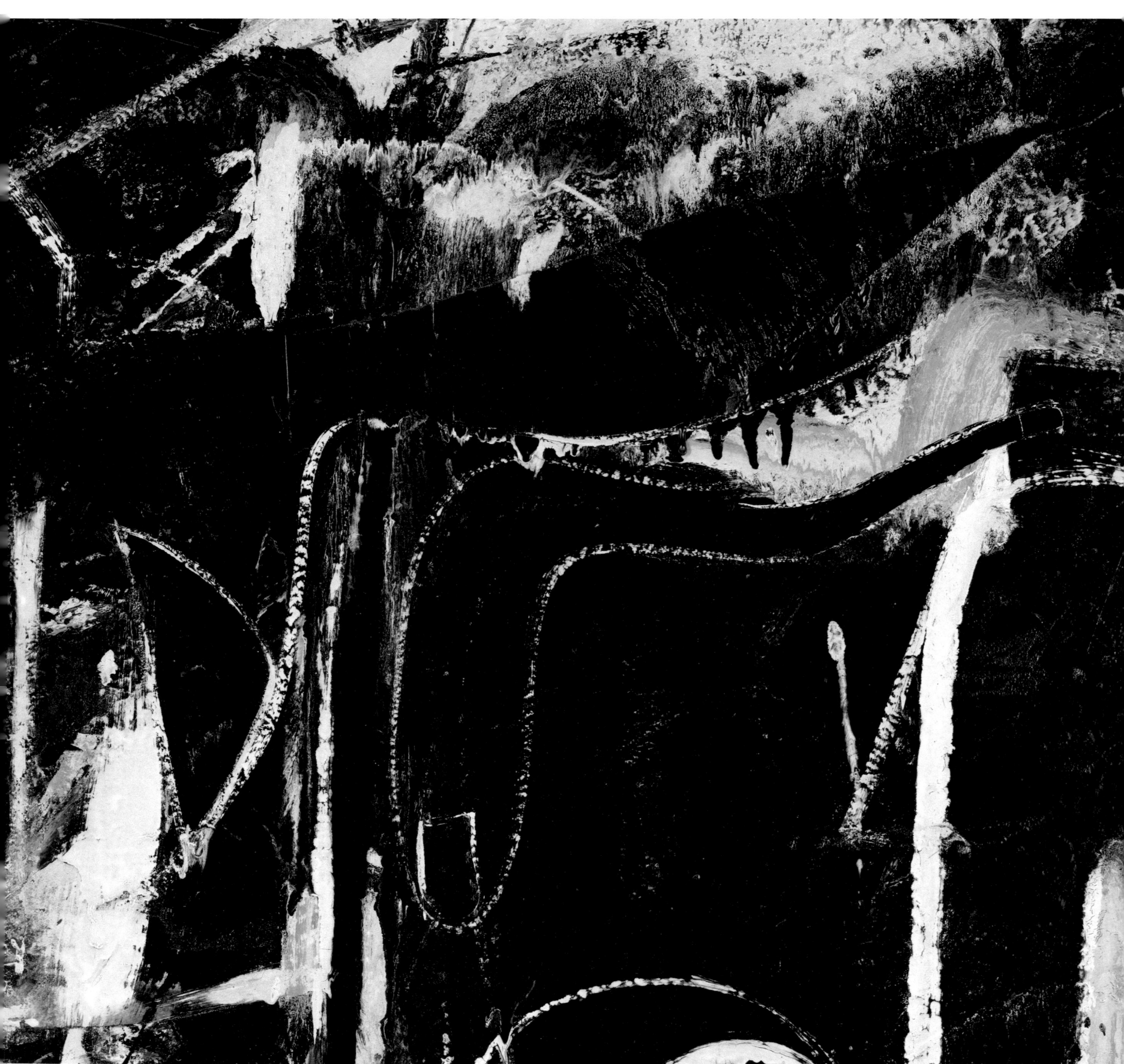

Use, Reuse, Work, and Rework: The Painting of *Black Friday*

JIM CODDINGTON AND BART J. C. DEVOLDER

His pictures represent the stages of the artistic process itself, including its pauses, frustrations and marginalia. His method amounts to a special variety of painted collage in which the individual shapes of a finished picture are a record of the studies involved in the work's development.

— Charles F. Stuckey [1]

The facts of a painting are prosaic at first. At least at first. A support to paint on, a preparation of that support, then paint. These facts, the materials of the painting, are choices the painter makes. In the case of *Black Friday* (see fig. 28), the support is a panel, a solid support, de Kooning eschewing the more historically common canvas support—something he particularly did in his works from the late 1940s.[2] The paint is both artist paint and retail trade paints.[3] Both choices are somewhat unorthodox. De Kooning made these material choices alongside choices of how to work with these materials, and his choices are reflected not only in the final image but also in the many traces of the labor and thought that preceded the completed work.

It is broadly understood that de Kooning's paintings evidence such labor, as he routinely engaged in multiple campaigns of painting on his works—and *Black Friday* is no exception. In writing about de Kooning's first solo exhibition, in 1948, which included *Black Friday,* the critic Renée Arb responded to de Kooning's working method: "the process of painting becomes the end itself."[4] The artist's extensive reworking of his surfaces is also no doubt much of what Harold Rosenberg had in mind when he wrote of "an arena" of action in his seminal essay "The American Action Painters" (1952), positing a formulation in which a painting becomes the residue of action on action.[5]

Returning, then, to the bare facts of this painting, *Black Friday.* It is painted on a four-millimeter-thin composition board, or fiberboard. This type of board was not a wholly unusual choice as a painting support for artists in the 1940s. Most such fiberboards have one smooth side, with the other side showing a crisscrossed pattern, the result of a wire screen pressed into the wet fibers

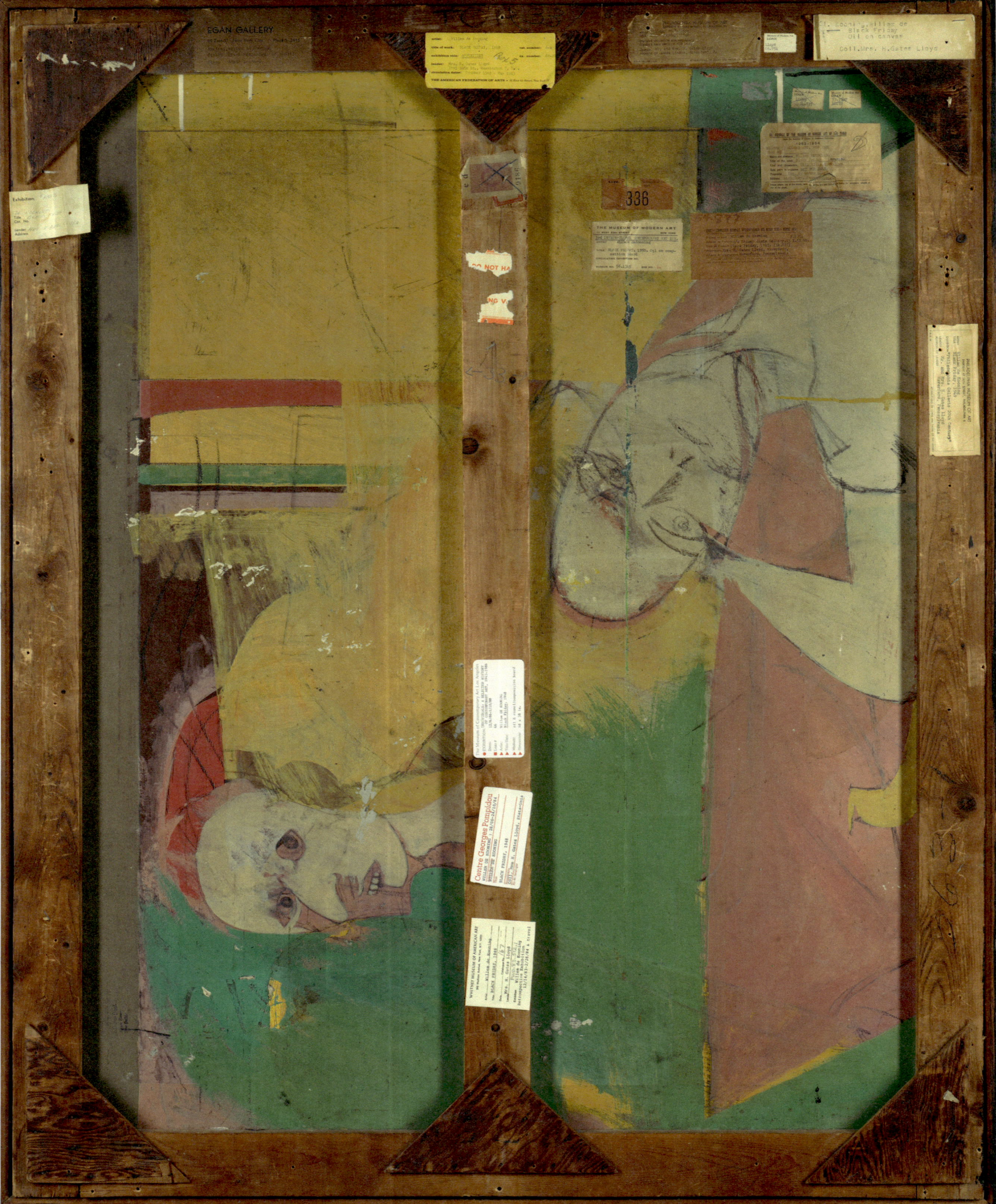

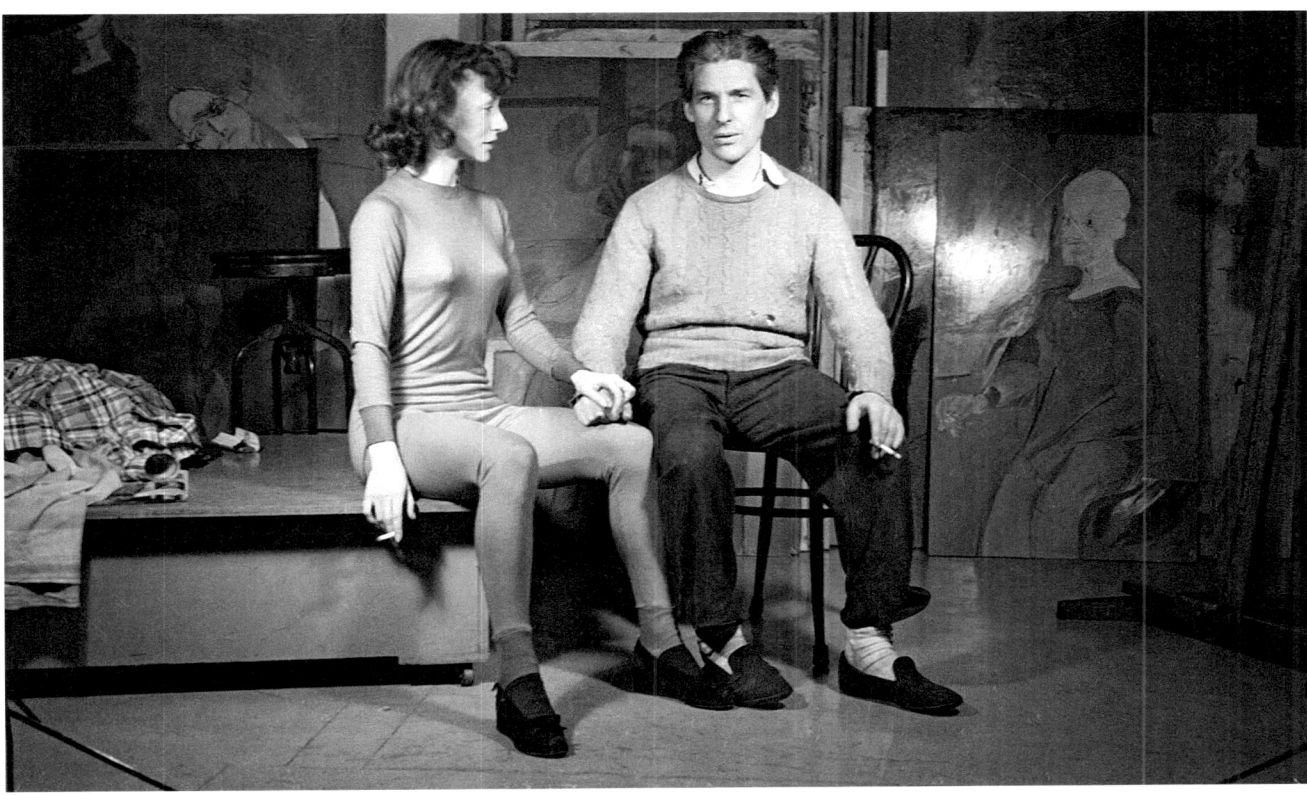

during fabrication.[6] De Kooning seems to have favored the smoother side for his paintings, including his first Woman series, until the mid-1940s. According to conservator Susan Lake, this preference originated when Arshile Gorky, John Graham, and de Kooning saw Jean Auguste Dominique Ingres's paintings at the Metropolitan Museum of Art and fell in love with his smooth surfaces. Subsequently, they started polishing the surfaces of their paintings with razor blades and sandpaper.[7]

The smooth side of the panel is, in fact, on the reverse of *Black Friday,* and it portrays two figures, one in the simplified style of de Kooning's first Woman series, and the other a head that de Kooning had reworked, yielding an even more ghostly face (fig. 103). The artist carried out several campaigns on this side of the board, the last of which had him block in an ocher color around the lower head and a green around the upper, a combination to be found in similarly unfinished paintings from the early 1940s.[8] The careful blocking suggests that at this point de Kooning may have considered integrating the two seemingly disparate figures into a single composition. Thomas Hess dated this

Figure 103
Verso of **Willem de Kooning,** *Black Friday*

Figure 104
Ellen Auerbach (1906–2004; born Karlsruhe, Germany; died New York, NY), **Elaine and Willem de Kooning in the Studio, New York, 1944.** 20.3 × 25.3 cm. Ellen Auerbach Kunstsammlung, Akademie der Künste Archive, Berlin (KS-Auerbach 851)

unfinished "sketch" to about 1943 and hypothesized that it may be the picture visible in the upper left of a photograph taken by Ellen Auerbach of de Kooning with his wife, the artist Elaine de Kooning, in his studio (fig. 104).[9] Our research, which included overlaying high-resolution images, confirmed that the painting seen in the background of this photograph is indeed what would become the reverse of *Black Friday.* From the photograph we can see that that the painting support was significantly reduced in size prior to de Kooning turning it over and painting *Black Friday.* It is well documented that from the 1930s to the mid-1940s de Kooning was plagued by self-doubt; during this time, he finished relatively few paintings, destroying and overpainting many. As the artist recalled, "I destroyed almost all those paintings [of the late 1930s and early 1940s], I wish I hadn't. I was so modest then that I was vain. Some of them were good, a part of the real me."[10] The writer Edwin Denby, a friend of de Kooning, also remembered from his studio visits in the mid-1930s: "There might be a terrific painting on his easel, maybe it needed a little something more in a corner, but Bill would never fix anything to make it acceptable. Instead, next time, you'd find a totally new picture painted over the earlier one, maybe disappointing."[11]

It seems likely that the resizing and the reuse of the fiberboard was not carried out with *Black Friday* specifically in mind. In addition to examining the painting in raking light and close observation, X-radiographic imaging (fig. 105) reveals several forms underneath the current painted surface. For example, a ball form and other organic shapes are reminiscent of abstract works that de Kooning made in the early 1940s, such as *Pink Landscape* (ca. 1942; private collection) and *Summer Couch* (1943; private collection).[12] The edges of the panel show drips of bright color (figs. 106, 107). Those at the left edge cannot be from the seated-woman composition on the reverse, as the artist used a saw to reduce the panel's size after that side was painted. It would thus seem that de Kooning may have been working on the smooth side of the panel and then worked on the rougher side, leaving the drips and a few passages of color from the reverse of the support in the *Black Friday* composition. The rough pattern of the fiberboard is only noticeable in a few spots on the surface of *Black Friday,* as de Kooning's compositional changes led to a buildup of paint and other materials that eventually filled the crisscross pattern and created a surface topography. The likelihood of an abstract composition with bright colors underneath *Black Friday* can be seen as an illustration of Hess's observations regarding the genesis of de Kooning's black-and-white-paintings: "The idea for these paintings started in his high-keyed color abstractions; then ochers gradually dominated; finally the color was drained out—but slowly; patches of color still appear as late as *Light in August* [see fig. 18] and *Black Friday*."[13]

Anecdotal descriptions of de Kooning's painting techniques and methods, recorded by visitors to his studio, also confirm his habit of reworking his compo-sitions. One recurring comment is a surprise that his working method was more protracted.[14] No matter what his actual speed or deliberateness was, examining the painted surface reveals a significant amount of action in Rosenberg's "arena." From the mid-1940s onward, de Kooning's surfaces gradually evolved toward greater texture. This is also the time when he started superimposing drawings, sketches, and torn-paper fragments into and onto his paintings.[15] *Black Friday* indeed includes fragments of paper—possibly newspaper and tracing paper—left in the paint-layer matrix (see figs. 102, 108, 109).

Additional evidence of a dynamic interaction between worked and reworked areas includes the thick impastoed areas rising from the panel, flanked by thinned-down washes of paint as well as traces of charcoal where de Kooning pulled charcoal sticks through a semi-wet layer of paint. There is also paint that was bulked up with sand (fig. 110); the artist Pat Passlof, who studied with de Kooning in 1948, commented that the mixing in of solid materials was a regular occurrence in de Kooning's oeuvre.[16]

In the center of the top half of the painting, a piece of paper with a distinct organic form is collaged into the paint matrix, perfectly integrated within the overall composition. The sequencing of the "action" in this area (see fig. 102) is demonstrative of the artist's continuous reworking of the materials. Once the shape was in place, and the black paint layer and white brushstrokes traversing the form had been applied, the artist reinforced part of the paper form by highlighting the shape with white paint applied with a swooping movement of the brush, visually pulling this collage element forward in the composition.

De Kooning carried with him a wide variety of painting experience, from his academic training to various stints as a commercial painter. This range of experience allowed him to push his painting medium and other materials to rather new and innovative levels. The purposeful juxtaposition of these different techniques reveal themselves in multiple areas. Painting wet-in-wet was a common technique for artists working

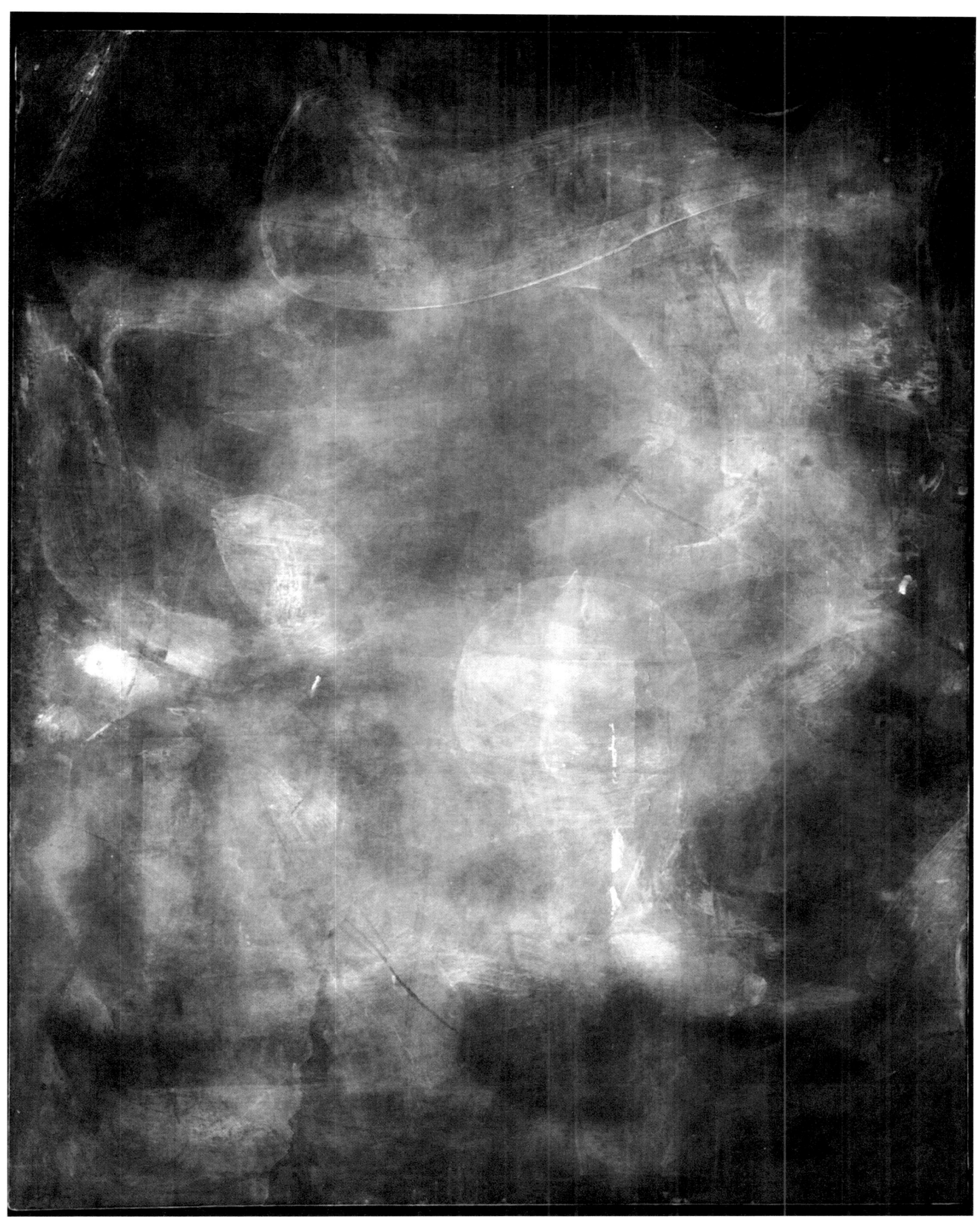

Figure 105
X-ray image composite of **Black Friday** (exposure: 40kV, 2mA, 2min),
revealing organic shapes not present in the painting's final composition

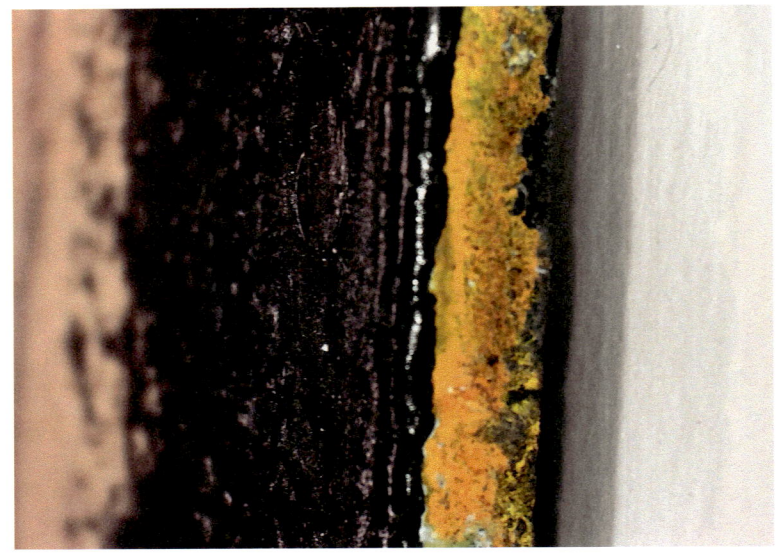
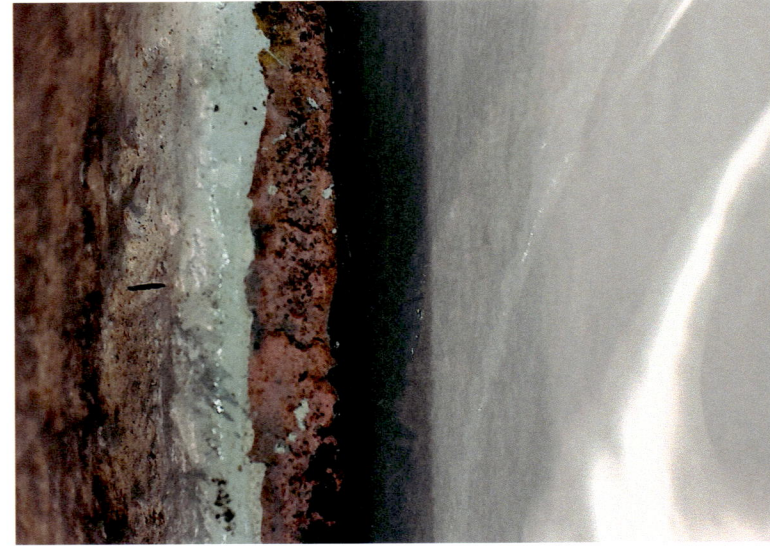
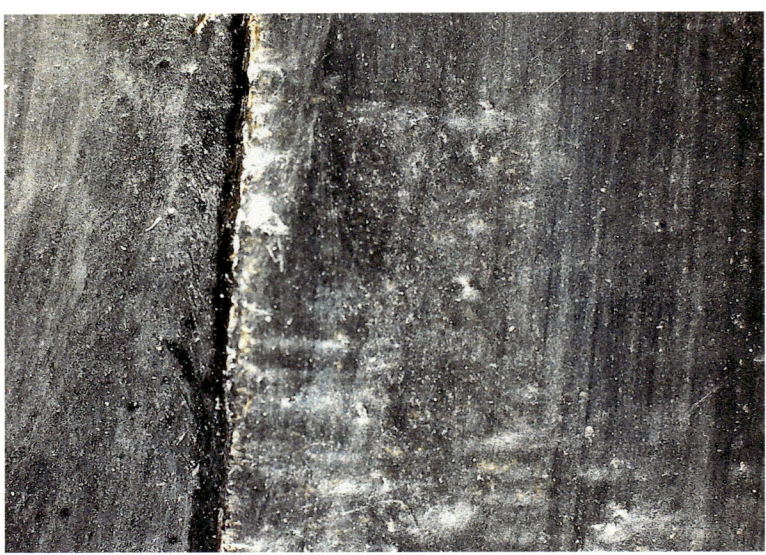
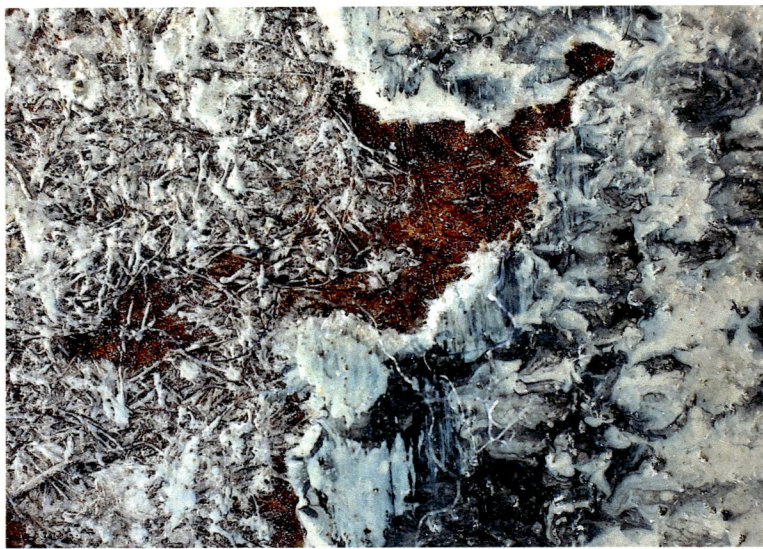

From top:

Figures 106 and 107
Micrographs of **Black Friday**, showing drips of color on the lower-right edge of the board's verso

Figures 108 and 109
Micrographs of the upper-left quadrant of **Black Friday**, showing paper in the paint matrix

with oil paints, as this method allows for subtle transitions and a smooth blending of colors. What de Kooning did in *Black Friday* is not quite a true wet-in-wet technique but instead was realized with paints that can be partially redissolved with the solvent originally used to dilute them. With the mechanical action of the brush, for example, application of the white paint can partially solubilize the already applied black paint, working the

lower layer back up in the new layer to create a lava-like or marbleized effect (fig. 111).[17] Such marble-like surfaces can be found throughout the entire surface of *Black Friday*.

Some of these painterly effects were only obtainable because of de Kooning's use of a variety of retail trade paints, including oil-based enamels, to create his black paintings. More specifically, Passlof remembered that the black paints were Ronan's drop black quick-dry lettering enamel and that the whites were paste-white house paints that de Kooning purchased at the Behlen Brothers paint store on Christopher Street in New York. Additionally, Hess mentions the enamel brands Ripolin and Sapolin.[18] Cans of these paints are visible in Rudy Burckhardt's photographs of de Kooning's studio taken

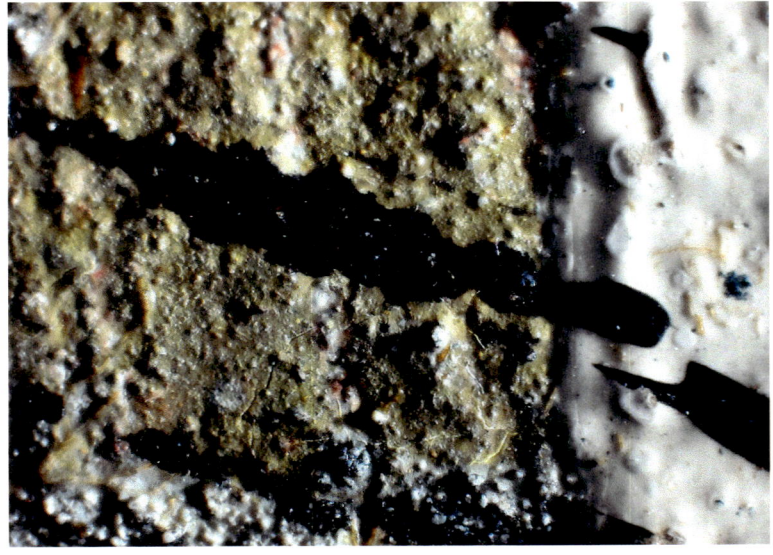

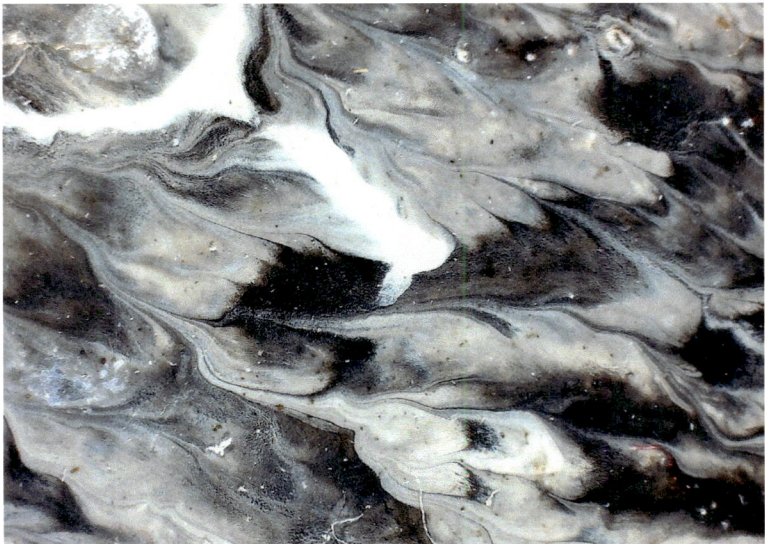

in 1950. Both Ripolin and Sapolin paints were also sold at Behlen Brothers.[19] The use of both retail trade paints and enamels has been confirmed in *Black Friday*: technical analysis of the painting identified white retail trade paints in the area near the artist's signature and retail trade black enamel paint at the top edge.[20] The artist himself referred to the use of retail trade paints in his black-and-white pictures in a 1959 interview: "I did it really because I wanted to be free of the material. I did not have any money, I did not have any particular aesthetic idea or theory, but I could go to a store and buy a gallon of white and a gallon of black and be in business."[21] In addition to the low cost of these paints, de Kooning likely employed them because he understood and valued their unique characteristics, different from those of more common artist paints.

One of the most persistent strategies de Kooning employed throughout his career was turning a painting on his easel to judge his composition from an entirely different perspective. As Hess notes, "It is not unusual for a painting to be turned upside down or 90 degrees at the last minute."[22] De Kooning used this strategy throughout his career—when he built his studio in Springs (East Hampton, New York) in 1964, he cut a wide recess into the studio floor, into which he could lower canvases. In this way he could easily access any point on a canvas in any orientation, even on very large canvases. No such device would have been necessary on an easel-size painting like *Black Friday,* which he could simply

lift and turn as he wished. Thus, it is instructive to look at the painting "upside down," as it is clear from the drip patterns that de Kooning did turn the painting, probably multiple times, and worked on it in these different orientations (fig. 112).

While *Black Friday,* seen right side up, shows a few easily recognizable features, notably the pitched-roof shapes at top left and the drooping figure at the center, an inverted view shows us not only a plausible composition but one that calls to mind another painting, Henri Matisse's *The Piano Lesson* (fig. 113), a work acquired by the Museum of Modern Art in 1946 and on view for all but a few months between then and 1948 (the year de Kooning finished *Black Friday*). Hess's observation that de Kooning's black-and-white paintings started out in high color, which was gradually drained out, leaving only patches of color to remain, supports the proposition that de Kooning may have used gray, red, and green in the initial stages of painting, echoing Matisse's palette. If so, the small passages in the lower-right corner were held in reserve, untouched by the multiple campaigns across the rest of the support. Recalling Denby's remarks,

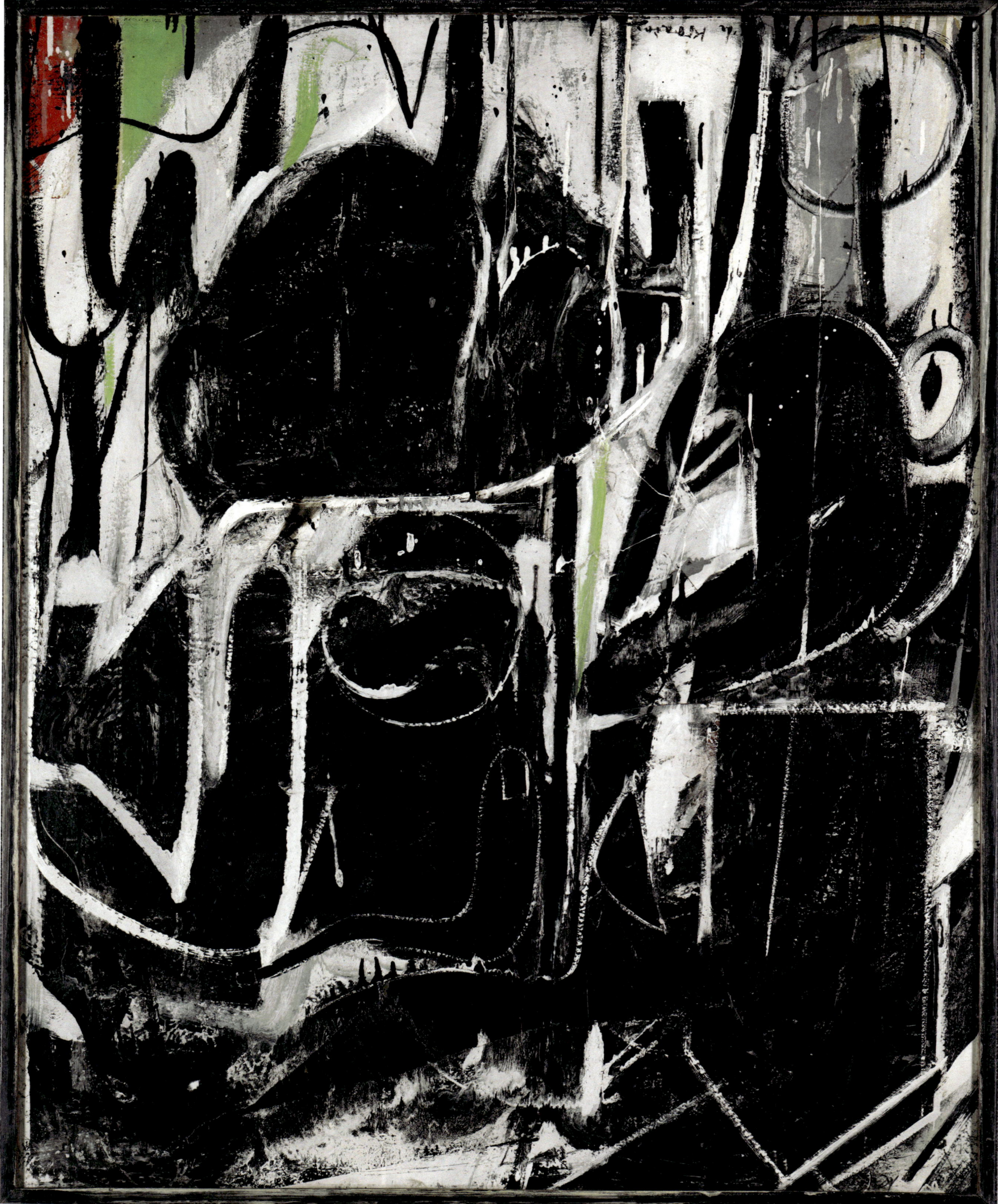

de Kooning may have thought that a painting "needed a little something more in a corner, but . . . would never fix anything to make it acceptable." [23]

De Kooning's active engagement with the surface of *Black Friday* has been outlined here, and *The Piano Lesson* also evidences a direct, active, even violent engagement with the canvas that surely resonated with de Kooning. We know from Matisse's son, pictured behind the piano, that his father had scraped down large areas of paint, most notably along the cast-iron railing in the window, two or three times before arriving at the final composition; hence, the battle-worn, pitted appearance of many areas.[24] Some of these scratches are deep and repetitive enough to become full erasures of the paint, not just points of emphasis. Most distinctive, though, are the deep, violent gouges in the upper left of the painting, in the grassy exterior landscape. Literal divots, these were done with the paint still somewhat wet, unlike the scratches elsewhere in dried paint, as Matisse pushed the paint, yielding a buildup of paint at the end of each gesture.

In the lower half of *Black Friday,* a flat black plane is supported by four legs, suggesting a table. Directly above it is a summary circle of paint, akin to those in the contemporaneous paintings *Light in August* (see fig. 18) and *Orestes* (see fig. 17) but also redolent of Pierre Matisse's head above his piano. In its inverted, "upside-down" position, the upper-right corner of *Black Friday* has a slash of black paint intersecting another simple circle, rather an oval, like the one that outlines the head of the figure in Matisse's 1914 painting *Woman on a High Stool,* shown on the wall behind the piano. We suggest not that de Kooning was in any way copying Matisse but instead that he was possibly finding a way into his own composition, a fully abstracted one, through Matisse's composition as well as his own technique.

The presence of an original strip frame (see fig. 28) is an interesting and unusual physical feature of *Black Friday.* Original frames on de Kooning's paintings are rare, but he may have made one in anticipation of his first solo exhibition at the Charles Egan Gallery in 1948. The painting was pressure-fit into the original strip frame

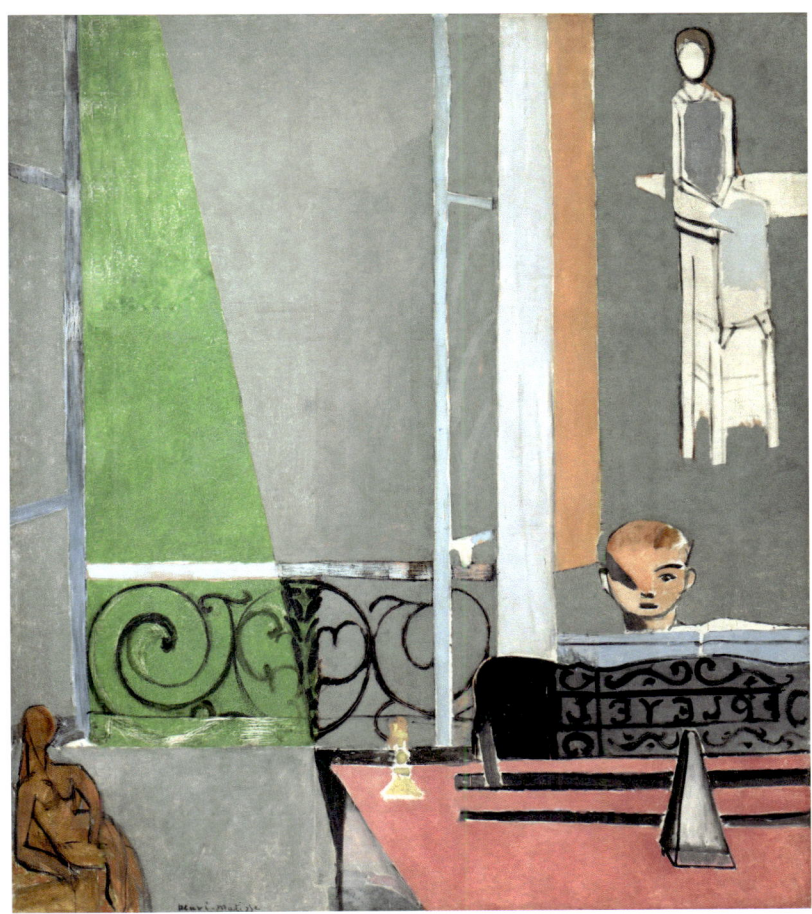

Figure 112
Willem de Kooning, *Black Friday*, rotated 180 degrees

Figure 113
Henri Matisse (1869–1954; born Le Cateau-Cambrésis, France; died Nice, France), ***The Piano Lesson*, 1916**
Oil on canvas, 245.1 × 212.7 cm. The Museum of Modern Art, New York. Mrs. Simon Guggenheim Fund (125.1946)

with a strainer, surprisingly crudely made despite de Kooning's woodworking skills. The fiberboard support is wedged between the strip frame and the strainer, kept in place with a series of nails connecting frame with strainer. On the reverse of the painting, in the upper-left corner of the strainer, a label from the Egan Gallery is still intact (fig. 114). Some of the labels on the strainer are glued upside down, and the word "TOP," written on the strainer, was for many years at the bottom of the painting suggesting that the frame, or at a minimum the strainer, has been oriented differently in the past. An archival photograph in the catalogue for Hess's 1968 exhibition at the Museum of Modern Art shows that the strainer was at that time oriented so that "TOP" was at

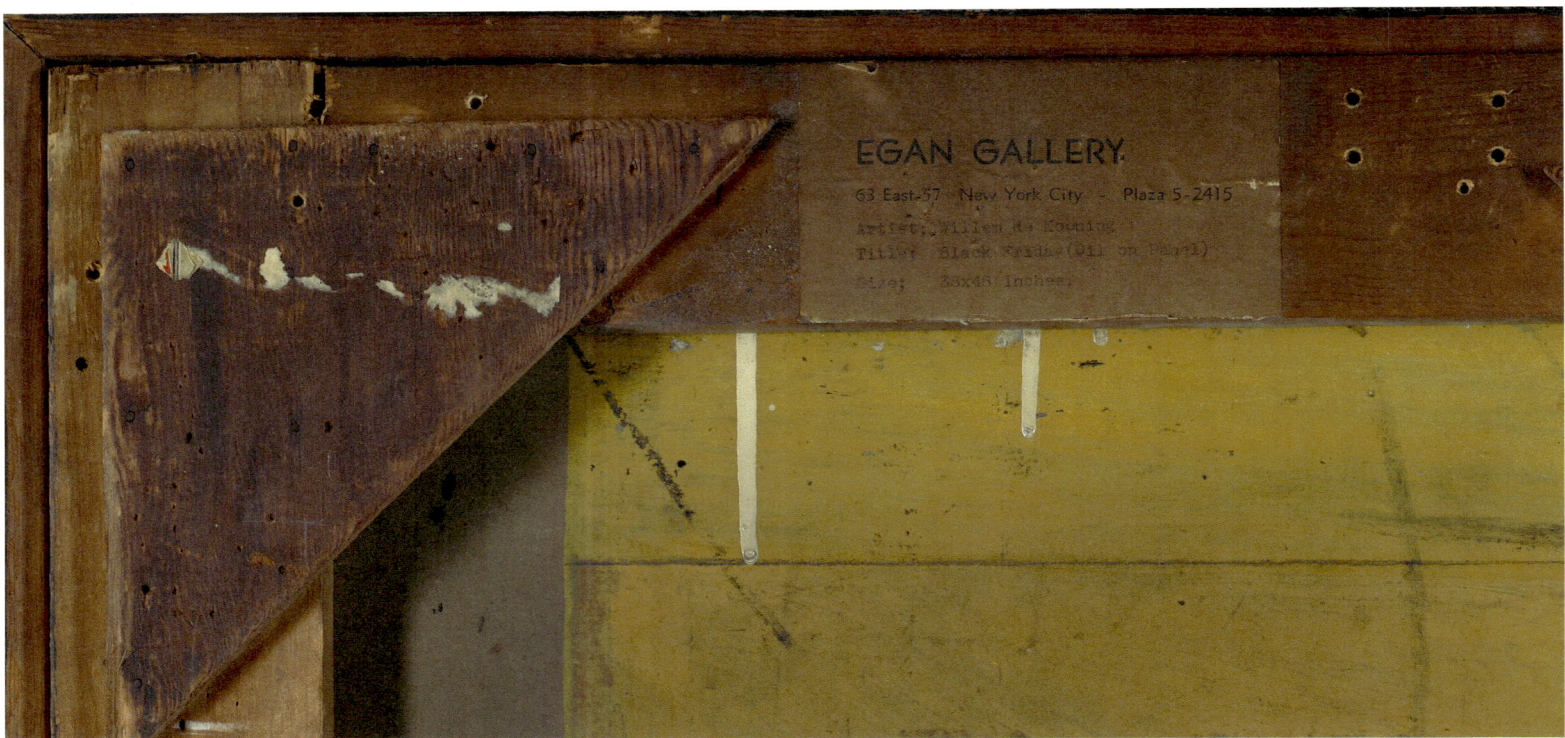

Figure 114
Charles Egan Gallery exhibition label on the reverse of
Black Friday

the top;[25] however, because the painting is not physically attached to the strainer, the painting was not in a different orientation. Closer examination of the original strip frame reveals that de Kooning worked on the painting after it was originally framed. Some of the brushstrokes on the frame no longer line up with their matching fragments on the painting. In order to reunite these marks, the strip frame (and strainer) needs to be rotated 180 degrees. The timing of, and reason for, the change to the frame is unclear, but it is possible that the painting was unframed for photography and simply slid back between the frame and the strainer incorrectly. The earliest published photograph of this incorrect orientation of the original strip frame is in the Princeton University Art Museum *Handbook of the Collections* (2007).[26] In June 2025, Princeton University Art Museum Chief Conservator Bart J. C. Devolder rotated the frame back to what is believed to be the original orientation so that the brushstrokes line up, the inscription "TOP" is at the top of the strainer, and the strip frame is in the same orientation as in the installation images from the 1969 exhibition.[27]

A close reading of *Black Friday* makes clear that the picture is an extraordinary document that illustrates de Kooning's groundbreaking working methods and creative processes in the 1940s. This singular object reflects a transition by the artist from his earlier approach to painting to the genesis of a new style culminating in the "black" paintings shown at the Charles Egan Gallery in 1948. In this new style de Kooning also found techniques that he would use repeatedly in the coming decades, even as he explored so many varied styles of painting throughout.

1. Charles F. Stuckey, "Bill de Kooning and Joe Christmas," *Art in America* 68, no. 3 (March 1980): 77.

2. Of the nine paintings we know were in the 1948 Egan exhibition, only *Light in August* (see fig. 18) and *Painting* (see fig. 27) were painted on canvas. From a letter from de Kooning to Miss [Virginia] Pearson dated January 20, 1953, we know that the artist wanted both of those canvases glued on panels for preservation concerns. The Museum of Modern Art, New York, Department of Circulating Exhibitions Records, II.1.74.11.2. This preference shows a high degree of understanding of the mechanics of paint films, as mounting canvas paintings to solid supports is a demonstrated way to stabilize unstable paint films.

3. The term "retail trade paints" comes from Marion Barclay, "Materials Used in Certain Canadian Abstract Paintings of the 1950s," in *The Crisis of Abstraction in Canada: The 1950s*, ed. Denise Le Clerc (Ottawa: National Gallery of Canada, 1992), 205–32. See also Susan Lake, *Willem de Kooning: The Artist's Materials*

(Los Angeles: Getty Conservation Institute, 2010), 23. Barclay uses this phrase to refer to products that are designed for interior and exterior use to coat architectural structures, signs, and furniture. They are different from industrial paints in that the latter are more difficult for the public to purchase.

4. Renée Arb, "Spotlight on de Kooning," *Art News* 47, no. 2 (April 1948): 33.

5. Harold Rosenberg, "The American Action Painters," *Art News* 51, no. 8 (December 1952): 22.

6. Claire Barry, "Across the Final Surface: Observations on Charles Demuth's Painting Materials and Working Methods in His Late Industrial Oil Paintings," in Betsy Fahlman, *Chimneys and Towers: Charles Demuth's Late Paintings of Lancaster* (Philadelphia: University of Pennsylvania Press, 2007), 158.

7. Lake, *Willem de Kooning,* 23.

8. See, for example, *Figure* (1944), illustrated in John Elderfield, ed., *De Kooning: A Retrospective*, exh. cat. (New York: Museum of Modern Art, 2011), 97.

9. Elderfield, *De Kooning: A Retrospective,* 99. The photograph is incorrectly referred to as figure 7; it should be figure 8. The photograph is in the Ellen Auerbach Kunstsammlung, Akademie der Künste Archive, Berlin, and can be seen online at https://archiv.adk.de/objekt/2462156.

10. Selden Rodman, *Conversations with Artists* (New York: Devin-Adair, 1957), 103.

11. Rudy Burckhardt, "Long Ago with Willem de Koning," *Art Journal* 48, no. 3 (Fall 1989): 223.

12. Illustrated in Elderfield, *De Kooning: A Retrospective*, 24, 27.

13. Thomas B. Hess, *Willem de Kooning* (New York: Museum of Modern Art, 1968), 50.

14. Lake, *Willem de Kooning,* 40.

15. On the use of drawings in the painting process, see Lake, *Willem de Kooning,* 27–28.

16. Lake, *Willem de Kooning*, 29.

17. Lake, *Willem de Kooning*, 33–34.

18. Lake, *Willem de Kooning*, 34.

19. Lake, *Willem de Kooning*, 33–34.

20. Lake, *Willem de Kooning*, 82.

21. Willem de Kooning, Kenneth Snelson, Michael Sonnabend, and Robert Snyder, "Inner Monologue," Summer 1959, recorded conversation transcribed by Marie-Anne Sichère.

22. Thomas B. Hess, *Willem de Kooning* (New York: George Braziller, 1959), 27.

23. See note 11, above.

24. See the discussion of *The Piano Lesson* in Stephanie D'Alessandro and John Elderfield, *Matisse: Radical Invention, 1913–1917* (New Haven, CT: Yale University Press, 2010), 291–93.

25. Hess, *Willem de Kooning* (1968), 24.

26. *Princeton University Art Museum: Handbook of the Collections* (Princeton, NJ: Princeton University Art Museum, 2007), 247. The images can be viewed at moma.org/calendar/exhibitions/3507?installation_image_index=27.

27. The images can be viewed at moma.org/calendar/exhibitions/3507?installation_image_index=24.

Selected Bibliography

Auping, Michael, et al., eds. *Abstract Expressionism: The Critical Developments.* Buffalo, NY: Buffalo Fine Arts Academy; New York: Harry N. Abrams, 1987.

Cooper, Harry, et al., eds. *Philip Guston Now.* Washington, DC: National Gallery of Art, 2020.

Curtis, Cathy. *A Generous Vision: The Creative Life of Elaine de Kooning.* New York: Oxford University Press, 2017.

De Kooning, Elaine. "De Kooning Memories." *Vogue,* December 1983, 350–53, 393–94.

Elderfield, John, ed. *De Kooning: A Retrospective.* New York: Museum of Modern Art, 2011.

Gibson, Ann Eden. *Issues in Abstract Expressionism: The Artist-Run Periodicals.* Ann Arbor, MI: UMI Research Press, 1990.

Greenberg, Clement. *Art and Culture: Critical Essays.* Boston: Beacon, 1961.

Guilbaut, Serge. *How New York Stole the Idea of Modern Art: Abstract Expressionism, Freedom, and the Cold War.* Translated by Arthur Goldhammer. Chicago and London: University of Chicago Press, 1983.

Hess, Thomas B. *Willem de Kooning.* New York: George Braziller, 1959.

———. *Willem de Kooning.* New York: Museum of Modern Art, 1968.

Janis, Harriet, and Rudi Blesh. *De Kooning.* New York: Grove, 1960.

Jones, Caroline A. *Eyesight Alone: Clement Greenberg's Modernism and the Bureaucratization of the Senses.* Chicago and London: University of Chicago Press, 2005.

Lake, Susan F. *Willem de Kooning: The Artist's Materials.* Los Angeles: Getty Conservation Institute, 2010.

Landau, Ellen G., ed. *Reading Abstract Expressionism: Context and Critique.* New Haven, CT, and London: Yale University Press: 2005.

Molesworth, Helen. *Leap Before You Look: Black Mountain College 1933–1957.* New Haven, CT: Yale University Press; Boston: Institute for Contemporary Art, 2015.

Morgan, Robert C., ed. *Clement Greenberg: Late Writings.* Minneapolis: University of Minnesota Press, 2003.

Mostafavi Mohsen, and Max Raphael. *The Color Black: Antinomies of a Color in Art.* London: MACK, 2024.

Motherwell, Robert, and Ad Reinhardt, eds. *Modern Artists in America.* New York: Wittenborn Schultz, 1951.

Naifeh, Steven, and Gregory White Smith. *Jackson Pollock: An American Saga.* New York: Clarkson N. Potter, 1989.

O'Brian, John, ed. *Clement Greenberg: The Collected Essays and Criticism.* 4 vols. Chicago and London: University of Chicago Press, 1986–93.

Passlof, Pat. "1948: The Author's Studies with Willem de Kooning." *Art Journal* 48, no. 3 (Fall 1989): 229.

Rose, Barbara, ed. *Readings in American Art, 1900–1975.* Rev. ed. New York: Praeger Publishers, 1975.

Rosenberg, Harold. *De Kooning.* New York: Harry N. Abrams, 1973.

Ross, Clifford, ed. *Abstract Expressionism: Creators and Critics.* New York: Harry N. Abrams, 1990.

Schaffner, Ingrid, and Lisa Jacobs, eds. *Julien Levy: Portrait of an Art Gallery.* Cambridge and London: The MIT Press, 1998.

Schloss, Edith. *The Loft Generation: From the De Koonings to Twombly; Portraits and Sketches, 1942–2011.* Edited by Mary Venturini. New York: Farrar, Straus and Giroux, 2021.

Seitz, William Chapin. "Abstract-Expressionist Painting in America: An Interpretation Based on the Work and Thought of Six Key Figures." PhD diss., Princeton University, 1955.

Stevens, Mark, and Annalyn Swan. *De Kooning: An American Master.* New York: Knopf, 2004.

Stone, Allan. Preface to *De Kooning: Liquefying Cubism.* New York: Allan Stone Gallery, 1994.

Stuckey, Charles F. "Bill de Kooning and Joe Christmas." *Art in America* 68, no. 3 (March 1980): 66–79.

Sylvester, David. *Interviews with American Artists.* New Haven, CT, and London: Yale University Press, 2001.

Wolfe, Judith L. *Willem de Kooning: Works from 1951–1981.* East Hampton NY: Guild Hall of East Hampton, 1981.

Yard, Sally. *Willem de Kooning: The First Twenty-Six Years in New York.* New York and London: Garland, 1986.

———. "The Angel and the Demoiselle: Willem de Kooning's *Black Friday.*" *Record of the Art Museum,* Princeton University 50, no. 2 (1991): 2–25.

Checklist of the Exhibition

Untitled (Reclining Figure), ca. 1945
Oil and charcoal on Masonite, 38.1 × 50.5 cm
Collection of Gene and Sueyun Locks
Figure 54

Bill-Lee's Delight, 1946
Oil on paper mounted on composition board,
80.3 × 122.9 cm
Eastman Collection
Figure 16

The Moraine, 1947
Oil on paper mounted on Masonite,
93.7 × 65.1 cm
Eastman Collection
Figure 14

Valentine, 1947
Oil and enamel on paper on board, 92.2 ×
61.5 cm
The Museum of Modern Art, New York. Gift
of Mr. and Mrs. Gifford Phillips (1093.1969)
Figure 20

Noon, ca. 1947
Oil and enamel on Masonite, 121.9 × 86.4 cm
Philadelphia Museum of Art. The Albert M.
Greenfield and Elizabeth M. Greenfield
Collection, 1974 (1974-178-24)
Figure 22

Night, 1947–48
Oil on board, 55.9 × 73 cm
Minneapolis Institute of Art. The John R.
Van Derlip Fund and The Ethel Morrison
Van Derlip Fund (63.36)
Figure 13

Secretary, 1947–48
Oil and charcoal on paper mounted on
fiberboard, 61.9 × 91.9 cm
Hirshhorn Museum and Sculpture Garden,
Smithsonian Institution, Washington, DC.
Gift of Joseph H. Hirshhorn, 1966 (66.1193)
Figure 12

Black Friday, 1948
Enamel and oil over paper collage on
fiberboard in painted wood frame; 125 × 99 cm,
128.3 × 102.2 × 7.3 cm (frame)
Princeton University Art Museum. Gift of
H. Gates Lloyd, Class of 1923, and Mrs. Lloyd
in honor of the Class of 1923 (y1976-44)
Figure 28

Black Untitled, 1948
Oil and enamel on paper, mounted on wood,
75.9 × 101.6 cm
The Metropolitan Museum of Art, New York.
From the Collection of Thomas B. Hess,
Gift of the heirs of Thomas B. Hess, 1984
(1984.613.7)
Figure 49

Mailbox, 1948
Oil, enamel, and charcoal on paper on
composition board, 58.7 × 76.2 cm
Collection of Bettina Bryant
Figure 21

Painting, 1948
Enamel and oil on canvas, 108.3 × 142.5 cm
The Museum of Modern Art, New York.
Purchase, 1948 (238.1948)
Figure 27

Attic Study, 1949
Oil, enamel, and graphite on paperboard
mounted on hardboard, 47.9 × 60.6 cm
The Menil Collection, Houston (X 422)
Figure 45

Town Square, 1949
Oil on paper mounted on Masonite,
44.2 × 60.3 cm
Seattle Art Museum. Gift of the Friday
Foundation in honor of Richard E. Lang and
Jane Lang Davis (2020.14.2)
Figure 43

Zot, 1949
Oil on paper, mounted on wood, 45.7 × 51.4 cm
The Metropolitan Museum of Art, New York.
From the Collection of Thomas B. Hess,
Purchase, Rogers, Louis V. Bell and Harris
Brisbane Dick Funds and Joseph Pulitzer
Bequest, and Gift of the heirs of Thomas B.
Hess, 1984 (1984.611)
Figure 42

Dark Pond, 1948
Enamel on composition board, 118.7 × 141.6 cm
Frederick R. Weisman Art Foundation,
Los Angeles
Figure 41

Gansevoort Street, ca. 1949
Oil on cardboard, 76.2 × 101.6 cm
Anderson Collection at Stanford University.
Gift of Mary Margaret Anderson (2019.1.1)
Figure 40

Landscape, Abstract, ca. 1949
Enamel on paper, 48.9 × 64.9 cm
Whitney Museum of American Art, New York.
Gift of Mr. and Mrs. Alan H. Temple (68.96)
Figure 48

Untitled (Black and White Abstraction),
1950
Sapolin enamel on paper, 55.9 × 76.2 cm
Private collection
Figure 52

Index

Photography Credits